AFGHANISTAN

NATIONAL GALLERY OF ART

Washington, DC | May 25 – September 7, 2008

This exhibition is organized by the National Geographic Society and the National Gallery of Art, Washington, in association with the Asian Art Museum of San Francisco; the Museum of Fine Arts, Houston; and The Metropolitan Museum of Art.

It is supported by a grant from the National Endowment for the Humanities and an indemnity from the Federal Council on the Arts and the Humanities.

At the National Gallery of Art the exhibition is made possible by the E. Rhodes and Leona B. Carpenter Foundation. It is also supported by The Charles Engelhard Foundation.

AFGHANISTAN

Hidden Treasures from the National Museum, Kabul

NATIONAL GALLERY OF ART

Washington, DC

MAY 25–SEPTEMBER 7, 2008

ASIAN ART MUSEUM OF SAN FRANCISCO

San Francisco, CA

OCTOBER 24, 2008–JANUARY 25, 2009

THE MUSEUM OF FINE ARTS, HOUSTON

Houston, TX

FEBRUARY 22–MAY 17, 2009

THE METROPOLITAN MUSEUM OF ART

New York, NY

JUNE 23–SEPTEMBER 20, 2009

PREVIOUS PAGE: *A gold boot-buckle, encrusted with turquoise, depicting a carriage drawn by dragons, dates to the second quarter of the first century* A.D. *It was found buried with its owner in a tomb at Tillya Tepe.*

OPPOSITE: *Limestone Corinthian capital found at Aï Khanum, older than 145* B.C., *is of the so-called "free" Corinthian type, where the volutes spring directly from the crown of acanthus leaves.*

Ceremonial silver plate found at Aï Khanum, depicting Cybele, the Greek goddess of nature. The plate is gilded with gold leaf and dates to the third century B.C.

A young man's long, wavy hair is held together with a thin band in this circular plaster medallion found in Begram, dating to the first century A.D.

Medallion on a gold belt shows a figure sitting on a panther. Found in a tomb at Tillya Tepe, this belt dates to the second quarter of the first century A.D.

Gold and turquoise clasp found at Tillya Tepe, dates to the second quarter of the first century A.D. *and shows Dionysus and Ariadne embracing while seated on a monster.*

FOLLOWING PAGE: *One of a pair, this gold, turquoise, garnet, lapis lazuli, carnelian, and pearl pendant showing the "Dragon Master" dates from the first century* A.D.

AFGHANISTAN

Hidden Treasures from the National Museum, Kabul

EDITED BY

FREDRIK HIEBERT AND PIERRE CAMBON

NATIONAL GEOGRAPHIC

WASHINGTON, D.C.

TILLYA TEPE

Appliqués once sewn to clothing long disintegrated, found in graves in Tillya Tepe.

Contents

Dear Friends:

I want to welcome you to this vibrant celebration of Afghanistan's beauty, culture, and history. Afghanistan stands at the crossroads of many civilizations. At the heart of the Silk Road, Afghanistan was the historic link between China, India, Persia, the Middle East, and the West.

Tragically, the troubles of the last several decades have distracted us from this rich history that spans centuries. This exhibition, "Hidden Treasures," is nothing less than a miracle. Held hostage in our own country seven years ago, we could not even dream that the finest American art museums would soon be celebrating Afghanistan's rich culture and history.

The brilliant sculpture, ancient jewelry, and magnificent gold that you will see were once described as the "lost" treasures of Afghanistan. But they were never lost. Priceless artifacts were hidden throughout Kabul, in dry wells, and behind false walls. Miraculously, our cultural inheritance was preserved and protected by a brave and selfless group of Afghan heroes. A single piece of gold would have been a ticket to escape the war and destruction that afflicted our country, but not a single piece was lost.

I would like to thank the National Geographic Society, who together with the National Gallery of Art created this exhibition. Many American and international scholars aided greatly in the new inventory of these artifacts, and I personally had the opportunity in 2004 to see with my own eyes the fabled treasures of Afghanistan's past. The American people have given us so much, and it is an honor to be able to share with you these exquisite treasures, most of which have never been seen in the United States.

When I was elected President of Afghanistan, one of my promises to the Afghan people was that the world would never again forget our country. "Hidden Treasures" will paint a panoramic picture of our wondrous country and let the beauty of Afghanistan come alive in the imaginations of our friends around the world.

Thank you for your interest in Afghanistan. I hope that someday soon we will have you as our own guests, to see these and other treasures in the rebuilt National Museum of Afghanistan.

President Hamid Karzai
Islamic Republic of Afghanistan

Golden ram's head adornment, found in a Tillya Tepe tomb from the second quarter of the first century A.D.

BALKH

Balkh, the major city of ancient Bactria, at the foot of the central highlands in northern Afghanistan, is said to have been home to legendary prophet Zoroaster, residing here centuries before the arrival of Alexander the Great

LETTER FROM THE EXHIBITION ORGANIZERS

Gold crown found in the Tillya Tepe tomb, from the second quarter of the first century A.D.

IT IS, INDEED, A SPECIAL OCCASION when two institutions such as the National Geographic Society and the National Gallery of Art, with historic commitments to documenting the cultures of the world, join on a project that combines the excitement of archaeological discovery with a celebration of truly extraordinary works of art.

This exhibition, "Afghanistan: Hidden Treasures from the National Museum, Kabul," presents the rich cultural heritage of one of the world's great nations. Strategically located in the heart of Central Asia, ancient Afghanistan was a dynamic and thriving economic power in Silk Road culture, leading up to the first century A.D. The surviving collections of the Kabul museum portray a nation richly diversified in its population, economic underpinnings, and cultural traditions. Today's images of war and suffering have clouded our understanding of the proud and prosperous history of this great nation. It is our hope that this exhibition will give rise to a new historical perspective, one that the Afghan people have taken tremendous risks to maintain and preserve for future generations.

This exhibition would not be possible without the vision and steady efforts of the Afghan people under the leadership of President Hamid Karzai. We offer special thanks to Abdul Karim Khurram, Minister of Information and Culture; Omar Sultan, Deputy Minister; and Omara Khan Massoudi, Director of the National Museum, Kabul, as well as the entire Afghan exhibition committee and archaeology committee, who graciously agreed to the extended loan of Afghanistan's national treasures and embraced our desire to present their cultural heritage to an American audience. We also express profound thanks to Ambassador and Mrs. Said Jawad, for their guidance and support.

The National Endowment for the Humanities, under the inspired leadership of its chairman Bruce Cole, has been another important partner on this project, providing invaluable assistance over the course of several years. For their great contributions to this exhibition, we also thank our museum partners and their directors: Emily Sano of the Asian Art Museum of San Francisco; Peter Marzio of The Museum of Fine Arts, Houston; and Phillipe de Montebello of The Metropolitan Museum of Art, New York. In addition, all those involved in this international effort are grateful to the Musée Guimet, Paris, under the leadership of Jean-François Jarrige, for its superb efforts in mounting the initial exhibition of these artifacts and for providing vital conservation services.

We and our museum partners are equally indebted to National Geographic Society Fellow, archaeologist, and curator Fredrik Hiebert, whose close relationship with colleagues in Afghanistan, France, and Russia provides the basis for this important project. His love of Afghanistan and infectious enthusiasm for this exhibition are at the very source of its success. To Fred Hiebert and to all of our colleagues on this project, we offer our gratitude for a job well done.

Terry Garcia
Executive Vice President, Mission Programs
NATIONAL GEOGRAPHIC SOCIETY

Earl A. Powell III
Director
NATIONAL GALLERY OF ART

REPORT ON THE EUROPEAN TOUR

JEAN-FRANÇOIS JARRIGE
President, Musée des Arts Asiatiques-Guimet

IN 2004, THE WORLD OFFICIALLY LEARNED THAT MANY IMPORTANT ARTIFACTS from the Kabul Museum had been saved and were preserved in the vaults of the Central Bank. Once the vaults were opened, the work of cataloguing the recovered objects could begin. This task was undertaken by the curatorial staff of the Kabul Museum and by a team of international experts, thanks to the generous financial support of the National Geographic Society, coordinated by Fred Hiebert. Then it was proposed that a selection of the preserved treasures of Afghanistan should go on tour. The Afghan authorities and our colleague Omara Khan Massoudi, director of the Kabul Museum, agreed to collaborate with the Musée Guimet and the French Archaeological Delegation in Afghanistan (DAFA) to plan a touring exhibition, that would display golden vessels from Fullol (ca 2000 B.C.), various remains from the Greek city of Aï Khanum, an outstanding set of the artifacts from the tomb at Tillya tepe (1st century A.D.) and a beautiful selection of the finds from two rich deposits from Begram (end of the 1st century A.D.).

After quite some time and many difficulties, the Ministry of Information and Culture of Afghanistan and the Musée Guimet signed a contract, allowing the transportation of the precious artifacts to Paris on two flights organized by the French army. Then we had to cope with the challenge of cleaning and restoring the antiquities in just three weeks, in order to set up the exhibition and hold an opening ceremony on December 5, 2006. The exhibition, which ran until April 30, 2007, met with tremendous success. The demand to see the treasures was so great that visitors waited in lines for more than two hours, but most of them did not complain since it was a great privilege to see so many outstanding masterpieces, which had been thought lost forever.

President Hamid Karzai and President Jacques Chirac visited the exhibition together. President Karzai expressed great satisfaction about the display of the exhibition at the

Musée Guimet. He was also pleased to get confirmation that the Ministry of Information and Culture in Kabul was already working with us on a European tour followed by an American tour. It was decided that the next venue after Paris would be the Museo di Antichità of Turin in Italy. The exhibition organized in Italy by the Fondazione per l'Arte della Compagnia di San Paolo was held from May to November 2007. Even during the summer months and throughout the fall, huge crowds of visitors attended what became a major cultural event for the whole of northern Italy and for many tourists.

After Turin, the exhibition was shown from December 22, 2007 to April 20, 2008, in Amsterdam in the Nieuwe Kerk, the great church where coronation ceremonies of the kings and queens of the Netherlands are held. The church also serves as one of the country's main exhibition halls. To accompany the exhibit, Musée Guimet also loaned a selection of sculptures from the "Greco-Buddhist" monasteries of Hadda. The Queen of the Netherlands and President Hamid Karzai were both invited to attend the exhibition.

We are, indeed, very happy that, after the European tour, these treasures from Afghanistan are going to be displayed in four major museums in the United States. This American tour is organized with the support of the National Geographic and begins on May 25, 2008 at the National Gallery of Art in Washington. We have no doubt that this exhibition will meet with the same success it had in Europe, as it reveals through priceless objects Afghanistan's historic role at the crossroads between the Mediterranean world, India, Central Asia, and China. As U.S., French, Italian, and Dutch soldiers continue to collaborate as peacekeeping forces in a country that still overcome enormous difficulties, such an exhibition symbolizes hope and the great contribution of the Afghan cultural heritage to world history.

AÏ KHANUM

The end of the royal Greek city of Aï Khanum (meaning "Lady Moon") came suddenly around 145 B.C. at the hands of nomads from the northeast, who set fire to the palace and robbed the treasury.

CURATOR'S PREFACE

BY FREDRIK HIEBERT
National Geographic Society

THIS EXHIBITION REPRESENTS ONE OF THE MOST EXCITING NEWS STORIES OF recent times from Central Asia—the amazing rediscovery of Silk Road treasures previously thought lost to the ages. This is a story, first, of the Afghans' heroism in saving their cultural heritage. The motto of the Kabul Museum "A nation stays alive when its culture stays alive" imparts an important lesson to the entire world. The second story—that of Afghanistan's pivotal role in world history—is equally significant. Central Asia is often marginalized, seen as "the periphery," but it appears here at the center of trade routes, connecting the ancient world.

Tissue is pulled back, after 25 years of safeguarding, to reveal an exquisitely carved ancient throne arm support: a woman riding a leogryph, a mythical creature with the body of a lion, the wings of an eagle, and the beak of a parrot. This ivory bracket found at Begram is from the first century A.D.

My own participation in this project began in 1987 when I went to the Soviet Union to work with Viktor Sarianidi in the deserts of Turkmenistan. He told me the story of his discovery of the Bactrian Gold in neighboring Afghanistan nearly ten years earlier, as the country teetered on the brink of political chaos. At that time, he had excavated six intact ancient burials hidden in the remains of an ancient fortress. These burials were the first evidence of ancient nomads in northern Afghanistan and their trading routes with China and Rome. The burial jewelry and offerings showed artistry unlike anything Sarianidi had seen. He shared this story with the world in NATIONAL GEOGRAPHIC in March 1990. In the last line of the article Sarianidi said: "Look well at these pictures of the Bactrian masterpieces that follow. Who knows when they will be seen again." This phrase had haunted me ever since, because I did not have a chance to visit Afghanistan before civil war tore across the country. I invited Sarianidi to the United States to speak about the fate of the Bactrian Gold, and we speculated, sadly, that it must have been long gone–either melted down or stolen.

However, in August 2003, President Hamid Karzai announced the discovery of several museum boxes in the presidential bank vault in Kabul. Could this possibly be the

Bactrian Gold? To resolve issues raised in the 1990 NATIONAL GEOGRAPHIC article, National Geographic Mission Programs sent me to Kabul to find out if these were, indeed, the museum treasures. In Kabul, I met with the then-Minister of Finance, Ashraf Ghani, and the Minister of Information and Culture, Sayeed Makhdoom Raheen. They sketched out a plan for opening the boxes, inventorying the contents, and creating an international traveling exhibition. This exhibit is the result of their vision.

For an exhibition like this one to happen, many people must make contributions, and it is my pleasure to acknowledge them here: Terry Garcia, Executive Vice President for Mission Programs at the National Geographic Society, had the vision to include this project as a part of the Society's long-standing commitment to Afghanistan. Sarah Laskin, Agnes Tabah, Kathryn Keane, Susan Norton, Susan Reeve, Bill Warren, Mimi Koumanelis, and Melissa Jordan have dedicated their efforts to making this a reality, as well as editor Susan Straight, cartographer Carl Mehler, and publisher Kevin Mulroy.

In Kabul, we worked closely with the Ministry of Information and Culture, in particular with Minister Abdul Karim Khurram and Deputy Minister Omar Sultan, and the Kabul Museum director, Omara Khan Massoudi. Massoudi specifically asked for Carla Grissmann, who had worked at the museum since 1973, to join the inventory team. Her role in the inventory was, and continues to be essential for long-term continuity, and she has been my treasured partner on this project from the beginning. For the opportunity to open the boxes in the presidential bank vault, we would like to thank President Karzai and his staff, the members of the Da Afghanistan Bank, and Minister Ghani and his staff, particularly Naim Dindar. Our work was also facilitated by UNESCO, SPACH, and ICOMOS while in Kabul. Both the inventory of the Kabul Museum and the exhibition have had the exceptional support of the chairman of the National Endowment for

BALKH. *The massive walls of this ancient city are built in an architectural tradition going back to the Bronze Age.*

the Humanities, Bruce Cole, as well as the tireless support of Ambassador Said Tayeb Jawad, and the entire staff of the Embassy of Afghanistan in Washington, D.C. I would also like to acknowledge the efforts of Professor Thomas Barfield, Dr. Charles Kolb, and Dr. Harry Iceland in their many efforts to support cultural heritage in Afghanistan.

In addition to acknowledging the enormous intellectual contribution by Viktor Sarianidi to this project, I would like to thank the co-curators of the exhibition—Dr. Sanjyot Mehendale and Professor Paul Bernard—as well as the other contributors to the catalog, for their keen scholarship.

I would also like to express my deep appreciation to the Kabul Museum inventory group. More than anything, I salute the Afghan heroes: Omara Khan Massoudi, Mir Ghulam Nabi, Sherazudin Saifi, and Abdullah Hakimzada, among others. Their safe care of these treasures preserved the heritage of Afghanistan for all of us.

TILLYA TEPE

The name should have given away the treasures buried in graves here. Tillya Tepe, as the Russians called it (the name has now been generally adopted) had long been known as Tilla tepa in the local Uzbek language, or "Hill of Gold."

INTRODUCTION

AFTER 30 YEARS OF AGGRESSION AND WARFARE, LIFE IN AFGHANISTAN has more or less returned to normal. These dreadful years of war have left unfortunate effects, but we have taken great strides in our transition from the culture of war to the culture of peace, fostering fraternity and cordiality and promoting the spirit of forgiveness.

The Ministry of Information, Culture, Tourism, and Youth of Afghanistan has tried to encourage these principles through cultural gatherings, cultural heritage events, and festivals, as well as popular events such as concerts, ceremonies, radio programs, and television shows. The psychological effects of such cultural events not only lift people's spirits but also help in promoting a culture of tolerance and understanding. We plan to continue these kinds of activities for a long time to rid the society from the effects of 30 years of war. Attention to arts and cultural activities will also help us in this regard. Our art objects and artists, especially under the government of the Taliban, were gravely affected, to the point of destruction.

Today we need a revival of the arts. For four years, we have worked toward this goal, but our success has been extremely limited. For the preservation and strengthening of our cultural heritage, we need your help.

At present, for example, in most regions of Afghanistan, folkloric music—the remnants of past centuries of artistic tradition—is about to disappear. It requires our protection, as do other arts such as calligraphy, tile work, and painting, which have existed in Afghanistan for many centuries. Our new generation has risen from the flames of war, and we are doing our utmost to alleviate the residual effects of war, brutality, and hatred.

Horses graze in green fields at the foot of Northern Afghanistan's rugged Pamir mountains.

The safeguarding of all aspects of cultural heritage in my country, both tangible and intangible, including museums, monuments, archaeological sites, music, arts, and traditional crafts, is of particular significance in terms of strengthening cultural identity and preserving a sense of national integrity. Cultural heritage can become a point of mutual interest for former adversaries, enabling them to rebuild ties, to engage in dialogue, and to work together in shaping a common future.

By organizing this exhibition, we want to affirm our commitment to the international community that Afghanistan is changing from a culture of war to a culture of peace.

As a further testament to Afghanistan's goals of peace and democracy, I am proud to inform you that, at the time of this writing, the people of Afghanistan have successfully, through a free and democratic election process, elected their representatives—including 68 women—to the National Assembly. I wish to express my gratitude to our partners in peace who, along with their brave citizens, the soldiers of peace, helped facilitate this feat of democracy.

The United States has profoundly contributed to the rehabilitation and reconstruction of Afghanistan. The warm, friendly, and historic relationship between the peoples of the Islamic Republic of Afghanistan and the United States of America and their shared commitment to the ideals of democracy, peace, and security has enabled this exhibit to safely come out of hiding and travel to the United States. This is the first time since their discovery that these precious cultural objects have been exhibited internationally.

We are also grateful to international cultural organizations such as UNESCO, the National Geographic Society, and the Society for the Preservation of Afghanistan's

Cultural Heritage, and others, which firmly responded to the challenges of rehabilitation of Afghanistan's endangered cultural heritage, which has suffered irreversible damage and loss during the past decades of civil unrest. This is especially true in their attention to the integrity of archaeological excavation sites and the prevention of illegal trafficking of cultural property.

It is a source of pride and a privilege to be able to show the rich and unique cultural heritage of Afghanistan through these priceless artifacts. Look at these precious objects from different parts of Afghanistan and you will see 4,000-year-old objects from Tepe Fullol—one of the great neighbors of Mesopotamia; you will also see the objects from Aï Khanum, which show the strong influence of classical Greek civilization; and you will see the treasures from Begram and Tillya Tepe with their cultural influences from such places as China, India, Persia, Siberia, Greece, and Rome. It is my sincerest hope that you will enjoy seeing these objects as much as we Afghans do.

Omar Sultan
Deputy Minister of Information and
Culture of the Islamic Republic of Afghanistan

BEGRAM

Excavation site of Begram's New Royal City, which yielded a dazzling, culturally diverse array of objects in ancient sealed-off rooms—glassware, bronzes, plaster medallions, porphyry and alabaster objects from the Roman world; fragments of Chinese lacquer boxes and bowls; and Indian-style objects carved in ivory and bone.

CHAPTER I

The National Museum of Afghanistan

OMARA KHAN MASSOUDI
Director of the National Museum in Kabul

Crystal beaker with carved image of the ancient lighthouse of Alexandria, Egypt, found at Begram, Afghanistan.

THE NATIONAL MUSEUM WAS BUILT IN 1922, DRAWING ON artifacts from excavations by local and foreign archaeologists. The museum was intended to provide a safe haven for the treasures of Afghan culture. By mid-century about 100,000 pre-Islamic and ethnographic objects were preserved in the museum. A large number of these objects were recorded on inventory cards. The National Museum of Afghanistan handled this task with great care so that thousands of students, teachers, official visitors, tourists, and other interested parties could view the artworks.

But then we entered the painful period in the 1970s, during which these treasures, of such immense historical and cultural value, became caught up in the political turmoil affecting the country, suffering terrible damage as a result. A coup d'état took place on April 27, 1978. Almost a year later, on April 17, 1979, in what proved to be a scientific and cultural disaster for Afghanistan, the objects from the National Museum were transferred to the home of Minister Sardar Mohammad Naim Khan. The artworks were removed hastily and handled without care, without regard for the scientific and technical standards that ought to have governed their packaging and transport. The transfer operation took 25 days, and the objects then remained in storage for a year. Luckily the objects themselves were not broken or damaged, but the glass cases and wooden and metal containers suffered badly from the effects of unsuitable storage spaces, rain, and snow. The museum pieces were then transferred to a restoration site at Darulaman, on the outskirts of Kabul. Following 18 months of effort by the conservators of the National Museum and the staff of the Archaeological Institute of Afghanistan, the museum was then reopened, as it had been in its original state. The restorers had the invaluable assistance of experts and scientists from around the country.

The Soviet invasion of Afghanistan on December 26, 1979 caused great political instability, developing into a popular uprising, that eventually claimed some 2 million victims. The invasion also led to the destruction of the economy and the cultural infrastructure. The superb museum at Hadda, 8 kilometers east of Jalalabad, was plundered and burned in 1981, a loss that can never be made good. The many treasures discovered by Afghan archaeologists at Hadda, stored at Jalalabad, were likewise looted and are lost forever. In 1988, with the security situation in Kabul continuing to deteriorate, the National Museum, in consultation with the Ministry of Information and Culture and the security forces, proposed that a number of works from the museum should be transferred to the custodianship of the then-President of the Republic, Mohammad Najibullah. This proposal was accepted. Objects from various collections, including those from Begram, Aï Khanum, and Hadda, as well as the gold from the Bactrian treasure, were transferred to a vault in the Central Bank in the Arg, the presidential palace. Finds from Fondukistan and Bamiyan were taken to the Ministry of Information and Culture. In the event of a problem with one of these hiding places, this measure would ensure that the others might still be safe. This approach paid off. The objects held in the National Museum at Darulaman suffered greater damage during the civil war than those taken to the Arg and to the Ministry, which have remained intact to this day. Despite the great difficulties, the hiding places of these works remained a secret throughout those years. In this manner at least part of Afghan history was preserved.

The removal of the Communist shackles in 1992 brought hope of a more peaceful future, but this was short-lived. The long war years had made the lives of Kabul's population hellish. Industry, all marks of civilization, state provisions, and private assets were plundered or left in ashes. Thousands of Afghan families had to leave the country. At the end of 1992, the personnel of the National Museum were placed on non-active status because of the dangers of the road accessing Darulaman. Staff had been arrested, mistreated, and even killed there for a variety of reasons. On the evening of December 31, 1992, two major works from Shotorak, which had pride of place in the hallway of the upper floor of the National Museum, were stolen. One piece, carved in slate and dating from the second or third century A.D., depicted a Buddhist legend, the adoration of the Buddha by the three Kashyapa brothers. This was bought in Peshawar, Pakistan, by a benevolent Japanese, and may eventually be returned to Afghanistan. The other is a bas-relief (Dipankara Jataka) 83.5 cm tall and dating from the same period. The government failed to take any action in response and so increased the likelihood of future thefts. Only days later the windows of the main storeroom of the National Museum were broken, and many pieces were stolen.

On March 12, 1994, the National Museum, which was being used as a military base and defensive position, was struck by a rocket during the fighting and burst into flames. On the evening of May 13, 1994, a BBC report declared that Afghanistan may have buried its children, but should not be burying its culture. This message created a great stir among the national and international cultural organizations, including the United Nations, and a worldwide alarm was raised. The heritage preserved in a country's museums—in this case the National Museum of Afghanistan, a very important museum representing the nation's values and its history—must be protected at all times. International treaties insist that such heritage must never be damaged; it must not be touched or moved to another location without the permission of the conservators, not even within the museum.

On November 29, 1994, the Special Representative of the Secretary General of the United Nations, Sotiris Mousouris, came to Kabul and visited the leader of the group holding this area. Mousouris asked the leader's permission to implement a plan for the rebuilding and restoration of the looted museum. The Representative's visit provided an opportunity for journalists, diplomats, and members of the United Nations and the Red Cross to visit various departments of the museum. Mousouris observed that a large number of works had been stolen from the National Museum, in particular a collection including some 40,000 coins from different eras. The same was true of a large portion of the floor coverings, including the superb Afghan carpets, which had decorated the entrance hall and the display rooms. The contents of several display cases, some donated by UNESCO, had been damaged by fire. Overcome by sadness, Mousouris said: "A museum is the major repository of history and represents the identity of a people so that even the smallest object must not be moved or interfered with. The removal of objects from a museum is an attack on the soul and spirit of the nation. The destruction of these works is an irreversible disaster, and their theft and looting are an unforgivable betrayal of the people." He made an immediate decision to throw a lifeline to the museum by pledging the financial support of the United Nations and the cooperation of the UN Office for the Coordination of Humanitarian Affairs (UNOCHA), the only UN organization still active in Kabul. The others had already transferred to Islamabad, Pakistan.

The National Museum's repository was provided with steel doors and a zinc roof covering. The windows were bricked up as protection against bullets, rockets, and other projectiles. Despite these measures, the roof was set alight during the bitter winter of 1994 and collapsed. Frescos in the Bactrian Hall and the Hall of the Ghaznavids were completely destroyed. Attempts were made to prevent snow and rainwater from penetrating the storerooms, using locally available materials such as clay-straw mortar. The Society for the Preservation of Afghanistan's Cultural Heritage (SPACH) was established in the same year, with indirect support from UNESCO. During that winter a team was brought in to rescue the collections on the upper floor of the museum from the rubble, taking a scientific approach. About 3,000 pieces, in stone, terracotta, and metal, many of them damaged, were saved and placed in storage.

In 1996 the Ministry of Culture and Information decided to remove the remainder of the works from the National Museum. Special committees were established to implement the project, dealing with recordkeeping, restoration, photography, packing, checking, transportion, and administration. A coordinating committee was also set up. All these committees were staffed by personnel from the National Museum and the Archaeological Institute. With the assistance of the National Security Forces, they managed to complete their task within six months. They worked in the storerooms by torchlight in an atmosphere choked with dust. The exhaustion could be seen on their faces. Many staffers developed allergies and had to cover their faces and mouths with masks. A total of 70 people were engaged in the work of recording, photographing, and packing the works, some of which were then transferred to the Hotel Kabul in the center of the city. Following the installation of the Taliban regime in Kabul, the pieces stored in the hotel were happily spared, but the museum's storerooms were looted and destroyed. Some months later the work of preparing an inventory of the remaining works in storage could be resumed, with the aid of equipment provided by SPACH.

At the beginning of 2001 the National Museum was faced with a further disaster as the Taliban decided that all images must be destroyed. A special group was charged with this task. They destroyed about 2,500 works of art. In March of 2001 they dynamited the giant Buddha statues at Bamiyan, which were 38 meters and 55 meters tall. These barbaric acts, which filled the heart of every decent Afghan with anger, represented an irreplaceable loss. Terrible damage was caused at every archaeological site in the country. Neither the coming generations of Afghans nor human history will forget this era of tyranny and destruction.

The Treasure of Tillya Tepe: The Work of Afghan Archaeologists

The treasure of Tillya Tepe was discovered in the ruined fire worshippers' temple of the second millennium B.C. behind the abandoned city of

Sheberghan in northern Afghanistan. In the winter of 1978-1979 the Soviet–Afghan Archaeological Expedition conducted excavations at Tillya Tepe under the direction of Viktor Sarianidi. The expedition found 21,618 gold, silver, and ivory objects in the six tombs there. The tombs were those of wealthy nomads, interred at the start of the Christian era in simple burial cists. The wooden lids had long since vanished, but the objects within remained undamaged and were of exceptional quality: Silver crescents, gold chains, a tree decorated with pearls, an engraved coin showing a mythological creature, an image of Aphrodite, a belt clasp depicting a man on a dolphin, a winged dragon, a gold crown, and Roman, Parthian, and Greek coins. The gold objects were photographed and listed by the expedition and presented to the National Museum by the Afghan Archaeological Department in 1979.

Part of the treasure was exhibited in the National Museum in 1980, but in 1985, as a precaution, the objects were moved to the Koti Baghcha palace. As has already been described, they were placed in the vaults of the Central Bank of Afghanistan in 1988. In July 1991 a limited number of objects were exhibited for a day at the Koti Baghcha palace. They were then withdrawn from public view. Only the museum staff who had brought the objects to the Central Bank knew the hiding place, which kept the objects safe from terror, violence, civil war, and the Taliban. At the end of 1992 officials visited the site to verify the existence of the crates. Numerous rumors circulated: The objects were said to be stolen, sold on the black market, or melted down. Those who knew the truth kept silent until 2002, when at the urging of the Director of Museums in the Ministry of Culture and Information a delegation was sent to the vaults of the Central Bank to investigate. The delegation reported that the crates were still sealed. In 2003 the Afghan government confirmed that the objects from Tillya Tepe were intact. In March 2004 the Minister of Culture, Information, and Tourism reached an agreement with the National Geographic Society on listing the works in the National Museum. In April 2004 an inventory of the objects was begun in the vaults of the Central Bank, with a data card in Dari and English for each item. Present on the first day were Viktor Sarianidi, Fredrik Hiebert, Carla Grissmann, and senior officials and members of the special committees of the National Museum and the Afghan Archaeological Institute. They listed 22,607 objects, 20,587 of them from Tillya Tepe. The remainder came from Begram, Hadda, Fondukistan, Tepe Fullol, Aï Khanum, and Surkh Kotal. There was also a set of gold and silver coins. Sadly, many of the objects that had not been moved were lost. Local and foreign experts were called on for assistance in listing the museum collections and setting up a database to record them. The National Geographic Society, UNESCO, and SPACH, in collaboration with the management of the National Museum, began the work of digitalizing the collections, one of the focal points of the museum's program of works.

Museum Inventory

In 2004, when the first boxes were opened at the Presidential Palace (*Arg*), a new inventory system for the National Museum of Afghanistan was implemented. A team of museum professionals from the National Museum of Afghanistan and from the Institute of Archaeology of Afghanistan was assembled, including collections managers, conservators, a photographer, and computer specialists. Together with museum specialists from abroad they were able to record all information about the objects in both Dari and English. The new inventory system employs international standards of museum description and scholarly access while preserving the traditional museum curatorial system of having a key holder (*tahilwidar*) for accountability and security.

International standards of object description were used to categorize each artifact. As of today, measurements have been taken for more than 23,000 objects—each object photographed, provided with a conservation record, and signed and returned to safe storage—thus allowing the collections to be studied throughout the world.

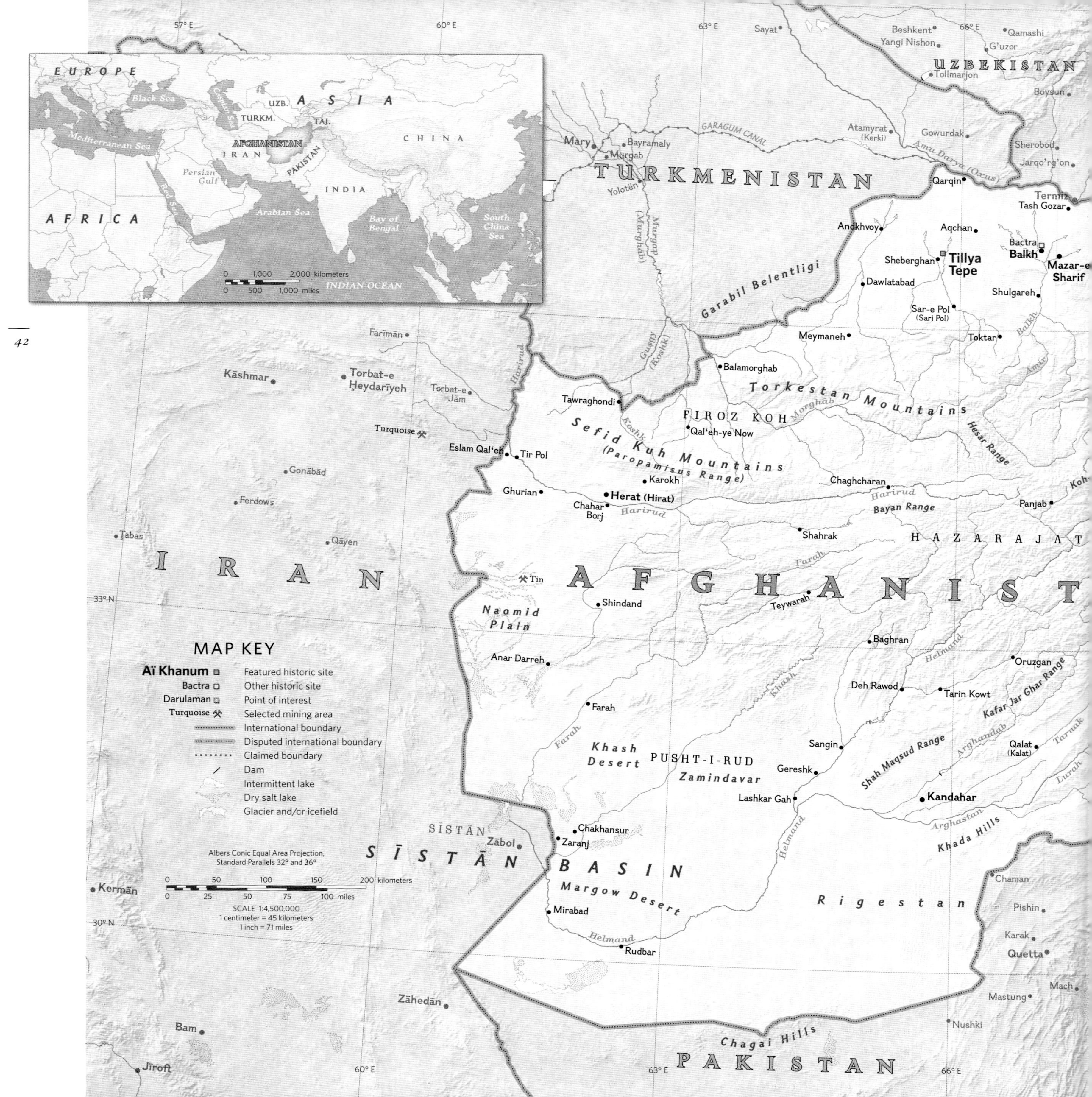
EUROPE
ASIA
Black Sea
Caspian Sea
UZB.
TURKM.
TAJ.
CHINA
AFGHANISTAN
IRAN
PAKISTAN
Mediterranean Sea
Persian Gulf
INDIA
Red Sea
AFRICA
Arabian Sea
Bay of Bengal
South China Sea
INDIAN OCEAN
0 1,000 2,000 kilometers
0 500 1,000 miles
57° E
60° E
63° E
66° E
33° N
30° N
UZBEKISTAN
TURKMENISTAN
IRAN
AFGHANISTAN
PAKISTAN
Sayat
Beshkent
Yangi Nishon
G'uzor
Qamashi
Tollmarjon
Boysun
GARAGUM CANAL
Atamyrat (Kerki)
Gowurdak
Sherobod
Jarqo'rg'on
Amu Darya (Oxus)
Mary
Bayramaly
Murgab
Yolotën
Murgap (Murghab)
Qarqin
Termiz
Tash Gozar
Andkhvoy
Aqchan
Bactra
Balkh
Mazar-e Sharif
Sheberghan
Tillya Tepe
Dawlatabad
Shulgareh
Garabil Belentligi
Sar-e Pol (Sari Pol)
Toktar
Balkh
Amir
Meymaneh
Gasgy (Koshk)
Balamorghab
Torkestan Mountains
Hesar Range
Harirud
Farīmān
Kāshmar
Torbat-e Heydarīyeh
Torbat-e Jām
Tawraghondi
FIROZ KOH
Morghab
Koshk
Qal'eh-ye Now
Sefid Kuh Mountains
(Paropamisus Range)
Turquoise
Eslam Qal'eh
Tir Pol
Karokh
Chaghcharan
Gonābād
Ghurian
Herat (Hirat)
Chahar Borj
Harirud
Bayan Range
Panjab
Ferdows
Tabas
Qāyen
Shahrak
HAZARAJAT
Farah
Tin
Shindand
Teywarah
Naomid Plain
Baghran
Helmand
Oruzgan
Anar Darreh
Khash
Deh Rawod
Tarin Kowt
Kafar Jar Ghar Range
Farah
Farah
Khash Desert
PUSHT-I-RUD
Zamindavar
Sangin
Gereshk
Shah Maqsud Range
Arghandab
Qalat (Kalat)
Tarnak
Lurah
Lashkar Gah
Kandahar
Arghastan
Khada Hills
SĪSTĀN
Chakhansur
Zābol
Zaranj
SĪSTĀN BASIN
Helmand
Margow Desert
Rigestan
Chaman
Pishin
Kermān
Mirabad
Karak
Quetta
Helmand
Rudbar
Mach
Mastung
Zāhedān
Nushki
Bam
Chagai Hills
Jīroft
MAP KEY
Aï Khanum Featured historic site
Bactra Other historic site
Darulaman Point of interest
Turquoise Selected mining area
International boundary
Disputed international boundary
Claimed boundary
Dam
Intermittent lake
Dry salt lake
Glacier and/or icefield
Albers Conic Equal Area Projection, Standard Parallels 32° and 36°
0 50 100 150 200 kilometers
0 25 50 75 100 miles
SCALE 1:4,500,000
1 centimeter = 45 kilometers
1 inch = 71 miles

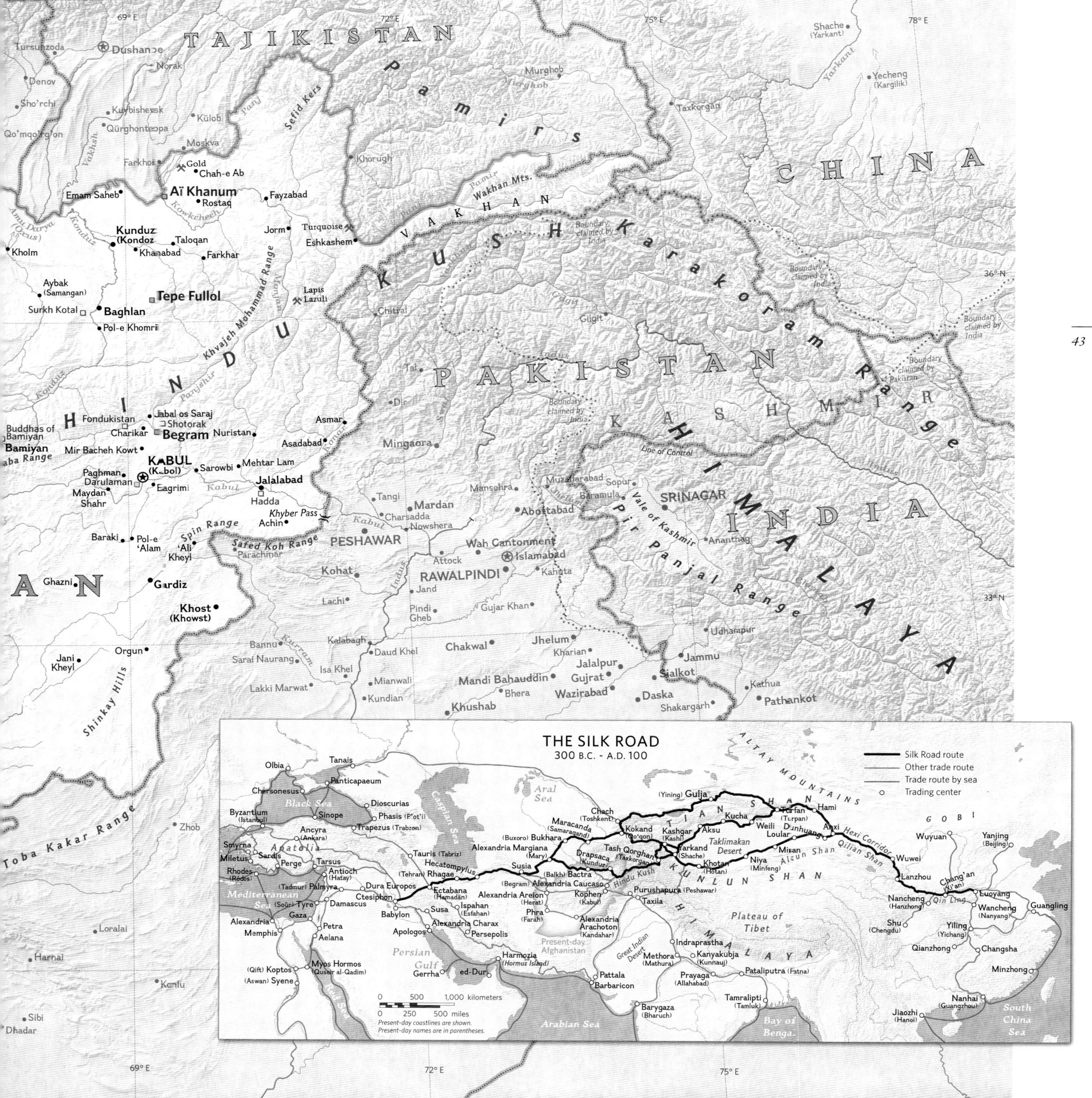

TAJIKISTAN
Pamirs
CHINA
HINDU KUSH
Karakoram Range
PAKISTAN
KASHMIR
INDIA
HIMALAYA
AN
Dushanbe
Tursunzoda
Denov
Sho'rchi
Qo'mqo'rg'on
Kuybishevsk
Qŭrghonteppa
Kŭlob
Norak
Moskva
Farkhor
Gold
Chah-e Ab
Aï Khanum
Rostaq
Fayzabad
Emam Saheb
Kunduz (Kondoz)
Taloqan
Khanabad
Farkhar
Kholm
Aybak (Samangan)
Surkh Kotal
Baghlan
Pol-e Khomri
Tepe Fullol
Lapis Lazuli
Jorm
Turquoise
Eshkashem
Khvajeh Mohammad Range
Sefid Kers
Murghob
Khorugh
Wakhan Mts.
WAKHAN
Taxkorgan
Shache (Yarkant)
Yecheng (Kargilik)
Yarkant
Chitral
Gilgit
Indus
Tai
Dir
Mingaora
Asmar
Asadabad
Nuristan
Fondukistan
Jabal os Saraj
Shotorak
Begram
Charikar
Buddhas of Bamiyan
Bamiyan
Mir Bacheh Kowt
KABUL (Kabol)
Paghman
Darulaman
Sarowbi
Mehtar Lam
Eagrimi
Maydan Shahr
Jalalabad
Hadda
Khyber Pass
Achin
Kabul
Spin Range
Safed Koh Range
Parachinar
Baraki
Pol-e 'Alam
'Ali Kheyl
Ghazni
Gardiz
Khost (Khowst)
Orgun
Jani Kheyl
Shinkay Hills
Toba Kakar Range
Zhob
Loralai
Harnai
Kohlu
Sibi
Dhadar
Tangi
Mardan
Charsadda
Nowshera
PESHAWAR
Kohat
Lachi
Attock
Wah Cantonment
Islamabad
RAWALPINDI
Kahuta
Jand
Pindi Gheb
Gujar Khan
Mansehra
Abbottabad
Muzaffarabad
Baramula
Sopur
SRINAGAR
Vale of Kashmir
Pir Panjal Range
Anantnag
Line of Control
Boundary claimed by India
Boundary claimed by Pakistan
Udhampur
Jammu
Sialkot
Kathua
Pathankot
Shakargarh
Daska
Wazirabad
Gujrat
Jalalpur
Kharian
Jhelum
Chakwal
Mandi Bahauddin
Bhera
Khushab
Kalabagh
Daud Khel
Isa Khel
Mianwali
Kundian
Bannu
Sarai Naurang
Lakki Marwat
Kurram
69° E
72° E
75° E
78° E
36° N
33° N
THE SILK ROAD
300 B.C. - A.D. 100
Silk Road route
Other trade route
Trade route by sea
Trading center
ALTAY MOUNTAINS
GOBI
TIAN SHAN
KUNLUN SHAN
Taklimakan Desert
Hexi Corridor
Qilian Shan
Altun Shan
Plateau of Tibet
Hindu Kush
Black Sea
Caspian Sea
Aral Sea
Mediterranean Sea
Persian Gulf
Red Sea
Arabian Sea
Bay of Bengal
South China Sea
Anatolia
Great Indian Desert
Present-day Afghanistan
Olbia
Tanais
Panticapaeum
Chersonesus
Dioscurias
Phasis (P'ot'i)
Byzantium (Istanbul)
Sinope
Trapezus (Trabzon)
Ancyra (Ankara)
Smyrna
Sardis
Miletus
Perge
Tarsus
Rhodes (Ródos)
Antioch (Hatay)
(Tadmur) Palmyra
(Soûr) Tyre
Damascus
Dura Europos
Ctesiphon
Babylon
Alexandria
Gaza
Memphis
Petra
Aelana
(Qift) Koptos
(Aswan) Syene
Myos Hormos (Quseir al-Qadim)
Apologos
Alexandria Charax
Gerrha
ed-Dur
Harmozia (Hormuz Island)
Tauris (Tabriz)
(Tehran) Rhagae
Hecatompylus
Ectabana (Hamadān)
Susa
Ispahan (Esfahan)
Persepolis
(Buxoro) Bukhara
Alexandria Margiana (Mary)
Maracanda (Samarqand)
Chach (Toshkent)
Kokand (Qo'qon)
Drapsaca (Kunduz)
Tash Qorghan (Taxkorgan)
Susia
(Balkh) Bactra
(Begram) Alexandria Caucaso
Alexandria Areion (Herat)
Phra (Farah)
Kophen (Kabul)
Alexandria Arachoton (Kandahar)
Purushapura (Peshawar)
Taxila
Kashgar (Kashi)
Tarkand (Shache)
Khotan (Hotan)
Niya (Minfeng)
Miran
Aksu
Kucha
Weili
Loulan
(Yining) Gulja
Turfan (Turpan)
Hami
Dunhuang
Anxi
Wuwei
Lanzhou
Chang'an (Xi'an)
Luoyang
Nancheng (Hanzhong)
Qin Ling
Wancheng (Nanyang)
Guangling
Shu (Chengdu)
Yiling (Yichang)
Qianzhong
Changsha
Minzhong
Nanhai (Guangzhou)
Jiaozhi (Hanoi)
Wuyuan
Yanjing (Beijing)
Indraprastha
Methora (Mathura)
Kanyakubja (Kunnauj)
Prayaga (Allahabad)
Pataliputra (Patna)
Tamralipti (Tamluk)
Pattala
Barbaricon
Barygaza (Bharuch)
0 500 1,000 kilometers
0 250 500 miles
Present-day coastlines are shown.
Present-day names are in parentheses.

CHAPTER II

Saving Afghanistan's Heritage

CARLA GRISSMANN
Member of SPACH and
Kabul Museum specialist

FREDRIK HIEBERT
National Geographic Society

Terracotta Buddha statue from the site of Hadda. The statue was photographed at the moment of unwrapping in the presidential palace, Kabul, 2004.

DURING THE LAST THREE DECADES, AFGHANISTAN'S CULTURAL heritage has been ravaged by war and neglect. Archaeological sites have been systematically plundered, the Kabul Museum has been destroyed, and its collections have been looted. The Kabul Museum itself, located in Darulaman, was in a particularly dangerous area, being far removed from the center of the city. It was occupied, shelled, and looted—yet miraculously many of the masterpieces of the museum survived.

A rudimentary inventory to ascertain what remained in the museum was begun in 1996, and the current and ongoing computerized inventory began in 2003. A brief chronological outline of the collection's recent history is presented here to set this exhibit in context.

The Kabul Museum During the Past Years

In April 1979, a year after the communist Saur Revolution, the Kabul Museum was abruptly ordered to move its contents from Darulaman on the outskirts of the city into a deserted house in western Kabul. The museum building was turned into an annex of the Ministry of Defense (located in the nearby Darulaman Palace), and the whole area became a military zone. The contents of the ground and first floor were carted away, and all underground stores were sealed off. At the temporary storage area, objects were piled up to the ceiling in hallways and basements; the garden was strewn with broken showcases, pedestals, office furniture, and metal coin cases. The staff moved into the servants' quarters, the library into a garage.

In October 1980, the contents of the museum were moved back to Darulaman. The building had been repaired, the rooms painted, proper toilets installed, and the grounds cared for. The collections were reinstalled in their original rooms, having miraculously suffered very little damage. All the exhibits were intact. New artifacts were installed: ancient frescoes from Delbarjin and Dashli Tepe, newly excavated objects from Aï Khanum, and a white marble Hindu Shahi Surya uncovered in Khair Khan by Soviet soldiers. The 1980s were tumultuous times for Afghanistan, yet the museum remained open. In 1982, Viktor Sarianidi was even able to return to photograph and study the 20,000 objects from the Bactrian gold collection.

In 1989, while Afghanistan was being relentlessly destroyed during the years of the war, Kabul and the museum remained relatively intact. However, the Najibullah government officially closed the vulnerable museum and ordered objects on exhibit (numbering approximately 600) to be prepared for moving. Again the collections were packed up. To minimize the risk of loss, some trunks were moved to the Central Bank treasury vault in the Presidential Palace and others to the Ministry of Information and Culture, while the rest remained in the various depots of the Kabul Museum. Some of the finest ancient coins, gold objects from Tepe Fullol, and the famous Bactrian gold were placed in the bank vault in the palace. The heavy stone sculptures and inscriptions and many of the artifacts in the storerooms were left in the museum building.

The tragic years of 1992–1995 saw the destruction of Kabul and the Kabul Museum. Looting began in 1993 and continued each time the area of Darulaman changed hands. In May 1993 the museum building was shelled and the roof and top floor destroyed. In early 1994, the United Nations Center for Human Settlements (UNCHS) weatherproofed the top floor, installed steel doors on the lower storerooms, and bricked up all windows. Fire had destroyed office records, including inventories, the photography room, the Delbarjin and Dashli Tepe frescoes, and most of the Islamic glass

Destroyed National Museum of Afghanistan, Kabul, 2001

and metal objects. Storerooms were pillaged, including much of the collection of 35,000 coins.

The Society for the Preservation of Afghanistan's Cultural Heritage (SPACH) was founded in Islamabad in 1994. Through a UNESCO grant, a member of the Guimet Museum came to Kabul for two weeks in the summer of 1995 to help the museum staff clean storerooms and to plan an inventory of what remained. Also in 1995, a liaison officer for SPACH began going to Kabul every year to facilitate the inventory process.

After 1995, the museum storerooms were again pilfered, leaving floors ankle-deep in rubble. The Kabul Museum had neither electricity nor water.

An Afghan girl stands next to a stone statue of a Kushan prince from the site of Surkh Kotal

Work was carried out by the light of kerosene lamps after the theft of the generator donated by UNCHS. Salaries from as low as $6 a month for the post of Director of Museums of Afghanistan to $2 a month for guards, went largely unpaid. Kabul was under attack almost daily. The massive schist sculptures in the museum had been wrenched off their iron hooks and carried away during the night curfew. Carved wooden Nuristani sculptures had been cut up for firewood. In the no-man's-land behind the museum, one locomotive from King Amanullah's railway stood rusting; the second one was stripped down for scrap metal. None of the collection of the king's cars remained at the museum.

The Ministry of Information and Culture of President Rabbani's government was anxious to safeguard what remained in the museum. In early 1996, the staff returned to the Kabul Museum and worked heroically for almost six months on this first and most difficult phase of the inventory. For the inventory process, space was cleared in the wreckage of the basement storerooms, with museum staff and two members from the Afghan Institute of Archaeology picking objects out of the debris around them. Each object, mostly fragments from the depots, was measured and briefly described in Dari and entered by hand into individual registers. The entries were copied by hand in English since there were no photocopy facilities or electricity in Kabul. The photographs of some objects were taken under extremely difficult conditions.

During the anxious two weeks before the arrival of the Taliban, more than 500 crates, trunks, and boxes were shifted from Darulaman to the deserted Kabul Hotel. This storage area was locked on September 28, 1996 by the Taliban government, and museum staff were no longer allowed to go to the museum.

Preparatory work to continue the 1996 inventory began in mid-July 1998. The Ministry of Information and Culture also planned restoration of the ground floor of the museum. Earlier in the year, the museum trunks and boxes had, once again, been shifted from the Kabul Hotel to the ground floor of the Ministry of Information and Culture. At the museum, the staff went back to sifting through the rubble that still littered the storeroom floors. Work stopped in August 1998, due to the U.S. bombing of Afghanistan. The museum staff had dispersed during the previous two years, coming to sign the register at the ministry and attempting to find odd jobs in the bazaars of Kabul. A senior staff member sold potatoes in the main market; the accountant ran a horse and buggy. Work started again in late May 1999. Unexpected objects were found in abandoned corners of the museum: 350 fragments from the Begram collection and 8 objects from Gul Darra, which had not been seen before. Still intact was the large ceramics storeroom in the basement of the right wing, the wooden drawers still bearing their original identification labels.

In 2000, the museum staff, now numbering only 20, continued the inventory. In October, the final total of objects inventoried since 1996 was 6,449.

Yet many museum artifacts were missing. SPACH—alerted that stolen museum objects were for sale in the markets—was able to purchase objects documented to have come from the Kabul Museum. Several of these were sent to the Guimet Museum for safekeeping and are on display in this exhibition: They are six rare fragments of Begram ivories and two plaster medallions, also from Begram.

On a positive note, in July 2000 a ministry commission unofficially confirmed that the seals on the Tillya Tepe gold and the numerous museum trunks in the bank vault and the ministry were still intact. Mullah Omar issued an edict protecting all cultural and historic relics of Afghanistan and making illegal excavation and smuggling of artifacts out of Afghanistan punishable by law.

The good news lasted only a short time. In March 2001, the world watched in impotent shock as the Taliban dynamited the Bamiyan Buddhas, destroyed major objects in the Kabul Museum, and vandalized the ministry and museum storerooms. Trunks were forced open, wrappings torn off, and objects smashed and left in chaotic disorder. Museum staff valiantly swept up the debris and repacked as much as possible.

By late 2001, at the request of UNESCO, the SPACH liaison officer assembled duplicate copies of all Dari and English inventories made between 1996 and 2000 at the Kabul Museum, as well as more than one thousand cards from the Délégation Archéologique Française en Afghanistan (DAFA) (some with photographs only, others with photographs and descriptions in French) from the 1970s that had been partially burned during the destruction of the museum in 1993. Duplicate copies of the Dari and English inventories were packed in separate trunks, one to go to the ministry for safekeeping, the second to stay at the museum for eventual reference purposes.

Already in 2002, the museum director had requested that all inventories be put in a database. The havoc caused by the Taliban destruction at the ministry and the museum rendered many of the rudimentary inventories on hand invalid. Thousands of artifacts had been separated from their identifying wrappings and packing cases, and were shattered into unrecognizable fragments. Others had been repacked in different boxes or swept together and packed in a jumble.

Further Inventory of the Kabul Museum Collections

In 2003, a report from the central bank in Kabul revealed that the museum trunks deposited there in 1989 were intact. During a visit to Kabul in October 2003, Fredrik Hiebert of the National Geographic Society and Thomas Barfield of Boston University were informed that the key holders of these trunks were now long gone and the labels unclear. Inventory of these objects became a priority for the Minister of Culture, and the museum director specifically asked for an inventory to begin with the Bactrian gold—as long as Professor Viktor Sarianidi of the Institute of Archaeology in Moscow would verify that these were indeed the actual artifacts. Funding for this inventory was secured from the National Geographic Society (NGS), along with an emergency grant from the National Endowment for the Humanities (NEH) to create a "mobile inventory lab"—a kit that would allow inventory in non-museum settings in Kabul. The kit included packing and conservation materials, along with laptop computers, digital cameras, and scanners to digitize the process for the first time. An Afghan inventory committee was appointed to approve an inventory protocol and the format of datasheets and to begin planning the actual inventory.

The team really did not know what to expect, despite the earlier ministry commission reports that the seals of the trunks were intact. A search was made for the former key holders with some success; a judge was appointed to take the place of the missing officials. The inventory team, led by Omara Khan Massoudi, director of the Kabul Museum, included Carla Grissmann and Fredrik Hiebert, tahilwidars (key holders), conservators, a photographer and computer specialist from the National Museum, and specialists from the Afghan Institute of Archaeology. With Viktor Sarianidi's assistance the team was prepared to confirm the authenticity of what he had last seen in 1982.

On the day of the opening of the vault in 2003, the Minister of Culture, along with diplomats, many officials, and the Afghan press squeezed into the cramped temporary inventory room. Viktor Sarianidi had arrived directly from his dig site in the deserts of Turkmenistan—traveling by truck across the desert, then by air from Baku to Kabul—and was now standing in front of the heavy safes that he had last seen more than 20 years before. When the first safe was finally cracked, the team saw piles of small plastic bags with old labels—each one containing beads and jewelry from Tillya Tepe tomb no. VI. These objects had been buried with a nomad princess 2,000 years ago and were only briefly revealed in 1978. Most of the people in the room had never seen these objects. Viktor Sarianidi examined several of the pieces. His expression changed, and he smiled broadly upon examining a pair of hairpieces. He pointed out a small wire repair that he had made with his own

Minister of Information and Culture Sayeed Makhdoom Raheen (center) turns to Viktor Sarianidi (left, front) as the inventory team opens the first safe of Bactrian gold in the presidential bank vault, Kabul, 2004.

hands, proving that these were the original items, not some copies replacing the originals.

The next step was more tedious: counting and assessing the 20,000 individual artifacts from the six burials. Viktor Sarianidi provided the team with the full documentation from the excavation inventory and returned to his dig in the Turkmenistan desert. The inventory progressed on a daily basis for the next three months. The team came to know the artifacts well. The manufacture of the jewelry from the six nomadic burials was so similar that it became clear that these were all locally made, possibly even in the workshop of a single goldsmith.

By June 2004, the Tillya Tepe collection had been inventoried, and the news was released that the entire collection of Bactrian gold was safe. President Karzai visited the now familiar inventory room and *The New York Times* first reported the story in the Western press.

A second inventory stage followed as more trunks came out of the vault. Funding from NGS and NEH allowed the inventory team to continue work late in 2004. In the second inventory, the team opened trunks containing objects that had been packed in 1989. The inventory system was streamlined by months of practice. From unwrapping an object to identification, description both in Dari and English, photography and conservation assessment, the team hardly had time to admire the artifacts. These included ivories, glass, and bronze items from Begram and other sites that had been thought lost, and fragile sculptures and frescoes from ancient sites at Bamiyan and Fondukistan. The important finding was that almost every object that had been on display at the museum (except for the collections left in the museum) was preserved. The condition of even the most delicate artifacts was remarkably good—all preserved during the 1990s and despite the unconscionable smashing of artifacts by the Taliban.

In 2005 the inventory continued in the storerooms of the museum, and many artifacts there were found intact—particularly amazing was the figurative sculpture that had narrowly escaped destruction in 2001.

Inventory at the museum continues. Indeed, the practice of inventory in a museum is never finished. Objects come to the museum from the new DAFA excavations at Balkh, and Professor Zemaryalai Tarzi's current excavations in Bamiyan. Items from clandestine digs are also being recovered and sent to the museum, and objects looted from Afghanistan are being repatriated from around the world. Training of museum personnel is a high priority. The ultimate goal is that at the time when the treasures of the Kabul Museum in this volume return to Afghanistan, conditions will allow them to be displayed permanently for all Afghans to see.

CHAPTER III

The Lost Worlds of Afghanistan

FREDRIK HIEBERT
National Geographic Society

The land of modern Afghanistan mirrors the lands of the eastern provinces of the Greek world as described by Herodotus.

OPPOSITE: *Modern horsemen near the ancient ramparts of Balkh, northern Afghanistan.*

WITHIN THESE "HIDDEN TREASURES," YOU WILL SEE SOME OF the most remarkable archaeological finds in all of Central Asia. These pieces are not only artistically splendid, but also unravel significant elements of the mystery of their ancient creators and owners and thus our ancient shared past. Each of the four collections included here relates the rich story of its particular site: from Fullol, a Bronze Age set of gold bowls that hint of the native wealth of Afghanistan; from Aï Khanum, artifacts from a Greek city in northern Afghanistan; from Begram, untouched treasures from a merchant's storeroom sealed up 2,000 years ago; and from Tillya Tepe, a selection of the golden jewels that six Bactrian nomads took with them to their graves.

When looking at the collection, visitors may be surprised by the wide range of styles and materials of the artifacts. To understand the pieces, it's necessary to find out a little more about the history of Afghanistan. Wrought from conflict, the country of Afghanistan was created in the late 19th century as a result of the competition between rival modern powers. In what historians call the "Great Game," British, Russian, and Persian leaders created Afghanistan as a buffer zone, unintentionally linking the edges of three distinct lands described by the ancient Greeks and Persians 2,000 years ago: Bactria (northern Afghanistan), Aria (western Afghanistan), and Arachosia (southern Afghanistan). Modern Afghanistan, once the borderland between ancient peoples, now encompasses the confluence of these regions and provides Afghanistan with its diverse and robust cultural heritage.

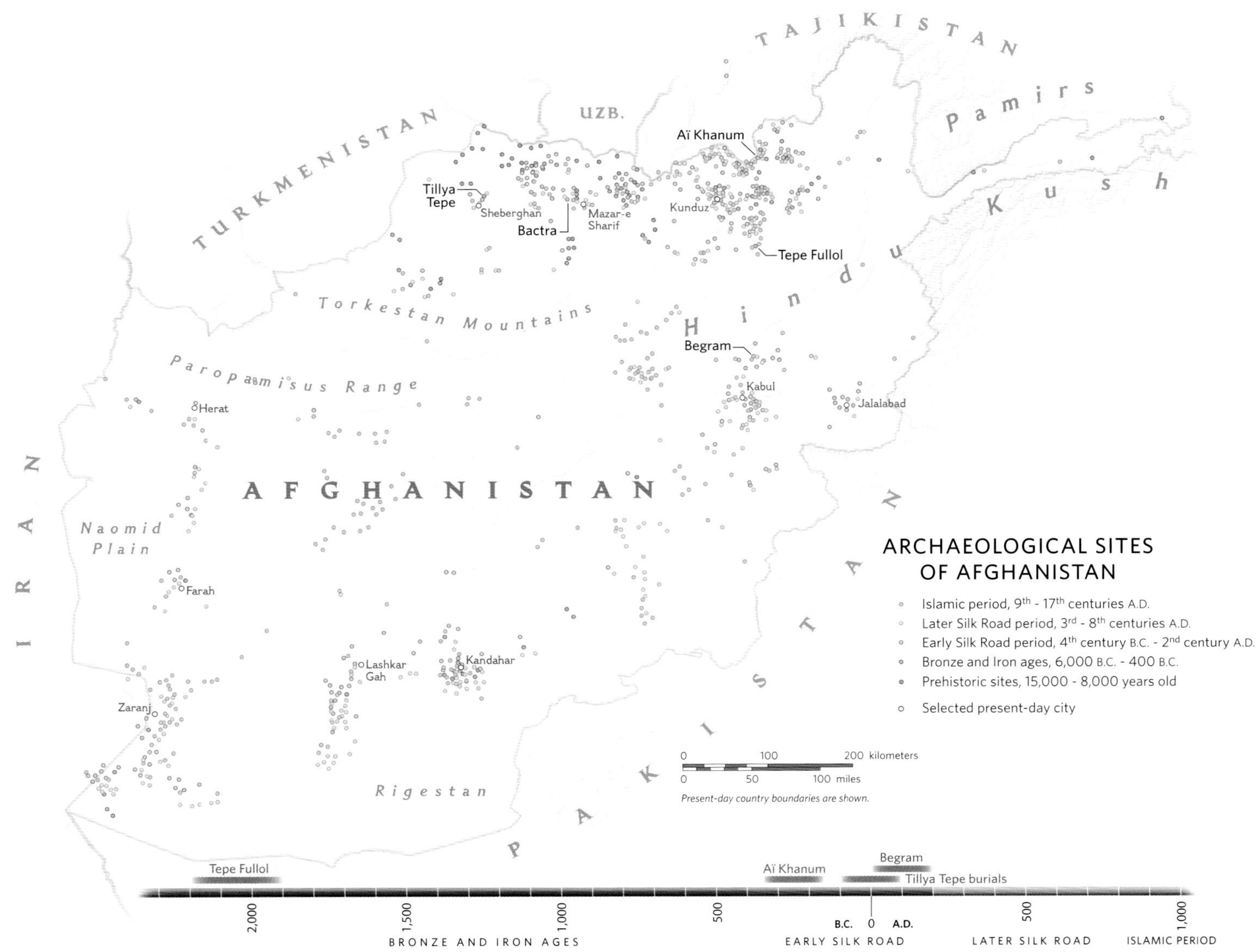

ARCHAEOLOGICAL AFGHANISTAN. *The above map reflects the distribution of the known archaeological sites in Afghanistan that span from the earliest remains, c. 15,000 years ago, through the 17th century A.D.*

Today more than 1,500 archaeological sites are known in the territory of Afghanistan, and surely many more are yet to be found. Artifacts from these sites document settlement of these lands from the Paleolithic (up to 8,000 years ago) through the historical periods. Throughout this time, the peoples of Afghanistan were central in the development of world religions, played a major role in trade and exchange, and at times dominated political and cultural life in Asia.

This exhibition presents but a selection of the historic and artistic treasures of Afghanistan. Aside from Fullol, the Bronze Age site, the collections relate to one of the most dynamic periods in Afghanistan's history, from the third century B.C. to the first century A.D.—which covers the beginning of Silk Road trade.

The Silk Road, the network of trade routes between early states, started with the exchange of goods between Rome and China in the first centuries B.C./A.D., and peaked with trade between the empires of Tang China and the Byzantines several hundred years later. There was, in fact, no "road" but a series of paths connecting cities, trading posts, caravan watering places, and hostels between the eastern Roman frontier in the Middle East and the Chinese frontier, and others going north through Afghanistan from the Indian Ocean to the Siberian steppe. People in those widely separated locations facilitated traffic and participated in this trade network.

Merchants seldom carried products from one end of the Silk Road to the other. The distances to be covered were so great, and the rigors of travel so daunting, that only goods that combined light weight with very high value were practical to transport the entire distance. Products traveled instead from hand to hand, from trading town to trading town. Goods were added to the caravans as they passed through markets—ivories from India; horses from Siberia and Mongolia; rubies, garnets, lapis lazuli, gold, and tin from Afghanistan; and carpets from Persia and settlements of the steppe. Some of the most important items traded to China were precious metals and coins, glass, and semi-precious stones. In return, China traded silk and other fine textiles, lacquered bowls, and other luxury goods to the West.

The Bronze Age Background to the Silk Road Trade

The exhibition begins with artifacts from Fullol, left by inhabitants of northern Afghanistan during the Bronze Age—a time long before the Silk Road trade began. The set of gold bowl fragments dates back 4,000 years.

The story of Afghanistan begins even before that. Farmers and herders settled in the plains surrounding the Hindu Kush as early as 7000 B.C. They brought traditions of building dwellings from unbaked mud brick and making pottery from local clay. These people may have grown wealthy off the lapis lazuli and tin they found along riverbeds, which they traded to early city sites to the west, across Iran and Mesopotamia.

As farms and villages grew and thrived in Afghanistan, these ancient people eventually devised methods of irrigation that allowed them to grow crops on the northern Afghanistan desert plains in what would later be known to the West as Bactria. Here constellations of sites located on deltaic plains formed man-made oases created by large irrigation systems some 4,000 years ago. These oasis peoples fortified their settlements against the elements, as well as their foes, in much the same architecture style the area's inhabitants do today. The oasis culture shared aspects of civilization with its Mesopotamian neighbors: artistic craftsmanship, presence of an elite class, and complex public rituals.

However, the one thing this civilization lacked was a writing system—giving us no clue as to even what the people called themselves. Today scholars call this un-named culture the "Bactria-Margiana Archaeological Complex" (BMAC), or the "Oxus civilization." The artistic decoration on the bowls of the Fullol treasure—part of the BMAC—shows both local motifs and designs better known in the distant cultures of the Middle East, suggesting that by the Bronze Age, the people of Afghanistan were already involved in international trade.

Unfortunately, much of what we know about this Bronze Age "Bactrian" civilization comes from clandestine excavations. Since the 1970s thousands of Bronze Age Bactrian objects were dug up, probably from ancient burials, revealing the art of these ancient people. When looting or other undocumented excavations take place, however, not only are the objects often taken out of their country of origin, but the significance of each object—

who owned it, what other artifacts were next to it, where it came from—is lost forever.

Afghanistan, revered as a crossroads of civilization, was also home to religion. The fortified 4,000-year-old oasis buildings appear to be the forerunners of fire-temples. Over the passage of time and political and cultural change, such structures developed into specialized buildings for the world's earliest monotheistic region: Zoroastrianism. Viktor Sarianidi was excavating just such a fortified site at Tillya Tepe where the intrusive burials, interred some 1,500 years later, were found containing the Bactrian Gold.

Aï Khanum

Neighboring empires did not ignore such riches. The splendid wealth of Afghanistan exerted such powerful sway over the Persians and Greeks that they were compelled to try to claim it for their own. The Persians' legends about these lands' natural resources and treasures first gave us the names of the regions that would one day become Afghanistan: "Bactria" in northern Afghanistan, "Sattagydia" in the mountainous center (later called "Parapamisadai" by the Greeks), "Aria" in the west around Herat, and "Arachosia" in southern Afghanistan near Kandahar. Cyrus the Great conquered these areas as part of the Achaemenid Empire, as recorded on the Behistun inscription in Iran in 519 B.C. From this time onward, Afghanistan would be known as part of the "Orient" by Western scholars. The riches of the lands in Afghanistan also attracted the attention of Alexander the Great.

The Greco-Bactrian site of Aï Khanum in northern Afghanistan revealed tangible evidence of these conquests and shows that the foreign influences became a persistent part of the local culture. The artifacts and architecture at Aï Khanum are truly a melding of Western (classical) and local ideas, products and culture. In the exhibition, different cases represent different parts of the site: the palace treasury, the temple sanctuary, the administrative quarters, the gymnasium, and the cemetery. Although the Greek influence and the legacy of Alexander the Great are evident, adaptations of traditions by the local culture of northern Afghanistan are also apparent.

Alexander the Great's conquest of the Persian Empire and eventual push to the borders of India established many cities associated with this period. A number of these, including Aï Khanum, were further developed by the generals he left in charge and their successors. Thus the Greek language (used by the ruling class and for official purposes) and aspects of Greek art and culture were implanted in Afghanistan—at their farthest extension from the Greek homeland. Non-Greek people in Afghanistan used the Greek language for some five centuries for at least certain formal purposes such as coin inscriptions. The Buddhist art of Afghanistan and Pakistan in the first through the fourth centuries A.D. shows clear connections with Greco-Roman art. And even many centuries later, in the Islamic period, legends continued to be told of a mighty hero named Iskandar—that is, Alexander.

The topography of Aï Khanum, protected by two rivers on a natural acropolis 60 meters higher than the surrounding plain, made it an ideal choice for ancient city planners. The residential quarters and public buildings—the gymnasium, temple, fortifications, royal palace, and administrative complex—were built on the lower part of the site, which was less exposed to the winds than the acropolis. The artifacts from the excavations include architectural elements, sculpture, and ritual and elite objects of great value. These objects and inscriptions provide a tantalizing insight into the local origins and foreign influences of ancient Afghanistan's Silk Road culture in the centuries following the campaigns of Alexander the Great in Afghanistan.

The earliest materials from the site can be dated to the fourth century B.C., as seen in the Clearchos inscription, though most of the finds date closer to the second century B.C. The site was abandoned around 130 B.C., likely due to fierce nomadic incursions, with evidence of intense fires from which the city never fully recovered. While finds of Greco-Bactrian coins across

THE BAMIYAN VALLEY. *High mountains and lush valleys characterize central Afghanistan, where trade and religion flourished together.*

Bactria show the influence of the culture, Aï Khanum is the only true Greco-Bactrian settlement ever excavated and documents the mix of local, other Asian, and Hellenistic traditions.

Begram and Tillya Tepe

The Begram and Tillya Tepe sites have yielded the greatest archaeological treasures found in Afghanistan, if not in all of Central Asia. The finds from both of these sites were discovered under remarkable, painstakingly careful circumstances of preservation. From the ancient city of Begram, two store-rooms containing luxury goods from the first century A.D. had remained untouched after the doors of the rooms were bricked shut and the site abandoned. From Tillya Tepe, six burials rich with gold ornaments remained untouched for 2,000 years, the remains of nomads hidden among more ancient ruins. Such instances of preservation are unusual in Central Asia and, in both instances, particularly unusual in that they include exceptionally rich artistic and cultural meaning.

Begram

Nearly 80 years ago, archaeologists digging in Begram came across two sealed rooms with an undisturbed array of ancient glassware, art, precious objects, and furniture decorations, fallen to the dirt floor directly beneath the places where the wooden structures they once adorned had long since decomposed. Since their discovery, art historians and archaeologists have puzzled over just how the marvelous and diverse objects came to be in the sealed rooms. Was it a royal treasure hoarded there over time by the Kushan emperors, or was the gathering of goods found in the two rooms actually mercantile stock? The assertion that the objects were a royal treasure might explain the otherwise confounding difference of one or two centuries between the proposed dates of a few individual pieces. Other scholars discount this difference in dates and point to a consistent pattern of first century A.D.

dates for most of the Begram finds. If the dates are viewed as contemporaneous, the gathering of goods found in the two rooms might be interpreted as a merchant's or trader's stock rather than a royal treasure hoard. In this light, Begram might be seen not only as a royal residence but also as an important trading center on the northwestern edge of the Kushan Empire, active in well-established trade routes between China, south-central Asia, and the Greco-Roman world. The objects thus provide a glimpse into the heart of the Silk Road at a time of intense commercial exchange.

Tillya Tepe

The gold artifacts unearthed at Tillya Tepe are nothing short of breathtaking, both for their design and for the light they shine on the lives of the ancient people they once adorned. More than 21,000 individual gold artifacts were found in the six burials excavated at the hill appropriately named "Hill of Gold" (Tillya Tepe) in 1978. When the discovery was first made, it was headline news around the world. The elaborate designs of the artifacts tell the story of a sophisticated group of nomads who were an essential part of the Silk Road—in contact with a vast array of peoples across Asia with goods both from Rome and from China. The Tillya Tepe collections document the metamorphosis of Silk Road art into unique, local iconography in a highly refined style with workmanship of exceptional quality. The nomadic treasures from Tillya Tepe represent the final stage in the development of Silk Road art—a synthesis of the ideas and beliefs into a unique art style, seen for the first time in Afghanistan with this single, spectacular find.

Owing to Viktor Sarianidi's careful excavations, it is possible to reconstruct the cut of the garments and how clothing and jewelry would have been worn. The gold pieces are even more remarkable in that, based on their workmanship and materials, they appear to be almost entirely locally made, possibly even coming from a single workshop.

While the cause of the nomads' death remains a mystery, the sumptuousness of their clothing and jewelry and the care with which they were buried indicates a people of high status, perhaps a family, who perished at the same time and were carefully buried—hidden among the walls of an even more ancient site.

Sarianidi's study of these finds was cut short by the ensuing war and chaos that extinguished this exciting moment of discovery. For a second time, the Tillya Tepe treasures were hidden—this time in the basement of the presidential bank vault. Only a few Afghans knew where they were, hidden with the other ancient treasures of Afghanistan's past. As the recent past becomes part of Afghanistan's history, we can now tell the story of the Afghan heroes who risked their lives protecting these treasures. When the boxes were finally opened, the world sighed in relief. Here these priceless objects were, preserved for all to see.

"Hidden Treasures" provides powerful impressions, not only of the rare and beautiful objects themselves but also of the history and significance of Afghanistan and its culture, aesthetics, and commerce. Ancient Afghanistan was a place of remarkable diversity, influenced both by a wide array of notable cultures and by its role as a key player along the Silk Road. The following essays and catalog descriptions outline in detail the context and significance of these finds and these peoples' role in world history.

Catalog

CHAPTER IV

The Treasure of Tepe Fullol

JEAN-FRANÇOIS JARRIGE
Director, Musée national des Arts asiatiques Guimet

Bronze Age gold beaker from Quetta, Pakistan

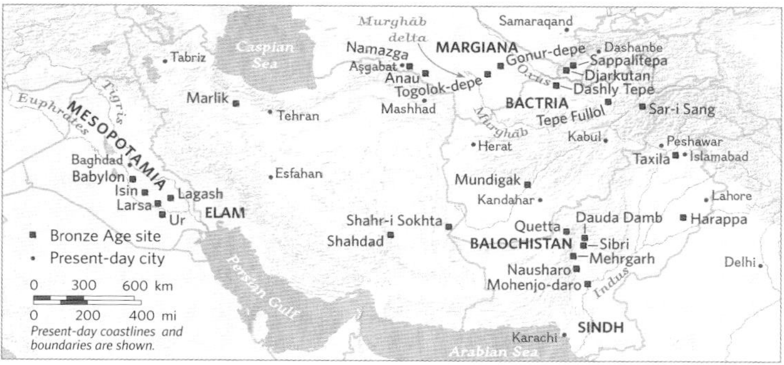

BRONZE AGE ARCHAEOLOGICAL SITES.
The map above showing parts of central and south Asia, reflects the distribution of Bronze Age sites mentioned in this chapter.

IN 1972 MAURIZIO TOSI AND RAUF WARDAK PUBLISHED a detailed article describing the discovery of the Tepe Fullol treasure (Tosi and Wardak 1972). On July 5, 1966 a group of farmers had made the chance discovery of a hoard of gold and silver bowls near a mountain pass, 2 kilometers from the village of Fullol in northeastern Afghanistan. Wishing to divide the booty equally among them, the finders hacked the bowls into equal pieces with an axe. However, local government agencies soon arrived on the scene and managed to recover five gold and seven silver vessels as well as a number of fragments. These were then entrusted to Wardak from the National Museum in Kabul. Wardak carried out a small excavation at the purported location of the find, a 14-by-8-meter hillock known locally as the Kosh Tapa. The dig revealed no further artifacts; however, a skeleton in very poor condition was exposed, lying in a bent posture with the head oriented toward the north. The location of a burial at the site of the Fullol discovery, which could be linked to pre-Islamic traditions by the flexed posture and the orientation of the head, suggested that the gold and silver bowls may have been grave goods.

Several of the bowls were decorated with geometric motifs or animal figures, primarily friezes with bulls, oxen, and wild boars. One fragment also showed a bird between two snakes. The decoration showed the use of a variety of techniques including engraving, hammering, and repoussé work.

The discovery of these objects came as a great surprise, all the more so since apart from some of the geometric ornamentation they bore little resemblance to other known finds from Afghanistan or the neighboring regions. The archaeological reference material available in Afghanistan at that time

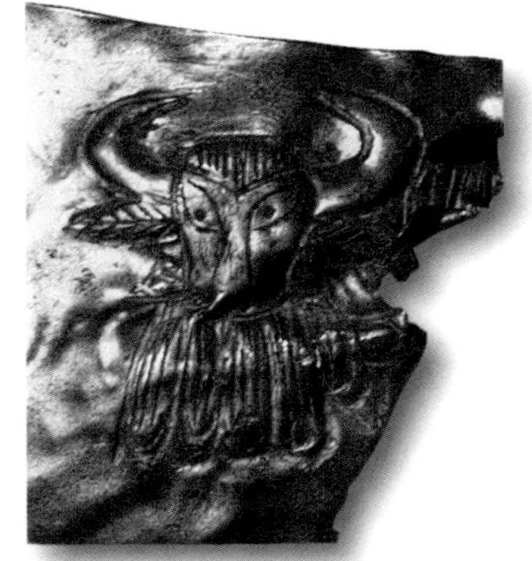

ABOVE AND OPPOSITE:
Silver beaker from Tepe Fullol, stolen from the National Museum of Afghanistan, Kabul. These objects were recovered and are temporarily stored at the Musée de Lattes, France.

came primarily from the site at Mundigak in the Kandahar region in western Afghanistan. Excavations were conducted there in the 1950s under the direction of Jean-Marie Casal in the context of the activities of the Délégation Archéologique Française en Afghanistan (DAFA). A settlement, dating to the fourth millennium B.C., was exposed. During the first half of the third millennium B.C., Mundigak had grown to true city status, covering an area of some 50 hectares and featuring a variety of monumental construction works and massive defense walls (Casal 1961). The exhibition "Afghanistan, une histoire millénaire" ("Afghanistan, a Millennial History") at the Musée Guimet in 2002 put on display a collection of objects from Mundigak, that the museum had held in storage. Ten years after the completion of the excavations at Mundigak, a team of Italian archaeologists went to work at the site of Shahr-i Sokhta in Sistan, Iran, the delta region of the Helmand River close to the Afghan border. These excavations revealed a town of some 100 hectares, displaying much cultural affinity with the golden age of Mundigak, between 3000 and 2500 B.C.

Tosi, who excavated Shahr-i Sokhta, suggested that these two major sites should be linked as forming part of a Helmand culture. The trading and administrative activities of this culture had clearly played a significant role in contacts between Proto-Elamite Iran and the sites in Balochistan and the Indus Valley, dating from the end of the fourth millennium B.C. to halfway through the third millennium B.C. Remnants of the workshops of precious-stone polishers, testifying to the importance of lapis lazuli, are found in both Mundigak and Shahr-i Sokhta. The sources of this blue mineral are near Sar-i Sang in Badakhshan Province in northeastern Afghanistan. It is well known that lapis lazuli from Afghanistan was highly sought after in Mesopotamia throughout the third millennium B.C. Tepe Fullol is barely 200 kilometers from the lapis lazuli quarries of Sar-i Sang. The rich assembly of gold and silver bowls from Fullol may therefore have been a result of exchanges with areas of western Asia, revolving in particular around the trade in lapis lazuli.

Nevertheless, it appears that the majority of the gold and silver vessels from Fullol belong to a cultural background differing from that of Mundigak and Shahr-i Sokhta; they do not appear to have been made at the time of the trade contacts between the two sites in the Helmand system and the West.

Some experts have therefore given the Tepe Fullol vessels a later date, based on comparisons with gold and silver vessels from the royal tombs at Marlik in the north of Iran. However, the decoration from Marlik, with rearing bulls and stylized trees inspired by Babylonian art of the 12th century B.C., bears only a distant resemblance to the ornamentation of the Tepe Fullol vessels. Several experts, in particular Tosi in his article with Wardak, but also Amiet, have emphasized that some of the decorations from the Tepe Fullol vessels, and in particular the bearded bulls, display similarities with iconographic themes from Mesopotamia at the end of the third and the start of the second millennium B.C. (the Ur III and Isin-Larsa dynasties) (Amiet 1986). However, the same authors have also acknowledged that the geometric motifs—cruciform or stepped, engraved or repoussé—on two of the Tepe Fullol vessels, one of which can be seen in this exhibition, also resemble earlier ceramic decorations, in a style from the first half of the third millennium B.C., referred to as Namazga III or Quetta. This style is also well represented in Mundigak and Shahr-i Sokhta.

In summary therefore, some experts felt that the Tepe Fullol "treasure" could represent a secret cache or a graveyard containing objects from several periods, some dating back as far as 2800 or 2500 B.C. and others from around 2000 B.C.

Placing Tepe Fullol Within a New Cultural Region

K. R. Maxwell-Hyslop was the first to convincingly link the Tepe Fullol vessels with a complex of new finds from the end of the third and the start of the second millennium B.C. (Maxwell-Hyslop 1982).

The exhibition "Afghanistan, une histoire millénaire" in the Musée Guimet in 2002 brought together a selection of objects forming part of what was then defined as an extensive cultural region taking in a major part of Afghanistan, Turkmenistan, and Uzbekistan, as well as areas of eastern Iran and parts of Balochistan as far as the western side of the Indus Valley.

A series of new finds from the 1970s onward and excavations in Dashli Tepe in Afghanistan, Sappalitepa and Djarkutan in Uzbekistan, and Togolok-depe and Gonur-depe in Turkmenistan, have revealed the existence of a whole network of settlements, sometimes extending over 40 hectares. These were walled cities containing a complex of buildings set in a symmetrical plan. The ground plans of some of these structures can be interpreted as palaces and religious buildings. On the periphery lay burial grounds, producing a wealth of grave goods where they had not been robbed: undoubtedly prestigious objects in stone, copper, gold, and silver, of a richness never previously encountered in any of these regions. It is largely thanks to Viktor Sarianidi that an exceptionally coherent set of new data covering this period is now available for both Afghanistan and Turkmenistan (Sarianidi 1998, 2002).

Grave goods have been found at the Shahdad graveyard in eastern Iran, which display many similarities with the finds from the sites in the Murghab Delta and at the Dashli Oasis (Hakemi 1997). Several sites (such as Sibri) and graveyards (particularly Mehrgarh VIII and Dauda Damb) are known in Pakistani Baluchistan, to the west of the Indus Valley, and show significant affinity with excavated finds from Afghanistan, Turkmenistan, and Uzbekistan (C. Jarrige et al. 1995). Numerous objects were found accidentally during construction work at Quetta in Baluchistan, including various gold items. These became known as the "Quetta treasure." A skeleton was found in the same pit, indicating that this was a graveyard. The treasure was therefore made up of grave goods, which, following comparison with the finds from the Mehrgarh VIII graveyards, belong to the same cultural complex that we have just mentioned (Jarrige and Hassan 1989).

It was later observed that combinations of stone objects—"scepters," carved disks, and miniature columns—are placed in the same manner in tombs and cenotaphs throughout the area from Turkmenistan to the west of the Indus Valley, in particular in the Mehrgarh VIII graveyards and the burial deposit from which the Quetta finds came. The individual objects from within this area also displayed many similarities. The stone figures, most commonly of steatite or chlorite, with hands and faces of alabaster and garments reminiscent of the kaunakes (woolen skirts) of Mesopotamia, are the most striking among the allegorical objects from this cultural region. Several of these images were to be seen in the exhibition "Afghanistan, une histoire millénaire" (cat. RMN 2002, figs. 8–11). The same figure appears on various objects, including a silver pyxis (a lidded box) from Gonur-depe. It is difficult to say who is represented in these images, which are almost always encountered in funerary contexts. The area of distribution is certainly very extensive, with one example found in the Quetta treasure, whereas in Harappa, a major city of the Indus civilization, fragments of a head covering usually associated with this type of sculpture were found in a layer dating from period III of the Indus civilization at the end of the third millennium B.C. (Meadow, lecture to the Académie des Inscriptions et Belles-Lettres 2005).

Composite female figurine from the looted sites of Bronze-Age Bactria, Musée du Louvre, Paris

Series of metal seals from this area display a wide range of iconographic themes, probably reflecting a religious ideology, offering many parallels with similar objects from several sites from the Middle East (Francfort 1992). Among them are many cylinder seals with parallels to Mesopotamia and Elam, distinguished by the stamp on the base. A similar type was found at the eastern limit of this cultural complex on the border of the Indus Valley, in particular at the site of Sibri (C. Jarrige et al. 1995).

All the new discoveries of the last 30 years have revealed an extended, relatively homogeneous cultural entity in various areas of Central Asia and

Composite female figurine "A Bactrian Princess" from the collections of the Musée du Louvre, Paris

the Indo-Iranian border regions. While this entity has its original characteristics, it also to a large degree bears the marks of many and diverse outside influences. Furthermore, besides these finds, originating from sites of more or less supervised excavations, there are also countless remarkable objects, which have found their way onto the international art market via clandestine excavations and have been added to public or private collections.

The Tepe Fullol vessels—a find that was a tremendous surprise—can now be understood within a better-known cultural context. They can be put on a rather long list of objects including gold and silver bowls, some with geometric motifs like the two Fullol vessels, and some with narrative scenes depicting banquets, hunting parties, and work in the fields (Francfort 2003, Francfort 2005a). The 1988 exhibition in the Musée Guimet "Les cités oubliés de l'Indus" ("Forgotten Cities of the Indus," AFAA cat. 1988) provided an opportunity to view the rich grave goods of the Quetta treasure. One of the objects on view was a footed gold drinking beaker. A frieze showing beasts of prey was applied as decoration, with the skin worked in exactly the same way as the wild bulls on the gold vessels from Tepe Fullol (Jarrige 1988, 115; Jarrige and Hassan 1989, figs. 6 & 7).

While the Tepe Fullol vessels, like most bowls from that extensive cultural region, have something of a local character, they also show signs of outside influences. Researchers had, indeed, noted these influences shortly after the discovery, in particular the representations of bearded bulls reminiscent of a generally recognized theme from Mesopotamia. The representation of a tree on a mountain on the golden drinking beaker from Tepe Fullol showing wild boars can be linked to decorations on Mesopotamian seals. The same theme is also found on a silver vessel from a burial tomb of Gonur-depe in Turkmenistan. Some of the various animals shown on this vessel can be compared to those on the Tepe Fullol bowls. They are shown against the background of a landscape symbolized by trees on mountains (Francfort 2005b).

We hope that more bowls from Fullol will find their way back to the National Museum of Afghanistan in Kabul. Nevertheless, the three examples which have been so far recovered are of a great symbolic value. They form part of the first group of objects heralding the discovery of a previously unknown larger cultural complex, whose precise definition has become a major topic of expert debate over more than 20 years. Some of our colleagues use denominations going back to Hellenistic geography, referring to the Bronze Age as the Bactria-Margiana Archaeological Complex (BMAC), while Henri-Paul Francfort proposed the term "Oxus civilization." This may be too restrictive, given the immense geographical area covered by this cultural complex. However, that is also the case with the term Indus civilization, which has been adopted to indicate a cultural complex extending well beyond the geographical boundaries of the Indus Valley. The term "Oxus Cultural Complex" will be adopted in what follows, in full awareness of the aforementioned limitations.

Allegorical figure with scarred face, likely from Iran or Afghanistan, from the collections of the Musée du Louvre, Paris

The Oxus Cultural Complex and Its Relationship With the Indus Culture

As we have explained, the Oxus Cultural Complex expanded as far east as the western edge of the Indus Valley during the period between 2200 and 1800 B.C. (Jarrige and Hassan 1989). We also now know that a set of finds, often defined as "exotic" objects, recovered in the cities of the Indus civilization, such as cylinder seals, various weapons, and metal objects, can be associated today with this previously unknown Oxus Cultural Complex. Questions arise about the contacts that may have existed between the Indus civilization and the Oxus Cultural Complex. Our excavations at the site of Nausharo, close to Mehrgarh on the fringes of the Indus Valley, cast new light on this question. After period I, dated to the first half of the third millennium B.C., Nausharo grew during periods II, III, and IV to form a complex, that was part of the Indus civilization. However, new elements appearing at the start of period IV, dating at the earliest from around 2200 B.C., can

Decorated silver beaker from the Bronze-Age site of Gonur-depe (Turkmenistan)

also be linked to the Oxus Cultural Complex. These finds come from layers that yielded material mostly belonging to the Indus civilization. It is notable that period IV falls within the third main period of the Indus civilization, from around 2200 to 1900 B.C., a period marking the urban and economic climax of the great Indus cities such as Mohenjo-daro and Harappa.

The occurrence around Nausharo and Mehrgarh of other sites with artifacts showing an affinity with those from the Oxus Cultural Complex has already been indicated, but it can also be associated with objects characteristic of the Indus civilization (Jarrige and Quivron 1999). It is therefore possible now to state that two groups with different cultural backgrounds lived apparently peacefully together on the western border of the Indus Valley between 2200 and 1900 B.C. Far from the Indus, in Gonur-depe in Turkmenistan, a cylinder seal of the Mesopotamian type in the style of Ur III was found by Sarianidi and can be dated to the end of the third millennium B.C. At the same site he found a seal with an image of an elephant below an inscription in the script of the Indus civilization (Francfort 2005b).

Such an increase in the available data allows an investigation of the types of contacts, that took place between the groups associated with this Oxus Cultural Complex—first brought to light by the vessels from Tepe Fullol—and the inhabitants of the cities of the Indus civilization. The archaeologists directing the major excavations of the first half of the 20th century in what is now Pakistan were struck by the extent of urbanization of the Indus civilization, their administrative capabilities, and the obvious economic prosperity. A notion quickly took root among many specialists that this civilization between 2500 and 1800 B.C. had rigid conservative tendencies so that any form of development was inhibited and all significant influence from outside was rejected. However, a good deal of the recent research, in particular the work in Nausharo mentioned above, and also the reassessment of the Harappa excavations by an American team, have shown clearly that the Indus culture did, indeed, undergo development over the course of time. The previous large excavations were in general limited to the exposure of the upper layers. Now that we have a much better understanding of the stratigraphy of several sites of the Indus civilization, we understand that cities like Mohenjo-daro and Harappa, discovered during the major excavations of the first half of the 20th century, only grew to metropolis status in the course of the third major era of the Indus culture, that is, between around 2200 and 1900 B.C. These relatively recent findings, showing that the successive periods of the Indus civilization were marked by important changes, have opened the way to investigations into the internal and external factors, such as the Oxus Cultural Complex, contributing to the evolution of the Indus civilization.

Hunting scene from the decorated silver beaker, cast, from Gonur-depe (Turkmenistan)

The Indus Culture and Mesopotamia, From the Third to the Start of the Second Millennium B.C.

We have already mentioned the existence of sites such as Mundigak and Shahr-i Sokhta around 3000 B.C. These sites, which could be part of a Helmand cultural system, have provided us with clear evidence of contacts between the Proto-Elamite world in Iran and cultures from Baluchistan (southwest Pakistan) and Sindh (southeast Pakistan). These sites also gave evidence of work using lapis lazuli from the mines of Sar-i Sang (Afghan Badakhshan). The strong links of Mundigak during its final period (IV C) with Mehrgarh (period VII C) and Nausharo (I C) between 2700 and 2600 B.C. tend to confirm that neither the Helmand culture sites such as Shahr-i Sokhta and Mundigak nor many sites in the upper valleys of Balochistan were occupied after 2500 B.C. These observations are based on intensive comparative research on the ceramics from these different sites. We can now refute the opinion of some scholars who still assert, without providing significant evidence, that Mundigak and Shahr-i Sokhta were still occupied at a later date. With a more precise chronology for these regions, it becomes evident that the sites of the Helmand cultural system were no longer occupied when what we call the Indus civilization appeared.

Composite female figurine, back view, collections of the Musée du Louvre, Paris

It is probably not a coincidence that during the first stage of this civilization, between 2500 and 2400 B.C., a settlement with all the features of the Indus civilization was founded at Shortughai, in northeast Afghanistan at the border with Tajikistan, close to the confluence of the Oxus and Kokcha Rivers (Francfort 1989). This seems to indicate that after 2500 B.C. groups of people belonging to the Indus civilization began to play a significant role in trade—especially lapis lazuli—with western Asia. Experts have agreed for years that the area of diffusion of the Indus civilization can be connected to the geographical term "Meluhha," mentioned on Mesopotamian clay tablets of the third millennium B.C. Reports by Sargon of Akkad from around 2300 B.C. about boats from Meluhha, Magan (Oman), and Dilmun (Bahrain and the island of Failaka, off Kuwait) have been well known. Mesopotamian clay tablets also stated that the successors of Sargon undertook military expeditions extending to the borders of Meluhha (Sollberger 1970; Maxwell-Hyslop 1982). Texts from the end of the third millennium B.C., in particular those associated with the ruler Gudea around 2100 B.C., reported improvement works in the city of Lagash involving the use of carnelian, copper, silver, gold, lapis lazuli, and valuable timber from Meluhha (Falkenstein 1966).

We may therefore suppose that the contacts between the worlds of the Indus, Elam, and Mesopotamia, as well as the consequences of military expeditions by the successors of Sargon, may have directly influenced the history of the groups populating the areas which, to the west and northwest, bordered the regions identified as the Meluhha of the clay tablets. We have also seen that, probably from 2200 B.C. on, a complete network of complexes with palace-like buildings grew up in the Murghab Delta in Turkmenistan and on either bank of the Oxus. The richness of the grave goods from some of the tombs testifies to the existence of elites, whose wealth in such a geographical context is no doubt the result of the active role they played in the great trading network between Mesopotamia, Elam, and the Indus Valley.

The chance discovery of the gold and silver vessels at Tepe Fullol can now be placed within this general cultural context, around 2200 to 1900 B.C.

Our present knowledge does not allow a precise determination of the exchanges between the groups occupying the area from Turkmenistan to the western boundary of the Indus Valley. But the data we have leads to the conclusion that this extended cultural region was so homogeneous—albeit with clear regional variations—that we may speak of a true civilization, which was unknown before the discovery at Tepe Fullol. There seems to be little doubt that this Oxus civilization had an impact on the history of the major civilizations of Mesopotamia and the Indus at the end of the third and the start of the second millennium B.C. Growing evidence appears to indicate that the economic prosperity of the cities of the Indus Valley from around 2200 B.C. is connected in significant ways with the dynamism of trade contacts, in which the groups occupying areas of the Indo-Iranian border regions and the south of Central Asia played an important role. It should also be noted that population groups related to the Oxus Cultural Complex on the southwest border of the Indus Valley lived closely together with peoples affiliated with the Indus civilization right before and shortly after 2000 B.C. This suggests that there were interactions, which surely made their mark on the period.

It is noteworthy that the Oxus cultural system was at its zenith when the Mesopotamian world under the Ur III and Isin-Larsa dynasties went through a period of economic prosperity. The discovery at Mohenjo-daro of round seals of the Dilmun type from the same period and finds at Bahrain and Failaka bearing inscriptions in the script of the Indus civilization (Kjaerum 1983) as well as at Ur (Gadd 1932) show how important the sea connections were (along with the land routes) mentioned on the clay tablets of Sargon of Akkad. When, according to Mesopotamian records, there was a break in trade with Meluhha in the 18th century B.C., the cities of the Indus civilization were no longer occupied and objects such as the gold and silver bowls from Tepe Fullol became scarce in the graveyards of Central Asia.

1 THE SHAPE AND DESIGN of this cup fragment is typical of the Bronze Age cultures of Central Asia. It likely had a stemmed foot with a flared base, similar to ceramic Bronze Age goblets found both in settlements and burials. Such a goblet made of gold probably came from a burial or ceremonial deposit. The "stepped square" motif is frequently found on artifacts from Afghanistan, Uzbekistan, and Turkmenistan. The motif inscribed within a square is distinctive of this region, first appearing some 7,000 years ago and common on ceremonial objects for the next 3,000 years.

2 THESE SIX FRAGMENTS derive from a single bowl, which was cut up for other purposes by the farmers who found it in 1966. Gold items are typically recycled to make new gold objects, so finds of ancient gold are quite special. This bowl is stylistically part of the "Bactrian Bronze Age" (also known as the Oxus Cultural Complex) artistic tradition. The decoration of these fragments shows a boar, trees, and mountains—perhaps a hunting scene. Such iconography draws heavily from the local environment of northern Afghanistan—a small picture of the actual surroundings 4,000 years ago.

3 LIKE THE OTHER GOLD and silver artifacts recovered from the Fullol hoard, this bowl was intentionally cut up. The bull imagery is Mesopotamian in inspiration, though the bowl was found in northern Afghanistan not far from the ancient lapis lazuli mines and appears to have been manufactured locally. Almost 1,200 miles (2,000 kilometers) of rugged mountains and deserts connected these Bronze Age cultures.

1
Goblet with geometric motif
Tepe Fullol
2200-1900 B.C.
Gold
Diam. 9.9 cm
National Museum of Afghanistan
04.29.1

2
Six fragments of a bowl
Tepe Fullol
2200–1900 B.C.
Gold
H. 11.6 cm (largest fragment)
National Museum of Afghanistan 04.29.3

3
Fragment of a bowl
Tepe Fullol
2200–1900 B.C.
Gold
H. 14.9 cm
National Museum of Afghanistan
04.29.5

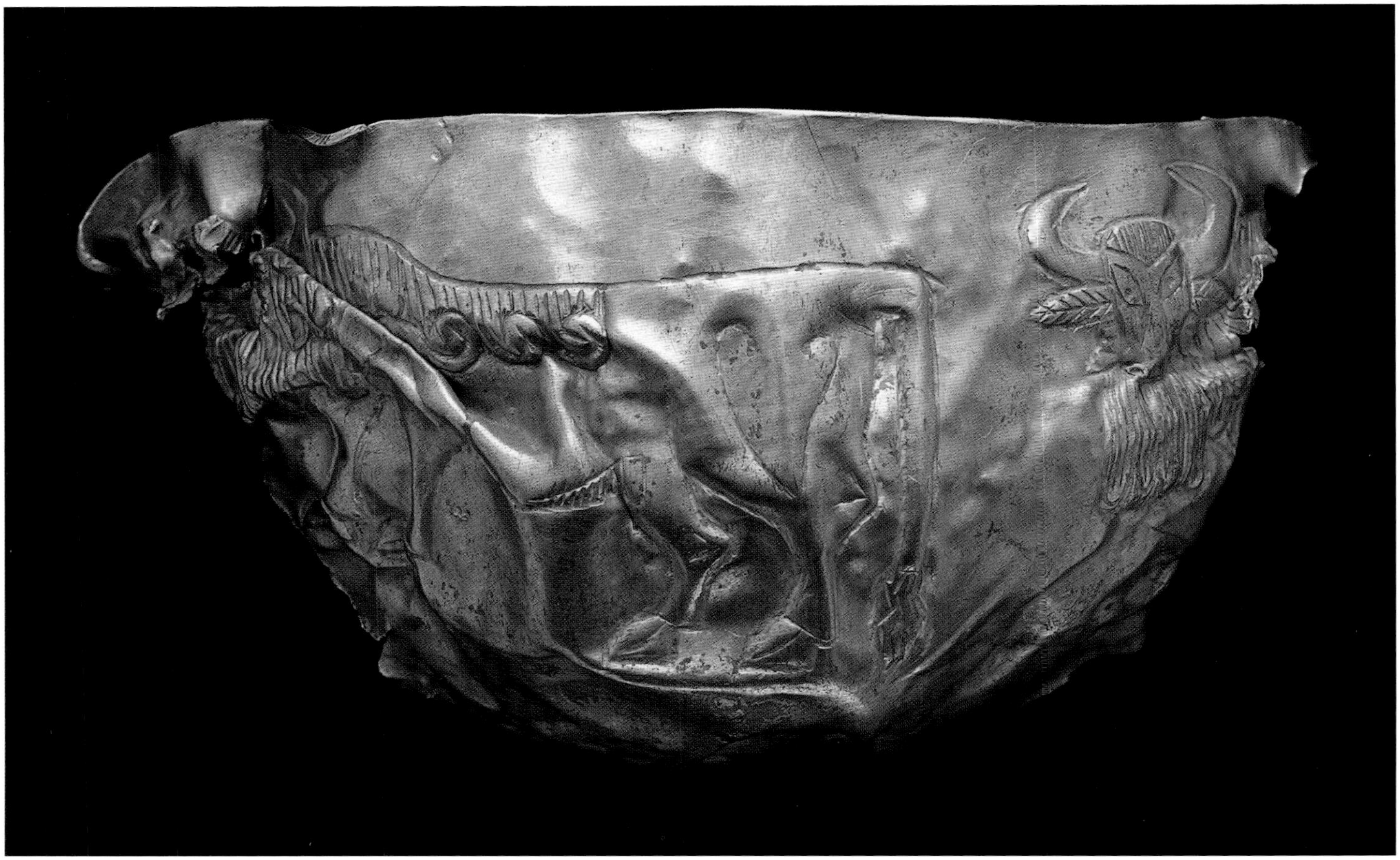

CHAPTER V

The Greek Colony at Aï Khanum and Hellenism in Central Asia

PAUL BERNARD
Member of the Institute
Former Director of
The Délégation Archéologique
Française en Afghanistan
(DAFA)

Moving a column capital. Aï Khanum, southern portico, palace main courtyard

OPPOSITE: *Corinthian capital. Aï Khanum, palace main courtyard, 1970*

WITH THE CONQUEST OF CENTRAL ASIA BY CYRUS THE GREAT (reigned 550–530 B.C.), founder of the ancient Persian Empire of the Achaemenids, Afghanistan and the neighboring lands entered the era of the great eastern empires. Alexander's conquest of the Persian Empire (334–323 B.C.) left much of the existing internal structures of this vast ensemble intact. However, the empire's integration into the newly settled Greco-Macedonian domination led to the progressive elimination of Persian culture, which was gradually replaced by Greek culture as colonists arrived. Bactria, the main province of the eastern area of the empire, in what is today northern Afghanistan, exemplifies the phenomenon.

Greek Bactria: A Concise Summary

In 327 B.C., as Alexander departed for India, he was conscious that peace and order in the hard-won region around the Oxus River (modern name: Amu Darya) required consolidation. He therefore left behind in Bactria a greater number of Greeks and Macedonians in military outposts or in real colonies than anywhere else in his empire. He named some of these colonies after himself, such as Alexandria in Aria (Herat), Alexandropolis in Arachosia (Kandahar), Alexandria of the Caucasus (Begram), and Alexandria Eschate (Khojand in Tajikistan), while other towns, even when reinforced by colonists, often retained their traditional local names like Bactra, the capital of the Bactrian province, in the middle Oxus River Valley.

Following the death of Alexander (323 B.C.), Bactria was absorbed into the Greek Syrian-Mesopotamian Empire founded by one of Alexander's

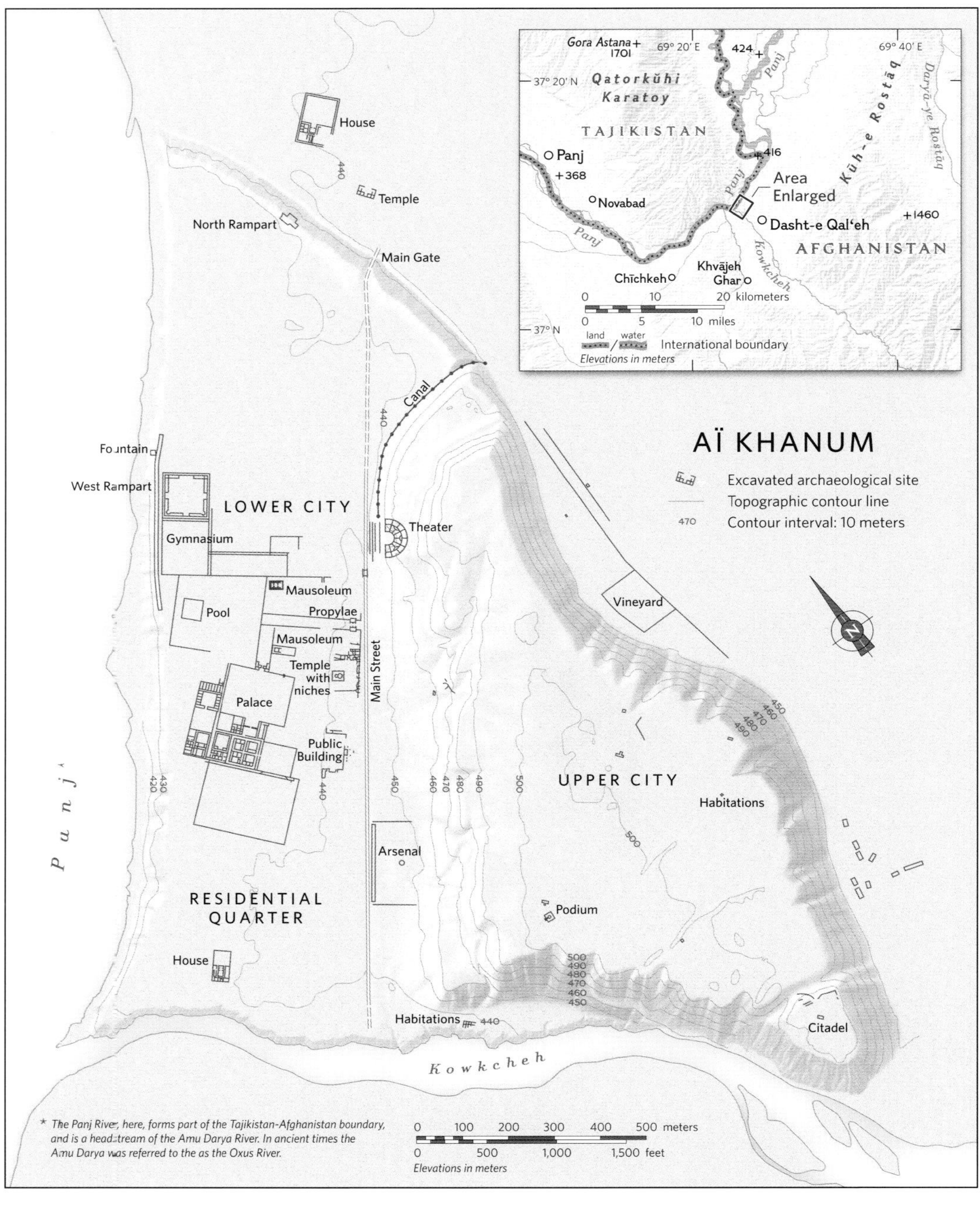

AÏ KHANUM
Excavated archaeological site
Topographic contour line
Contour interval: 10 meters
House
Temple
North Rampart
Main Gate
Canal
Fountain
West Rampart
LOWER CITY
Gymnasium
Theater
Vineyard
Mausoleum
Propylae
Pool
Mausoleum
Temple with niches
Palace
Main Street
Public Building
UPPER CITY
Habitations
Arsenal
Podium
RESIDENTIAL QUARTER
House
Habitations
Citadel
Panj
Kowkcheh
Gora Astana
TAJIKISTAN
AFGHANISTAN
Qatorkühi Karatoy
Kūh-e Rostāq
Daryā-ye Rostāq
Panj
Novabad
Area Enlarged
Dasht-e Qal'eh
Chīchkeh
Khvājeh Ghar
International boundary
Elevations in meters
* The Panj River, here, forms part of the Tajikistan-Afghanistan boundary, and is a headstream of the Amu Darya River. In ancient times the Amu Darya was referred to the as the Oxus River.
Elevations in meters

former commanders, Seleucus (311–281 B.C.). He and his son Antiochus I (281–261 B.C.) continued a policy of active colonization and so established the foundations of the Greco-Bactrian state. They founded new cities that became bulwarks of Hellenism, and so it was for Aï Khanum. Aï Khanum, meaning "Lady Moon," refers to an Uzbek princess who was said to have inhabited a medieval castle on the acropolis. The name applied both to the neighboring Uzbek village and to the archaeological site, since the original Greek name is lost to us.

Around 250 B.C. Bactria became an independent state under the governor Diodotus. The Greco-Bactrian state was initially concentrated along the Oxus River Valley, but its territory increased enormously from the second century B.C. onward with the adoption of a policy of expansion. South of the Hindu Kush, the Greek provinces of Arachosia and Paropamisadai were lost to the Mauryan Empire, the first great empire in India (ca 321–185 B.C.), after Alexander's death. These areas were soon reconquered by the north, and Greco-Bactrian control was even extended as far as the northwest region of the Indus Valley. In time, however, it became clear that this policy had undesirable consequences. Weakened by the very magnitude of its expansion and the diversity of local cultures—whether Iranian or Indian—within its own borders, compounded by rivalries among the ruling class, the Greek Empire began to fall apart, forming independent principalities, a development that particularly affected the Indo-Greek area. Around 145 B.C., the Greeks were driven out of Aï Khanum by nomads, who in 20 years would become masters of the entire Oxus River Valley. The Greek kingdoms south of the Hindu Kush held out for another century, but by the first century A.D. the last remnants in the eastern Punjab, around modern Lahore, of what has been called the fourth great Hellenistic monarchy, had vanished, as had the Seleucids of Syria-Mesopotamia (311–64 B.C.), the Lagids of Egypt (305–31 B.C.), and the Attalids of Pergamum (283–133 B.C.).

Images from explorer Jules Barthoux's mission report, "Travels in Turkestan and Badakshan," 1926. At the confluence of the Amu Darya and the Kokcha Rivers, several kilometers to the south of Aï Khanum, Barthoux reported that villagers had shown him a vast cemetery. "The bones were, as stated by the inhabitants, gathered pell-mell into immense terracotta jars with diameters of three to four meters. These are similar to the Persian tombs found in Mesopotamia. It is certain that excavations in this area could be fruitful. The cemetery, however, might not provide anything and, on the other hand, I would have a great deal of enthusiasm in the area of the fort. I have identified this site with the ancient city of Amu, which gives its name to the river Amu Darya."

Jules Barthoux at the site of Aï Khanum: "From the north-west of Rustak and at the mouth of the Kokcha River there is an extended ancient site. The fort, which wrapped around a small plateau on its southern extremities, is some 300–400 meters long by 150 meters in breadth (approximately). Between the fort and the river, and at approximately the middle of the northern surrounding wall, was found a fragment of a column some 2 meters long and 80 cm in diameter, which seemed to have fallen from the edge of the wall. There had been in the past, I'd like to say 10 years ago, a plinth or column alongside it, however, so close to the river that it had slid into the riverbed, some two meters below."

Mission Report from Jules Barthoux, "Travels in Turkestan and Badakshan," 1926. Archives of the Musée Guimet.

Excavations in progress. Aï Khanum, main entrance to the palace

The Discovery of the City

While the attention of the historians of the classical age was always focused on the empires surrounding the Mediterranean, they were also aware of the proverbial riches of Greek Bactria, with its "thousand cities" and its fertile land, where everything but olives would grow. They recorded the names of certain notable rulers: Diodotus, Euthydemus, Demetrius, Eucratides, and Menander, the latter known for his connection to Buddhism. A number of their fine coins had found their way to the collections of museums in Europe and India. However, it was a long time before the archaeologists discovered the remnants of this Greco-Bactrian state, which had existed for two centuries. In 1924-25 the Délégation Archéologique Française en Afghanistan (DAFA), headed by Alfred Foucher, made a first attempt to excavate around Bactra, which was known to have been the main city of the area even before the Greek conquest, but it came to nothing. The failure was aggravated by the erroneous conclusion drawn by Foucher that the Hellenistic conquerors, while successful warlords, were neither builders, nor people of culture. It seemed to him that if he had found no trace of their civilization, it was because it had no material reality. It was only 40 years later, in 1964, that the DAFA succeeded in locating and excavating the first monuments bearing witness to the Greek presence in Central Asia, at the site of Aï Khanum. This site, at the easternmost extremity of the Bactrian plain, had first been visited in 1838 by the English explorer John Wood, then in 1926 by the French archaeologist Jules Barthoux, who was investigating the Buddhist monuments at Hadda. Although both realized it was an important ancient settlement, there was no clue indicating the presence of a Greek city, and neither suspected that Hellenistic ruins lay buried here, so their testimony went unnoticed. The actual discovery was memorable for its unusual circumstances where luck connived with sound reasoning. The chance element was a carved stone, shown to the Afghan King Zahir Shah by the occupants of the hamlet of Aï Khanum, close to the border of Soviet Tajikistan, as his hunting party crossed the game-rich marsh areas of the Oxus River one day in 1961. But it was not by chance that the king, a real expert in his country's antiquities, reported the puzzling find to Daniel Schlumberger, then director of the DAFA. Schlumberger recognized in the damaged stone a Corinthian capital and concluded that the site where it was found must have been a Greek city. On a cold and rainy day in November 1964, French archaeologists, under his direction, arrived for the first time at the majestic site on the banks of the Oxus, under the watchful eyes of Soviet border guards. They immediately confirmed the nature of the site by finding shards bearing Greek letters. The excavations, began in 1965 and continued until they were interrupted by the Soviet intervention in Afghanistan in 1979.

The Founding of the City

Evidence gradually accumulated that the city had been founded on the eastern border of Bactria around 300 B.C. by Seleucus I, to control an access road from the northeast leading to a fertile plain, long occupied and developed thanks to a network of irrigation canals. The city came to occupy a triangular location, with sides roughly a mile long, delimited by the confluence of the two rivers, the Oxus and the Kokcha, a tributary on the Afghan left bank, and, on the third side, by a 60-meter-high tabular acropolis. This natural defensive position was reinforced with a belt of solid city walls made of sun-dried bricks, and to the southeast of the acropolis by a citadel overhanging the Kokcha River. The surrounding countryside was inhabited by native farmers, who worked the land on behalf of the colonists and the local aristocracy. In the city, the Greeks played a dominant but not exclusive role. They formed the ruling class, as evidenced by the Greek and Macedonian names of the high and middle level officials who oversaw the palace treasury. Lesser posts in the financial administration were held by officials of local

Aï Khanum, palace, reception rooms

origin, with such typically Iranian names as Oxeboakes, Oxybazos, Aryandes, and Oumanos.

Most of the public and religious buildings were erected in the lower town, alongside a quarter of residential mansions.

The Palace

The city plan was conceived to devote the center of the lower town to a royal palace, a clear indication that Aï Khanum was itself a royal city. To make room for this palace, the main street, which ran from the gate in the northern rampart down to the Kokcha, was moved to the foot of the acropolis. In devising the ground plan of the palace, which used a type of construction that bore no relation to their national architectural tradition, the Greeks drew inspiration from the Eastern models offered by the royal neo-Babylonian palaces and, even more, by the palaces of the Achaemenid kings. Courtyards and buildings, grouped by blocks corresponding to their residential, administrative, or economic function, and forming a compact mass of constructions crisscrossed by numerous corridors, are reminiscent of the palace of the Iranian King Darius I (reigned 522-486 B.C.) in Susa. A grandiose forecourt (137 by 108 meters), surrounded by four Corinthian colonnades of 108 pillars, greeted visitors. Opposite the entrance, the southern portico opened wide at the back to a monumental hall with 18 Corinthian columns through which one entered various adjoining buildings, including twin official reception halls, a double chancellery section, a large bath house, two private residences, an inner courtyard with 60 Doric columns and a treasury with its storage rooms set around another courtyard. Apart from the ceremonial rooms, the walls of which were decorated with stone pilasters and reliefs in unfired clay, there was little interior decoration and the earth floors must have been carpeted in accordance with Eastern practice. As usual in all Greco-Bactrian architecture, walls were made of sun-dried bricks, sometimes with some rows of baked bricks at the foot. Roofs were flat, according to the Asian building technique, but the edges were lined with a typically Greek decoration of terracotta plates known as antefixes, adorned with vegetal motifs (cat. nos. 25–28).

The local natural stone, a soft whitish limestone, was used for most of the columns and pilasters and the main thresholds. All three of the classical orders were present: Ionic columns, with their capitals of a more strictly codified geometry than the other two orders, were something of a rarity; Doric columns were not infrequent; but the Corinthian order, with its more florid decoration of acanthus leaves, was the favorite with the Greco-Bactrian architects who proposed a lush and exuberant version (nos. 4, 24). Circular elements such as the drums of the column shafts and the bases were wrought speedily using an old Greek mechanical turning process, which required a less skilled workforce and which the Greco-Bactrian architects used systematically. Taken all together, this grandiose but sober architecture, despite the somewhat profuse and overblown decoration of stone columns, with an almost obsessive predilection for symmetry and orthogonality, was of the same vintage as the haughty and impassive imperial architecture of its illustrious predecessors, the Achaemenid palaces. The Greek touch was provided by the columns and the antefixes. All the buildings at Aï Khanum demonstrate, more or less, the same grand style, designed more to impress and subjugate than to please and seduce.

Aï Khanum, palace, courtyard

Gymnasium and Theater

Like every Greek city of any significance, Aï Khanum had its gymnasium, devoted to intellectual and physical training, and its theater, both of them primary institutions for the maintenance and spread of Hellenism. Their typically Greek architecture was inspired by similar buildings fulfilling the same function in the Greek world. An inscription revealed that the gymnasium had been placed under the traditional double protection of Hermes and Heracles (cat. no. 32). Apart from other structures intended for sports in the same complex, a very large lecture hall, composed of an inner court-

Aï Khanum, fountain spout in situ, Oxus rampart

yard, surrounded by a series of rooms, had a ground plan one hundred meters to a side. What set it apart from its Greek models was its enormous dimensions, the recurrent symmetry on each of the four sides with a porch in the axis, and the presence of an uninterrupted corridor extending all around the perimeter of the building, permitting interior circulation and providing covered ambulatory space necessary in the harsher Central Asian climate, functions which in Greek gymnasiums were normally performed by large porticoes opening into the inner courtyard.

The theater, the easternmost of its kind in all of Hellenized Asia, further east than the examples at Babylon and Seleucia on the Tigris (near Baghdad), was built against the lower inner slope of the acropolis. The theater was built in a semi-circle with steeply rising tiers, made of sun-dried bricks that could seat several thousand spectators. In the absence of an agora, the theater would serve as a meeting place for the citizens of the town and of the whole province when they had to deliberate. The theater's main function was to stage performances, either popular spectacles like pantomime and jugglers, or the Greek classical repertory made famous by the plays of the three great tragic poets Aeschylus, Sophocles, and Euripides. For works by comic authors like Menander, the actors wore masks, such as the one sculpted to decorate a water-spout in a fountain next to the Oxus (no. 33). These theatrical performances fostered among the audience a sense of cultural identity and the feeling of belonging to the nation of the Hellenes. Spacious *loggias,* honorary seats, were located halfway up the rows of seats, a feature unknown in contemporary Greek theaters, where distinguished guests were instead honored simply by being seated in the first row. The presence of these *loggias* are a clear indication of a society in which men of power—the ruler, his court, and high officials—did not hesitate to demonstrate publicly their rank. It was an unmistakable sign of the decline of the democratic ideal in Greek colonial Bactria, an ideal that continued to be of importance in the cities around the Mediterranean, even when these were incorporated in the Hellenistic kingdoms.

Aï Khanum, gymnasium, excavations of the main courtyard

Domestic Architecture

The homes of the leading colonial families were isolated from the common folk in an exclusive residential area at the southern extremity of the city, at the confluence of the two rivers behind the palace. Some 40 patrician residences (65 by 35 meters) lined parallel side streets branching off from the main street at right angles. In a traditional Greek house, the rooms were set around an inner courtyard, which was the hub of domestic life, but at Aï Khanum the central space was reserved for the main reception and living room, while the other rooms and service areas were disposed around it horseshoe fashion along a corridor, which provided access to the central unit, but which at the same time isolated it from them. Removed from its central position and pushed to the northeastern side, the courtyard became a forecourt with privileged access to the reception room through a porch with two columns protected from the prevailing winds blowing up the Oxus River

Valley. Outside the northern rampart a mansion of monumental dimensions (107 by 72 meters) displays a similar ground plan that, with a few alterations, occurs again in the palace in its two residential sections. This type of design did not take shape all at once in the minds of the Greco-Bactrian architects: Before it attained its final form in the second century B.C., it went through formative stages, which could be observed in the earliest houses excavated in the residential quarter near the Kokcha River. One thing seems sure: This original plan of an aristocratic mansion was elaborated in Central Asia in Greco-Asian settlements, as can be inferred from the recently excavated "Red temple" at Nisa (Turkmenistan), the first capital of the Parthian Empire, which offers a striking resemblance to the Greco-Bactrian residences.

This ground plan, which made the reception room the epicenter of the living area and reserved the courtyard for the preferential if not exclusive use of the lord of the house, suggests a stricter hierarchy in family relationships, with an increased ascendancy of the master of the family, an arrangement characteristic of colonial communities. Although this type of house is very different from what is found around the Mediterranean, there was nevertheless one facility that was entirely in keeping with the Greek lifestyle: the bathroom. These bathing facilities, even the best-finished, were relatively simple, as bathing was a question of pouring water, from buckets over oneself, and not bathing in a tub.

Religion and Religious Architecture

The greatest degree of innovation was found in the religious architecture. The typical rectangular plan of Greek temples built in stone with their columns, pediments, and exterior sculptural decoration was abandoned. The city's principal temple, the so-called "temple with niches," which stood on the main street, was a compact building of sun-dried masonry on a 20-meter-square ground plan, set on a high three-stepped podium (1.5 meters). A wide vestibule led directly to the smaller cult room containing the statue of the god, flanked with two narrow sacristies on either side. The plan, the raised podium, the exterior decoration of indented niches, and the flat roof all point toward the religious architecture of the East, from Mesopotamia to Central Asia. A similar building, even more monumental, with three juxtaposed cult rooms, outside the northern rampart, close to the entrance gate of the city, confirms that this was the standard plan of Greco-Bactrian temples.

If these buildings could barely be termed Greek, the same cannot be said of the deities who were worshipped in them and who were closely linked to the Greek pantheon, as can be inferred from the coinage minted by the Greco-Bactrian rulers. Hermes and Heracles were the patrons of the gymnasium (no. 32). Hestia and Cybele (no. 23) were also honored. The sandal of the surviving marble foot of the cult statue of the main temple is decorated with the images of winged lightning, signifying Zeus, even if the unmistakably Eastern character of the building suggests a syncretic deity of mixed Greco-Asian parentage, probably a Zeus-Mithra, as he appears with a Persian cap and a halo of rays on Indo-Greek coins. A beautiful disk of gilded silver representing Cybele, the goddess of nature, cannot be taken as evidence of a specifically Eastern cult, for although of Anatolian origin, the goddess had been adopted by the Greeks long before Alexander's conquest of Central Asia and the founding of the city. If the pervasive Eastern flavor of the sacred architecture induces us to assume some degree of religious symbiosis between the colonists and the native population, the exact extent of it remains a matter of speculation. On the other hand, no doubt exists about the Iranian character of the monumental stepped platform built of sun-baked bricks, which stood in the middle of an open-air shrine on the southwest extremity of the acropolis, where the priest would officiate turning his face to the rising sun. This platform is indisputably reminiscent of the religious monuments of the Persians who, as recorded by Greek historians, worshipped their gods without representing them in human form, on elevated sites in the open air.

Aï Khanum, temple with niches

Honoring the Dead

The inhabitants of Aï Khanum conformed to the traditions of their ancestors when it came to the treatment of the dead. These were normally buried outside the city, where the richest families owned multi-chambered mausoleums that half-protruded from the ground as solid cubes. The vaulted burial chambers were periodically emptied and the bones assembled in jars upon which the names of the deceased were inscribed in ink. Some inscriptions on jars that were recovered read, in Greek, "he and she, the little ones" (either children who had died shortly after birth and had not yet been named, or young slaves), "Isidora", "Lysanias" (a typically Macedonian name) and "Cosmas." It was also a Greek practice to bury important personages and city benefactors in highly visible locations in the city, to honor their memory and extoll their accomplishments. To this custom we owe the discovery of what must have been, in spite of its rather modest appearance, an illustrious monument. In the heart of the lower town, close to the entrance of the future palace, stood a simple funerary chapel on a podium, its porch flanked by two wooden columns. Buried underneath lay the sarcophagus of one Kineas, who had been mandated (probably by Seleucus I) to found the city. His name is known to us thanks to a Greek inscription discovered in the porch, which records the visit of a certain Clearchos, who had traveled from Greece at the start of the third century B.C., and is probably none other than the philosopher Clearchus of Soli, a pupil of Aristotle. Anxious that the inhabitants of the recently founded city keep to their Hellenic traditions, he had a copy of the 150 maxims of wisdom, ascribed to the famed Seven Sages of Greece who had dedicated them to the god Apollo in his oracular sanctuary of Delphi, engraved on a stele over the grave of Kineas (no. 29–30). Presented in the form of aphorisms, these sayings defined the ideal virtues of the Greek man. Formulated by the highest moral authorities of ancient Greece and exhibited to be read in its entirety on the most sacred site in the city, this pledge to the moral and civic values of Hellenism is an illuminating testimony to the will of the colonists to preserve intact their ancestral inheritance. A second mausoleum in the city, of later date, lacks the emotional charge of the Kineas monument, no doubt in part because of its anonymous nature. Nevertheless the building, planned as a small temple (30 by 20 meters), with an underground stone burial chamber, had a monumental character and must have radiated an air of dignity. It stood on an elevated terrace, surrounded by a 6-meter-high stone colonnade with Ionic capitals, an order that, as we have noted, was quite uncommon at Aï Khanum, and the choice of which reflects the deliberate intention to make this a special monument.

The Greek Language as the Cement for National Identity

The preservation of the Greek language is further indication of the colonists' attachment to national culture. They continued to speak and write Greek in an uncontaminated form right to the end, as evidenced by inscriptions found during the excavations. The various types and styles of script (cursive for handwritten documents on papyri, parchments, and vases; capitals for inscriptions in stone) reflect a linguistic development similar to that found in the documents from the Mediterranean. Numerous handwritten documents were found in the palace treasury. Short texts, written in ink on ceramic jars and other vessels, reporting the date of storage and the quantity stored, as well as the names of the officials involved. The contents of the jars included silver coins, representing the cash reserve of the palace, incense, wine, and oil. These documents indicate that and the system of control was identical to that employed in treasuries elsewhere in the Greek world (cat. nos. 10–11). One of the inscriptions on a bowl, used as the lid of a jar containing olive oil, is of special significance (cat. no. 11) It is dated to the year 24, which certainly refers to the reign of King Eucratides, and thus allows us to date to 145 B.C. the destruction of the treasury. In that year nomads burned the palace, and the Greek city came to an end. Three receipts for payments written on parchment, chance finds from other places in Bactria, are indistinguishable from those produced by the hand of Ptolemaic or Seleucid clerks in Egypt or Mesopotamia.

Inscriptions on stone are rare, but fortunately the few that were discovered are of great interest. The dedication of the gymnasium to Hermes and Heracles has already been mentioned, as well as the now famous inscription by Clearchos with the Delphic maxims. Also significant are a funerary epigram from the city necropolis and two other inscriptions in verse found outside Aï Khanum. All of them demonstrate the local poets' command of Greek poetic language and meter. In one originating probably from an area not too far from Aï Khanum, the king's official, Heliodotus, dedicates an altar to Hestia "the most venerable of the goddesses", protector of the holy fire of the family and of the state, and asks her protection for "the greatest of all kings," Euthydemus (230–200 B.C.), and his son Demetrius (200–180 B.C.), "splendid victor," who was destined, in the following years, to start the conquest of northwest India. The exalted triumphant tone of these verses, which ring like a Pindaric ode, reflects the euphoria, that swept Greek Bactria after the successful resistance of Euthydemus, besieged for two years (208–206 B.C.) in Bactra, his capital, by the Seleucid ruler Antiochus III (223–187 B.C.). The latter was eventually forced to officially acknowledge Euthydemus as King of Bactria and to treat him as an equal.

The other inscription, probably from Kandahar, is a long funerary epigram, written by the deceased himself during his life and cryptically signed by means of an acrostic. His name, Sophytos, sounds quite Hellenic, but is, in fact, the transcription in Greek of a good Indian name. The poem tells us that this Sophytos, the scion of a wealthy family, had been in his youth duly initiated into the art of Apollo and the Muses, that is to say into Greek poetry, and had fully assimilated Greek culture. While still young he had been left a destitute victim of a disaster that befell his family. Borrowing some money, he had decided to emigrate and to try his luck in trade abroad. He returned many years later immensely rich and now feted. He restored his family's long-neglected house and rebuilt the ancestral mausoleum in which he had this stele inscribed with his poem to celebrate his hard-earned successes and propose them as a model for his heirs. This exceptional document demonstrates how vigorously Hellenism had taken root in the province of Arachosia, south of the Hindukush around Kandahar, since Alexander the Great had left thousands of soldiers there, in 330 B.C. After his death, the colony had gained in strength under the supervision of a remarkable governor, Sibyrtius, who had played host to the historian Megasthenes, the future author of the best book ever written by a Greek about India.

Hellenism had flourished under the benign rule of the Indian Maurya dynasty in the third century B.C. to which Arachosia had been lost at the end of the fourth century B.C. Then, in the beginning of the second century, the conquests by Demetrius I, Euthydemus's son, restored the unity of the Greek state in Central Asia from Bactra to Kandahar. Thanks to the example provided by Sophytos we can better understand how Plutarch could write, without shocking his readers, albeit with some exaggeration, that the people of the East, or, to be more accurate, the more or less Hellenized local aristocracy, were still in his time (middle of the second century A.D.) several centuries after Alexander's conquest, reading Homer and reciting the tragedies of Sophocles and Euripides. It was in gymnasiums and theaters like those at Aï Khanum that local elites could absorb the best that Greek culture had to offer.

Like Sibyrtius before them, the Greco-Bactrian rulers were far from being uncivilized condottieri. Following the examples of the Hellenistic rulers, patrons of arts and letters, they had stocked their palace at Aï Khanum with a collection of literary manuscripts, probably brought from the West. We have come to know this through a surprising find in one of the rooms of the treasury that served as a library. The parchments and papyri on which the texts had been written had disintegrated, leaving behind only a thin layer of white powder. But the ink of the letters had been imprinted by pressure on

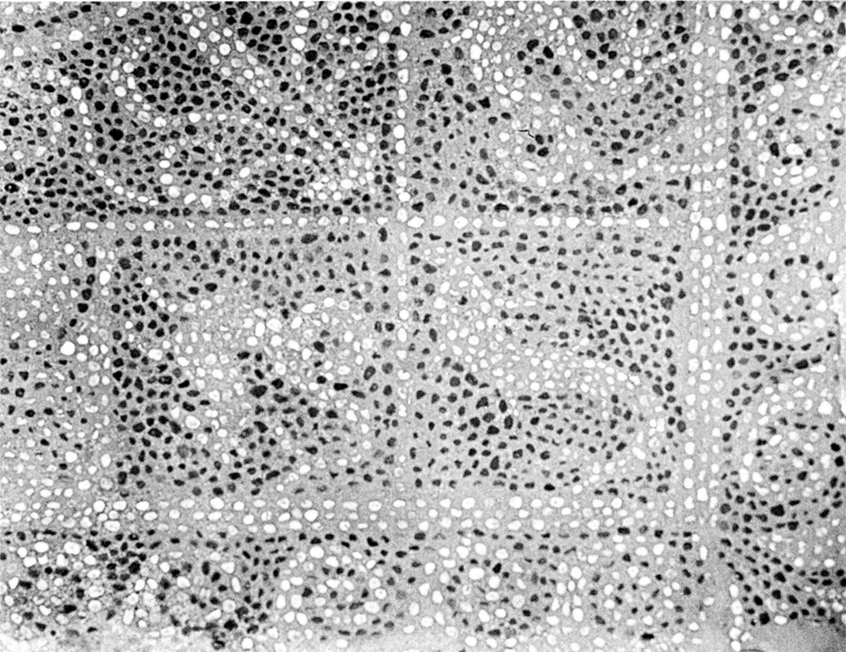

Aï Khanum, palace bath, floor mosaic made of river pebbles

the fine dust produced by the decomposition of the mud-brick walls. It was therefore possible to read, on clods of earth, some pages of a lost philosophical treatise by Aristotle, wherein he critically discussed Plato's theory of ideas, and next to them, some fragments of a text in verse!

Figurative Arts and Traditionalism

The traditionalism of the figurative arts in Bactria, which seemed to have fallen under the spell of a kind of late classicism, was the result of several causes. First, a great distance separated Bactria from the major Mediterranean centers where a powerful artistic renewal was taking place. Further, the political break around 250 B.C. of Bactria from the Seleucid Empire caused it to lose the royal patronage and dynamism of the Seleucid cities, one of the main actors of this cultural revolution. Lastly, a barrier, even if it was never completely hermetic, developed between Bactria and the Mediterranean world by the emergence and the expansion of the Parthian kingdom. While in the West mosaics could be found in rooms of different function, mainly in the dining rooms, they were limited in Bactria to the dressing rooms of the bath sections. They were made using an already obsolete technique of pebbles laid in cement. The traditional geometric and vegetal motifs, the sea-creatures, reduced to opaque silhouettes by the juxtaposition, widely spaced, of fairly big pebbles, of only two or three colors, had little in common with the creations of the Mediterranean mosaic workers of the time who composed with minute, multicolored stone-inlays illusionist tableaux that could pass for real paintings in stone.

The Greco-Bactrian sculptors, inspired by the creations of their Seleucid colleagues, employed the Greek technique of *acroliths,* where only the undraped parts (faces, hands, and feet) were made in stone; the remainder consisted of a timber framework, covered in fabric or modeled in clay or stucco. This technique was used for the larger-than-life cult statue in the main temple at Aï Khanum, the work of a true master; of which only one marble foot in a sandal, together with some finger fragments survive. Apart from the acrolithic sculpture, a soft limestone, the same as that used by the architects, was employed only for small to medium statues. They were carved in a conservative style, but with great skill. A good example is the statue of a nude young man, crowned with a leaf wreath (symbolizing victory in a competition?). The anatomical detail is impeccable, as is the case for the statuette of another naked youth with a cloak wrapped over his left arm, depicted in relief on a funerary stele found in the necropolis (no. 34), another typically Greek genre. The most representative piece is a Hermes-pillar, another common type in Greek sculpture, so called because such pillars were originally crowned with a Hermes head. At Aï Khanum the pillar bears the bust of an old man in a cloak, probably the master of the gymnasium where the statue was discovered, his lively and sensitive face contrasting with the heavy, rather clumsy drapery (no. 32). In a more modest example, but of no lesser Greek workmanship and treated with gusto, is the grotesque grinning mask, worn

Aï Khanum, a finely carved statue of a youth (no. 34) two views of the sculpture, painstakingly pieced together by French archaeologists, before it was smashed by the Taliban in 2001

in Greek comedy by the slave-cook, which served as a water spout in a fountain overlooking the Oxus, near the gymnasium (no. 33). Bronze statues, more likely to disappear than their stone counterparts, have left only minimal fragments, enough however to attest to their existence.

The Greco-Bactrian sculptors did at least contribute one major innovation to their art by introducing and perfecting a technique used only to a limited extent in the Greek world and which was to maintain an immense and lasting success in Central Asia: statues modeled in unfired clay or stucco on wooden frames and lead sticks (for the hands).

The minor art forms, more easily influenced by the native arts, were more open to Asian traditions, as can be seen from some figurines of naked women (or goddesses), plump and in stiff attitudes, made in bone, or molded in terracotta, and overburdened by heavy draperies of vaguely Hellenistic style. Only a few objects demonstrated an attempt to fuse Greek and Eastern traditions. The most remarkable of these is a large impressive disk of gilded silver showing Cybele, the goddess of nature, passing through a mountain landscape on a carriage drawn by lions and driven by a winged Victory attended by two long-robed priests. Features borrowed from the Hellenic tradition (the type of Cybele, the allegorical representation of Victory as a winged Nike and of the sun as the haloed bust of Helios, the feminine draperies, the lions parading) are juxtaposed to conventions of Asian art (composition without perspective, juxtaposition of motifs without any overlapping, absence of transition between contrasting profile, and frontal views of the various parts of the bodies) without really being harmonized and fused.

Dynamic Craft Workshops

Greco-Bactrian craftsmanship was a particularly dynamic area of activity, with Greek techniques used to meet the requirements of day-to-day living. Ivory was imported in quantity from neighboring India, providing the raw material for a bustling center of production. This was particularly the case for the manufacture of chairs and beds, with bell-and-disk profiled legs, which are derived from Greek prototypes. Locally produced imitations of Western objects include heavy mortars used with a horizontal pestle, bronze ink pots, and the so-called strygils with which athletes used to scrape their bodies clean from oil and sweat after competing. Time was measured by typically Greek hemispherical sundials (no. 30). However, one peculiar specimen consists of a squared block of stone, having a large cylindrical opening with the hour lines engraved within. This represents a unique type of equatorial sundial (no. 31), probably a pedagogical instrument to teach astronomy in the gymnasium. A state armory produced all kinds of military equipment, stored in a large arsenal on the main street, the excavation of which unfortunately had to be interrupted almost as soon as it was begun after the last 1978 campaign because of the Soviet military intervention of 1979. One remarkable discovery made there consisted of substantial remnants of iron armor used by the *cataphractarii*, horsemen who were famed in antiquity and covered in mail from head to toe, as were their horses. This heavily clad cavalry was mainly used by the Parthians, but it had also been adopted by the Hellenistic armies. This is confirmed by the finds from Aï Khanum, which offer the best-preserved and most ancient examples of this type of armor to date.

The bulk of the earthenware vessels were in specifically local forms, such as cylindro-conical beakers. Nevertheless there were also a large variety of Greek forms, for example the so-called fishplates, drinking bowls, and, among the latter, the so-called Megarian bowls decorated with vegetal motifs in relief, jugs, and amphorae. Frequent use was made of a black or red slip, reminiscent of Hellenistic monochrome vessels, often in combination with impressed palmette ornamentation. Local workshops had made a specialty of decorative stone vessels carved from a blue-gray schist with various engraved motifs and incrustation of multicolored ceramic inlays forming geometric design: Specimens include plates and hemispherical lidded boxes with internal radiating compartments, which are the direct precursors of the globular Buddhist reliquaries (nos. 18–20).

Imported Luxury Items

Imports are represented by a fine collection of semi-precious stones, originating primarily in India, and by some pieces of exceptional interest. Half a dozen plaster casts, impressed from the decoration in relief of vessels in precious metal from the western Hellenistic world and depicting mythological and epic scenes, are among the earliest examples of these types of molded copies used by local goldsmiths and silversmiths. Numerous similar finds from Egypt to Begram and now Aï Khanum in Afghanistan testify to the wide diffusion of these molds and casts and to the role they played in the dissemination of classical iconography.

Another unique piece is without parallel even in its country of origin, India (no. 9). It is a large disk made up of an assemblage of small plaquettes of a kind of mother of pearl, with a decoration of tiny inlays of colored glass delineated by gold threads. The plaquettes form a complex composition that might depict a famous Indian myth, the love story of king Dushyanta and of the fair nymph Shakuntala who bore Bharata, the eponymous ancestor of the Indian nation. Not only does this prestigious object furnish us with precious information about the earliest figurative art of India, but it was also directly involved in the last events of the history of Aï Khanum. Discovered in the layer containing the burned remnants of the royal treasury, where it had been stored shortly before the palace was pillaged and destroyed by nomads around 145 B.C., it may very well have formed part of the booty collected by Eucratides, the last great king—who reigned in eastern Bactria around the area of Aï Khanum—during one of his campaigns in India. It is a strong argument in support of the idea that the city of Eucratidia in Bactria, mentioned by the geographer Ptolemy (VI, 11, 8), was Aï Khanum, refounded as

Gold medallion of Eucratides I, Greco-Bactrian king (170–145 B.C.)

his capital city and given his own name, to which he would repair after his Indian expeditions.

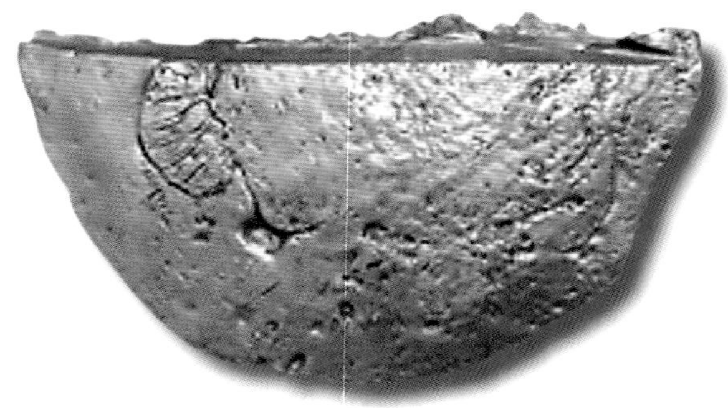

Backside of gold ingot (no. 8), an amalgam of jewelry, coins, and other booty melted after the sacking of Aï Khanum

The End of the Greek City

The end of the Greek city came suddenly around 145 B.C. Nomads from the northeast, perhaps Sakas on their way to plunder Bactria, set fire to the palace of Aï Khanum, the seat and symbol of authority, and robbed the treasury. It seems the Greek population had fled before the attack of the invaders. The local people, until then living outside the city, settled down en masse inside the ramparts and reoccupied the buildings abandoned by the Greeks, making no distinction between public and private areas, and systematically plundered all the goods and possessions left behind by the former owners. The burned-out palace was razed to the ground wherever building materials could be recovered (stone, metals, particularly bronze cramps, baked bricks). Some time later another, equally unexpected attack by nomads occurred. This time the perpetrators were the Yuezhi—migrating from Chinese Turkestan—and future founders of the Kushan Empire that extended from the Oxus to the Ganges Rivers, who now brought the brief post-Greek reoccupation to an end. They marked their passage by setting fire to the temple with niches, which the post-Greek "squatters" had converted into a storage space for every kind of rare and valuable item. By around 140 B.C. the city of Aï Khanum was a wasteland of ruins, gradually disappearing under its own rubble. Only the citadel on the acropolis continued to be occupied, from time to time, up to the Timurid period (15th-16th centuries A.D.).

The Greek Legacy

The end of Greek power in Bactria (around 130 B.C.) and the Punjab (around the beginning of our era) did not mean the immediate and complete disappearance of Hellenism from Central Asia. The civilizations that

succeeded the Greeks continued to draw on their legacy for a long period, right up to the Islamic conquest. Examples include the use of the Greek alphabet by the Kushan state to write the Bactrian language, which became the official tongue from the beginning of the second century A.D., the regular functioning of a royal mint, elements of architectural decoration like the Corinthian capital and the ubiquitous acanthus leaf with its endless variations, the ground plan of some buildings, and the modeling of statues using unfired clay and plaster. Generally speaking, in spite of ever-recurring tendencies toward abstract or decorative conventions, the artists continued to adhere to the conception of art as the representation of physical reality, but without crude naturalism. Greek art made man the center of its vision: In northern Afghanistan, the lesson was never entirely lost.

AÏ KHANUM, 2002. *Since the 1980s, it has become impossible to continue excavating at Aï Khanum. Civil war raged, and the location of the site, at the confluence of two major rivers, once again became a strategic place as a base for military operations. This photo shows the result of looting of the ancient city: Soldiers systematically pockmarked the site searching for antiquities. The remaining DAFA excavations are visible only in the distance. Today, site guards protect the site, but the looting has caused extensive damage.*

4 THIS CAPITAL IS CONSTRUCTED WITH four superposed and alternating rows of acanthus leaves, which are large and high, so that the capital seems to be fully enveloped by the bouquet of leaves. Behind the leaves, the central body of the column takes the form of an inverted cone, as is usual for a Greek capital.

The outermost protruding parts of the acanthus leaves have been cut off when the capital, some time following the Hellenistic period, was roughly reworked, together with other stone architectural elements and re-used in the construction of an embankment close to the old walls of Bactra, on the edge of the eastern section of the lower town now known as Tepe Zargaran (the "Hill of the Goldsmiths"). The badly eroded block and the ferruginous discoloration of the surface indicate that the stone was exposed for a long period to a powerful stream, probably from a branch of the river that flowed close to Bactra. Many Greco-Bactrian architectural elements were found together with this capital, in particular capitals of the same order, column bases and drums, pilaster bases and threshold stones. These were dug up from 1992 onward during clandestine excavations at the Tepe Zargaran site. Their discovery led to the initiation of an excavation project in 2004 by the French DAFA, with the aim to fix the exact location of these finds and to systematically explore the site.

A great number of similarly worked stones have been discovered since that time. However, the exact reason for the construction on the embankment, hastily made with second-hand materials is still unclear, as are the circumstances under which it was decided to dismantle some of the monumental buildings erected here by the Greek colonists, in what was the capital city of their realm. And it is still not known what exactly these monuments were.

4
Corinthian capital
Balkh (ancient Bactra)
3rd–2nd century B.C.
Limestone
82 x 48 cm
National Museum of Afghanistan
06.18.01

The Palace Treasury

5–8 THESE FOUR GOLD INGOTS WERE discovered hidden in a shallow cavity under a thin layer of earth in the floor of Room 115 in the royal treasury. They were made by melting down previously worked objects. They were found together with eight silver ingots weighing 12.574 kilograms, a bronze scale from a balance, and a lead weight.

Immediately after the arrival in 145 B.C. of the first invading nomads, who brought about the fall of the Greek city, craftsmen were active using this room for the processing of metals. They had close connections with the nomadic conquerors, since they transformed objects of precious metals looted from the town into ingots, probably mainly from the palace and the treasury itself.

One of the silver ingots bears an inscription in an unknown script. Although we are unable to read the script, we are certain that the language, which is not Greek, is not that of the local Bactrian population either. The alphabet closely resembles that of an inscription on a silver bowl from the famous burial mound called "the Barrow of the Golden Man," far to the north at Issyk in Kazakhstan, where a nomad chief had been buried in sumptuous attire decorated with gold.

The metalworkers must have ceased their activities suddenly, because they had barely time to bury the valuable ingots in an improvised hiding place. Whether or not they belonged to the nomad community, this sudden interruption of their activity can only be explained by the hasty departure of the nomads themselves; the reasons remain unknown to us.

The local population then entered the buildings abandoned by the Greeks, in particular Room 115 in the palace treasury, but this cache was not discovered. This second reoccupation was itself brought to an abrupt end by a second wave of invading nomads, this time the Yuezhi, the ancestors of the Kushan rulers. The history of the precious metal ingots is therefore closely bound up with the first attacks on Bactria by nomadic tribes, which led to the destruction of the Greek city of Aï Khanum.

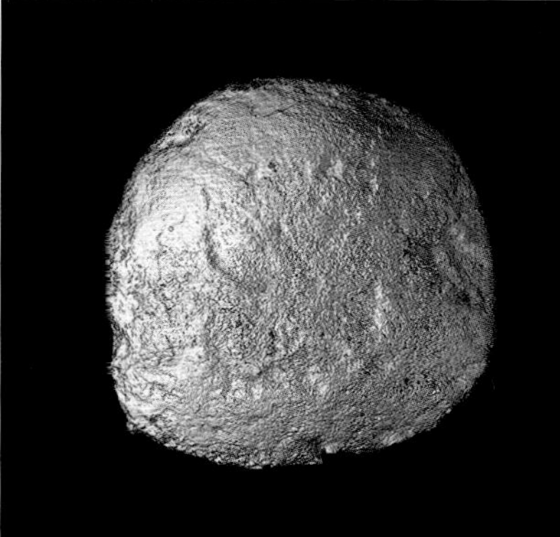

5–8
Gold ingots
Aï Khanum,
Palace treasury
Shortly after 145 B.C.
National Museum
of Afghanistan
04.42.1
5.23 x 5.90 cm, 322 g
04.42.2
4.32 x 4.99 cm, 189 g
04.42.3
3.21 x 3.31 cm, 103 g
04.42.4
7.4 x 7.44 cm, 259 g

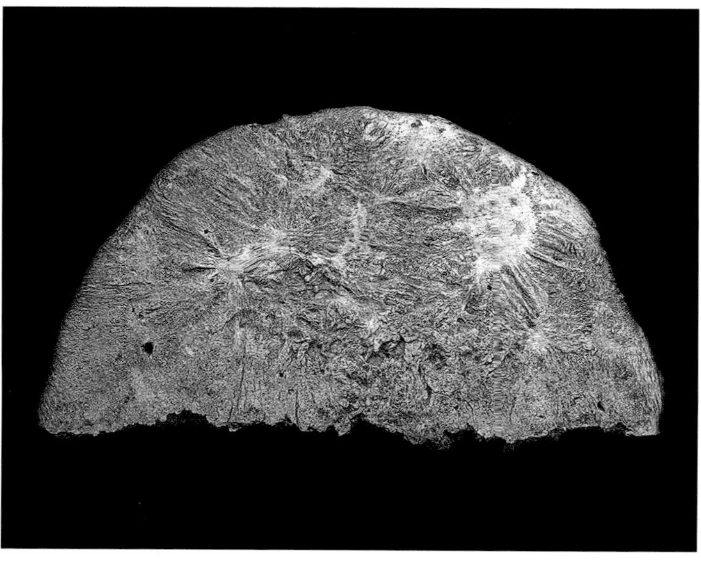

9
Engraved disk
Aï Khanum,
Palace treasury
Before 145 B.C.
Scallop shell (*Xancus pyrum*), colored glass and gold thread
Diam. 20.5 cm
National Museum of Afghanistan
05.42.25

9 THIS DECORATIVE DISK CONSISTS OF A main central panel surrounded by two circular frames. The missing parts have been reconstructed by Claude Rapin on the basis of Indian parallels. The lower part of the central panel shows a royal procession, shielded by a parasol, consisting of three persons on a chariot, escorted by three riders, and passing before a number of spectators through a landscape of flowers and various animals typical of the Indian fauna, including peacocks and deer. To either side are four pillars with bulging bases. In the upper part are depictions of various personages near a typically Indian building, whose bowed roof can be reconstructed with certainty on the basis of the three remaining peaks. The circular frieze, more static and less narrative, shows groups in conversation, buildings with curved roofs and peaks, peacocks and deer and, as elsewhere, blossoming branches.

Rapin interprets this as a very free and allusive depiction of the famous Indian legend of Shakuntala, foster daughter of the hermit Kanva. She was seduced by King Dushyanta, who entered the garden containing the hermitage (with the pillars, perhaps indicating the boundary of the garden) during a hunting party (the chariot, the parasol, and the escort), and then left her, pregnant with Bharata (eponym of India). Eventually he acknowledged Shakuntala as his spouse and Bharata as his lawful son. The seated group in the round frieze may depict the two main protagonists in the center of the park, repeatedly represented in support of the main theme.

The dating of this object, prior to the fall of the Greek city of Aï Khanum in 145 B.C., makes this disk one of the oldest examples of Indian figurative art. The disk displays a complex narrative grammar and is witness to the craftsmanship involved in decoration, using inlaid fragments of glass, the contours of which are delineated by gold threads. These have survived the ages without losing anything of their bright and lively color.

A great name from the history of the Greeks in Central Asia is also linked to this unique object, that of King Eucratides, who probably collected it on one of his campaigns in India and stored it in the treasury of the city he made his capital, calling it Eucratideia. In around 145 B.C., returning as he had so many times from India, he was murdered by his son, Heliocles. This event opened the gates of Bactria to the nomads, who were always alert to any sign of Greek vulnerability.

10
Amphora fragment inscribed in ink
Aï Khanum,
Palace treasury
ca 145 B.C.
Earthenware
H. 41 cm; Diam. 28 cm
National Museum
of Afghanistan
05.42.608

10 ON THE SHOULDER OF THIS HANDLELESS amphora, two previous inscriptions were purposefully scratched out to allow a new message of three lines to be added: "(deposited) by Cosmus in legal silver currency, checked by Nikeratos; sealed by Nikeratos himself."

This inscription indicates that the amphora contained silver currency, deposited by an assistant treasury official named Cosmus Nikeratos who verified that the silver was of good quality and the coins of the correct weight, so that they conformed to the so-called Attic standard for Greco-Bactrian coinage. This precautionary measure was taken to prevent mingling with Indian coinage, which had a lower silver content and was regulated by a different standard. When Indian coins (known by numismatists as "punch-marked") were deposited, they were identified as such and treated separately. The checker, Nikeratos, had also sealed the vessel containing the money. The inscription shows that the notations made in ink on these clay vessels were simply labels indicating the contents. In the case of this amphora, the exact amount was not registered, but in other cases this is done. Neither was the amount recorded when part of the content was withdrawn, whether it was coins or other items. The actual bookkeeping was carried out separately (on tablets, papyrus, or parchment) in a different room. This method was also usual elsewhere in the Greek world.

11 THIS IS A FRAGMENT OF A BOWL WITH A pointed base which was inscribed after it was broken. The bowl had been inverted and used as a lid for an amphora (it is probably for this reason that the writing is upside down).

a) "Year 24, the...
(contents) olive oil;
The vessel A incompletely filled
With the contents of two vessels (keramion)
decanted by ...
(In total) One and a half (hemiolion) (?) unit
(stamnos) (of oil)"

The inscription has the following explanation: two vessels, A and B (the latter mentioned in the lost part of the text), were filled with "hemiolios" or "one and a half units" of oil in total. Item A, identified as "incomplete," "... contained oil, transferred from two vessels" designated as "keramion" (different from A and B). Two officials sealed A and B. However, rather than meaning "one and a half units", the word "hemiolios," which is also known as an official title could very well have designated the person who made the decanting operation, which accompanied the deposit of oil in the treasury. In that case, combining with the inscription on the vessel that had our bowl as a lid gives a more satisfactory sense, which would read: Year 24 .../ (contents)olive oil;/ vessel A incompletely filled into which were decanted / two vessels (keramia) by Hippias / the hemiolios and A was sealed / by Molossos (?) and B by Strato, (?).

b) On the same bowl, but to the left of the previous inscription, is a later, badly damaged text on the same pattern:
"On behalf of Philiskos
... olive oil
...
Incompletely filled ... from the three...
...
Theophrastus / sealed.".

The exceptional fertility of the region of Bactria was widely known: Everything grew there except the olive tree, which could not withstand the harsh winters (Strabo 2, II, 1, 14). Olive oil was seen as essential by the Greeks, and therefore was imported from the Middle East or the Mediterranean. Because of its high price it was probably used not so much in the kitchen but more as an ointment for athletes and in preparing medicines and perfumes.

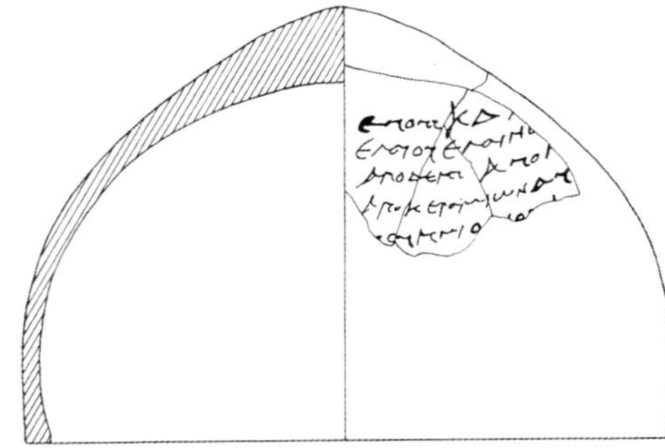

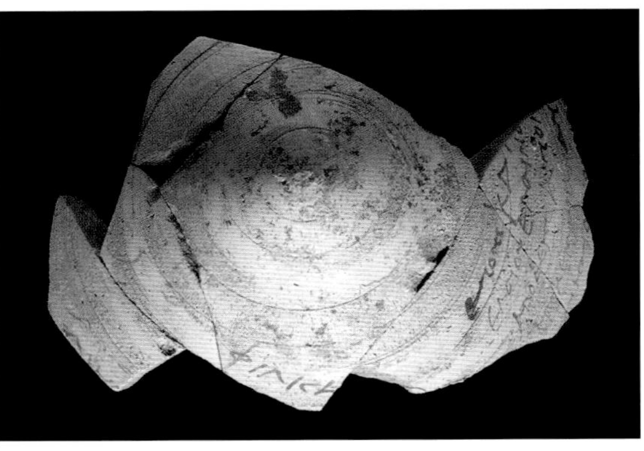

11
Fragment of vessel inscribed with ink
Aï Khanum,
Palace treasury
147 B.C.
Earthenware
H. 12.5 cm; Diam. 18 cm
National Museum
of Afghanistan
05.42.611

The inscribed bowl is particularly important because it is dated. The year 24 can only refer to the reign of Eucratides, the last ruler of Aï Khanum. A historical text (Justin XLI, 6) demonstrates that his reign coincided with the administration of the Parthian ruler Mithridates I, which commenced in 171 B.C. As regards the various administrators of the treasury at Aï Khanum, the Philiskos mentioned in 1 b must have succeeded the person whose name is missing from inscription 1 a. Philiskos was the last but one on the list, whereas Nikeratos, mentioned in cat. no. 10, and known to have been general administrator from another text, was the last one. On the basis of these facts it has been concluded that the date must be 171 - 24 = 147 B.C., two years before the treasury suddenly ceased operations, as a result of the looting associated with the take-over of the city during the first wave of nomad invasions and the burning of the palace. It is for this reason that a date of 145 B.C. has been adopted as marking the end of the Greek city of Aï Khanum.

The Temple With Niches

12
Male or female head
Aï Khanum, Temple
with niches, Courtyard
2nd century B.C.
Unfired clay
21 x 15 cm
National Museum
of Afghanistan
05.42.74

12 FOUND IN 1968 IN THE VESTIBULE OF THE temple with niches, only the outermost layer of the relief survives. The entire middle section of the forehead and the cranium of the relief are missing. The locks of hair, made separately and fixed on later, have also disappeared, apart from the four above the temples. The ashy grey color was caused by the heating of the clay during the fire that destroyed the temple.

This high-relief statue is one of two sculptures that stood on masonry bases against the separating wall between the vestibule and the cult room. The sculpture was made by applying ever-thinner layers of clay to a wooden armature.

Clay and plaster sculpture was much employed by the Greco-Bactrian artists. The material was air-dried, quickly made, less costly than stone or bronze, and lent itself well to the decoration of interiors. At Aï Khanum limestone, or occasionally marble, was used for small and middle-size statues placed in interiors and also for acroliths. In the latter case the monumental proportions were achieved with the use of a minimal quantity of marble. But the main legacy of Hellenism to the arts of Central Asia was the modelling of statues in clay or stucco.

The full, soft features and the stern yet tender expression suggests a feminine head in a very classical style, but recently it was noted that the short curling hair around the forehead is a characteristically male hairstyle. Remnants of red pigment on the right cheek and temple may be traces of adhesive used to secure gold leaf, as on a plaster male head found at the same location, which had clearly been gilded in this way.

All we can say about the identity of the individuals depicted is that they were important enough to have their statues dedicated in the main temple of the city in the last period of its existence.

13
Handle of a bowl
Aï Khanum,
Temple with niches,
Courtyard
ca 145 B.C.
Bronze
13.7 cm
National Museum
of Afghanistan
04.42.6

13 HANDLE OF A LARGE BOWL OR BASIN, IN the form of a flattened arch, attached to the vessel by two vine leaves serving as background to a pair of female busts. The busts are covered with stiffly folded cloaks, set off by a border engraved with a herringbone motif, which depicts an animal-skin cloak. One of the breasts is uncovered, its nipple marked by a circular incision. The vine leaves, on which the veins have been carefully indicated, are covered with small dots. The handle has a rounded annulus at its midpoint; a leafy branch is engraved on the exterior of its curve.

The Dionysian nature of the image is suggested by the vine leaves. The female busts depict a type of maenad—a follower of Dionysus, generally recognized by the animal-skin garb, exposed breast, and tangled hair, often crowned with vine leaves. The maenads are depicted as inebriated individuals with an ecstatic expression on the face or with closed eyes. Here, we are immersed in a more primitive peasant world, where these female followers of the god of wine, with their pointed ears and horns are more satyresses than maenads. Satyrs, with large animal ears, are part of the Hellenistic iconography of Central Asia, such as those gambolling on the famous ivory rhytons of Nisa. But they are seldom horned, as if the artists thought that their large, bald foreheads and animal ears, together with their animal skins, were enough to make them easily recognizable. Their female companions are characterized only by the animal skin they are wearing and by their dancing. Normally the Greeks did not make any attempt at bestializing the feminity of these wild companions of Dionysus, but here we are in faraway Bactria, where Hellenism was under pressure from foreign popular traditions. This iconographical peculiarity sets the handle from Aï Khanum apart from other documents of Dionysian character in Hellenistic Central Asia.

Found in the courtyard of the temple with niches, in the layer associated with the "squatter" reoccupation, the handle from Aï Khanum cannot be later than 150-145 B.C. Its style, already strongly provincialized, should rather be compared to a female head on a bronze appliqué from Takht-i-Sangin (northern Bactria), manufactured in a workshop which, at around the same period, also betrays a disintegrating Hellenism.

14
Statuette of Heracles
Aï Khanum,
Temple with niches,
Sanctuary
150 B.C.
Bronze
H 18.2 cm
National Museum
of Afghanistan
04.42.8

14 A BEARDLESS HERACLES STANDS ON A high base, his weight on his right leg. He holds in his left hand a club that rests against his upper left arm. With his right hand he places a crown of leaves on his head. This statue is poorly cast, with the upper part of the thighs below the crotch fused together. The style is rustic and heavy, with a disproportionately short and massive trunk, arms without muscles and enormous hands, in particular the left hand that doesn't quite grasp the club. This type of standing youthful Heracles, placing a crown on his own head, is represented in a similar way, but in masterly style, on Greco-Bactrian coins of King Demetrius (190–175 B.C), with the addition of a lion skin over the left arm, a pose later imitated by the Indo-Greek kings Lysias (120–110 B.C.) and Theophilos (around 90 B.C.). Together with the inscription in the gymnasium, this statuette bears witness to the enormous popularity of the worship of this hero in Greek Central Asia and throughout the Hellenized East. The left leg has been summarily repaired. The foot, which had been broken off, was joined to the lower leg by a metal pin replacing the ankle. The base, separately cast and hollow (wall thickness 1.5–2 mm), left open underneath, included two holes for the feet. During the repair the small pegs under the feet were reinserted in the holes and secured in them with molten lead. But the hasty repair fixed the feet higher than the base (by 5 mm) and the right foot protruded slightly from the base. The base fits the feet so badly that it is perhaps not the original one.

15
Moon crescent with a human head
Aï Khanum, Temple with niches, Sanctuary
Before 145 B.C.
Copper(?), bronze, iron, lead
H. 14 cm
National Museum of Afghanistan
04.42.10

15 A LARGE CAST BRONZE PLAQUE IN THE form of a moon crescent with small finials at the pointed extremities. A hollow image of a human head is attached in the center by three rivets, and the hollow interior is filled with lead. In the middle of the lower edge of the reverse were found heavily corroded remnants of a rectangular iron plate, possibly intended as an attachment to a vertical shaft. In that event, the crescent may be a religious insignia. The central appliqué is poorly preserved, making speculation on the figure's identity difficult. The object may be associated with a moon cult.

The probable (but not certain) male head in full front view has elongated oval features, with a stern expression. Under the chin there seems to be a beard. The style is of good quality, as far as this can be judged given the condition of the appliqué, which has deteriorated since its discovery. The voluminous compact mass surrounding the head and descending below the chin depicts a head covering, perhaps made of some sort of animal mane or skin. To either side of the appliqué the crescent is decorated with an engraved vegetal tendril, which undulates up to the finials.

Just like the disk depicting Cybele (no. 23), the moon crescent was discovered in the later occupation layer in the shrine, which by that time had been converted to domestic use by the local population, who collected materials there from all over the city, which the Greek colonists had abandoned. The object could therefore have been looted from some other place and does not necessarily provide us with information about the cult practiced in the shrine.

16 THIS STATUETTE WAS DISCOVERED IN Room no. 32 in the sanctuary of the temple with niches, in the post-Greek occupation level, dating to shortly after 145 B.C.

The statuette was carved from a long section of bone, with the central cavity sawn off at the base, under the stool supporting it, and closed off at the top by the hair. Remnants of red paint (on the tips of the breasts, lips, and forehead) and black paint (alternating red and black necklace pendants, pubis) are visible. A bone plate, now lost, must have originally been inserted in a vertical slot and had been cut at the base of the neck so that its sides would protrude enough for the arms, made separately, to be attached to it. The figurine has been erroneously restored (and photographed) with associated arms. The two upper arms may belong to another bone statuette, more feminine in appearance, which was also found in the area of the temple with indented niches.

The nude woman is shown frontally in a hieratically rigid pose, the legs stiffly pressed together, separated only by an engraved line. This astonishing and crudely explicit rendering of a fertility idol, with its heavy and fat body, an enormous neck with folds of flesh, an oversized "mons veneris", symbol of sexual power, covering the whole groin, embodies a type of naked mother goddess, which is a rarity, even during the Greek period in Central Asia, where there was a clear preference for clothed feminine deities. The features of the face are rudely stylized, with harshly incised eyes, eyebrows, and mouth; the ears are pierced for jewelry. The hair, short and smooth, probably painted formerly, forms a roll above the forehead. A necklace with pendants and a colored dot between the eyebrows in the Indian fashion play with the nakedness. The pedestal on which the goddess stands is unusual, clearly a stool, normally made as a footrest, not a base or a podium. Such miniature stools in stone, each around 10 centimeters in height were found in abundance in shrines and private houses. They were certainly used as stands, but we do not know for what objects. Without any parallel in the Greek world, they are one of the many riddles at Aï Khanum.

Although its feminine characteristics are somewhat exaggerated, this nude statuette of a goddess was nevertheless probably intended to represent the canons of oriental feminine beauty.

16
Female figurine
Aï Khanum,
Sanctuary,
Temple with niches
Before 145 B.C.
Bone
16.2 x 3.4 cm
National Museum
of Afghanistan
04.42.11

17
Decorative plate
Aï Khanum,
Temple with niches
Early 3rd century B.C.
Bronze
44 x 42 cm
National Museum
of Afghanistan
04.42.12

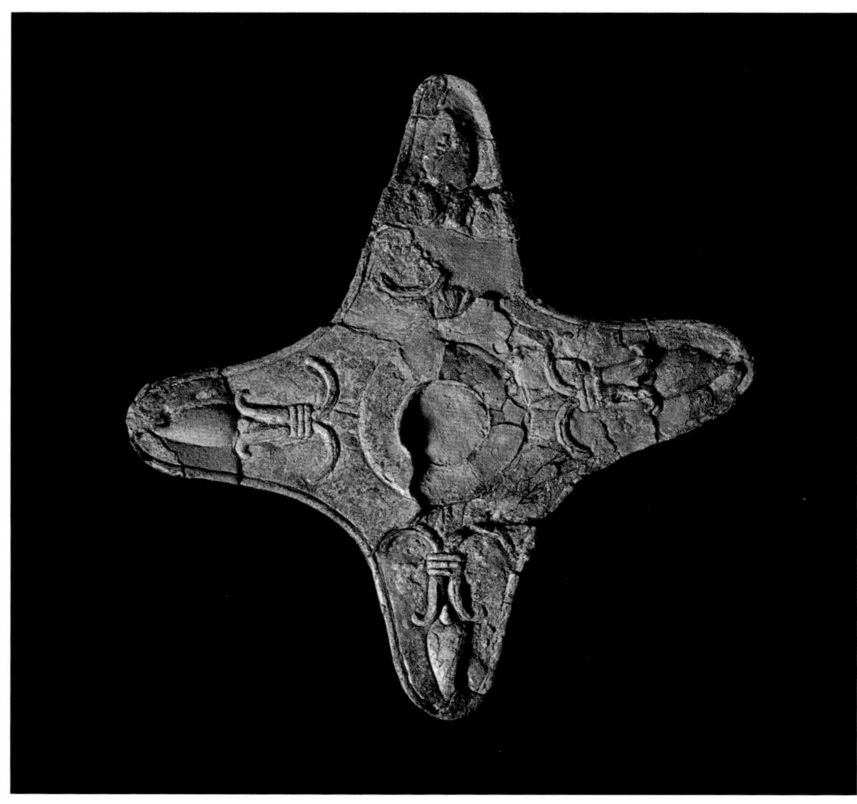

17 THIS BRONZE PLATE RECONSTRUCTED OUT of numerous fragments was damaged by a fierce fire that destroyed the temple and was found in the destruction layer of the vestibule (Room 3).

It is a cruciform decorative appliqué, probably for one of the two doors of the temple, with four equal, triangular arms. A circular central opening, with its slightly protruding edge upturned, must have been fitted with a door knob. Each arm is decorated with a flower bud sprouting from two leaves tied at their base by a triple binding, while their stems curve outward, their junction being marked by a short peduncular motif. The style of this piece suggests that it predated the temple with niches and originally belonged to an earlier temple built in the same area.

18–19
Stone compartmented bowls (pyxides)
Aï Khanum,
Temple with niches,
Sanctuary
Before 145 B.C.
Schist
National Museum
of Afghanistan
04.42.397
Diam. 9 to 18 cm
04.42.398
Diam. 5.9 to 18 cm

18–20 LOCAL WORKSHOPS PRODUCED A large number of schist objects. The stone is greyish, more rarely bluish, obtained from the mountains of Afghanistan. Fragments were found everywhere on the site, mainly in sanctuaries. They are hemispherical boxes, with a slightly flattened bottom. Inside they are generally divided into two, three, or four compartments by thin dividers. The lip is flat and has its inner side lined with a fillet in relief which helps maintain the lid in place. The slightly convex lid has a mushroom-shaped knob, which was glued or pinned in place. The lids often display an engraved decoration, inlays of colored ceramic plaques, or both. The engraved decoration consists of simple geometric patterns: triangles, rectangles, circles, bars, etc., and plant or animal motifs. The last two present leafy branches, rosettes, suns, horses, and ibexes and are treated in a linear stylized manner, which evokes rock engravings. The inlay decoration, which plays on the contrast between the dark stone and the vivid colors of the incrustations, is purely geometric.

These are similar to small Greek compartmented vessels known as *pyxis* (sing.), *pyxides* (plur.), round or square, often divided into compartments, though rarely made in stone. Here, the systematic manufacture in stone and the engraved or inlaid decoration are characteristic of the local craft industry. The carving of hard stones for vessels and various objects and the use of inlays for decoration goes back to an ancient Bactrian tradition of the Bronze Age.

These compartmented bowls were undoubtedly used by women for all kinds of purposes—cosmetics, jewelry, etc.—were widely circulated, and came to serve as a model for a type of spherical Buddhist reliquary very common in the Gandhara area.

20
Stone vessel (pixides) lids
Temple with niches, Sanctuary
3rd-2nd century B.C.
Diam. 4.3 to 26.5 cm
National Museum of Afghanistan
05.42.229

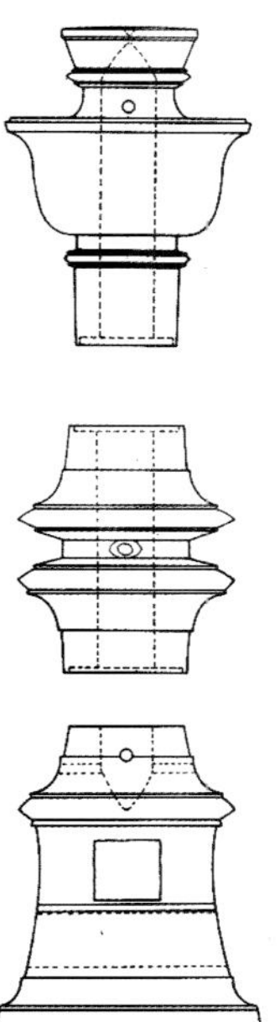

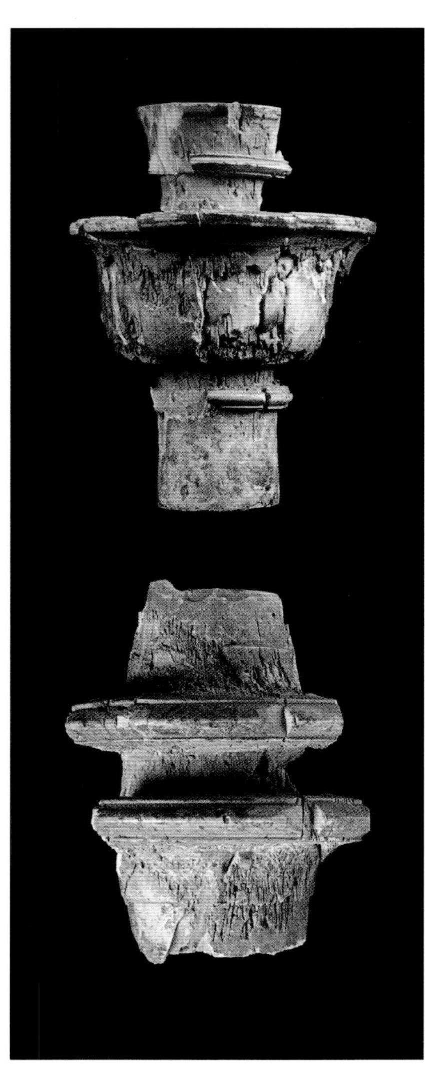

21–22
Fragments of a chair leg
Aï Khanum,
Temple with niches
Before 145 B.C.
Ivory
National Museum
of Afghanistan
05.42.582: H. 10.7 cm
05.42.583: H. 13.8 cm

21–22 THESE TWO IVORY PIECES ARE PARTS OF the legs of a stool, typical of Greece, found in the burned debris of the vestibule of the temple. Each leg originally consisted of three cylindrical ivory parts, carved from sections of elephant tusks, turned on a lathe in sections.

This type of Greek stool was not uncommon at the time, but few examples have survived in the East. The proximity of India was undoubtedly a factor in the development of an exceptionally active ivory industry in Bactria, much evidence of which has been found at Aï Khanum.

23
Ceremonial plate with a representation of Cybele
Aï Khanum,
Temple with niches
3rd century B.C.
Gilded silver
Diam. 25 cm
National Museum
of Afghanistan
04.42.7

23 THIS GILDED SILVER PLATE WAS ORIGINALLY nailed to a wooden disk. The plate's design was embossed and gilded with gold leaf, 1/10,000 to 1/15,000 of a millimeter thick. It was looted in antiquity and violently torn from the wood backing. Cybele, the Greek goddess of nature, is crowned with a *polos* (head covering), a symbol of her godly status. She rides through her mountain domain in a chariot drawn by two lions. Beside her stands the winged goddess Nike, body facing forward with head in profile. She grasps a goad and the reins and drives the team through a rocky landscape strewn with small flowers. She is attended by two of her priests who wear the *tunica talaris* (a ritual garb) with wide belts tied thrice around their waists and conical hats. One of the priests walks briskly on tiptoe behind the chariot, with his back and head tilted back, so as to better hold aloft the heavy, broad parasol above the goddess. The other priest stands opposite the chariot, on a high-stepped altar, built of six tall blocks of stone, making an offering. He burns incense in a small censer. Three heavenly bodies shine down from the sky: the sun in the guise of the bust of the god Helios, the moon crescent, and a star with multiple rays.

The subject is typical of a hybrid Greco-Oriental art, particularly in its iconography. Cybele in her chariot drawn by lions is a motif from the Greek Mediterranean and Asia Minor. The winged Nike, personified as a charioteer, embodies the Greek symbol of Victory. By contrast, the typically eastern elements include the priest with the parasol (a royal symbol), his walking behind the chariot, the bare feet of the two priests (a symbol of ritual purity in Asia), the chariot with its large wheels and high balustrade, resembling Achaemenid chariots, and the altar with its high steps, comparable examples of which are known from Syria and Iran.

Although the object was found in one of the sacristies, it is far from certain that it belonged to the temple. In fact, the silver plate had been hidden under the floor of the southern sacristy some time before the second and final invasion of nomads (Yuezhi) by one of the "squatters" who, after the first nomadic assault (Saka), had desecrated the temple and made it a storage place. It could therefore have been picked up anywhere on the site before being deposited in the temple.

Based on stylistic analysis, this plate dates to around 300 B.C.—before the foundation of Aï Khanum. It probably does not predate the Greeks, as there is no evidence that the cult of Cybele had spread to Iran and Central Asia prior to Alexander the Great's conquest.

The Southeastern Citadel

24 THE CAPITAL WAS EXCAVATED FROM THE citadel. It surfaced when soldiers from the Northern Alliance were installing heavy artillery directed against the Taliban, who occupied the opposite site of the river. It was recently taken to Kabul by the DAFA.

This capital must have come from an important building, either a temple that would have stood within the defensive perimeter of the promontory (similar to the Parthenon on the Acropolis of Athens) or the residence of the military governor. The capital is virtually intact: almost unique at Aï Khanum except for those displaced and reused in a modern teahouse not far from Aï Khanum.

Most capitals from Aï Khanum, including the present example and the one from Bactra also exhibited here (no. 4), are of the so-called "free" Corinthian type where the volutes spring directly from the crown of acanthus leaves.

While the capitals from Aï Khanum belong formally to the "free Corinthian" type, they nevertheless have very distinctive features that differentiate them from their Greek counterparts. The ascending part of the angle volutes is extraordinarily wide and massive and partly overlapped by the spirals of their upper end terminating around a large protruding eye. On each of the four sides the large triangular space between the angle volutes is left empty, without the pair of smaller interior volutes that one finds at that place on the Greek exemplars. This amorphous, slightly concave surface has lost any structural function, while the Greek specimens and the capital from Bactra show, at that place, the rounded surface of an inverted cone, which, emerging from underneath the external decoration, plays the role of a real bracket sustaining the roof.

This original variant of the Corinthian order was created in Syria-Mesopotamia at the beginning of the third century B.C. and took its inspiration from an ancient type of Greek and Near Eastern capital with ascending volutes, called Aeolic, which was "Hellenized" by means of the Greek acanthus. The leaves in high relief, boldly detached from the background, with pending extremities displaying pulpy and luxuriant forms, are typical of these Greco-Bactrian capitals, the vigor and leafy exuberance of which prevail over elegance.

24
Corinthian capital
Aï Khanum
Before 145 B.C.
Limestone
H. 74 cm; Diam. 90 cm
National Museum
of Afghanistan
06.42.640

25–26
Two sets of antefixes with palmettes, type I a and b
Aï Khanum, Palace
Terracotta
3rd century B.C.
National Museum of Afghanistan
05.42.84/1-8
05.42.84/12-19

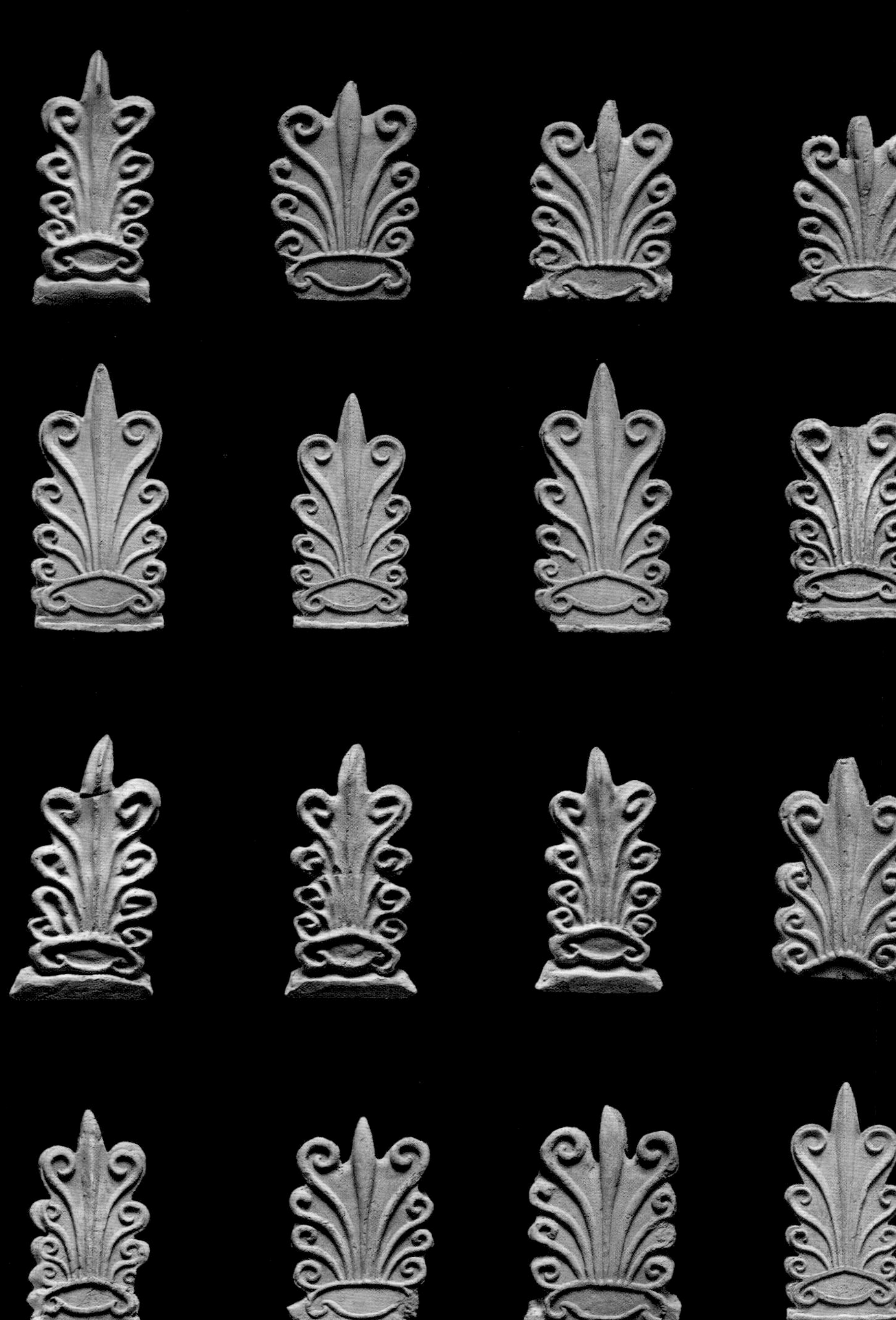

The Palace Antefixes

27
Winged antefix, type II
Aï Khanum, Palace,
Main entrance
3rd century B.C.
Terracotta
50 x 42 x 8 cm
National Museum
of Afghanistan
05.42.84/1

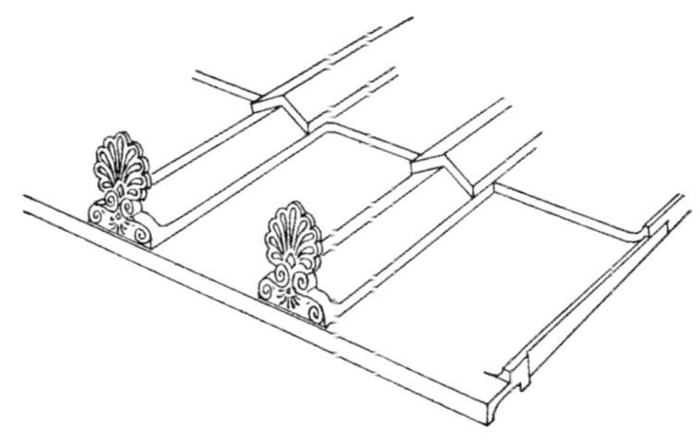

25–27 ANTEFIXES. In the Greco-Bactrian architecture as in all of Asia, the roofs had only one slope and not two as was customary in classical architecture. Another major difference: The roofs were not completely covered with terracotta tiles but made of earth. The ceiling of reed-mats supported by the beams was covered with a mattress of freshly cut reeds over which a thick layer of earth was spread; the latter was made watertight by a thick lining of a mixture of clay and straw. The gentle slope of this last protective layer was carefully calculated so that the rainwater neither pooled nor ran down too quickly and washed away the lining of clay.

At Aï Khanum, the top layer of clay was reinforced only along the edge of the roofs with one or two rows of terracotta flat tiles of the so-called Corinthian type, which protected the edge of the roof from erosion by dripping rain. This detail was evident in Greco-Bactrian architecture in the buildings of any importance (generally public buildings), including the palace and the patrician private mansions. The narrow pentagonal-shaped cover-tiles superimposed over the lateral joints between the main tiles to prevent rain infiltration had, attached to their front face, decorative plates ornamented with motifs in relief, most frequently—but not exclusively—palmettes. These so-called "antefixes" represent another typically Greek system of architectural decoration.

The antefixes with palmettes exhibited here are examples of two main types, the first of which has a long history. Type I had an attractive shape with sharp contours, slender leaves with acute edges, and a narrow base with a flat profile: height 35 cm; width 17.5 cm; width of base 16.5 cm. According to the Greek system, the antefix was stuck to the pentagonal cover-tile, forming one piece. In another variant the leaves became gradually thicker, the contours less sharp, the forms less precise. The ultimate outcome of this degeneration is evident in the flabby palmettes of the inner courtyard of the palace with Doric columns, dating from the last period of the Greek city (second quarter of the second century B.C.). This stylistic development was accompanied by a technical change. The antefix was separated from the cover-tile and fired separately. The plate was provided with a horizontal triangular peg protruding from the lower part of the back, which was inserted in the pentagonal front opening of the cover-tile. This change was probably motivated by the difficulty of firing both the cover-tile and the antefix as one piece, which would leave the antefix eminently fragile and prone to break easily from the cover-tile; in fact, the two parts were always discovered separately. But the new technical system to which the Greco-Bactrian architects resorted was not effective either, for the back-pegs themselves broke easily from the antefix-plates. Among the tens of antefixes recovered from the excavations only one was discovered still attached to its unbroken peg.

Type II. Despite the obvious affinity with type I, type II was not derived from it, but created independently. This large type of antefix is characterized by a pair of wings combined with vegetal motifs. The composition is dominated by the two large outstretched wings, like unfurled banners, the lower part of which are made of two rows of short horizontal feathers and the upper one of three rows of long feathers strongly curving inward like sickle blades. Near the base, are depicted two thick leaves or petals with out-turned extremities. These form an open calyx for the whole composition, which sits on a base imitating a column base with two bulging tori separated by a groove. To each side of the base, the palmette leaves are closer to each other; the arched motif at the base of the palmette is almost flat.

The outside façade of the main entrance to the palace was decorated with this type of antefix. The highly unusual hybrid composition of animal (feathers) and vegetal motifs (leaves) is unique, and unknown from the Greek repertoire. But its powerful assertiveness and monumentality compensate for whatever it lacks in elegance and good taste.

The Funerary Monument of Kineas

28
Lower left corner fragment of the stele
Aï Khanum, the funerary monument of Kineas.
Beginning of the 3rd century B.C.
Limestone
14 x 15 cm
National Museum of Afghanistan
05.42.190

29
Inscribed base for the stele
Aï Khanum, the funerary monument of Kineas.
Beginning of the 3rd century B.C.
Limestone
65.5 x 46.5 cm; H. 28 cm
National Museum of Afghanistan
05.42.13

28–29 THESE TWO STONE FRAGMENTS belong to a single funerary monument dedicated to Kineas, one of the founders of Aï Khanum. A man named Clearchos donated a copy of the Delphic Precepts to the town of Aï Khanum, after having them engraved at the most sacred spot in the city, the *temenos,* or sacred precinct of the founder of Aï Khanum, Kineas.

The Delphic Precepts contain some 150 maxims, said to have been presented to Apollo at his sanctuary in Delphi by the Famed Seven Sages of ancient Greece, which laid down the rules for a Greek man's conduct in private and public life.

The only part of the upper stele preserved at Aï Khanum (no. 28) includes the start of the maxim "practice wisdom," number 48. Thus, we know that the whole series of maxims must have been engraved on the stele of Aï Khanum, extending over three columns. These last maxims formed a group apart, for they enumerate the chief virtues to be cultivated by a Greek man during the different phases of his life: "As a child, learn good manners/as a young man, learn to control thy passions/in middle age, be just/in old age, give good advice/then die, without regret."

For lack of space the last five sayings were engraved on the base (no. 29), on its upper right-hand part, forcing the engraver to push to the left the dedicatory poem by the man who had donated the copy of the Delphic maxims to the city.

The donor, Clearchos, mentions his own name in the four-line poem to the left of the maxims:

"These wise sayings of the illustrious men of old have been consecrated at the Sacred Pytho [the former name of the oracular sanctuary of Apollo at Delphi]. There, Clearchos transcribed them carefully, coming here to display them so that they shine in such a distant place, in the sacred precinct of Kineas."

This Clearchos has been identified as a famed Greek philosopher from Soli, a disciple of Aristotle. He immersed himself in the study of human behavior and the moral rules governing social relations, which led him to attempt an authentic list of the Delphic aphorisms. He was also interested in the origins of religious thought, which he believed to come from the East: first expressed by Iranian magi, then transmitted to the Indian philosophers, and onward to the Jews. This would explain his exploratory trip through Bactria and Aï Khanum and further on to northwest India, at the start of the third century B.C.

The Gymnasium

30–31 THIS SUNDIAL IS A RECONSTRUCTION based on eight fragments. The instrument was carved from a block of limestone and takes the form of a throne supported by two lion legs in front. The seat of the throne forms the dial face, a section of hemisphere. Seven horizontal month lines are inscribed on the dial face, together with eleven vertical hour lines, along which travels the lengthening and shortening shadow of the style (the rod provided to create a shadow), representing the earth's axis. At the summer and winter solstices, the shadow reaches the two outermost curves, whereas at the spring and autumn equinoxes, it stands on the central line. The horizontal metal style, now lost, was fixed at the rear using a claw with five pegs, the holes for which are still visible. The fixation point for the style coincided with the theoretical center of the sphere and its length was equivalent to its radius.

The inscribed curves show that this sundial was designed for a latitude between 38° 28′ and 35° 51′ north, values that take in Aï Khanum (37° 10′), with a margin of around 1°. This was the most widespread type of sundial in ancient times. The Chaldaean priest and historian Berossus (third century B.C.), born in Babylonia, is said to have been the inventor of this type of sundial.

THE SECOND SUNDIAL IS MADE OF A SQUARED block of limestone that once stood on a horizontal base. Placed on its beveled edge, the stone makes an angle of 37°4′ with the vertical. A cylindrical hole, 22 cm in diameter, perforates the block. Two arcs of a circle are inscribed along both outer edges of the lower part of the cylinder, creating two curved strips. Hour lines are engraved transversely to these, dividing the strips into 12 sections. A 15-cm-metal rod or gnomon (polar style) in the axis of the cylinder throws a shadow that moves through this network of engraved lines to mark the passage of time. The gnomon is held in place by a metal rod fixed in a hole in the top of the block. All the original metal elements were pulled out when the gymnasium was looted in antiquity.

Among all the ancient sundials, the Aï Khanum instrument is unique: It is the only type of cylindrical equatorial sundial that we know. The instrument betrays a significant discrepancy in the astronomical data that was used in its design. The hour lines within the cylinder are calculated for a latitude of around 23°, notably more to the south than Aï Khanum, while the inclination of the stone on its base has

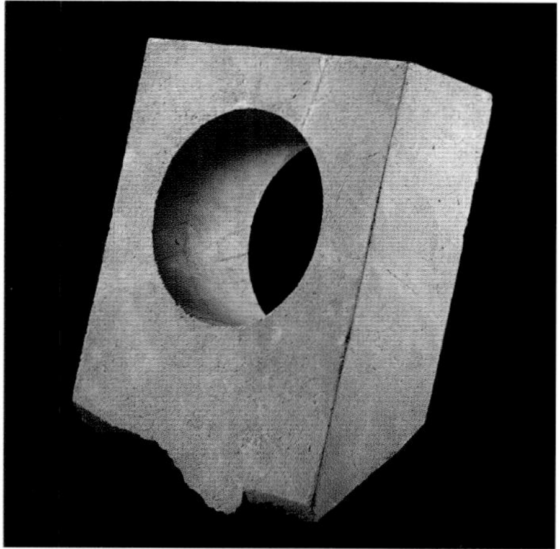

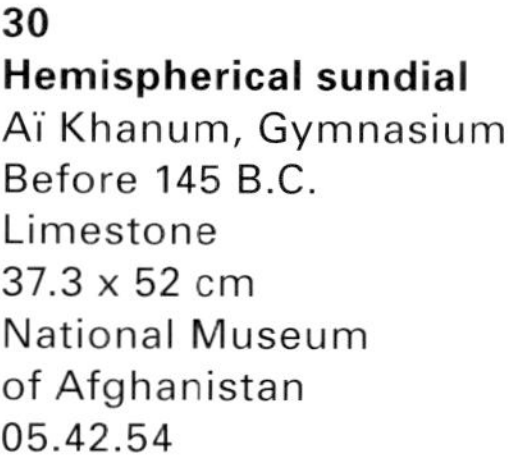

30
Hemispherical sundial
Aï Khanum, Gymnasium
Before 145 B.C.
Limestone
37.3 x 52 cm
National Museum
of Afghanistan
05.42.54

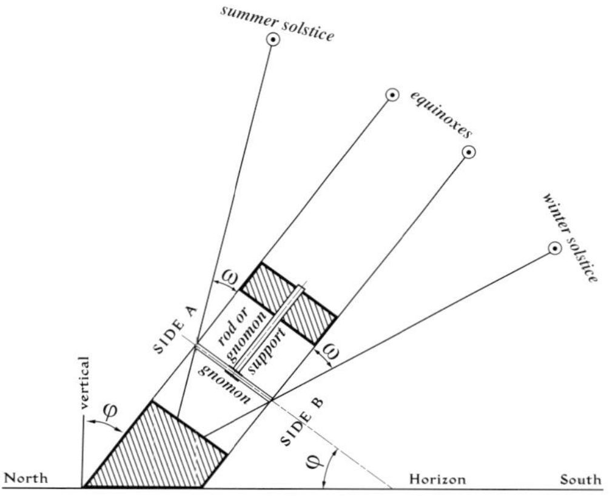

31
Cylindrical polar sundial
Aï Khanum, Gymnasium
Before 145 B.C.
Limestone
44.5 x 34.5 cm
National Museum
of Afghanistan
05.42.55

been calculated for a latitude of around 37°, which is the real latitude of the site. The result was that the time indicated by the sundial was some 20 minutes behind the real time of the Greco-Bactrian city. It is unlikely that the designer of a sundial displaying such originality and ingenuity could have committed such a grave error in calculation. Looking more closely at the data, one cannot fail to notice that a latitude of 23° north brings us close to ancient Syene, modern Aswan, Egypt (24°). This city had a conspicuous place in the history of ancient astronomy: Eratosthenes famously used the location and its distance from Alexandria to calculate the circumference of the earth. It cannot be ruled out that the difference in time indicated respectively by the hemispherical and the polar sundials (both of which stood in the gymnasium), serves as evidence that the reading of time is correlated to the latitude. The Aï Khanum polar sundial must therefore be seen as a demonstration model for astronomy lessons, which would be appropriate in an educational establishment like a gymnasium.

In the same line of thought we may even wonder if the latitude of 23° that regulated the engraving of the hour lines on the polar sundial could not be also interpreted as that of the Indian city of Ujjain (23° 1′), a place with the same significance for India as Syene had for the Greeks, and the meridian of which served as a reference point for the Indian astronomers. The city that the Greeks knew by the name of "Ozene, royal city of Tiastenes" (Ptolemy VII, 1, 63) lay on an important route connecting ancient Barygaza (Bharuch) with the valleys of the Yamuna and the Ganges. It was already an important center of the Mauryan Empire in the third century B.C. when Ashoka lived there as viceroy. In the second century B.C. the Indo-Greeks of the Punjab and the Indus Valley must have established contacts with the state of Ujjain. At the end of the same century an ambassador of the Indo-Greek King Antialcidas visited the sovereign of Vidisa, which is not very far from Ujjain, and dedicated to the god Vasudeva, a monument that still bears his Greek name and that of his master. It could very well be that the Greco-Bactrian astronomers of Aï Khanum knew Ujjain and that it had, like Syene, a special meaning for them because of its location on the Tropic of Cancer.

The discovery at Aï Khanum of this unique piece should give a fresh insight to the study of exchanges between Greek and Indian astronomy. Thanks to the Greek colonization of Central Asia these could have started in the Hellenistic era, much earlier than previously thought. Greco-Bactrian and Indo-Greek astronomers would thus have paved the way for the massive introduction of astronomical knowledge during the Roman period to India

32 THE SCULPTURE FOUND IN THE CENTRAL niche in the gymnasium's northern colonnade is a rectangular pillar with the bust of a bearded old man. A broad, heavy cloak covers his arms. The right hand grasps from inside the cloak at the level of the stomach. The left arm extends forward a little, leaving the hand bare and holding a metal rod, now lost. The drapery falls halfway down the thighs where it ends horizontally.

This particular type of pillar with a human bust was common in Greek sculpture. The Hermaïc pillar became associated with the activities of the gymnasia, of which Hermes and Heracles served as protectors. The heads increasingly took on the distinctive features of other gods and even of prominent people, as well as of persons who had played an important role in the activities of the gymnasia. There arose a tendency to replace the simple head by a bust, as is the case here.

This bust is probably the portrait of one Strato, whose two sons, Triballos and Strato the Younger, are thought to have financed the rebuilding of the gymnasium, as can be deduced from a Greek inscription at Aï Khano commemorating the dedication of the new building by them to Hermes and Heracles. This inscription was engraved on a high pedestal, in which the Hermaïc pillar was inserted. The pedestal was found in its original location, together with the Hermaïc pillar, head included, in a niche in the northern portico of the gymnasium. The elder Strato probably held the office of director of the gymnasium (gymnasiarch), a position that brought with it considerable responsibility. This would explain why he was represented with a rod (of metal, now lost) in his left hand, a symbol of his function, as well as a fillet crowning his head. According to the archeological data, the dedication of the new building and of the Hermaïc pillar must be dated to the early part of the second century B.C.

32
Hermaïc pillar
Aï Khanum, Gymnasium
1st half of the 2nd century B.C.
Limestone
77 cm
National Museum of Afghanistan
05.42.14

The Fountain of the Oxus

33 THE WATERSPOUT WAS FOUND IN SITU IN A fountain built against the outside of the western city wall, rising above the Oxus. It is probable that the fountain also served as a bath for visitors to the gymnasium immediately adjacent. The water for the fountain was drawn from irrigation canals on the plain, where it ran into the soil and then resurfaced here.

This strikingly expressive mask betrays the hand of a first-class sculptor well versed in the knowledge of theatrical portrayal. The water spout was installed at the time of the last repair to the fountain, in the first half of the second century B.C., when the other outlets—some of which were found with their own gargoyle (lion and dolphin heads)—became blocked by mineral deposits, necessitating replacement. This find is all the more remarkable because a mask is quite unusual as a decorative element in a fountain.

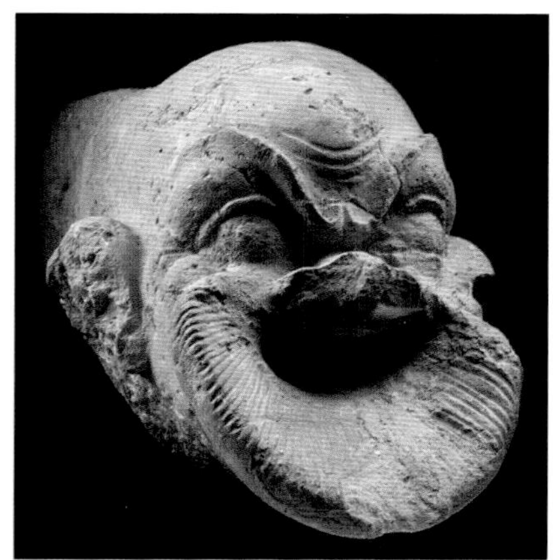

33
Gargoyle water spout
Aï Khanum,
Fountain of the Oxus
2nd century B.C.
Whitish limestone
21 x 40 x 19 cm
National Museum
of Afghanistan
05.42.17

The Necropolis

34 WHEN IT WAS DISCOVERED IN 1971, THE stele had been broken into pieces. Its fragments were reused in clay masonry, blocking the entrance to a mausoleum in the necropolis lying outside the ramparts (see p. 100). It was later severely damaged once again, this time in the Kabul Museum by Taliban religious fanatics, and subsequently restored by Afghan specialists.

The stele represents in high relief (6.5 cm) a naked youth leaning on his left leg. His only garment is a long cloak, draped around his neck and attached by a brooch on his left shoulder, falling down his back and continuing in front on the left side, hanging loosely over the left lower arm.

Above the left shoulder a small curved rib is visible: It has been suggested that it represents a Greek *petasos,* the typical head covering of the *ephebes* (a youth performing his military service), but the interpretation remains tentative. Untypical for Greek tradition, his hair falls in long waves to his shoulders.

Could it be that the Eastern style of long hair had gradually become more usual among the Greco-Bactrian ephebes in training, or is this a Bactrian youth who has adopted Greek ways and attended the gymnasium, but wished to display his Eastern origins?

A comparison with the exuberant waving hairstyles of the Greco-Scythian warriors shown on a pair of brooches from Tillya Tepe (cat. no. 79) is an argument for the second interpretation. Stylistically the rendering of this athletic nude whose statuesque forms are softened by the delicate modeling of the musculature belongs to the best tradition of the Late Greek classicism in the fourth century B.C. The raised glance of the deep-set eyes gazing at the heavens, still preserved when the stele was discovered, added an emotional note in harmony with the sensitive treatment of the waving locks cascading to the shoulders: an echo of the lessons of the great fourth century innovator Scopas of Paros and of his romantic style had passed to this Greco-Bactrian sculptor.

34
Stele with a youth
Aï Khanum, Necropolis
Before 145 B.C.
Whitish alabaster
50 x 26 x 11.5 cm
National Museum
of Afghanistan
05.42.15

CHAPTER VI

Begram: At the Heart of the Silk Roads

SANJYOT MEHENDALE
Lecturer, Department of Near Eastern Studies
University of California, Berkeley

Excavations at Begram, doorway of Room 10, 1937

OPPOSITE: *Excavations of Room 13, Joseph Hackin and Jean Carl cleaning the back of a throne, 1939*

THE RUINS OF ANCIENT BEGRAM LIE CLOSE TO THE MODERN town of Begram (Bagram) in a fertile valley to the south of the massive Hindu Kush mountains, near the confluence of the Ghorband and Panjshir Rivers in modern Parwan Province, Afghanistan. To fully appreciate the nature of the site and its finds, it is important to understand that Begram also sits at the confluence of ancient and modern Silk Road trade routes, which continued on to Kabul in the south and then toward the Khyber Pass connecting Afghanistan to Pakistan. The location was also strategic from a military perspective, which has contributed to the proposition of some scholars that ancient Begram had, indeed, been Alexandria ad Caucasum, a fortified post founded by Alexander the Great in the fourth century B.C.

The fame of ancient Begram rests on the 1937 and 1939 discoveries of a large number of extraordinary objects in two ancient sealed-off rooms in a part of the site excavators called "New Royal City." Many of these pieces evinced a high degree of artisanship and had their origins in various and distant parts of the world: glassware, bronzes, plaster medallions, porphyry and alabaster objects from the Roman world; fragments of Chinese lacquer boxes and bowls; and Indian-style objects carved in ivory and bone. Since their discovery, scholars have puzzled about how such a wonderful and geographically diverse array of objects came to be stored at Begram. Based upon several factors and inferences, some epigraphic, others drawn from in situ archaeological evidence, these objects from Begram's New Royal City have been referred to as a "treasure," hoarded there over time by Kushan emperors. However, some recent studies have shown that virtually all of the hoard can be safely assigned to the first century A.D., which, although not entirely discounting the notion of a royal "hoard," leaves open the intriguing possibility that these objects were instead part of a commercial stock that had traveled along ancient trade routes. In either view, the extraordinary finds make Begram one of the most spectacular repositories of commodities traded along the Silk Roads during the first century.

Exploration and Excavation

Archaeological remains in Afghanistan initially became known in the West through the accounts of European travelers and amateur history sleuths. One of these was British explorer Charles Masson, who in the 1830s followed the path of Alexander the Great's journey east and gave an account of the Begram site, where he had discovered many coins of Mauryan and Greco-Bactrian origin. Masson's reports resulted in extensive coin hunting at Begram throughout the 19th century, and a wide range of coins were uncovered from Mauryan to Ghurid. Systematic exploration of the area, however, did not commence until the early 1920s when the Afghan government granted the French Délégation Archéologique Française en Afghanistan (DAFA) a near monopoly on archaeological research in Afghanistan for the next 30 years.

Alfred Foucher directed the first systematic surveys of Afghanistan in the years following the 1922 treaty, in the region of Kabul, Bamiyan, and Begram, which Foucher believed had been the ancient Kushan capital Kapisi in the early centuries A.D. On the basis of Foucher's explorations and Jules Barthoux's initial surveys at Begram, a plan was devised for systematic excavations. These commenced in 1936 when, under the direction of Jean Carl, work was begun to uncover what is referred to as Site I in the New Royal City. The first step was the making of a north-south oriented trench that corresponded to one of the main arteries of the ancient town, referred to as the "Bazaar." This was followed by the release of several workshops bordering this road. Work on Site I was taken up again in 1937 under the direction of Joseph Hackin. In the same year, directed by Ria Hackin and Ahmed Ali Khan Kohzad, work began on Site II, some two hundred meters east of Site I. Again digging north-south, a few meters from the enclosure wall, they released several rooms and lower layers, and mud brick for the upper part of the wall.

Most of the rooms uncovered during the 1937 excavation failed to reveal any spectacular finds until the excavators came across an ancient passageway sealed off by bricks, leading to a similarly blocked-off door in the excavations at Site II. Behind this door was a room containing a vast number of extraordinary finds of great diversity. In what was designated Room 10, numerous glass objects of Roman design were found, as well as a number of Roman bronze objects including dishes, scale-weights or *balsamaria* (a type of vessel) and coins, plus an alabaster dinner plate and amphora. There were also a great number of carved ivory and bone bands and plaques, analogous in style to ancient Indian stone carvings, most of which had formed the decorative outer layers of wooden structures, perhaps chests or small footstools. Over time, however, exposure to humid soil had pulverized the wood of these bands and plaques so that only the bone and ivory remained. The 1937 excavation ceased not long after the discovery of Room 10, and the site was abandoned for almost a year while the DAFA carried out excavations elsewhere. In 1938, more excavations were carried out at Site II of the New Royal City, as well as in other parts surrounding it.

In 1939, Joseph Hackin returned to Begram to continue work in Site II. This excavation, in a section north-northeast of the rooms uncovered in 1937, released a spacious new room, Room 13, the door of which, like that of Room 10, had been sealed off in ancient times by a brick wall. In this room were found still more and diverse objects from the Roman world: plaster medallions, painted glassware, and bronzes. The finds in Room 13 also included a number of carved ivory and bone objects similar in style to the ones

Begram. Plan of the ancient site

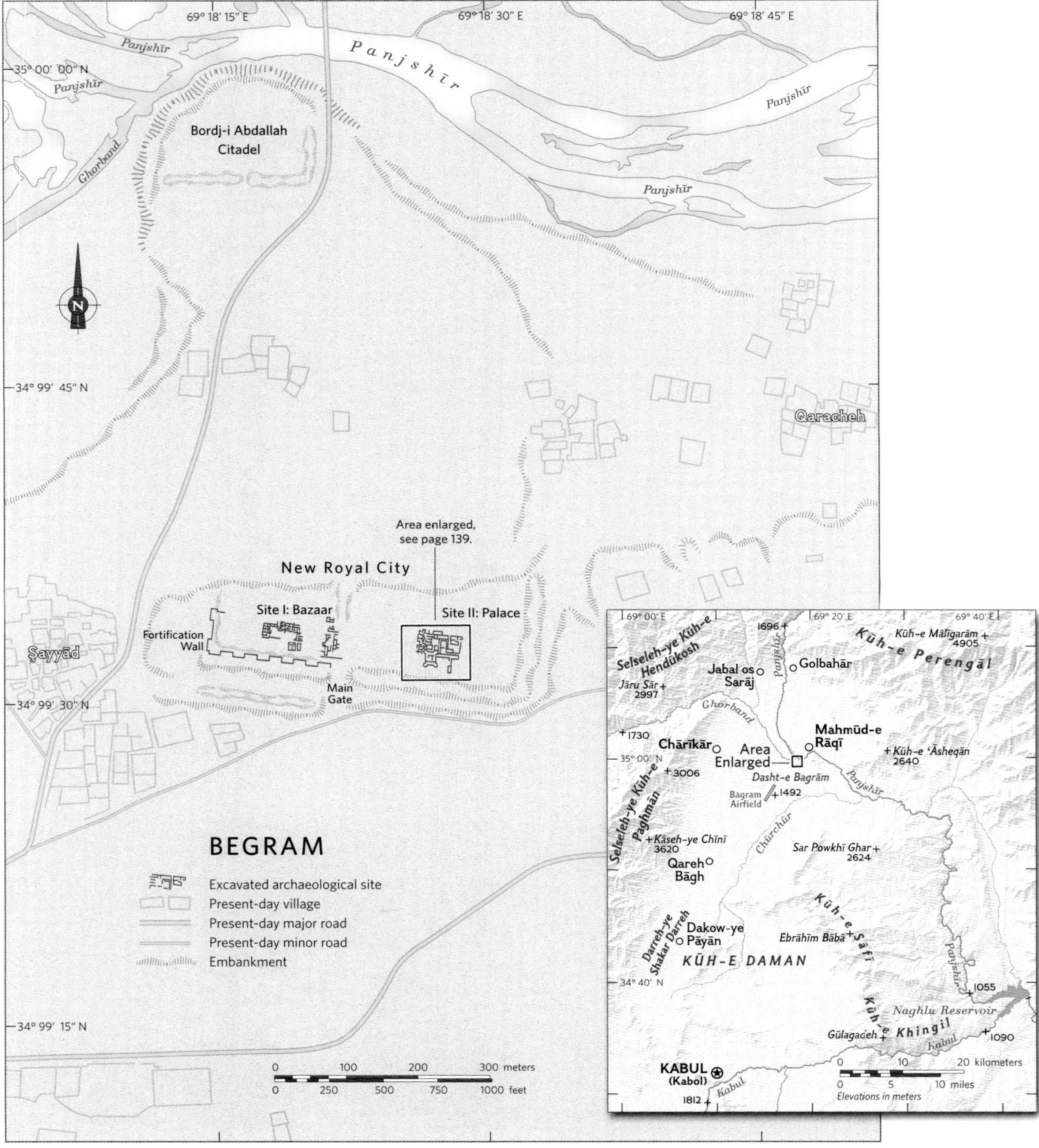

found in Room 10, and once again, long contact with the humid soil had caused irreparable damage to many of them. An interesting addition to the objects in Room 13, spreading the breadth of the finds' origins still further along the trading routes, was a number of lacquer fragments of Chinese origin.

With the outbreak of World War II, the Hackins returned to France; both lost their lives during the war. Their notes of the 1939 excavation and the catalogue of finds were preserved and later published in Volume XI of the "Memoirs of the French Archaeological Delegation in Afghanistan (MDAFA)," together with a series of comparative studies. In 1941–42 and 1946, two more DAFA excavations took place. But, except for a survey conducted in the 1960s, no comprehensive excavation has taken place at Begram since the 1940s. The remarkable collection of finds was divided between the French and Afghan archaeological delegations and ultimately found its place in the National Museum of Afghanistan in Kabul and in the Musée Guimet in Paris.

Begram. Satellite image

The Begram "Treasure"

Although not all are represented in this exhibit, many different types of objects were uncovered in the two sealed rooms at Begram, the majority of which were originally divided into three regions of origin: the Roman world, China, and India. Continuing study suggests, however, that yet another region—Afghanistan itself—might be included. That Afghanistan may not have been a mere thoroughfare for, and passive recipient, of goods traveling from elsewhere, but a participant in the actual production of some of these objects is demonstrated by close examination of some of the ivory and bone carvings and plaster medallions.

The Ivory and Bone Carvings

The Begram hoard included hundreds of individual pieces of ivory and bone that had formed the decorative outer layer of furniture. These pieces consisted of plaques and bands, either engraved or in relief, and sculptures in the round. On some ivory and bone objects traces of red and black paint were found. So many of the ivory and bone carvings were preserved thanks to a special method of excavating utilized by Jean Carl, who realized that to save these pieces it was necessary to recreate their structure, lost due to burial in the humid soil. A warm gelatinous substance was poured onto the pieces and, while the gelatin was still soft, tissue paper was attached to the back surface to hold the pieces together. After the gelatin had set, the embedded pieces could be safely detached from the soil.

The majority of the ivory and bone objects discovered in Room 10 consisted of plaques, which formed the outer decorative layer of footstools as indicated by the existence of small holes for attachment. In addition, several furniture legs and three sculptures of women were also found. The exact function of these is unclear, but it is probable that they, too, formed part of some type of furniture. From Room 13, delicately carved and sculpted objects apparently formed parts of the backs of elaborate chairs or benches, which were often decorated on both sides. That the remaining parts of the chairs were not discovered suggests that they were made of wood, which has long since decayed in the humid soil.

The decorative motifs on the ivory and bone artifacts consist of engraved or sculpted women, mythical creatures, floral and faunal designs, and architectural constructions. It is striking there are so few male figures depicted in these decorations; only occasionally are a king and a few horsemen or hunters recognizable. The scant number of men depicted, plus the particular nature of the many scenes involving women, have led most scholars to believe that the ivory and bone artifacts from Begram most often represent scenes from the women's quarters. Although entry to a harem itself would have been forbidden to the carvers, the artisans might well have had drawings or descriptions of these quarters. On the other hand, access to courtesans' quarters would have been possible, so the artisans could have taken much of their modeling from there.

What then of the provenance of these ivory and bone carvings? Many scholars have attempted a stylistic comparison with the monumental art of Mathura, Sañci, and Amaravati, the most common argument holding that they were carved in India and then transported north to Begram. Although these stylistic analogies are certainly valid, three uncarved and unworked pieces of ivory uncovered at Begram suggest the intriguing possibility of an ivory- and bone-producing workshop at Begram itself. That some of the carvings carried marks in the Kharosthi script may confirm the hypothesis that these were carved locally in Afghanistan or in Pakistan, perhaps by artisans who relocated to Begram after training further to the south. Textual sources, too, provide evidence that artisans were itinerant.

That Begram was part of an ivory distribution network is suggested by analogous ivory finds elsewhere along the ancient Silk Roads. Three, in particular, compare favorably. An ivory comb from the Kushan site of Dal'verzin Tepe in present-day Uzbekistan presents the first engraved ivory object identical in form and content to one discovered at Begram. The second is an ivory comb from the Tillya Tepe necropolis in northwest Afghanistan. The third, underscoring the reach of the trade in ivory, is a figurine uncovered at Pompeii. Dating to the first century, the Pompeian statuette, which formed part of a small table, is very similar in style to two of the three larger statuettes discovered in Room 10 at Begram.

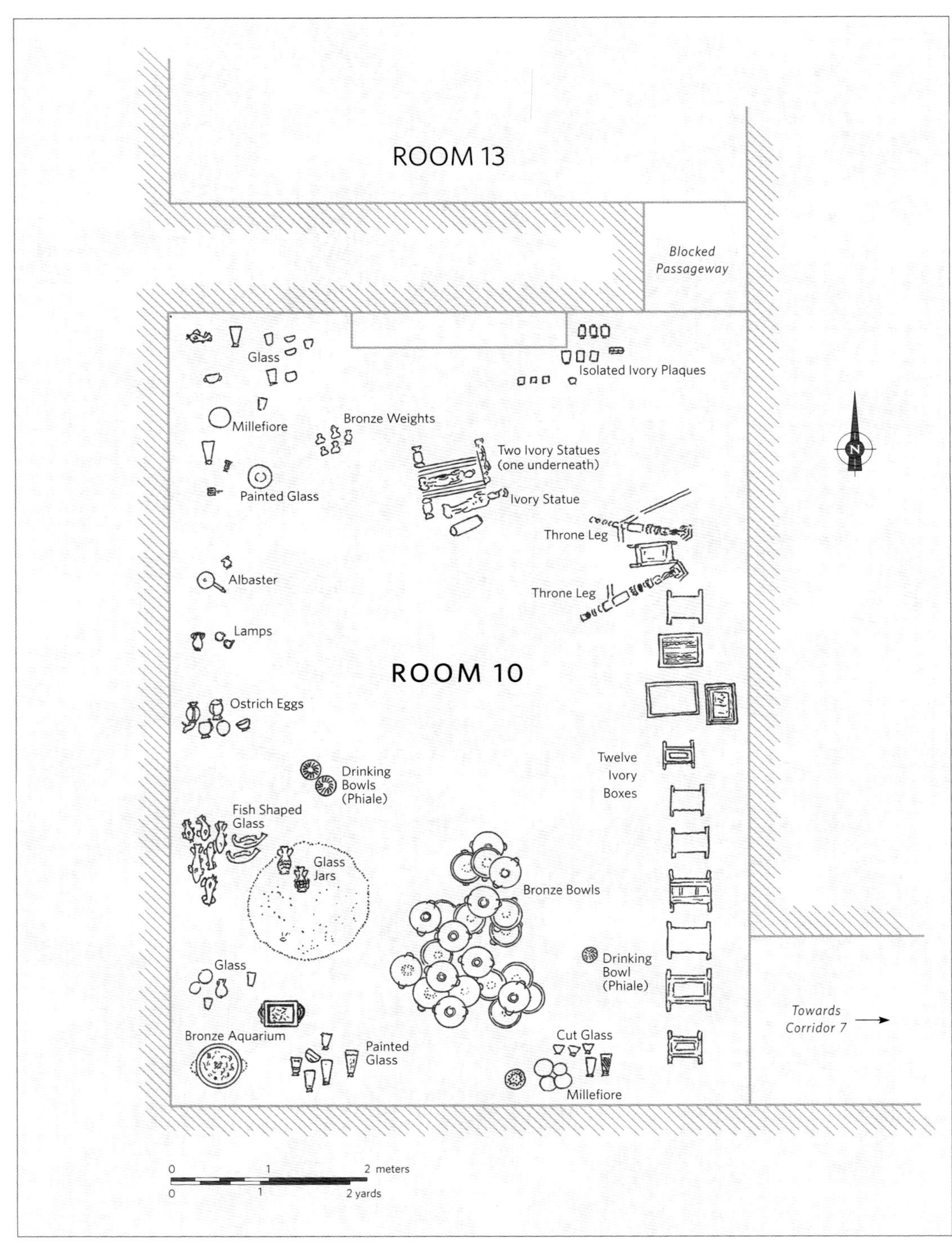
ROOM 13
Blocked Passageway
Glass
Isolated Ivory Plaques
Millefiore
Bronze Weights
Two Ivory Statues (one underneath)
Painted Glass
Ivory Statue
Throne Leg
Albaster
Throne Leg
Lamps
ROOM 10
Ostrich Eggs
Twelve Ivory Boxes
Drinking Bowls (Phiale)
Fish Shaped Glass
Glass Jars
Bronze Bowls
Glass
Drinking Bowl (Phiale)
Towards Corridor 7
Bronze Aquarium
Painted Glass
Cut Glass
Millefiore
0 1 2 meters
0 1 2 yards

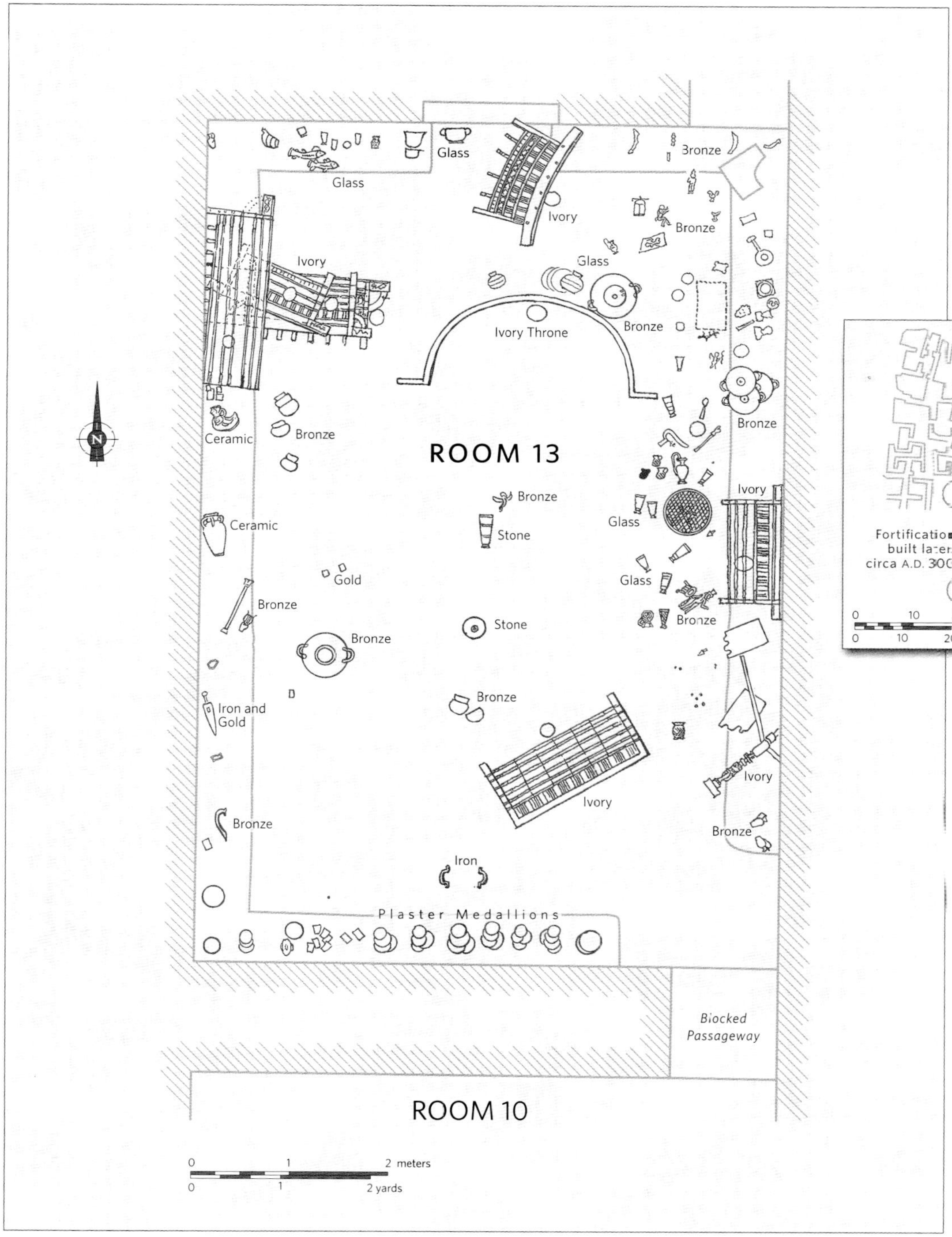

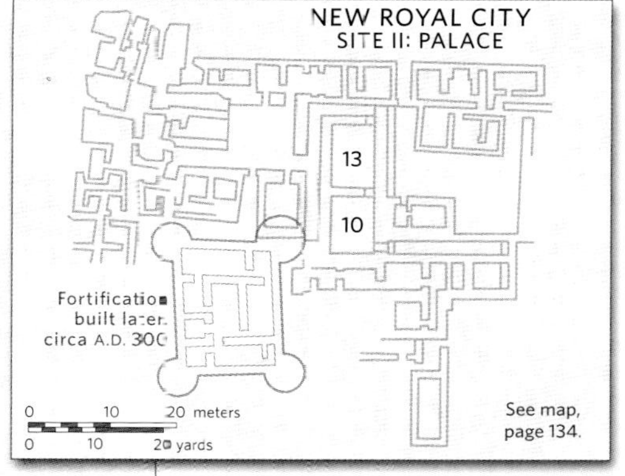

Field drawings of the "Treasure" of Rooms 10 and 13. The artifacts were found exactly as they were left 2,000 years ago and uncovered in two excavation seasons, 1937 and 1939.

Glassware, Bronzes, and Plaster Medallions

Most glassware uncovered at Begram has Roman parallels and is thought to have been transported along the Silk Road to Begram. The mosaic or "Millefiori" bowl and a large number of glass goblets with decorative patterns consisting of honeycomb designs find their parallels in Roman Egypt and Europe. Analysis of Begram's fascinating painted glass beakers has revealed that the base glass is of a soda-lime-silica variety, a type analogous to ancient glassware found in Egypt and the Near East. Supporting the theory of Egyptian provenance are ancient sources that mention Egypt in general and Alexandria in particular, along with Syria, as centers of glass manufacturing.

If Roman Egypt or Syria was the place of origin of much of the Begram glassware, the exact route by which the commodities traveled to Begram might be indicated by the distribution pattern of the ribbed bowls uncovered at Begram. Examples of such ribbed bowls are known throughout the Roman world, and a number of them have been discovered at the site of Ed-Dur in the Arabian Gulf Emirate of Umm al-Qaiwain, on the island of Bahrain, and in the coastal site of Arikamedu in Tamil Nadu, southern India. Dated firmly in the first century, their coastal distribution seems to suggest that some, if not all, of the Begram glassware first traveled by sea to the ancient port cities of the Indian Ocean and then was distributed overland to the north. The Periplus of the Erythraean Sea, a first century trading manual, mentions that Barbaricum near modern Karachi, Pakistan, and Barygaza in Gujarat, western India, were the two main ancient ports where Roman products were offloaded in return for goods produced in India and silk yarn and cloth from China.

Two bronze statuettes from Room 13 clearly display Egyptian origin. A small statue of a young man with a finger pointed toward his mouth can be identified as Harpocrates (Horus the Child); a statue not unlike this one was discovered at Taxila in Pakistan. Another is that of Serapis-Heracles, depicting the god naked with arms spread, legs slightly apart and the right foot placed just in front of the left. His right hand rests on a club while his left holds a ball. He is shown with a beard and a full head of hair on which he wears a *calathus,* the primary source of identification. Like the Harpocrates statue, this one is a typical representation of a Greco-Egyptian god; the head attire is characteristic of the god Serapis, while his attributes and pose are typical of Heracles. Another beautiful bronze object is a mask of Silenus, who became the nurse, teacher, and follower of Dionysus and is usually presented as a fat and jolly old man, his head crowned with flowers.

Many of the objects with Roman parallels excavated in 1939 from Room 13 consist of circular plaster medallions with scenes depicted in low or high relief. Many of the scenes are well known from classical mythology and most scholars have no doubt about the medallions' general place of origin. For example, one plaster medallion portrays the head and torso of a child with the child's head nearly detached from the surface of the medallion. On the child's back are traces of wings and his small fleshy arms clutch a butterfly against his breast. The scene has been identified as Eros and Psyche—the ancient Greek name for butterfly being Psyche, also meaning soul—in their allegorical union. Similar depictions are known from Roman Europe. Other plaster medallions in relief portray the beautiful boy Ganymede feeding the eagle of Zeus, as well as the Sleeping Endymion who was adored by Selene, the Titan goddess of the moon who visited him every night on Mt. Latmos. Many scholars believe these objects to be models, reproductions of perhaps metal originals, and have assigned them to Alexandria in Egypt. Others have suggested that they were made in Begram itself. The fact that some carried fingerprints on the front could suggest that they were not decorative pieces but models used in a workshop or examples of trade ware.

Lacquer Ware from China

Of all the finds from Begram, the Chinese lacquers were the most poorly preserved; only a few pieces survive in the Musée Guimet in Paris. Due to their fragility, only a small number of heavily damaged fragments were recovered from the humid soil, which had destroyed the supporting wood leaving only extremely thin and delicate pieces of lacquer. Though small in number, they are nonetheless of considerable importance for dating the Begram finds; stylistic comparisons with similar, precisely dated Han dynasty lacquers found in East Asia make it possible to assign them with a high degree of certainty to the first century.

Royal "Treasure" or Commercial Depot

Since their discovery, scholars have hypothesized how these remarkable objects came to be stored at Begram. In the 1920s, Alfred Foucher, director of the French Archaeological Delegation, identified the site at Begram as ancient Kapisi, believed to be a summer capital and residence of the Kushan emperors. Foucher based this identification in large measure on the records of the Chinese pilgrim Xuanzang who had traveled through the area in the seventh century and who had surmised that he had found Kapisi in the area where Foucher came upon Begram. In the 1930s, when the extraordinary objects were found together in the sealed chambers, the excavators deduced, from Foucher's description of the site as a royal Kushan residence, that the structures were an ancient palace; and from the value and distant origins of the objects, that they were part of a royal Kushan buried treasure. Initial efforts at dating the objects also placed several pieces two or three centuries apart, which supported the notion that they had been gathered over several centuries and were, indeed, a sealed-up royal "hoard."

More recent research suggests that the underpinnings of the royal hoard theory are subject to a number of doubts. Archaeological evidence from the site itself fails to support either that Begram had been Kapisi or that the site—Kapisi or otherwise—had been a royal residence. The intrinsic value of some of the artifacts discovered could reasonably lead to an inference of some royal presence at the site. But the fact that some valuable artifacts might have passed through, or were yet intended for, royal control does not necessarily imply a royal residence at the site where they were stored.

Begram's strategic location toward the edge of the Kushan empire, plus its naturally fortified spot at the juncture of two rivers, may indeed have made it one of the empire's important transit and trading cities. But nothing in its location or in the nature of its structural remains suggest that it served as a royal residence for a substantial part of the year. There is also the fact that many of the Greco-Roman artifacts were plaster medallions of no intrinsic value, taken probably from metal originals; it is difficult to conceive why mere plaster would be included in a royal collection. On the other hand, such plaster copies might well have been of interest to a merchant as examples of wares, which could be obtained in trade or which could have served as models for artisans to create trade wares in situ.

Finally, the assertion that the objects were a royal treasure has remained current at least in part because it might explain the otherwise confounding one or two century difference between the proposed dates of a few individual pieces. But these wide differences in the contended dates of a few pieces all can be effectively rebutted, leaving instead a consistent pattern of first century dates for all the objects of the Begram finds. Once the dates are viewed as contemporaneous, the gathering of goods found in the two rooms can just as well be viewed as a merchant's or trader's stock rather than as a royal treasure hoard. Moreover, the presence of unworked and uncarved ivory and the many plaster models at Begram also presents the possibility that Begram was not merely a crossroads storage site but a trading center with its own workshops or ateliers. This conclusion may shed a different light on the nature of the Begram settlement itself, seen now not simply as a royal residence but as an important trading and manufacturing center on the northwestern edge of the Kushan empire, strategically located along—and active in—well-established trade routes among China, Central and South Asia, and the Roman world.

Begram: Alexandria of the Caucasus, Capital of the Kushan Empire

PIERRE CAMBON
Scientific researcher, Laboratoire d'archéologie, ENS Ulm-CNRS, Paris
Corresponding member of the French "Académie des Inscriptions et Belles-Lettres"

Begram. Bronze figurative weights, Room 10, 1937

There are hardly any regions in Asia, which are as picturesque as Kabulistan. Because the ground level is situated nearly twelve thousand feet above sea level, the air is absolutely pure. Vast mountains can be seen, where an untainted nature reveals a harsh but vigorous beauty; the herds graze on fertile and sweet-smelling meadows in the hills, open plains and valleys supply every product available in a temperate climate, and everywhere, crystal-clear streams bring this spectacle to life. Nothing is as regal...as the Hindu Kush covered with eternal snow and framed by a pristine blue sky in good weather in the spring and autumn seasons! Such natural beauty is extremely rare.

GENERAL CLAUDE-AUGUSTE COURT, 1843
(unpublished manuscript in the Musée Guimet)

SYSTEMATIC ARCHAEOLOGICAL RESEARCH DID NOT COMMENCE until the creation of the Délégation Archéologique Française en Afghanistan (DAFA) in 1922. In 1923, the DAFA archaeologist Alfred Foucher started recording the descriptions of Begram. He stated that Begram is Kapisi, the ancient capital city of the Kapisa region, mentioned in the traveling accounts of the Chinese pilgrim Xuanzang or Hsan-Tsang (A.D. 602–664). In 1936, the DAFA began the excavation works at the place Foucher called the "New Royal City." In 1937, a second archaeological excavation was begun, in the east of the city, beside the main road that travels from north to south. It is here that the Begram treasure was discovered. This treasure was carefully hidden in two adjacent walled chambers (Rooms 10 and 13), revealed in 1937 and 1939, respectively.

Begram, 1926

Overview of the Begram Excavations

The excavations in Begram spanned a total of ten years, although publication was sporadic and there is no final summary:

- 1936, April–July, Site I, under the supervision of Jean Carl and Jacques Meunié, the Bazaar
- 1937, Site II, under the supervision of Ria Hackin, Room 10 (the first treasure chamber)
- 1938, April–June, Site II continues, under the supervision of Jacques Meunié: extension of Room 10 to the west, the Qal'ah new project started; Site III, under the supervision of Jacques Meunié: a building with four round turrets, 400 meters south of the city wall, the same type as the Qal'ah in Site II
- 1939–1940, Site II, under the supervision of Ria Hackin, Room 13 (the second treasure-room, immediately to the north of Room 10)
- 1941–1942, under the supervision of Roman Ghirshman, west of the previous excavations
- 1946, September–October, under the supervision of Jacques Meunié, south entrance of the "New Royal City." Attempt to connect with the Bazaar excavations and the so-called "city wall road" by Ghirshman.

Interpretation of the Excavations

The rather spectacular finds of Begram were nearly overlooked in 1936 and only found by accident in 1937; at that time, the explorers did not really appreciate what they were excavating, and the research is not entirely completed, even now.

When looking at the ground plans of the excavations, there are no doubts whatsoever that once there was an authentic city here. The aforementioned Xuanzang named it Kapisi, capital city of Kapisa (a power center and summer residence of Emperor Kanishka from the Kushan Empire). However, the question of whether Begram was the actual "Alexandria of the Caucasus" remained controversial for a long time. The discovery of the treasure upset everything, as it confirmed that the archaeological sources in Afghanistan were not limited to the Macedonian warrior's expedition, since the treasure also contained Chinese lacquer ware and Indian ivory, as well as artifacts from the Mediterranean area.

The Controversy Concerning Begram

The controversy about the treasure still exists due to several causes: First, the excavations remained unfinished. The archaeologists of 1937 were thwarted by the war, and although their death gave their work a heroic importance, the reports remained incomplete. And they were published by others right after the Second World War. Between 1938 and 1946, some excavations were done, but without any structural character. No general drawings were published, nor have the various approaches been itemized to create an overall picture of the excavations. There is no understanding of the context of the most famous excavation, Site II, although Ghirshman did publish a general ground plan. The Buddhist monuments around the city have not been mentioned either. One drawing of Site II is available, but this was only made much later: in 1947 to be precise, by DAFA architect Marc Le Berre, because an earlier sketch made by Jean Carl in 1940 was lost. If we compare it with a drawing of the extension excavations in 1938 toward the west of the site, it appears clearly that at Qal'ah, a building with four round turrets was built on older layers and that this Qal'ah annexed part of the older building where the treasure was found.

The second problem is the treasure itself. Although it generates admiration, it creates problems for those who wish to interpret it. First, there is virtually no reference material pertaining to the exact age of the Roman artifacts, more particularly the glassware; and second, because no comparative material is known for the ivory, except for one piece originating in Pompeii.

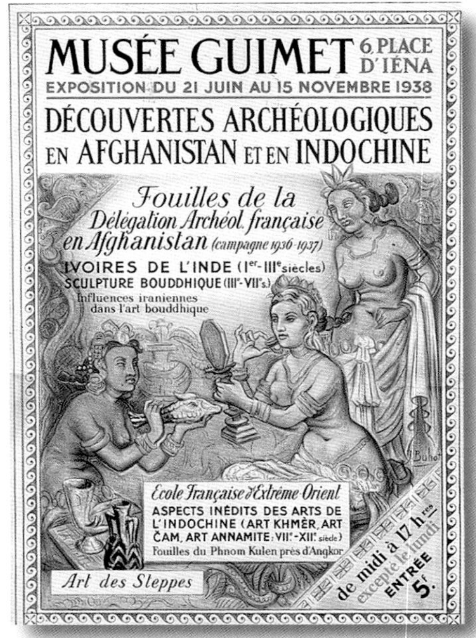

Poster of the first Afghan Exhibition, at the Musée Guimet, 1938

In fact, the chronology sometimes changed during the excavations. Hackin had various opinions in his publications, although he had practically no time to consider the differences. In the 1939 Begram report, Hackin estimated that the treasure dated back to a period between the first and fourth centuries A.D., based on the Western artifacts and the Indian ivory. "The abundant glassware (found in Room 10) undeniably originates from the small glass workshops on the Phoenician coast (Tyre, Sidon, etc.), which were extremely famous in antiquity. Most of the glassware we excavated has been dated and classified. For instance, the exquisite millefiori-type plate (first century A.D.), the ribbed phial (first or second century A.D.), the vase and goblets (third century A.D.), the small fish-shaped flagons (third century A.D.), and the vases and goblets with résille patterns (late third-early fourth century A.D.)... The bronze bowls and weights could be from the second or even third century A.D., and it is interesting to point out that a bronze coin from Kanishka was found alongside another bronze bowl, and that two Kushan coins (he does not indicate which ones) were found in the hollow space of the holder for these bowls." He ends on a positive note: "This part of our discovery, which originates from the eastern Roman Empire, can therefore be dated back to a period between the first and fourth century A.D.... The Begram treasure proves that interactions between this part of Asia and the eastern Roman Empire continued at least until the beginning of the fourth century A.D." He uses the same argument for the ivory, this time based on the ornamentation of the famous "casket" (footstool) IX. His conclusions are unequivocal: "I certainly don't hesitate," he writes (op. cit. p. 22), "to place all ornamentations of casket IX, the zoomorphic representations and scenes of human figures on large panels, within the margins of Gupta art.
I expect the approximate dating to be between the end of the third and the beginning of the fourth century A.D., because these ivory sculptures are the precursors of the extraordinary imperial Gupta art."

However, later Hackin changes the chronology. In Nouvelles Recherches Archéologiques à Begram (1954), he associates the treasure of Begram with the rise of the Kushan Empire, which occurred in the first part of the first century. With as much verve as in his previous publications he states: "The Begram discoveries, Hellenistic plaster casts, Greco-Roman or Alexandrian bronze statues, Roman utensils, Indian ivory, and Chinese lacquer ware all show an exceptional synchronism in time, and they mainly involve the first and second century A.D."

Ivory depicting young girl and a duck, Begram, 1937

Subsequent Research and Questions About the Treasure of Begram

The questions generated by the treasure of Begram are extremely diverse:

- THE EARLIEST DATE: The oldest coins from the Begram excavations are coins associated with Hermaeus, the last Indo-Greek monarch to rule in the valley of the Kabul River before the nomadic invasion. Unfortunately, Hermaeus's precise reign is not known. Some believe he ruled over the Kabul Valley until 70 B.C. If Hermaeus's fall is attributed to the arrival of the Indo-Scythians, then the treasure must originate some time during the Indo-Parthian period, during king Gondophares's reign over Taxila (ancient Sirkap in western India) around A.D. 30.
- THE LATEST DATE: Should this be placed in the Kushan dynasty, just before the Sasanian ruler Shapur I invaded Kapisi (Begram) in A.D. 241, as implicitly suggested by Hackin? The French scholars R. Ghirshman and P. Stern suggest this as well, based on the date of Vasudeva's rule (an image of his head is minted on the latest coin), whose rule ended in A.D. 241.
- THE LOCATION IN THE EXCAVATION COMPLEX: Why was it situated in what was called the "New Royal City" by Foucher and not in the citadel or the upper town?
- THE MEANING: Joseph Hackin in his original field reports suggested that this is a royal treasure. In her Ph.D. thesis, Sanjyot Mehendale suggests that the treasure represents a supply of commercial goods.

Begram, 1939, excavations of Room 13

And Paul Veyne has suggested that it might have been a votive present from nomad caravans.

THE LAYOUT OF THE TREASURE: In two closed chambers with small benches along the walls and with rational categorization are placed bronze objects with bronze, glass with glass, ivory with ivory, and even the glass artifacts are sorted into painted or cut glass. The reason for this arrangement is unknown.

THE COLLECTION: The artifacts from Room 10 and Room 13 are extremely diverse and on the whole, of very good quality, although they have no financial value (the coins and modest gold found in the treasure were not used as a means for payment, and there were no precious stones). Various curiosities were found, such as an ostrich egg in a rhyton (drinking horn), a type of bronze aquaria in which fishes would float around on a miniscule chain as soon as the tanks were filled with water, porphyry pieces, and two golden appliqués shaped like elephant heads. In addition, there are pieces of coral and cut glass with lapis lazuli beads, and delicate pieces that nevertheless were used as daily implements by the nobility, including a dozen bronze bowls that were found as a matching set. These objects of diverse quality caused no end of amazement. In a review of the second volume of the Begram finds, Ernst Will wrote, "How can one reconcile the fact that valuable objects such as Indian ivory furniture was found next to Greco-Roman plaster casts of objects, which only had practical functions?"

The Ivories

The treasure enigma may never be solved completely because of a lack of written documents. The archives left by Hackin and the drawings from Carl are often incomplete and difficult to decipher. We must therefore take the excavations as they come, with their limitations, and place them in the 1930s context. Even so, Pierre Hamelin, who worked as a restorer in Begram on behalf of Hackin, tried to reconstruct as much as possible based on his own experience and Carl's entries. He became involved with the glass and ivory both at the Musée Guimet in Paris and at the National Museum of Afghanistan. After a bit of hesitation, he suggested considering the ivory pieces as furniture, a type of throne with an ivory canopy and footstools.

The ivory was very cleverly carved and intricately engraved with every technique available, as was the glass, varying from decorative trim reliefs to high relief carvings. The ivory is reminiscent of the Jaggayapeta and Amaravati styles of southern India. It has been fastened with tiny copper nails to the wooden frame, which is decorated with intricate floral work. It consists of different size panels, on which there is a contrast between empty and full, with openwork motifs. Great care was taken in the composition and decoration of each panel. In fact, the ivory pieces were considered too beautiful to be very old.

Whoever looks at the famous casket IX will notice that the carvings are no less exceptional than the most beautiful paintings in the Ajanta rock temples (western India), which are supposed to date from much later, not only because of the animation and space, but also on account of the depictions of extremely graceful and provocative female figures. This rather puts into perspective the notion of Gupta art as the apex of Indian antiquity.

The ivory from Begram is striking as a result of its freshness, inventiveness, and diversity; it reveals the work of a master's hand. The griffins accentuated with red or black seem to move in a nearly abstract way. However, casket IX also demonstrates a candid naturalism; the cow lifting its leg, the lion full of pride, and the elephant wandering by. The ducklings on casket I are also fairly realistic, even if humor and fantasy have not been omitted. The adornments consist of a mixture of Indian themes, such as the Vase of Abundance, the gana (attendant of Shiva) who carries the sling, and motifs from Iranian culture and even from the Middle East, for instance, monsters with human heads that resemble

Begram, Room 10, skeleton found in upper levels

Begram, 1937, Room 10, bronze bowls in situ

Gorgons, the Greek mythological monsters. With regard to style, some of the engraved figures are similar to the ivory pieces found in Sirkap in the Indo-Parthian strata. Others have a completely different style, with sleek and unexpectedly tall silhouettes, while several others have shorter and bulkier shapes. There is also a contrast between, on the one hand, very comely young girls, represented by the artist with astonishing grace and a feeling for fine distinctions, and on the other hand, the nude adult female figures, which appear completely relaxed and without any sense of modesty. Female couples with round faces and opulent forms lie entwined voluptuously alongside a graceful lady getting dressed and combing her hair or hairpiece. This astonishing diversity in style and aesthetics even appears on a single piece of furniture (see for instance the back of the chair). The ivory shows an exuberance and imagination that could never have been suggested by the stone sculptures: The weeping willow evokes a landscape, the charming nonchalance with which the cat lies in wait for the bird reminds us of daily scenes. Some pieces are true paintings, for instance casket X, depicting what appears to be a lively village meeting. Besides these daily scenes with simple details, there are also adornments with a *makara* (type of crocodile), which is, in fact, rather typical of the Indian art of that period. Nevertheless, there seems to be a consistency in the decoration of these different objects, which hints at a single context.

The Glass

The blown glass with the résille pattern (nos. 158–160) is unique, the engraved glass with the resting *ephebe* (adolescent male) kept in the Musée Guimet is the oldest example of this decorative trim technique, and the enameled goblets are the only ones that have been found up to now, except for a piece from the Hans Cohn collection, which presumably came from Egypt. This is why they provide plenty of information regarding painting in the Pompeii era in the eastern Mediterranean. The glass depicting the

Pharos of Alexandria is still the most reliable and maybe oldest representation of the lighthouse, which was one of the classic Seven Wonders and known far and wide at that time.

All the analyses of glass from Begram show that they are solely classical Roman pieces. Besides, glass as a product can travel far; the Chinese and Korean excavations confirmed this. A report from the Ernest Babelon Research Centre for archaeological material states: "Although the glass ware from Begram displays important typological diversity, it still belongs to the same chemical family," and then it continues: "The analyzed pieces belong to a well-defined type of glass, namely Roman glassware. The geographical origins can be situated in the Mediterranean area or the Middle East." The analyses of the painted glassware kept in Paris and Kabul provided identical data: "Both items are enameled drinking vessels consisting of sodium glass rich in quartz. The adornment consists of an opaque, vitreous substance, which contains antimony, the primary means to create contrast in classical glass working until the Roman era."

To judge from the themes and motifs, the "Western" pieces seem to have originated in Egypt (this for instance is the reason why the Egyptian goddess Isis appears on some of the enameled glass). This is also confirmed by the porphyry vase, because the Romans could only find this type of stone in Egypt. As well as the depiction of Harpocrates, the child Horus (no. 225), the bronze statue of Heracles-Serapis illustrates how much this Roman Empire province combined different styles.

Begram, 1939, Room 13

The Plaster Medallions

Another noteworthy fact is the similarity between the Begram plaster medallions *(emblemata)* and the emblemata that were found at the ancient city of Chersonesus on the Crimea. They appear to have been made for the same purpose, namely as a model for the decoration of the silverware. Perhaps they were used by the nomadic "barbarians." The ancient potter

Begram, Room 13, wall painting depicting the interior of a room with columns

seems to have made these molds not by independent modeling, but by taking impressions from metal, stone, or clay. The general style points to the second half of the third century B.C., when medallions in high relief were much in fashion for adorning the bottoms of silver vessels and were imitated in clay. Several of these molds, made from emblemata in silver vessels, were intended for producing such imitations. The best of these represents Omphale teaching Heracles to spin: It must have been taken from an original of a period earlier than anything in the collection. Similar emblemata have also been found in Memphis in Egypt. One silver emblemata from Sirkap (near Taxila) consists of the torso of a hairy and bearded man holding a kantharos (drinking vessel), perhaps an eastern version of Dionysus, as suggested by Benjamin Rowland. O. Kurtz, who studied the emblemata, stated: "This series forms a virtually unparalleled treasure with regard to composition and Hellenistic motives. Many are known from other objects, but none attain the refined shapes and artistic quality of the Begram relief.... They were regularly used as molds for artists or as samples for potential buyers and most likely for both purposes." The series shows the cycles of Aphrodite and Dionysus, daily scenes, torsos, and portraits in profile. Despite the "Parthian restrictions," the treasure of Begram proves that an effective contact between East and West continued to exist due to the coastal trade in the Indian Ocean. At that time, relations between Rome and the Iranian Empire of the Parthians were extremely strained; the defeat of the consul Crassus during the battle of Carrhae in 53 B.C. brought Roman expansion in the Middle East to an end. There are similarities with the discoveries in Sirkap. The treasure of Begram demonstrates the exchanges between Alexandria, Taxila, and Begram, including interactions with Tillya Tepe: A small bronze Harpocrates from Begram is related to an example found in Taxila (Sirkap); and the golden statuette of Aphrodite that was found in Sirkap reminds us of the Aphrodite statue from Tillya Tepe.

Chronological Issues

During its exhibition in the United States in 1966, the curator, Benjamin Rowland, suggested that the Begram finds, "one of the greatest treasures in the history of Asian Archaeology," caused confusion because of their profusion and unfathomable variety. It appeared to Rowland that this treasure stood outside of any context, since it was discovered walled up, presumably hidden at the approach of a dangerous invader. Rowland dismissed the theory of protection against the approaching invasion of A.D. 241 through logical reasoning. If the Western and Chinese objects were from the early first century (or a little earlier) and if the ivory were from the second century, then it would be very odd if at least one hundred years later a secret store was created, whether it was a royal collection or commercial goods. Rowland suggested the possibility that the treasure was hidden due to an internal succession problem during the Huvishka era (A.D. 126–164, successor of Kanishka), in light of the "barbarization" of the coins minted in his period.

Sanjyot Mehendale opts for the consistency perspective and suggests a date somewhere in the first century A.D. In spite of their diversity, the finds from Begram suggest a synchronism in the date of accumulation and may then help to understand the evolution of Gandharan art at the beginning of the school.

A final interesting interpretation is that the Begram ivories can be compared with earlier ivories (third century B.C.) from the Parthian capital of Nisa, in modern Turkmenistan. In fact, there already existed a scenario with a justification for an earlier date at Begram. John Marshall hypothesized—in 1913, long before the discovery of the treasure of Begram—the occupation of the Kabul River Valley in A.D. 30 by King Gondophares, who would have brought his own Indian and Greek influences. This scenario was unambiguous and coherent and also explained the concurrence of the findings in Sirkap and Begram. In fact, the treasure of Begram is situated

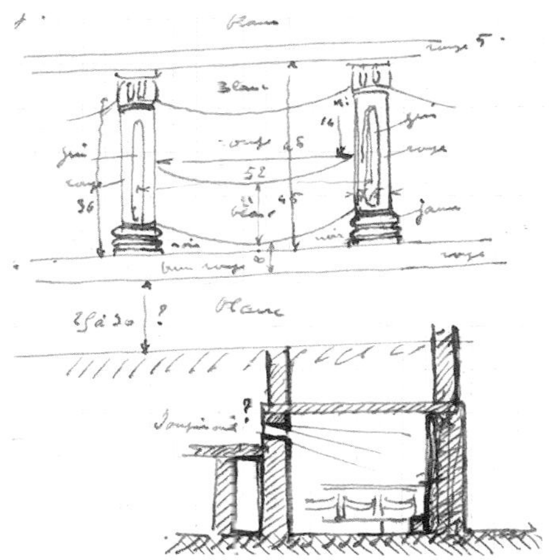

Field drawing by Jean Carl of the wall paintings, Begram, Room 13, 1939

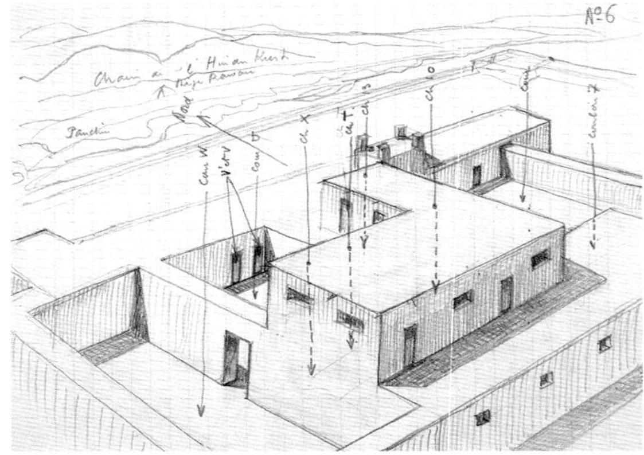

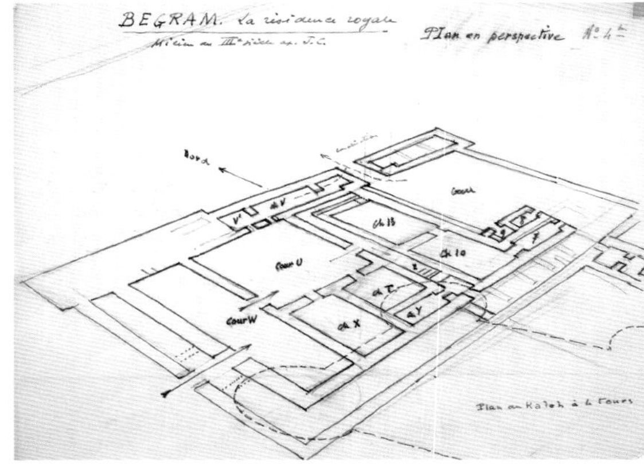

Architectural renderings of the excavations at Begram, Pierre Hamelin

at a crossroads, both in time and space; it sits right in the middle of the Kushana (Indian), the Greco-Roman, and the Parthian conjectures. In each case, an image is given of a world where ideas and shapes traveled a lot, despite borders, hazards, and wars.

The Building Where the Treasure Was Found

Next, we still have the building to consider. Strangely enough, only two out of all the aerial photographs of the excavations have been published: an overview photo by Ghirshman and an enlarged detail in an article by Hamelin. Hamelin uses this detail as proof for the ground plans of excavation Site II. On these ground plans, he attempts to reproduce the original shape of the building where the treasure was found. It is also strange that neither the photographs of the wall paintings in Room 13, nor the coins found during excavation Site I have ever been published. Hamelin suggests in a reconstruction that the building where the treasure was found extends further to the west, past the Qal'ah with the four turrets. He believes that the treasure chamber must have had an upper floor, because of the double walls, which he considers to be support walls. Hamelin states: "Based on the very accurate ground plans of Le Berre, we have outlined all the buildings of the royal palace of Begram. A large rectangular wall with a succession of small chambers and corridors surrounded the main building situated in the middle; this was designed as an L-shaped building oriented to the north-west; we believe that an upper floor was built on this main building.... At the back of the inner court there was a door, which gave access to corridor E, which led to Room 13 via a detour, and then to Room 10.... The double walls have been interpreted as serving to hide the walled-up doors, but we believe they were used as a support for the upper floor." He adds: "We have not found any traces at all of charred wood, thus the idea of destruction by fire can be ruled out.... And now that we are discussing architecture, attention needs to be drawn to the fact that the walls of Rooms 10 and 13 were plastered and covered with paintings. Light-green paint residues have been found in Room 10, and wainscoting decorated with drapery suspended from small columns in Room 13, in terracotta-brown, gray, white, and black (see the sketch from Carl)." Claude Rapin recently suggested that perhaps a building with a similar shape as the excavated treasure building from Aï Khanum can be distinguished in these ground plans. Rapin's references are based on the notes from Le Berre, although he does not mention the essays from Hamelin. Rapin says: "Although the archaeologists never mention the relics, the likelihood of an earlier building in the middlemost and eastern parts of the 'palace' is corroborated in several places, both by the coping, which can be seen in the floor and doorsills, and by the use of square clay bricks, which are typical of Hellenistic architecture in Central Asia and which were found during the excavations of the small shops on the north side of the 'palace.'... The ground plans of this earlier building, however, can only be reconstructed partially.... Based on the ground plans of the remains in the northwest of the middle part of the 'palace' and the remarkably thick walls in the elevation, a rectangular building can be reconstructed with walls of at least 1.90 to 2 meters thick. This building would be positioned around a large square space, possibly an inner court. Along the northern, western, and southern sides there was a narrow corridor. Because of the strict symmetry and the rectangular shape, which stands out against the 'palace' from the Kushan era, one wonders if this earlier building did not belong to a Hellenistic building style, which could be similar to the Aï Khanum style." In 1937, however, Hackin compared the masonry of the treasure chambers with the architecture of Taxila, where he refers to Marshall's report of a strong connection in the masonry work, which could point toward Scythian-Parthian layers.

Conclusion

The discoveries made in Begram, Taxila, and Tillya Tepe display a shared link. Obviously, in the first case there is a treasure, in the second case there are relics of a city, and in the third case there is a nomadic "barbarian" necropolis. However, all three excavations indicate the same fascination with the Greco-Roman civilization, the importance of Roman traditions from the early Christian era, and the Hellenistic influence, which seems to be directly connected with the cities of Chersonesus (Black Sea) and Alexandria (Egypt). The three excavations also show Indian influences, and the similarities between the ivory artifacts from Begram and Tillya Tepe indicate that they originated in the same period. Despite their strongly profane nature, these findings also show the role of Buddhism although in a subordinate way: According to Alfred Foucher, two ivory pieces from Begram depict a Jataka tale, and one gold coin from Tillya Tepe clearly refers to the Three Jewels of Buddhism (Buddha, Dharma, and Sangha). Further, Buddhist stupas have been unearthed in Taxila, perhaps inspired by Hellenistic examples much older than the Buddhist Gandharan art (dating back to the first century B.C.—the famous Scythian-Parthian period). The three excavations reveal an unexpected convergence between India and the Greco-Roman civilization, at the time when its limits were on the Black Sea coast, and also with Egypt when Alexandria was its capital city. Like Tillya Tepe with the Chinese mirrors, Begram extends the reach of its contacts throughout the whole of Eurasia, especially with the lacquer ware from the Han dynasty period. And although, just like in Tillya Tepe, Buddhism in Begram was merely incidental, it was still very much present. In both cases it harks back to relatively old and sometimes unexpected models. The Jataka tales are rather unusual in Gandharan art, but the few illustrations of them are increasingly humanized with time; the examples in Begram are already fairly humanized. On one side of the gold coins found in Tillya Tepe, there is a lion, often the symbol for Buddha, and on the reverse side there is a naked hero depicted as Heracles. These cases reveal a world in which extremely dissimilar traditions cohabit with each other, although they still have visual and aesthetic similarities. All this is far removed from the standard Greco-Buddhist art from the Kushan period, which is often compared with the late Roman Empire. The entirety is very similar to the oldest Gandharan reliefs inspired by Hellenistic examples which, according to Rowland, date back to the Antonian period (A.D. 96–192), when Greek tradition flourished for a second time. These reliefs suggest a remarkable connection to classical references. Begram, Taxila, and Tillya Tepe had demonstrable contact with each other around the beginning of our era, which could be a sign that they had developed a common artistic tradition in earlier times. This may have come from the ivory found 200 years earlier in the Arsacidian capital Nisa. Ghirshman connects the ivory, which shows a true eastern Hellenistic character, to Greco-Bactrian art. Moreover, nearly 200 years later, Hellenism was still thriving, despite (or maybe as a result of) the Parthian obstacle. The Parthian king Orodes II, for instance, was at a performance of Euripides's "The Bacchae," when he learned about the defeat of Crassus (53 B.C.). In any case, during the Roman Empire, the Parthians were passed up by the trade on the Indian Ocean. Begram, Sirkap, and Tillya Tepe had an amazingly coherent network, with vital commercial relations across the sea and on land.

The three excavations point to an Iranian culture with strong Hellenistic and Indian traditions. On this culture, the Kushan Empire was built, which was more receptive to Hellenistic influences than to the dominant Iranian culture; it also embraced Indian and Chinese connections. As highlighted by Foucher (1942), this Indo-Afghan world had a distinctive nature. It was an extensive region on the border between India and Iran, with access to the steppes, and a surprisingly deep-rooted Greek cultural tradition. In this world, art prospered, sometimes a little on the clumsy side, but growing stronger every day and developing into the flourishing Gandharan art form with its apex of stucco modeling in the Hadda district.

Begram, 1939, Joseph and Ria Hackin

Kapisa, the Last Hellenistic Kingdom, and its Conquest by the Indo-Parthians

The culture of Begram can be summed up as follows: Indo-Greek (Hermaeus) or Parthian, but not Greek or Kushan. The Greeks were gone long before the Kushan period (with the nomad invasions). The Kushana came much later and nothing truly supports the theory that Kujula Kadphises arrived via the Hindu Kush in A.D. 30. If we accept Marshall's thesis that Hermaeus ruled until the beginning of our era, the treasure of Begram originated during the reign of Hermaeus (Indo-Greek). But if we believe that Hermaeus fell in 70 B.C. because of the Indo-Scythian nomads' advance, the treasure has to have originated during the Parthian period. In the first case, the Indo-Greeks are the link between Tillya Tepe in the north and Sirkap in the south; in the second case, an Indo-Parthian presence would have spread from the Hindu Kush in the north to Taxila in the south. This group is believed to have been in contact with the Parthian Empire (Iran) on the one hand—and thus with the Roman Empire—and with the Scythian realm (Tillya Tepe) on the other hand, and as a result, with the Chersonesus and Greco-Scythian settlements on the Bosporus banks, too. Both datings appear more logical than a treasure from the time of the Kushan kings, who, according to their coins, still lived as nomads in Central Asia and who were rather primitive (Foucher describes them as "Tartars"). Thus the Roman association (Alexandria and the Persian Gulf) and the profound Hellenistic-Scythian relationship can be explained without being too inconsistent. This also brings more credibility to the Christian myth that Gondophares was one of the Three Wise Men from the East and to the legendary travels of St. Thomas to India (which previously appeared impossible because of the "Parthian boundary" in Iran).

The treasure of Begram shows obvious similarities with the findings in Taxila (Sirkap), dated by Marshall to the first century A.D. based on the bronze statuette of Harpocrates (an identical statuette was also found in the treasure of Begram). The treasure also shows similarities with the Tillya Tepe excavations (for instance, the ivory comb, the construction of which greatly resembles that of casket X from Begram). Based on the Chinese mirrors from the Han dynasty and coins dating back to the reign of the Roman Emperor Tiberius (A.D. 14–37), Tillya Tepe dates from the beginning of our era. A link between Tillya Tepe and Sirkap is easily found, too, for example in the Tillya Tepe Aphrodite and the one found in Taxila, in the Greek city of Sirkap, stratum II, Saka-Pahlava period. Consequently, placing Begram in the Kushan dynasty is more a matter of belief and assumptions rather than being based on reality, particularly because the Chinese Hou Hanshu does not provide any indication whatsoever to date the creation of the Kushan Empire before A.D. 30–35.

A comparison of Begram and Tillya Tepe reveals even more similarities. Obviously the context is different, but the gadrooned golden goblet found in Tomb no. IV in Tillya Tepe is quite similar to the blue glass beakers from Begram, the shapes of which were inspired by metallic objects. The chalice from Tillya Tepe has a Greek inscription, just like a number of glass pieces from Begram. The plaster emblemata with the Heracles representation found in Begram have the same ideography as the enigmatic representation of a man on a wheel on the golden coin from Tillya Tepe. This representation seems to refer to the Vajrapani theme, which symbolizes the power of the Buddhist doctrine and tuition in Gandharan art. The treasure of both Tillya Tepe and Begram are awash with Hellenistic themes with Indian influences (and vice versa, for that matter).

Begram, Room 10

147 A WOMAN IS DEPICTED STANDING ON a *makara,* a hybrid mythical creature composed of body parts of an elephant, crocodile, and fish. Her legs are pressed together and her right hip is bent outward, giving the body a swaying pose, with the upper body tilted to the left. Her left arm hangs down along her body and her hand grabs a branch of a fruit-bearing vine. Her right arm is flexed upward, her hand damaged. In contrast to the next two figurines, who wear an Indian-style lower garment *(dhoti),* she wears a clinging tunic more reminiscent of Greek styles.

This statuette is one of three (nos. 147–149) that were found in close proximity to each other in Room 10 at Begram. All three statuettes, though differently executed, share the same iconography, each standing on a makara. This has led many scholars to believe that the statuettes represent the Indian river goddess Ganga, whose animal mount is a makara. Although the exact function of the three ivory statuettes cannot be determined with certainty, considering the nature of the other ivory and bone pieces discovered at Begram, it seems reasonable to assume that these figurines, too, embellished furniture.

148 SIMILAR TO THE PREVIOUS FIGURE (147), A woman is standing on a mythical makara with legs together and right hip bent outward giving the body a swaying pose. The top of the head is too damaged to see what kind of headdress she wore, but some stylized curls are visible, as well as a rosette-shaped ornament on her forehead. Her upper body is nude except for a necklace, which bears a centrally placed pendant, and a cross-shaped chest ornament with a rosette medallion in the middle. Bracelets of thin plain rings, ending in larger more elaborate ones, are worn on either arm. She wears an Indian-style lower garment with thick pleats falling in front. Her right arm is broken off; her left arm, slightly extended, hangs alongside her body. Iconographically, she resembles the Indian river goddess Ganga.

149 A WOMAN IS SHOWN STANDING cross-legged on a makara. The right arm of the figurine hangs alongside her slightly tilted body while her left arm is flexed upward toward her earring. Her hair is covered by a kind of turban consisting of a twisted piece of cloth. On top of the turban rests something in the shape of a column. A rosette-shaped ornament adorns her forehead. Her upper body is naked except for what may be a necklace or chest ornament of which only a piece remains over the left breast. Bracelets of thin plain rings, ending in larger more elaborate ones, are worn on either arm. She wears an Indian-style lower garment with long pleats falling in front.

147
Woman standing on a makara
Begram, Room 10
1st century A.D.
Ivory
45 cm
National Museum of Afghanistan
04.1.14

148
Woman standing on a makara
Begram, Room 10
1st century A.D.
Ivory
45.6 cm
National Museum of Afghanistan
04.1.15

149
Woman standing on a makara
Begram, Room 10
1st century A.D.
Ivory
56 cm
National Museum of Afghanistan
04.1.16

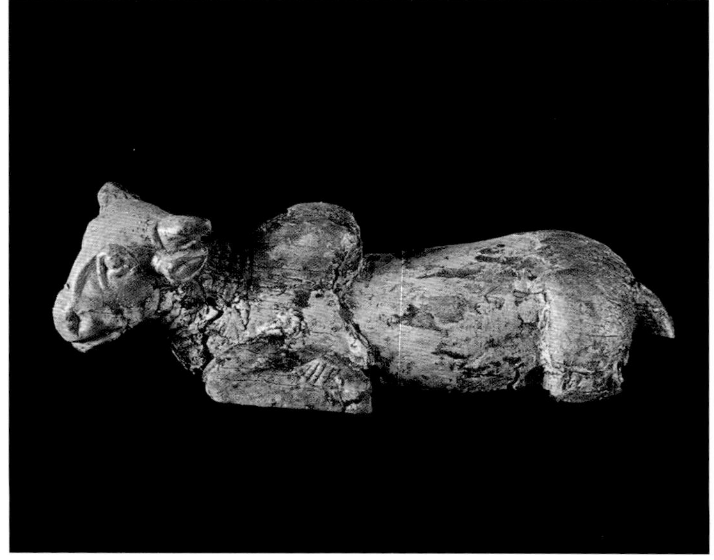

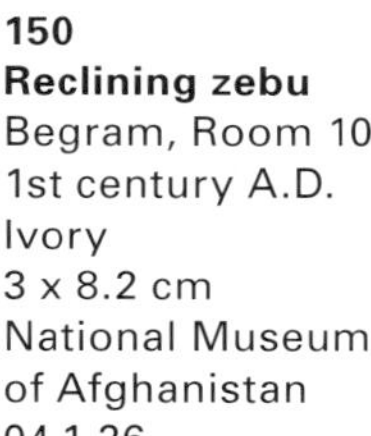

150
Reclining zebu
Begram, Room 10
1st century A.D.
Ivory
3 x 8.2 cm
National Museum
of Afghanistan
04.1.26

151
Fantastic creature
Begram, Room 10
1st century A.D.
Ivory
8.1 x 10.5 cm
National Museum
of Afghanistan
04.1.115

150 A SMALL FIGURE OF A HUMPED ZEBU ox lying down with its front legs folded underneath its body. Originally, this object was one of a set of four that may have belonged to a piece of furniture.

151 A SMALL SEATED FIGURE DEPICTED holding the leaf-like tails of two makaras, hybrid creatures with elephant, crocodile, and fish features. The figure wears a necklace and bracelets, as well as a cross-shaped chest ornament from which hangs a triangular, short leaflike undergarment. The mouths of the makaras, which are depicted in profile, are open and seem to be devouring the snakelike legs of the small figure.

152 A LEG OF A PIECE OF FURNITURE CARVED in the shape of an elephant. The top consists of an elephant's head, the bottom of an elephant's leg with the trunk wrapped around the middle.

152
Elephant protome
Begram, Room 10
1st century A.D.
Ivory
26 x 6.5 cm
National Museum
of Afghanistan
04.1.34

153
Four plaques of Footstool IX
Begram, Room 10
1st century A.D.
Ivory
6.8 x 17 x 0.2 cm
National Museum of Afghanistan
58.1.46(e)
58.1.48
58.1.51

154
Decorative plaque of Footstool IX
Begram, Room 10
1st century A.D.
Ivory
19 X 5.1 x 0.2 cm
National Museum of Afghanistan
58.1.59

155
Decorative plaque of Footstool IX
Begram, Room 10
1st century A.D.
Ivory
18.7 x 5.0 x 0.3 cm
National Museum of Afghanistan
57.1.81

156
Head of a zebu
Begram, Room 10
1st century A.D.
Ivory
2.8 x 5.5 x 3.2 cm
National Museum of Afghanistan
59.1.55

157
Forepart of a lion
Begram, Room 10
1st century A.D.
Ivory
4 x 5.5 x 2 cm
National Museum of Afghanistan
59.1.57

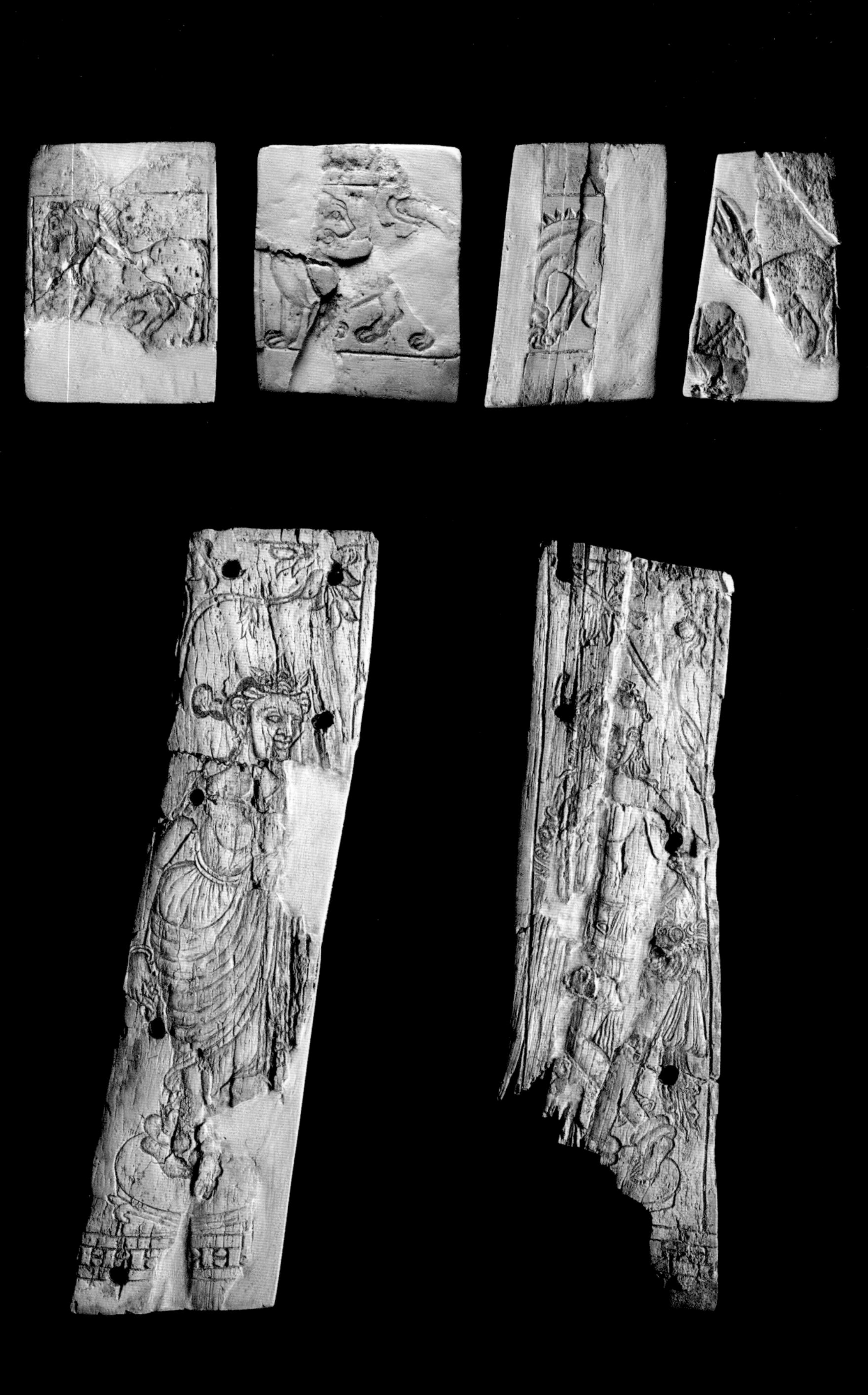

153 FOUR ANIMALS ARE SHOWN ON FOUR separate decorative plaques belonging to the same footstool. From the left, the animals are a horse, a feline with pointed ears, another horse, and a gazelle.

Together with objects 154 and 155, these small ornamental plaques formed part of an elaborate footstool, consisting of corner plaques depicting women standing on small platforms with the main horizontal register showing alternating plaques with animals.

154 PLAQUE DEPICTING A WOMAN STANDING cross-legged on a circular platform below a flowering branch. She wears a dress, the bottom part of which is held up by and probably draped over her left arm. Her right arm is held alongside her body. Her hair is tied in a bun, and she wears a three-leaf tiara on her head.

155 PLAQUE DEPICTING A WOMAN STANDING cross-legged on a circular platform below a flowering branch. She is dressed only in an Indian lower garment, her torso is bare. Her right arm is flexed upward and her left arm holds a pleat of her garment. Her hair is gathered in a tight ponytail, and she wears elaborate jewelry on her arms and legs.

156 TOGETHER WITH NO. 150, THIS BROKEN-off head of a humped zebu ox formed part of a set of four, which may have belonged to a piece of furniture.

157 A SMALL BROKEN-OFF OBJECT SHOWING the head and paws of a lion. Originally it seems to have formed part of a set of three similarly sculpted lions that may have served as part of a piece of furniture.

158 A VASE OF BLUE GLASS SURROUNDED BY openwork trailing of the same material and color. The openwork trellis consists of wavy horizontal and vertical trails, attached to the inner vase at intervals. The two handles are also decorated with wavy trails.

159 A LARGE GOBLET CONSISTING OF AN INNER beaker surrounded by openwork trailing of wavy horizontal and vertical bands, attached to the inner part at regular intervals.

160 SMALL VASE WITH A NARROW NECK AND bulging belly, consisting of an inner vase surrounded by openwork trailing consisting of wavy horizontal and vertical bands attached to the inner part at regular intervals. Two handles at the top are also decorated by wavy openwork trailing.

161 A SMALL CUP WITH A HANDLE, DECORATED with a honeycomb pattern between two plain top and bottom bands.

162 A SMALL CUP WITH A HANDLE, DECORATED with a honeycomb pattern between two plain top and bottom bands.

158
Blue vase with openwork trailing
Begram, Room 10
1st century A.D.
Glass
H. 17.7 cm; Diam. 7.3 cm
National Museum of Afghanistan
04.1.35

159
Large goblet with openwork trailing
Begram, Room 10
1st century A.D.
Glass
H. 17.8 cm;
Diam. 10.2 cm
National Museum of Afghanistan
04.1.37

160
Blue vase with openwork trailing
Begram, Room 10
1st century A.D.
Glass
H. 22.7 cm; Diam. 8 cm
National Museum of Afghanistan
04.1.41

161
Cup with a handle
Begram, Room 10
1st century A.D.
Glass
H. 11 cm; Diam. 9.2 cm
National Museum of Afghanistan
04.1.42

162
Cup with a handle
Begram, Room 10
1st century A.D.
Blue Glass
H. 8.9 cm
National Museum of Afghanistan
04.1.44

163 A LARGE BEAKER SHOWING TWO FEMALE and two male figures between two circular double-bands of yellow and ochre-red. The women, one of them seated, both wear aureole type headdresses and are fully clothed. Both men are standing, each facing one of the women as if attending her. According to their attire, the women appear to be of higher standing than the men. One of the men holds a large jar in his hands. The decor consists of date palms, and all the personages seem to be involved in harvesting the dates.

163
Painted beaker
Begram, Room 10
1st century A.D.
Glass
H. 12.6 cm; Diam. 8 cm
National Museum
of Afghanistan
04.1.43

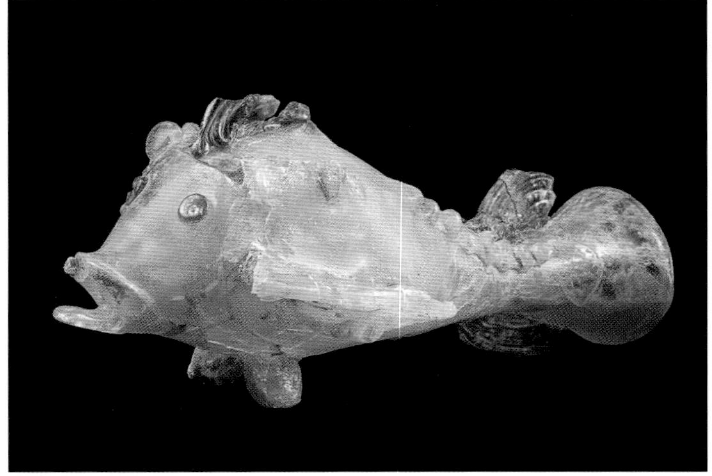

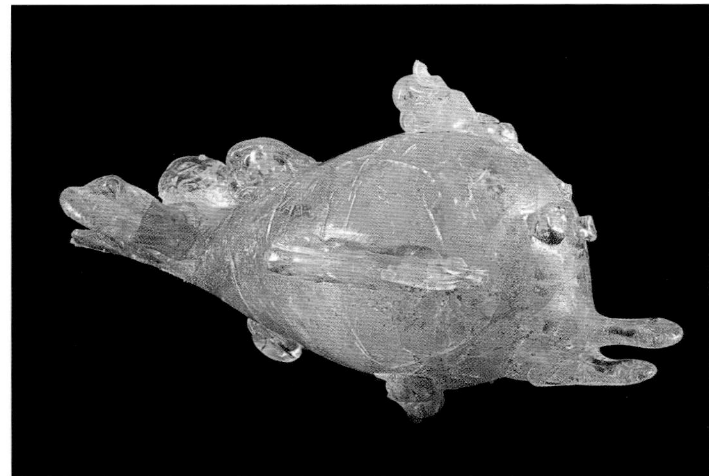

164 (top left)
Fish-shaped flask
Begram, Room 10
1st century A.D.
Glass
8.7 x 10.7 x 20 cm
National Museum of Afghanistan
04.1.45

169 (top right)
Fish-shaped flask
Begram, Room 10
1st century A.D.
Glass
7.3 x 20.2 cm
National Museum of Afghanistan
04.1.56

166 (bottom)
Fish-shaped flask
Begram, Room 10
1st century A.D.
Glass
7.2 x 30.5 cm
National Museum of Afghanistan
04.1.47

164 FLASK MADE OF YELLOW and blue glass shaped like a fish with tail, top and bottom fins. Its mouth is held ajar. The exact function of these fish-shaped flasks is unclear but they seem to be some sort of receptacle.

165 A CYLINDER-SHAPED goblet made of blue glass.

166 FLASK MADE OF BLUE glass in the shape of a fish with fins.

167 GLASS BOWL CONSTRUCTED with a series of vertical exterior ribs.

168 GLASS BOWL, THE SURFACE DESIGN of which is made up of small "cells" of various shapes surrounded by black dots. The central part of each cell is green or yellow and bordered by a stripe of ochre-red, and within each cell are four black dots arranged cross-wise.

169 FLASK MADE OF TRANSLUCENT glass in the shape of a fish with fins.

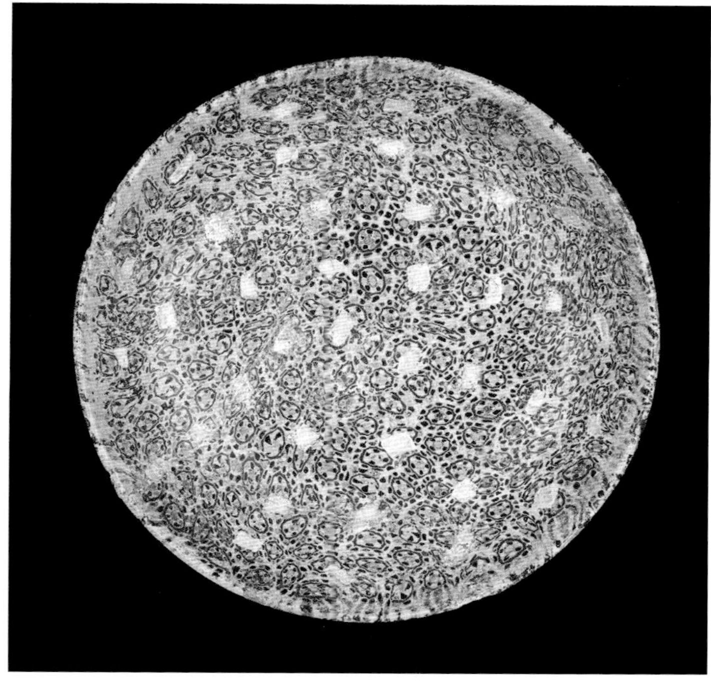

167
Ribbed bowl
Begram, Room 10
1st century A.D.
Glass
H. 7 cm; Diam. 23.5 cm
National Museum
of Afghanistan
04.1.54

165
Goblet
Begram, Room 10
1st century A.D.
Glass
H. 9 cm; Diam. 6.5 cm
National Museum
of Afghanistan
04.1.46

168
Mosaic
("Millefiori") bowl
Begram, Room 10
1st century A.D.
Glass
H. 4 cm; Diam. 17.7 cm
National Museum
of Afghanistan
04.1.55

170 A CURVED FOOTED RHYTON made of glass with the narrow end representing the head of a horned animal. A similar item was uncovered at Begram in the shape of a goat's head holding the remains of an ostrich egg.

171 A WIDE ELEGANT BOWL made of glass in imitation of agate.

172 LARGE GLASS GOBLET narrowing at the bottom. Between two plain bands at the top and bottom, the goblet is decorated with a honeycomb pattern.

170
Footed rhyton
Begram, Room 10
1st century A.D.
Glass
16.5 x 13.9 cm
National Museum of Afghanistan
04.1.57

171
Large bowl
Begram, Room 10
1st century A.D.
Glass
Diam. 17.2 cm
National Museum of Afghanistan
04.1.82

172
Large goblet
Begram, Room 10
1st century A.D.
Glass
H. 22 cm; Diam. 10 cm
National Museum
of Afghanistan
04.1.112

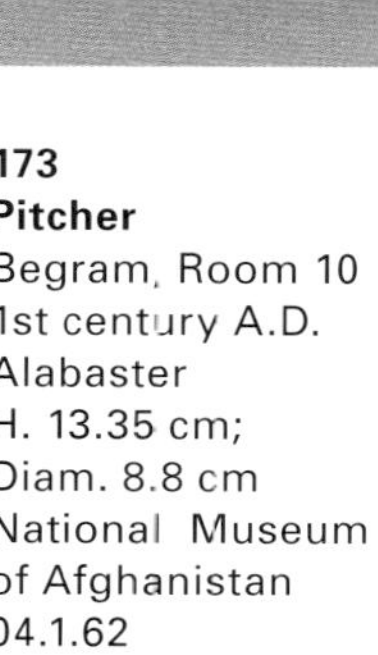

173
Pitcher
Begram, Room 10
1st century A.D.
Alabaster
H. 13.35 cm;
Diam. 8.8 cm
National Museum
of Afghanistan
04.1.62

174
Amphora
Begram, Room 10
1st century A.D.
Alabaster
H. 27.3 cm;
Diam. 13.5 cm
National Museum
of Afghanistan
04.1.77

175
Handled Dish
Begram, Room 10
1st century A.D.
Alabaster
Diam. 19.3 cm
National Museum
of Afghanistan
04.1.83

173 A PITCHER with a trilobate mouth.

174 A LARGE AMPHORA with two handles.

175 A BROAD SHALLOW DISH with a thin circular foot and a handle terminating in the shape of a ram's head.

176
Maple leaf
Begram, Room 10
1st century A.D.
Bronze
12 x 12.6 cm
National Museum
of Afghanistan
04.1.64

177
Handle
Begram, Room 10
1st century A.D.
Bronze
14 x 4 x 6 cm
National Museum
of Afghanistan
04.1.85

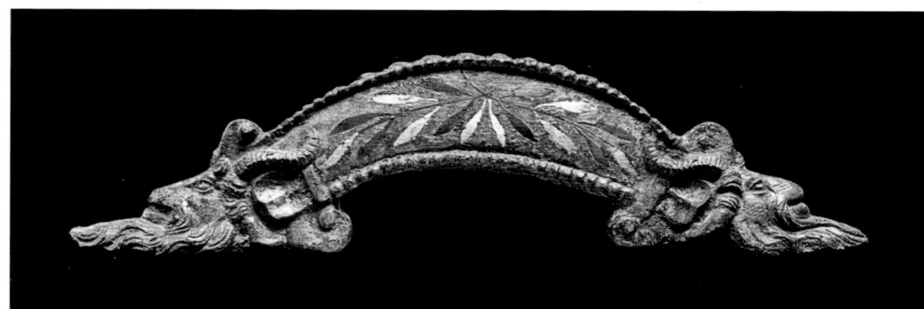

176 A SMALL BRONZE OBJECT in the shape of a maple-leaf with a small loop for attachment.

177 SMALL BRONZE HANDLE with terminals in the shape of fauns' heads decorated with goat horns.

178 FISH WITH MOVING FINS decorated this basin, a so-called aquarium. Originally this piece consisted of two circular bronze plaques fixed to each other. The remaining upper piece is decorated on one side by a Medusa head in the center, around which fish with moveable tails and fins are presented. The decorations are in repoussé. The exterior of the front was protected by a thick plate of uncolored glass separated from the movable decorations by a circular piece of wood. The movable parts of the obverse are connected by metal wiring to small weights attached to its bottom.

179 A BRONZE BOWL with a slightly raised center, a circular decoration and two handles.

179
Shallow bowl with two handles
Begram, Room 10
1st century A.D.
Bronze
H. 9 cm; Diam. 28.5 cm
National Museum
of Afghanistan
04.1.89

178
Circular basin decorated with fish
Begram, Room 10
1st century A.D.
Bronze
H. 3.4 cm; Diam. 46 cm
National Museum of Afghanistan
04.1.85

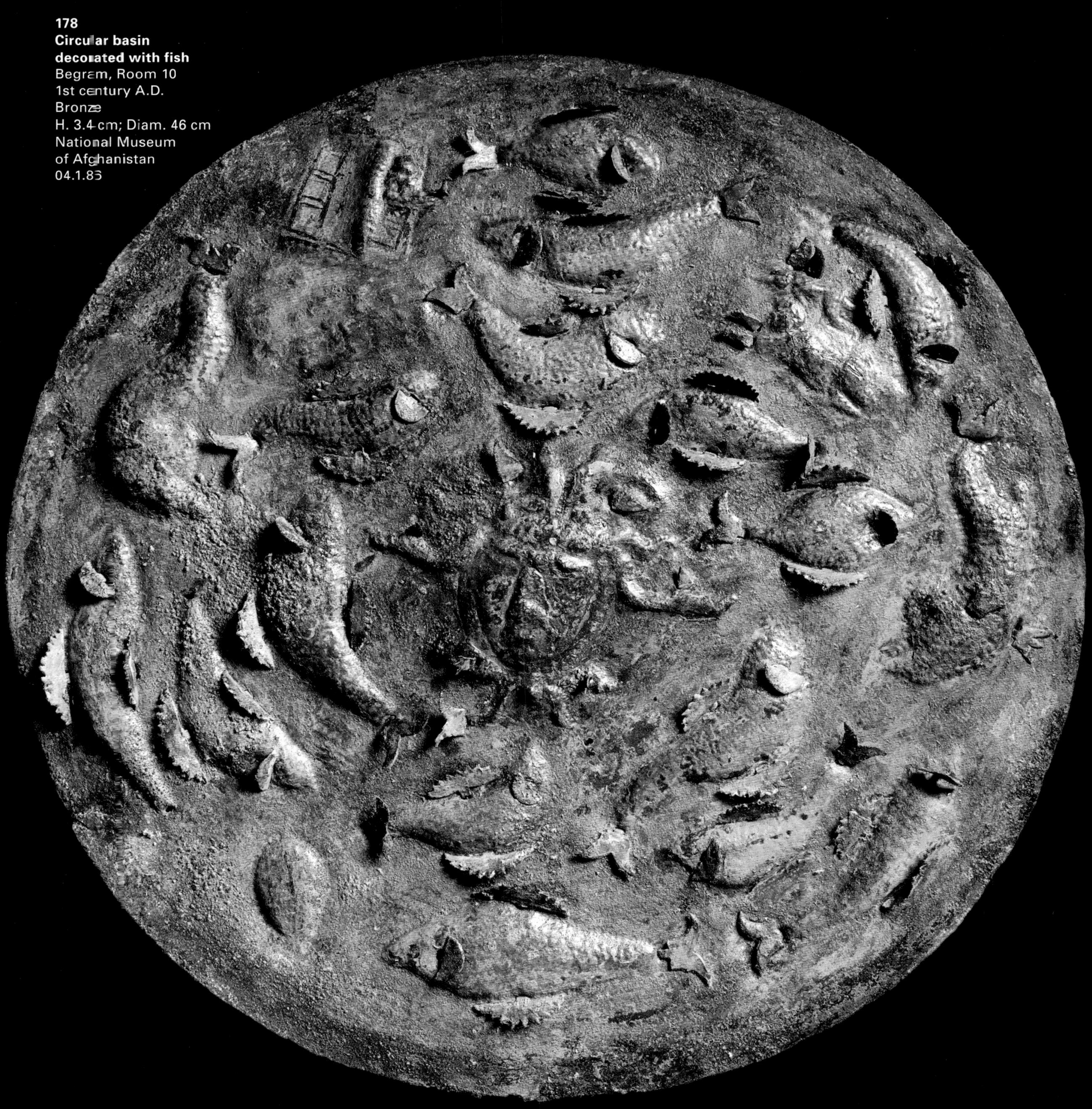

180
Scale weight
Begram, Room 10
1st century A.D.
Bronze
8.9 x 7.8 x 5.1 cm
National Museum
of Afghanistan
04.1.100

180

180 A SMALL OBJECT depicting the bust of the goddess Athena, which may have originally been a cosmetic jar and was later reused as a scale weight. The object is hollow and fitted with a plug on top of the head. Athena's chest armor is decorated in the center by the head of a Gorgon and serpents. She wears a helmet, on each side of her head are two loops, and on the back of her head is a handle.

181 SMALL VASE in the shape of a woman's head and neck.

182 A SMALL BRONZE scale weight, which originally may have functioned as a cosmetic jar, depicting the bust of a helmeted individual wearing a cuirass, perhaps the god Mars. The object is hollow, and the top of the head is fitted with a plug. The back of the helmet carries a handle and there are a number of loops fixed onto the helmet for suspension of a chain.

181
Vase in the shape of a female head
Begram, Room 10
1st century A.D.
Bronze
10.6 x 5.2 cm
National Museum of Afghanistan
04.1.104

182
Scale weight
Begram, Room 10
1st century A.D.
Bronze
9.8 x 7.9 x 8 cm
National Museum of Afghanistan
04.1.108

183
Circular medallion
Begram, Room 13
1st century A.D.
Plaster
22.3 cm
National Museum
of Afghanistan
04.1.17

Begram, Room 13

184
Circular medallion
Begram, Room 13
1st century A.D.
Plaster
15.2 cm
National Museum
of Afghanistan
04.1.18

185
Circular medallion
Begram, Room 13
1st century A.D.
Plaster
12.5 cm
National Museum
of Afghanistan
04.1.19

186
Aphrodite
Begram, Room 13
1st century A.D.
Plaster
26.7 cm
National Museum
of Afghanistan
04.1.20

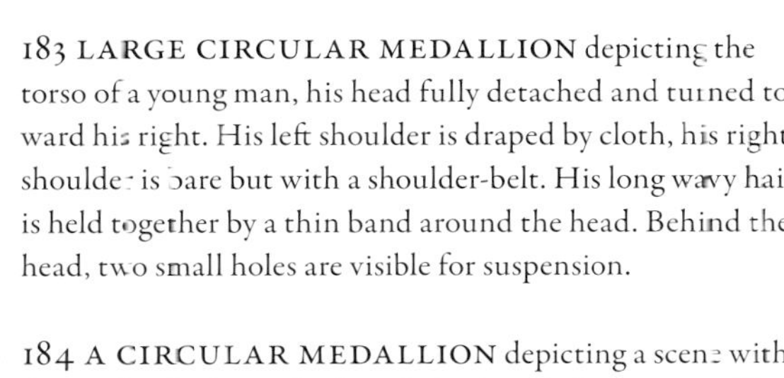

183 LARGE CIRCULAR MEDALLION depicting the torso of a young man, his head fully detached and turned toward his right. His left shoulder is draped by cloth, his right shoulder is bare but with a shoulder-belt. His long wavy hair is held together by a thin band around the head. Behind the head, two small holes are visible for suspension.

184 A CIRCULAR MEDALLION depicting a scene with four individuals. In the front left, a bearded man in profile reclines on a stool draped with a piece of cloth, his feet positioned on a footstool. His right hand is pointed toward a musical instrument held by a young man standing before him. On the right, another individual is depicted with body bent, arms resting on his right knee which is raised with his foot resting on a stepped platform, and his right hand holding a club resting on the ground. A fourth figure is depicted on the left, behind the bearded reclining individual.

185 A CIRCULAR MEDALLION depicting a young man in profile to the left wearing a helmet.

186 A SMALL STATUETTE of a naked woman cast from a mold. The left arm is stretched out, her hand holding a piece of fruit, perhaps a pomegranate. Her right arm is flexed upward, with her hand resting on her shoulder.

187 ON THE LEFT, a seated young man in profile is holding a vessel resting on his legs. An eagle with spread wings is depicted in profile on the right eating from the vessel. The scene has been identified as the beautiful boy Ganymede feeding the eagle of Zeus.

188 THE MEDALLION depicts the head and torso of a child with the child's head nearly detached from the surface. On the child's back are traces of wings, and his small fleshy arms clutch a butterfly against his breast. The scene depicts Eros and Psyche—the ancient Greek name for butterfly, also meaning soul—in their allegorical union. Psyche, a beautiful princess, incurred the jealous wrath of Aphrodite, who sent her son Eros to poison Psyche only to see him fall in love with her.

189 THE MEDALLION depicts a long grapevine that winds in a circular manner.

190 IN THE LOWER HALF of the scene, a nude male, probably the young manEndymion of Greek mythology, is shown lying stretched out on his back with his hands behind his head. He is mounted by a nude winged woman who appears to have descended from the sky. In her left hand she carries a lyre, her right hand clutches her right wing. A winged Eros is depicted above the head of the young man. In one version of Greek mythology, the handsome Endymion was the son of Zeus and the nymph Calyce. He was adored by Selene, the Titan goddess of the moon. Selene asked Zeus to grant Endymion eternal youth. Zeus blessed him with eternal sleep, and every night he was visited by Selene in a cave on Mount Latmos.

188
Circular medallion with Eros and Psyche
Begram, Room 13
1st century A.D.
Plaster
16.5 cm
National Museum of Afghanistan
04.1.117

187
Circular medallion with Ganymede and the eagle of Zeus
Begram, Room 13
1st century A.D.
Plaster
12.8 cm
National Museum of Afghanistan
04.1.22

190
Circular medallion depicting Endymion and Selene
Begram, Room 13
1st century A.D.
Plaster
16 cm
National Museum of Afghanistan

189
Circular medallion decorated with grapevines
Begram, Room 13
1st century A.D.
Plaster
12 cm
National Museum of Afghanistan

191 AN ENGRAVED IVORY PLAQUE showing two women under a gateway within a vegetal décor. The woman on the right taps a tree with the heel of her foot and holds a small flower in her right hand. The woman on the left plays a flute. Both are shown wearing Indian-style lower garments with multi-strand girdles, broad bracelets, anklets, and turban-like headdresses. Above, a balustrade is depicted.

This plaque, together with nos. 194–199, and 208, formed part of what was classified as ensemble 34, an elaborate chair back decorated on both sides by, among others, a series of broad registers with representations of women under gateways, alternating in relief and incised.

192 AN ENGRAVED IVORY PLAQUE with painted background shows a group of men and women visiting a hermit or sage. On the left is a simple hut, in front of which lies a doe. Next to this scene, a hermit is shown greeting three women and a man who seems to be another hermit, recognizable by the loose hanging hair. The woman in front is on her knees and holds her hands in the gesture of reverence or añjali. Some scholars have identified this scene as part of the Rsyariga (or Isisinga) Jataka, a story of the Buddha's previous lives. This particular Jataka tells the story of the seduction of a young hermit, born to a doe, by the princess Nalini who was sent by the god Indra to damage his virtue.

193 AN ENGRAVED IVORY PLAQUE with a painted background that might depict a scene from Buddhist Jataka no. 253, the story of a merchant who buys a thoroughbred horse and sells it to the king; the horse is not treated properly and so goes on a hunger strike. The scene depicts from left to right the noble steed, the queen, the horse trader, the king and his female warriors. The horse trader, who is depicted in a heavy costume and so thereby is meant to be from the northwest, holds up a small oil lamp for the night visit of the king and his entourage.

191
Decorative plaque with musician and dancer
Begram, Room 13
1st century A.D.
Ivory
34.6 x 15.4 cm
National Museum of Afghanistan
04.1.21

192
Decorative plaque with a narrative scene
Begram, Room 13
1st century A.D.
Ivory, paint
5.9 x 11.3 cm
National Museum of Afghanistan
04.1.23

193
Decorative plaque with a narrative scene
Begram, Room 13
1st century A.D.
Ivory, paint
5.8 x 11 cm
National Museum of Afghanistan
04.1.27

194 A SERIES OF WOMEN depicted under three gateways. On the left, partially damaged, a woman is depicted holding a bowl under a gateway topped by an Indian arch. In the middle, a woman is shown under a gateway with three architraves. Her right lower leg is flexed backward, touching the column supporting the arch. She carries a small child in her arms. The scene on the right depicts two women under an Indian arch. All women are shown wearing Indian lower garments.

195 TWO WOMEN ARE SHOWN, each standing in a gateway. The woman on the left has her head turned to her left and her legs crossed, with her foot touching a column. She wears a short skirt over a lower garment and a girdle made of large round balls. She is holding a long curved

194
Decorative plaque with women standing under gateways
Begram, Room 13
1st century A.D.
Ivory
13.8 x 24.7 cm
National Museum of Afghanistan
04.1.48

195
Decorative plaque with women standing under gateways
Begram, Room 13
1st century A.D.
Ivory
16 x 15.3 cm
National Museum of Afghanistan
04.1.49

196
Decorative plaque with women standing under gateways
Begram, Room 13
1st century A.D.
Ivory
15.8 x 16.1 cm
National Museum of Afghanistan
04.1.52

instrument below her chin. The scene on the right depicts a woman standing under an Indian arch.

196 ON THE LEFT, half of a scene depicting a small woman standing cross-legged under a gateway topped by an Indian arch. A parrot is perched on her shoulder. On the right, a woman stands under a gateway with three architraves, holding a long plait of hair along the right side of her body and wearing a striped lower garment.

197 ON THE LEFT, half of a scene depicting a woman standing under an arched gateway. Her left arm is flexed upward. The scene on the right depicts a woman standing cross-legged under a gateway with three architraves. Her right arm is flexed upward, with her hand holding a branch of a tree.

197
Decorative plaque with women standing under gateways
Begram, Room 13
1st century A.D.
Ivory
16 x 13.3 cm
National Museum of Afghanistan
04.1.53

198 A WOMAN IS SEATED, turned toward the right. A woman on the right is turned toward her. Between these two personages is a stool in the shape of an hourglass. In the next scene, to the right, another woman is represented frontally, her left hand touching the beak of a bird. Next to her, another woman is shown. On the right, a gateway is depicted with doors left slightly ajar.

The great majority of images presented on the Begram carvings are of women, and most of the scenes are set in semi-enclosed spaces suggested by gateways, doors and fences. Larger settings, in which groups of women are depicted, are offered in a series of plaques in relief (nos. 198–207). Small gateways are depicted at regular intervals, either topped by an Indian arch or joined by slightly curving architraves. Parts of balustrades are shown on either side of the gateways, which seems to indicate that the area was enclosed but not completely sealed off. This is also indicated by the doors of the gateways, which are left slightly ajar, as if to invite the viewer to contemplate the secrets behind them. Between the gateways are scenes of women relaxing and playing musical instruments.

199 FROM LEFT TO RIGHT, two women are shown frontally, carrying weapons in their girdles. The next scene shows a woman lying on a bed supporting her head with her left hand, her right leg is slightly raised. To the right, another woman is holding her weapon on her left hip. The scene is bordered below by a band with stylized flowers.

200 ON THE LEFT IS A GATEWAY with its doors ajar. On the right are two women seated on a round stool and a four-legged bed. The woman seated on the stool has both legs raised onto the seat. The woman on the bed is depicted in three-quarter profile with her left foot on the bed and her right foot on the ground.

201 A GATEWAY TOPPED by an Indian arch is depicted on the left. To the right, two attendant women are standing behind a woman seated on a small round stool. One of the standing women seems to be adjusting her companion's headdress.

198
Decorative plaque with a scene from the women's quarters
Begram, Room 13
1st century A.D.
Ivory
7.6 x 17.4 cm
National Museum of Afghanistan
04.1.58

199
Decorative plaque with a scene from the women's quarters
Begram, Room 13
1st century A.D.
Ivory
7.5 x 18.2 cm
National Museum of Afghanistan
04.1.59

200
Decorative plaque with a scene from the women's quarters
Begram, Room 13
1st century A.D.
Ivory
8.3 x 15.1 cm
National Museum of Afghanistan
04.1.68

201
Decorative plaque with a scene from the women's quarters
Begram, Room 13
1st century A.D.
Ivory
8.1 x 13.8 cm
National Museum of Afghanistan
04.1.69

202 TWO WOMEN in three-quarter profile are sitting on small four-legged stools, facing each other. To the left, a small table on which a basket rests. On the right is a gateway topped by an Indian arch. The scene is set in a garden with trees bearing fruit.

203 IN A GARDEN SETTING with trees bearing fruit, two women are reclining on a bed. One is depicted frontally, with legs spread and left knee raised. The other woman is shown sitting in three-quarter profile, leaning on her right arm. To the right, a woman is playing with a duck. Behind the bed is a small column surmounted by a vase.

204 ON THE RIGHT, a gateway is shown with doors ajar. On the left is a scene with three women. The central figure directs her attention to the woman on the right. The woman on the left is near a basket with fruit. Her left hand is directed toward a bird.

205 THE SCENE DEPICTS two women seated on a bed. The woman on the right is shown frontally, her right leg resting on a small footstool in front of the bed, her left knee raised. The woman on the left is depicted in three-quarter profile. Two other women are on either side of the bed. On the left is a gateway with two arches and door ajar.

202
Decorative plaque with a scene from the women's quarters
Begram, Room 13
1st century A.D.
Ivory
8.9 x 15.2 cm
National Museum of Afghanistan
04.1.70

203
Decorative plaque with a scene from the women's quarters
Begram, Room 13
1st century A.D.
Ivory
8.7 x 15.5 cm
National Museum of Afghanistan
04.1.71

204
Decorative plaque with a scene from the women's quarters
Begram, Room 13
1st century A.D.
Ivory
8.2 x 14.7 cm
National Museum of Afghanistan
04.1.72

205
Decorative plaque with a scene from the women's quarters
Begram, Room 13
1st century A.D.
Ivory
9.1 x 15.1 cm
National Museum of Afghanistan
04.1.73

206 THE CENTRAL SCENE shows a woman seated on a horse facing right with its head turned to the left. On either side, a woman is facing forward, holding objects. The woman on the left also holds the whip held by the woman on the horse. The woman on the right carries two cymbals in her flexed arms. On the far right is a gateway topped by an Indian arch.

207 TO THE RIGHT is a gateway with two arches and its doors left ajar. To the left are three seated women and one standing woman.

208 TWO WOMEN are shown under a gateway topped by three architraves. Their hair is arranged in loops and buns. Above, curtains are suspended from a semi-circular arch. Between the architraves are two *kinnaris* (bird-women) and a series of fantastic creatures separated by small pillars. The uprights of the gateway are joined with the lower architrave by two leogryph brackets, similar in style to the actual bracket shown next (no. 209) in this catalog.

206
Decorative plaque with a scene from the women's quarters
Begram, Room 13
1st century A.D.
Ivory
8.4 x 20 cm
National Museum of Afghanistan
04.1.74

207
Decorative plaque with a scene from the women's quarters
Begram, Room 13
1st century A.D.
Ivory
8.3 x 20 cm
National Museum of Afghanistan
04.1.75

208
Large decorative plaque with women under a gateway
Begram, Room 13
1st century A.D.
Ivory
42.7 x 24.6 cm
National Museum of Afghanistan
04.1.113

209 A BRACKET IN THE SHAPE of a leogryph or śārdūla, a mythical creature with the body of a lion, wings of an eagle, and the beak of a parrot. The śārdūla sprouts out of the mouth of a makara and has wings consisting of both feathers and fish scales, which are bordered on top by a row of pearls. On its back, a woman is seated holding a bridle. Between the lower paws of the śārdūla is a small yaksa figure who supports with his left hand the leg of the female figure.

210 PITCHER WITH GOLD-LEAF DECORATION. The neck is encircled by a band consisting of two fillets with a row of square shapes between them. Below, also encircling the neck and shoulder of the pitcher, are a laurel branch and branches with heart-shaped leaves. On the belly of the pitcher, three individuals are represented, including Dionysus wearing the *nebride* or fawn's skin and holding the *thyrsos,* a staff encircled by vines and topped by a pine cone.

209
Leogryph bracket
Begram, Room 13
1st century A.D.
Ivory
H. 30 cm
National Museum
of Afghanistan
04.1.116

210
Pitcher with a raised handle
Begram, Room 13
1st century A.D.
Glass
H. 21.4 cm
National Museum of Afghanistan
04.1.33

211 A LARGE GOBLET decorated with a battle scene in the center. Above and below are circular bands consisting of two rows of ochre-red and yellow lines with a series of five-petaled flowers in between. The central scene consists of two parts. Above, a small band shows combatants armed with shields and spears, three on foot and one on horseback. Below this is the main scene depicting three persons on horseback and two on foot. Two others lie mortally wounded on the battlefield. Some scholars have identified this scene as that of the battle between Hector and Achilles, the heroes of the Trojan war.

212 A LARGE GOBLET divided into two zones, enlarged at far right, with the scenes in each separated by a circular band running around the cup. At the top and bottom, the scenes are bordered by circular stripes in the familiar ochre-red and yellow. In the lower zone, three fishermen are shown among depictions of fish: One of the men appears to be seated in a small boat; another carries a fish over his shoulders. The upper zone depicts hunting scenes: the hunters, one on horseback, carry bow and arrow, which are pointed at an antelope, a tiger, and another unidentifiable animal.

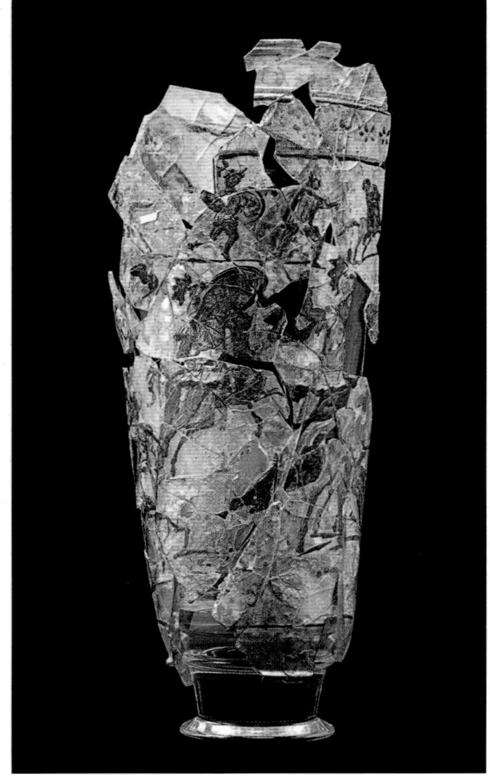

211
Large painted goblet
Begram, Room 13
1st century A.D.
Glass
H. 24.3 cm;
Diam. 13.4 cm
National Museum
of Afghanistan
04.1.38

212
Large painted goblet
Begram, Room 13
1st century A.D.
Glass
H. 24.8 cm;
Diam. 11.7 cm
National Museum
of Afghanistan
04.1.39

213 A PITCHER made of blue-black glass with a raised handle.

214 A DRINKING CUP furnished with handles, or *kantharos,* made of transparent glass, carrying a gold-leaf decoration of grape leaves and a knotted vine shoot. The kantharos was an attribute of Dionysus, who is often depicted holding the drinking cup in his hand.

215 A TALL CYLINDRICALLY shaped vase on a round foot; near its top and bottom are four and three circular grooves, respectively. Porphyry is a type of rock found primarily in Egypt, consisting of feldspar crystals embedded in a compact red or purple ground mass.

216 A SMALL BOWL made of porphyry, similar to No. 215.

213
Pitcher
Begram, Room 13
1st century A.D.
Glass
H. 28 cm
National Museum
of Afghanistan
04.1.66

214
Kantharos
Begram, Room 13
1st century A.D.
Rock crystal
H. 9 cm; Diam. 14.5 cm
National Museum
of Afghanistan
04.1.36

215
Porphyry vase
Begram, Room 13
1st century A.D.
Porphyry
H. 25.38 cm;
Diam.11.8 cm
National Museum
of Afghanistan
04.1.65

216
Porphyry bowl
Begram, Room 13
1st century A.D.
Porphyry
H. 4.5 cm; Diam.18.5 cm
National Museum
of Afghanistan
04.1.67

217 ORIGINALLY, A SMALL COSMETIC JAR, which may have been (re)used as a scale weight. It shows the bust of a young man with a small cylindrically shaped headdress. On either side of the headdress is a small ring, probably designed to have a chain or necklace fastened on to it. In the back is a small handle. He is identified as the Roman god Mercury by the two wings on either side of his forehead and the two horns on top of his head.

218 SMALL FIGURE of a naked winged Eros standing with his right leg positioned slightly ahead of his left. In his right outstretched hand he carries a torch, and in his left, his bow.

219 A MINIATURE DRAPED tripod with a slightly raised rim and three legs terminating in lion paws.

217
Scale weight
Begram, Room 13
1st century A.D.
Bronze
8.4 cm x 6.8 cm
National Museum
of Afghanistan
04.1.30

218
Eros
Begram, Room 13
1st century A.D.
Bronze
H. 15.2 cm
National Museum
of Afghanistan
04.1.31

219
Tripod
Begram, Room 13
1st century A.D.
Bronze
H. 9 cm; Diam. 9.5 cm
National Museum
of Afghanistan
04.1.32

220 A STATUE of the Greco-Egyptian god Serapis-Heracles depicting the god standing naked with his legs slightly apart and his right foot placed slightly in front of the left. His right hand rests on a club, while the left holds a ball. He is shown with a beard and a full head of hair on top of which he wears a calathus, the primary source of identification. Like the small statuette of Harpocrates, this statue is a typical representation of a Greco-Egyptian god: the head attire is characteristic of the god Serapis, while his attributes are typical of Heracles.

220
Serapis-Heracles
Begram, Room 13
1st century A.D.
Bronze
24.1 cm x 6.45 cm
National Museum
of Afghanistan
04.1.90

221 SMALL MASK OF SILENUS who became the companion of Dionysus and is usually respresented as a jolly, old bearded man wearing a crown of flowers.

222 A MALE HORSE-RIDER without his steed is shown in a slightly bent seated position with his legs spread as if to accommodate a horse. His torso is nude, and he wears a short loincloth. His right hand is raised in a fist as if he were originally holding a spear or lance, and his left hand rests on his left leg, perhaps originally holding the reins of a horse.

221
Masque of Silenus
Begram, Room 13
1st century A.D.
Bronze
9.5 cm x 7.9 cm
National Museum
of Afghanistan
04.1.91

222
Horse-rider
Begram, Room 13
1st century A.D.
Bronze
14.7 cm x 4.7 cm
National Museum
of Afghanistan
04.1.92

223 A BRONZE PITCHER with a handle. On top of the handle, nearly along its entire length, a serpent is represented.

224 BRONZE PITCHER, the handle of which is decorated with a serpent terminating at the bottom in a small head.

225 A STATUETTE OF A CHILD with his left hand raised and his finger on his chin. He is identified as Harpocrates, a Hellenistic version of the Egyptian god Horus, son of Isis and Serapis.

226 A SMALL FIGURE of a rooster with a human face, similar in iconography to the mythological harpy.

223
Pitcher with a decorated handle
Begram, Room 13
1st century A.D.
Bronze
H. 17 cm; Diam. 10.3 cm
National Museum of Afghanistan
04.1.94

224
Pitcher with a decorated handle
Begram, Room 13
1st century A.D.
Bronze
H. 15.2 cm;
Diam. 10.6 cm
National Museum of Afghanistan
04.1.95

225
Harpocrates
Begram, Room 13
1st century A.D.
Bronze
H. 13.3 cm
National Museum of Afghanistan
04.1.101

226
Rooster with a human head
Begram, Room 13
1st century A.D.
Bronze
5.4 x 6 cm
National Museum of Afghanistan
04.1.102

227
Young horse-rider
Begram, Room 13
1st century A.D.
Bronze
13.5 x 3.5 cm
National Museum
of Afghanistan
04.1.28

228
"Kinnari" jug
Begram, Room 13
1st century A.D.
Ceramic
20.2 x 13 x 21.8 cm
National Museum
of Afghanistan
04.1.84

227 A YOUNG MAN in a cuirass is depicted in the position of a horse-rider with his legs spread and his knees slightly bent. A shawl is tied over his right shoulder and under his left arm. His right hand is raised and originally held a lance or spear. The left hand is clenched as if holding the reins of a horse.

228 A CERAMIC JUG, covered in blue-green varnish, in the shape of a bird-woman—a combination known in Indian mythology as "kinnari." The human part consists of the head, bust and arms of a female figure, with the remaining part presenting a combination of bird and fish features. Her mouth is held open and functions as the spout of the jug. Her hair is tied in a tight ponytail which reaches all the way down the back of the jug and serves as the handle. Her arms are bent in front of her with her hands held in 'anjali' or the gesture of reverence. On top, just behind the handle, is an opening larger than the mouth for liquid initially to be poured into the jug. In Indian mythology, kinnaris function as celestial musicians and singers. Their closest counterparts are the sirens of Classical mythology, sea nymphs who were part woman, part bird, and who distracted sailors with their songs, causing ships to wreck. The Indian version is much more benign but shares the same iconography.

CHAPTER VII

Ancient Bactria's Golden Hoard

VIKTOR IVANOVICH SARIANIDI
Senior researcher, Institute of Archaeology
Russian Academy of Science, Moscow

Russian and Afghan archaeologists work throughout the cold winter to excavate the six golden burials.

OPPOSITE *First glimpses of a Bactrian princess, Tomb I, excavations at Tillya Tepe*

THE DARK PERIOD, IT WAS CALLED—the period of the shadowy first two centuries A.D., just preceding the Kushan Empire in the land of Bactria, on the northern plains of today's Afghanistan.

In the rainy fall of 1978 that darkness lifted. Digging in an unassuming mound known as Tillya Tepe, the "Hill of Gold," we chanced upon the graves of six ancients who had lived within that unknown period some 2,000 years ago. And with their bones we found the wealth they were to carry to the afterlife—more than 20,000 artifacts, mostly crafted of gold and semiprecious stones—a treasure of such artistic and descriptive richness that to speak of it was already to begin to understand that distant time.

But before we had a chance to make plaster copies of the pieces, before they could be studied or displayed, war and confusion closed in on Afghanistan. We quickly transferred the treasures to the museum officials in the capital for safekeeping. For years, the priceless hoard from Tillya Tepe lay hidden in Kabul, its condition clouded in mystery, and scholars had no access to study the pieces. Under vigilant guard by Afghan museum and bank officials, these priceless treasures were saved. Today we can finally tell their story, the story of a unique and original culture in Afghanistan at the heart of Silk Road trade 2,000 years ago.

More than three eventful decades have passed since I first went to Afghanistan from Moscow's Institute of Archaeology in 1969. We arrived as part of the joint Soviet-Afghan Expedition to examine the antiquities that lay beneath the fabled Bactrian Plain, once an important crossroads on the great Silk Route from the varied lands of the Roman Empire in the West

The Tillya Tepe burials were made in wooden coffins. Traces of leather, fine fabric, and gold ornaments adorned the coffins.

to the Chinese cities protected by the Great Wall in the East. We based our camp in Sheberghan, a large village set on the dry plain between the bleak foothills of the Hindu Kush and the desert valley of the Amu Darya.

It reminded me of home, for I was born in Tashkent, in Soviet Central Asia where my father, looking for a more meaningful life, had immigrated from a village in Greece. Sheberghan was on the frontier of the struggling Afghan nation and mired in poverty. Cotton fields pressed against the mud-brick houses, and merchants sat stoically among their stacks of melons and eggplants at the central bazaar. When night fell, everything was still. Neighbors talked to neighbors in the darkness between the houses, and packs of hungry dogs circled in the streets. It was much as Bactria must have been during the dark period. Only in the morning, when the trucks started up, did the 20th century return.

On and off for nine years we dug into the mounds near Sheberghan. At first we focused on an obvious site called Yemshi Tepe, the ruins of a monumental city dating from the first century A.D. Inside its walls we found a citadel, perhaps the palace of the local ruler who controlled a cluster of smaller villages that now appeared as small swells of sunbaked earth.

But surely an earlier people had farmed this plain. Day after dusty day I drove from mound to mound, searching for some sign of Bronze Age life, my specialty. In the brittle grass on one such mound my eyes fell on a type of painted potsherd I recognized from a prior dig in Central Asia. It pushed the date of habitation in this area back a thousand years, to the beginning of the second millennium B.C. A fantastic find! While others were excavating nearby Yemshi Tepe, my team set out to see what lay beneath this simple hillock.

Amid its top layer we found a village from the third century B.C., as we had expected. But from the layer beneath emerged the outline of a massive edifice. Inside, within a double line of columns, stood a mud-brick altar coated with ashes. We speculated that this was a temple for the worship of fire, built 3,200 years ago.

As we excavated in late 1978, Afghanistan was inching toward a civil war. A new socialist republic had been declared. We were not caught in any fighting, but one morning armed tribesmen came on horseback, like sand devils off the desert, circling Tillya Tepe, asking angry questions. The frightened workmen implored us not to say anything or we would be shot. And then the riders were gone. Despite the growing danger, our fascination with the ancient temple urged us on, while clouds that rolled in from the Hindu Kush each day grew darker, promising the heavy, prolonged rains of winter. A cold drizzle started late at night on November 12 and forced us to break off work at noon the next day. But that morning we had found several rusted fragments of iron bands with nails sticking from them. One was bent at a right angle and looked a lot like a bracket from a wooden coffin.

When the weather cleared, a workman suddenly turned up a disk that gleamed among the clods of damp earth. Gold! We called a military guard and waded in with pounding hearts. And soon a grave emerged from beneath our picks and scoops. Staring at us were the hollow eye sockets of a skull, a young woman between 25 and 30 years old, perhaps a princess. A nomadic princess from ancient Bactria looked straight at us after being hidden for 2,000 years. Surrounding her were layers of gold jewelry and ornamentation that had collapsed from her disintegrating clothing. The brilliance of her "dark period" finery astonished us.

The potent word "gold" soon spread across the plain, and a pilgrimage began of village people, tourists, and authorities from Kabul. Some came on donkeys, others walked in. One constant visitor was the farmer whose cotton fields lay next to our excavation. He would sit for hours on the edge of the dig, looking sad. "My wife has chased me from the house," he told us. "She yelled at me, 'All my life you've kept me in poverty, with gold lying under your feet every day!'"

But what was the mound of Tillya Tepe? Who buried the princess here, and why?

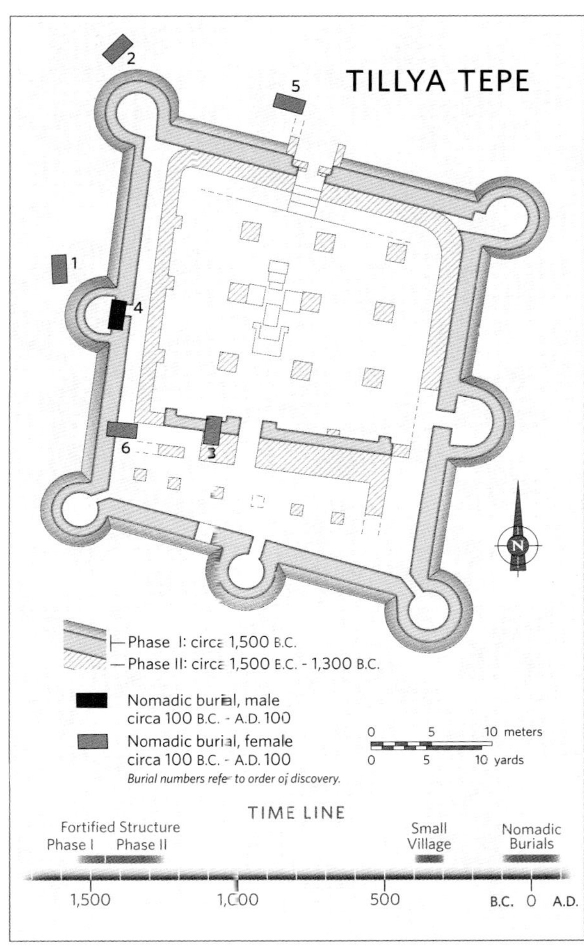

In typical nomadic fashion, the burials were dug into a hill or mound. Here the mound was actually an even older building in ruins, the plan of which is shown in outline. It is unlikely that the ancient nomads knew it was a building when they interred the group.

This is what we know: Four thousand years ago the first agricultural settlers appeared on the Bactrian plain; those who built the earliest structures at Tillya Tepe must have been among them. They constructed a small, fortified settlement at Tillya Tepe that we think may have been a temple. During the next thousand years the site was rebuilt several times. When it fell out of use, the mud-brick walls crumbled into a low mound. Tillya Tepe lay still for 600 years until a small village grew on the remains of the long-forgotten temple. The village did not last long, and again the site crumbled into ruin. So it would remain for 400 years until A.D. 100, when the golden graves were dug into the site's layered history.

While Tillya Tepe lay abandoned, Bactria was buffeted by the growing empires of the Achaemenid Persians and the Greek followers of Alexander the Great. Bactria itself grew into an independent state, known as the Greco-Bactrian kingdom. But the nobles buried in the humble mound were newcomers to Bactria; they had come from the East to plunder the Greco-Bactrian cities.

On the other side of Asia another drama was unfolding. Where wandering tribes had clashed for centuries on the frontiers of China, an aggressive group of nomads called Kushan was pushed west by the Huns into the bleak and limitless expanse of southern Siberia. There the Kushans encountered the Scythians, another nomadic tribe that had coveted the flourishing oasis cities on the trade routes to the south but dared not act alone. United, the horde gathered courage and raged across the Central Asian steppes 2,130 years ago, leaving charred fields and human suffering. When they crossed the Amu Darya—the Oxus River to Alexander the Great—they laid waste the Greco-Bactrian lands.

At first contemptuous of city life and Greek culture, the nomads gradually became enamored of the seductive Hellenic tradition. They rebuilt the cities they had sacked and created the great Kushan Empire on their own debris. In the time between the Greco-Bactrian period and the flowering of the

The crown from Tomb VI (no. 134) was a truly nomadic headpiece. It was collapsible, with five removable tree decorations, which could be attached to the golden band.

Kushans, ancient records fail us. As these nomads struggled with the ways of urban life and empire, the chroniclers of Rome did not visit them. The period was dark until our own time, when the Tillya Tepe treasures speak of those days with resonance and clarity.

The gold of Bactria shook the world of archaeology. It was compared by critics to the treasures of King Tutankhamun's tomb in Egypt. The artifacts were found in context, not in some antique shop, not isolated from their owners or their time.

They gave us a chance to glimpse the extensive trade between the East and the West. Nowhere in antiquity have so many different objects from so many different cultures—Chinese-inspired boot buckles (no. 106), Roman coins (no. 95), daggers in a Siberian style (no. 114)—been found together in situ. The local art of Bactria discovered at Tillya Tepe is a tantalizing amalgam of influences. Never has there been an artifact like the chubby little gold Aphrodite (no. 135), who is Grecian in concept but has the distinctly

The outline of a princess emerges from Tomb VI, Tillya Tepe

non-Grecian wings of a Bactrian deity and an Indian forehead mark that indicates marital status!

We labored into the winter with fingers numb and shriveled from the bitter winds that leaked through the plywood huts we had erected. Each thin gold platelet had to be cleaned and inventoried. We could barely hold the pincers. We slept in Sheberghan, but ate noodles and canned meat from Moscow while sitting in the truck, embarrassed at how little the workers had. The plan was to return the following fall, in 1979. We posted an Afghan guard over the necropolis and headed for the Kabul Museum with the crates of excavated treasures. But conflict soon erupted, and we left Afghanistan in a hurry in February 1979, never to return to the dig.

We had excavated six tombs of what may have been the family cemetery of the rulers of a large Kushan princedom. Tomb no. II held a bespangled matriarch between 30 and 40 years old. In Tomb no. III lay another female, perhaps a teenager. A tall warrior, the only male found, was buried in Tomb no. IV. In Tomb no. V was a young woman whose relative lack of ornaments suggests she was of lower rank. From Tomb no. VI emerged another woman, also perhaps a princess, who wore a collapsible crown. The seventh tomb had not yet been examined and simply disappeared with the rains, as we sat in Moscow.

And then the country plunged into more than two decades of strife that prevented us from returning to the excavation site or the treasures. The last two graves were looted, the artifacts never recovered. The heroic efforts of a small circle preserved the excavated artifacts—20,578 objects—for our current age. Look well upon these treasures—their beauty, craftsmanship, and originality defies the ages. Here we have an original art style from the heart of the Silk Road. I believe that some time in the future, we will be able to return to the fabled land of Bactria and discover more about the mysterious culture that linked the ancient civilizations of East and West.

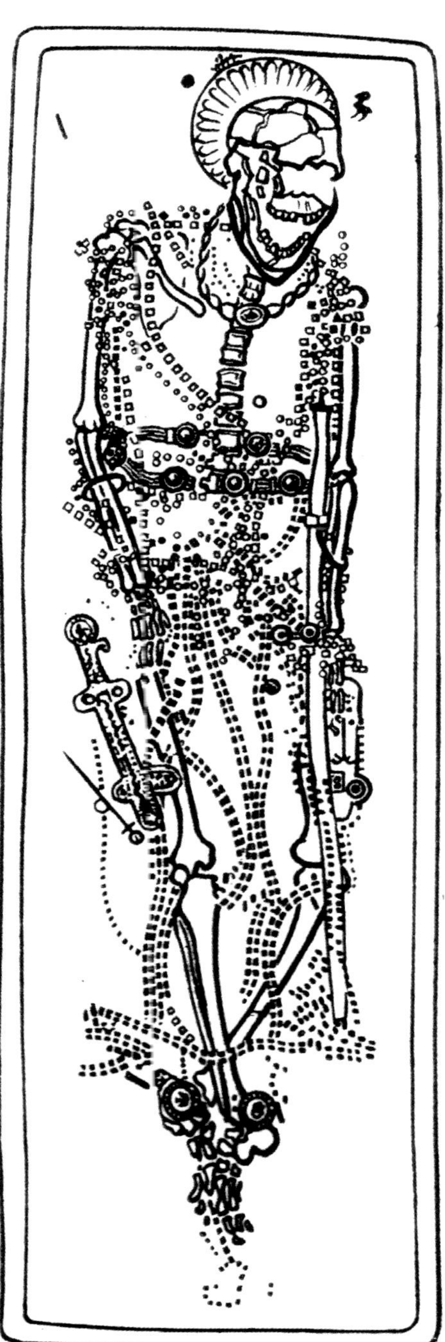

Field drawing of Tomb IV, Tillya Tepe

Tillya Tepe, the Hill of Gold: A Nomad Necropolis

VÉRONIQUE SCHILTZ
Scientific researcher, Laboratoire d'archéologie, ENS Ulm-CNRS, Paris
Corresponding member of the French "Académie des Inscriptions et Belles-Lettres"

For the man who rides across the wilderness, there comes a rising longing within him for a city.

ITALO CALVINO

Armed guards were brought to the site after the six golden tombs were found.

OPPOSITE: *"Man with Dolphin", one of seven appliqués from Tomb I, Tillya Tepe (no. 36)*

IT IS NOVEMBER 1978 IN KABUL. AN INTERNATIONAL CONGRESS on the Kushan dynasty for historians and archaeologists is being held there. The Russian Viktor Sarianidi, who has just arrived from the Tillya Tepe excavations, a Bronze Age mound, meets with a French colleague, Paul Bernard, who has been working on the excavation of the Hellenistic city of Aï Khanum. The Russian archaeologist takes out of his pocket a golden dress clasp, which has been carefully wrapped in a piece of newspaper. He shows it to his French colleague, eager to have his opinion. In uncovering the brick walls of the monumental building he had been exploring, his excavators discovered gold. It was a tomb. His Russian-Afghani team immediately had it subjected to a detailed study. The gold object is the "Man With Dolphin" (no. 36). The grave is Tomb I. In three short months another five graves would be opened.

After studying the little gold plaque for a long while, the two scholars go their separate ways. The Russian returns to his excavations at Tillya Tepe, which he brings to a satisfactory conclusion despite the vicissitudes of the Afghan winter. In February 1979 he leaves the country, which is now descending into chaos. The Frenchman returns to Paris and then has to wait a quarter of a century before he is able to revisit the devastated site of Aï Khanum.

At the time of their encounter in 1978, they were still unaware that the necropolis where Viktor Sarianidi's work was interrupted—the discovery of which could be seen as the crowning glory of a life entirely devoted to archaeology—was actually one of the missing pieces in the puzzle, which had been

Afghan excavator uncovering the dagger from Tomb IV, Tillya Tepe

sought so assiduously, the missing link between the end of Aï Khanum, the Greek city on the Oxus River laid waste by nomads, and the foundation by nomads of the great Kushan kingdom.

For if it is still to be demonstrated that the occupants of Tillya Tepe were the famed Yuezhi nomads, originating in the area bordering China, ancestors of the Kushan and founders of their empire, this site nevertheless threw a sharp light on the little-known period between the fall of the Greco-Bactrian rulers and the emergence of a power that would dominate this part of the world for four centuries. What Tillya Tepe shows, both historically and as an element of this exhibition, is that the nomads occupy an important position in the Afghan region.

Their significance went long unnoticed: After all, what traces do nomads "without walls and houses" (Herodotus, IV, 46) leave behind them, apart from their graves? If they appeared in the accounts of Bactria at all, their role was limited to a series of acts of destruction.

As so often happens, it wasn't exactly this kind of discovery that Viktor Sarianidi expected to make in the winter of 1978–1979 on the hill of Tillya Tepe, or more precisely, it was not only that. The objective of the Russian-Afghan archaeological collaboration, established in 1969, was to carry out new archaeological investigations on the Afghan left bank of the Oxus River, in addition to the excavations in Turkmenistan and the south of Uzbekistan, both then part of the Soviet Union, to gain a better understanding of the urban civilization of the former Bactria during the Bronze Age (the second millennium B.C.).

The French were the first to undertake excavations in Afghanistan, but the Russians also had a long-standing interest in Afghanistan and its archaeology. As early as 1850 Boris Dorn had conducted linguistic investigations. Vasily Grigoriev was active from 1867 onward in Kabulistan in the south and Kafiristan in the east, while the enthusiasm of Vasili Barthold initiated the archaeological investigations in Bactria (Gorshenina and Rapin 2001).

The Discovery

The Afghan-Russian team had decided to investigate a site at the oasis of Sheberghan, around a hundred kilometers to the west of Bactra (Balkh). From this island of green in a barren plain rose the ruins of Emshi Tepe, an ancient walled city with a citadel and palace. The excavations revealed that the city, probably founded in Greco-Bactrian times, had flourished by the time of the Kushan dynasty.

Some five hundred meters beyond the city walls lay a mound 3 to 4 meters high with a diameter of about 100 meters. Scraping away the upper layers, the archaeologists discovered pottery characteristic of the end of the second millennium B.C., comparable with fragments found in southern Turkmenistan. Investigating the mound further, they soon encountered the remnants of a monumental work of mud-brick construction, a terrace and columned hall, surrounded by a thick wall. Among Sarianidi's great achievements is his successful completion and publication of the excavations of this complex from the end of the Bronze Age and the beginning of the Iron Age, which he interpreted as a temple (Sarianidi 1989). Sarianidi might have been simply tempted to leave everything else aside to dig up only the gold.

The excavations showed that there had been a settlement for a brief time upon the ruins of the temple. At the start of the present era, the mound was no more than a heap of soil and clay. While carting away large quantities of earth, one of the excavators found gold. The name of the site ought perhaps to have alerted the archaeologists from the start: Tillya Tepe, as the Russians called it (the name has now been generally adopted) was known as Tilla Tepa in the local Uzbek language, meaning "Hill of Gold."

Six graves were found, set partly into the side of the mound, partly into the thick walls of crumbling brick. They were set close together, on the side facing the city of Emshi Tepe. With the assistance of Zemaryalai Tarzi, the Afghan head of the archaeological mission, Terkesh Khodzhanyazov, his trusted friend and archaeologist from Soviet Turkmenistan, and other Afghan

Visitors at the site of Tillya Tepe, with Viktor Sarianidi

colleagues, Sarianidi succeeded in carefully exposing all six graves. About 20,000 objects were revealed in the process, all to be cleaned, recorded, and packed up for transfer to the National Museum in Kabul. Just days before the excavations were to conclude, a seventh grave was located, and, who knows, maybe other graves could have been found, but time ran out with the onset of winter, and the grave was carefully covered over with the intention of investigating it further the following year. But in December 1979 the Soviet army invaded Afghanistan and war broke out. Nevertheless, Sarianidi returned to Kabul in 1982, with two photographers. A magnificent book of photographs entitled *The Golden Hoard of Bactria* was published in several languages in Leningrad in 1985. With superb photographs by Vladimir Terebenin and Leonid Bogdanov, this book was for many years the only way in which either art-lovers or specialists were able to examine these objects.

Enormous praise is due to Sarianidi for his generosity in so quickly making his findings internationally known. As a supplement to the countless articles, which immediately appeared in the international press, he wrote another two lively books, widely popular in Russia, which are also filled with precious information. In 1989, while continuing to work on important Bronze Age sites in Turkmenistan (ancient Margiana), he published what still counts as the only scientific publication on the excavations, *The Temple and Necropolis of Tillya Tepe* (Sarianidi 1989). In this work, he wisely called on the knowledge of colleagues like Gennadi Koshelenko to supplement his own expertise, which until then had focused more on proto-history. This publication formed a supplement to the book of photographs mentioned above, amending and clarifying the text in various areas. We discover that it was not only gold, silver, and other beautiful objects that were found at Tillya Tepe (providing the subject matter for superb full-page photographs), but also anthropological material such as skulls and other bones, organic residues, imprints of textiles, fragments of two bows, the remains of a folding throne, and many other items of great value to those interested in things other than precious jewels. And while we may not nowadays share all the author's conclusions, basing our knowledge on more recent research or new hypotheses, nevertheless, we continue to rely to a great extent on this publication, starting naturally enough with the structure of the tombs and their layout.

The Structure and Position of the Tombs

Leaving aside the objects lying concealed within them, it is first and foremost the structure of the tombs, laid out as they were within a mound, which points to the close involvement of the dead with the nomadic tradition. However, what we have at Tillya Tepe is far from a princely kurgan (tumulus). There is no funeral pit with a lateral burial niche and no wooden burial chamber at all. Instead, there are simple trenches covered with timber planking, spread with earth, with a lidless, cloth-wound burial coffin lying directly on the floor or positioned slightly elevated. Faced with this simple arrangement, so different from graves found elsewhere in the world of nomads, Sarianidi formulated the hypothesis that these were clandestine burials, hastily conducted by night and without the knowledge of the people of the neighboring city of Emshi Tepe, perhaps out of fear of grave robbers. But it is rather difficult to imagine that the digging of these graves and the funeral ceremonies could have taken place unnoticed by the locals, living as they did a couple of hundred meters away. Furthermore there are enough instances of tribes deviating from their usual nomadic circuits, perhaps because they were in the midst of a migration or, indeed, because they were moving to a more settled existence. In such circumstances they often turned to existing burial mounds or even natural hillocks. For the nomadic tradition required that the dead be buried within some kind of mound.

Viktor Sarianidi and Terkesh Khodzhayazov inspecting the finds from Tomb IV, Tillya Tepe

In Kossika for instance, between the Volga and the Don, at a time when nomads, probably the Alani, were moving to the west, a similar type of grave, also containing a dagger with a four-lobed sheath as at Tillya Tepe, was laid out on top of a natural mound. It appears that time or means were lacking to

Northern Afghanistan near Sheberghan

build a "proper" kurgan mound. It seems, therefore, that these were nomads whose normal rhythm of life had been disturbed. They no longer had access to the sites of their ancestral burial grounds, nor did they have the relationships and alliances with other groups that were required to move tons of earth to build a mound. Nevertheless, they found it important that their dead should be interred in the manner of their forebears. For we know that no matter how easy it is to adapt ourselves to new customs in life, when it concerns death, it is always done the old way. Even in present-day Kazakhstan one may encounter huge nomad tents of white felt (yurts) placed between two buildings to honor the dead and as a substitute for a traditional funeral.

The people of Tillya Tepe dealt with images and symbolic language in the same way as with the layout of graves: They took the local traditions into account, but modified them to suit their own customs.

The briefest glance at the plan of the necropolis makes it obvious: The position of the graves does not appear to be merely coincidental or dictated by the terrain. Not only do the five females surround the male, the male is also at the top of the mound, flanked by the most richly ornamented females in Tombs VI and III. They were, for example, the only ones to have the large, symmetrical paired clasps (nos. 79 and 136). These clasps are quite similar to 14 ancient clasps from Siberia, displayed in the Hermitage in St. Petersburg from the famous collection of Peter the Great. In addition, these three primary persons were interred within the ancient walls, while the other women (Tombs I, II, and V) lay at the foot of the mound. Moreover, the girl in Tomb V, so modestly adorned that the workers nicknamed her "Cinderella," seemed to lie quite aside.

Is it possible for us to conclude on these grounds that these graves were laid out according to a clear plan, all at once? And what are the criteria for dating the graves?

Coins and Dating the Tombs

Until now the archaeological evidence that would allow us to establish the relative chronology of these burials has not been available. Only the coins permit their placement within a broad time frame. Setting aside the Indian medallion, there are five coins to consider. Three of these are more or less connected to Parthian coinage. In addition there is an obol of Heraios, connected to the Yuezhi, and a Roman Tiberian aureus (no. 95), struck in Gaul between A.D. 16 and 37 and certainly not after A.D. 37, which provides the most precise date. The fact that there were two different types of coins (nos. 95 and 96) in a single grave, with at least a century between them, demonstrates that we must be cautious and not underestimate the period of circulation of these coins.

Tomb IV, Tillya Tepe. The preserved back of the prince's body revealed the exact placement of each appliqué, allowing the team to reconstruct the ancient garments the nomads wore.

This is especially true in the case of nomads, for whom prestige weighed more heavily than monetary value. This is well exemplified by the Scythian *bracteates* (a metal clothing adornment made to look like a coin) depicting an owl or a rooster, derived from Greek coins, and by the manner in which nomadic women from Central Asia still sew pre-1917 rubles or kopecks on their veils or use them to decorate necklaces. Nevertheless it seems reasonable to assume that the most recent coin, the Tiberian aureus, which must date from A.D. 37 at the latest, and probably reached Tillya Tepe fairly quickly (by sea, and then via southern or central India, where such coins have not infrequently been found) must be fairly close in date to the burial itself. The fact that no coins of later date were encountered supports this assumption.

To go further than this we would need clear indications about the relative chronology of the individual graves. Certain factors suggest that they all date from the same period. First there is the similarity of the structure of the graves, then the strong consistency between certain objects found within them, and most of all the premeditated, hierarchical manner of the burials, with the females surrounding the solitary male. It would be reassuring if this could be explained as the consequence of a bloody battle or an epidemic, since the notion of five or perhaps even more women following their lord and master to their deaths is not terribly appealing. However, we know from Herodotus (IV, 71), as well as from various other excavations, that after his death a man did not go alone to the hereafter, but was accompanied by his "household." And if we are to believe the same Herodotus (IV, 72), they did not scruple to sacrifice 50 young people in honor of the deceased, a year after his death. It is therefore quite possible, even probable, that we have here a leader accompanied in death by the womenfolk among his followers. If that were the case, the funerary rites must have taken place at the end of the first quarter or during the second quarter of the first century A.D.

The Parthian coins tell a different kind of story. The Parthians had a good deal of contact with nomads in the second and first centuries B.C. Sometimes they attacked them directly, other times they drove them back, or at any rate held them at bay sufficiently to stabilize the situation on their eastern borders. According to the travel journal *Parthian Stations* written by Isidore of Charax at the start of the first century A.D., the whole of the west of modern Afghanistan (the Herat region and the Sistan Province) was under Parthian rule at the start of the modern era. Parthian coins with a countermark were also found, raising the suspicion that tribal leaders and minor nomad rulers had acquired the right to mint coins. This is confirmed by the imitation in gold of a Parthian coin from Tomb VI (no. 146). This was an unexpected find, since all coins, whether of Greco-Bactrian or Parthian origin, as well as those that may have been struck by local chiefs, were of silver or bronze. A coinage system based on a gold standard was only introduced later under Vima Kadphises and the rule of the Kushans. So, the discovery in the hand of the female in Tomb VI of a gold coin displaying affinities with Vima Kadphises (Parthian) coinage points to her clan's link with the Parthians.

Bejeweled dagger and sheath from an ancient nomadic burial at Dachi, near the Black Sea

Garments, Weapons, and Jewelry

One can read in the catalog entries about the function and nature of some of the garments, jewelry, and weapons. It is important to remember the difficult and uncertain nature of certain identifications. Since virtually no textiles have survived, the clothing of these long-dead people can only be reconstructed by looking carefully at the gold jewelry—brooches, clasps, appliqués, and bracteates—and the manner in which these were placed. However, this is anything but simple. How are we to distinguish, among a profusion of materials, almost all stitched with gold thread, between the veil over the cist, the shroud, and the dead person's own clothing? The clothing itself also consisted of various layers: a shirt, tunic, jacket, and cloak, one on top of the other. The male probably wore a short jacket and a kaftan, with trousers tucked into high leggings, as can be seen on the large bronze statue of a Parthian ruler from Shami (southwest Iran) in the museum in Tehran.

The costumes of the women from the different graves were not identical. This may be because the women did not necessarily belong to the same tribe, or more probably because they did not all have the same social status. It has been suggested, for example, that the female in Tomb V was a young woman, who had not yet had children. All the women did, however, wear the type of garb that is still very common in this part of the world, the *shalwar kameez,* a tunic over trousers.

The man's weapons—two bows, a long sword, a dagger with a four-lobed sheath, and an additional sheath for various knives—are all characteristic of the nomads. Like the horse, present here but no longer buried next to its rider, and the four-lobed sheath, which was originally intended to secure the weapon tightly to the upper leg so that it could not hurt the rider when galloping, but which has here obviously a ceremonial function, it seems that the belt was worn more as a sign of power than to gird the waist. We are dealing therefore not with a common horseman but with a knight, a warlord, buried without a helmet or armor, probably because these were part of the actual fighting equipment and could not be counted as symbols displaying power. Head ornaments, pendants on either side of the face, earrings, necklaces, bracelets, anklets, rings in abundance—the briefest glance at these objects leaves no doubt as to their magnificence and great variety. What is less clear are the traditions, models, and influences that determined the forms and decoration of these objects and which the catalogue entries attempt to point out. One significant step forward came from the investigation of the gold and gems conducted by Thomas Calligaro of the Laboratoire des Musées de France, to whom we are indebted for their identification. Perhaps one day we will be able to gain a greater understanding of the relationship between the objects from Tillya Tepe and those of Peter the Great's Siberian collection, the world of nomadic tribes like the Sarmatians, the Alani, and others of the Great Migrations.

Even though the iconography of the Tillya Tepe artifacts may sometimes seem strange to us, because the models that inspired them have been misinterpreted by their makers, nevertheless the astonishingly high standard of the goldsmith's work can only stir our admiration. Little or no filigree work is evident, but there is surprisingly deft granulation and virtuoso inlay work.

Who were the makers of these superb objects? All the evidence indicates that a good number of the objects came from the same workshop. In the absence of a visual vocabulary, which would have required adaptation if borrowed from an external source, the tricks of the trade were transmitted from generation to generation in the same manner as can still be observed today in goldsmiths' shops in India.

Composite Art

As has been said—and can also be seen in the catalog entries—the art of Tillya Tepe is a mixture. There are Chinese objects or imitations, objects from India or those which reflect Indian traditions, and above all objects that follow Hellenistic traditions, which is even more apparent in the style than in the thematic repertoire, the latter being closely associated with ancient animal motifs from the art of the steppes. Nomadic art is almost universally characterized by its eclecticism, except perhaps at Arzhan (southern Siberia), but that is perhaps due to our lack of knowledge about it. One thinks, for example, of the art of Altai (also in Siberia), which both in the east and the west is largely based on borrowing, or of the finds from the site of Filippovka in the southern Urals, and, of the highly detailed and diverse style that characterizes Greco-Scythian art, an admireable monstrosity in terms of aesthetics.

The mixture we see here is sometimes bizarre in effect, and the images are not always free of visual misunderstandings. For example, we have the goddess Athena, her arm extended to hold a lance, but the lance is absent. In another case she is shown sitting, but without a seat. Elsewhere the small Kushan Aphrodite figure is standing erect between what can only be the pillars of a throne. It is also puzzling that certain well-known motifs are absent, such as the Bactrian camel, which oddly enough is found on the

Handle of the dagger from the site of Dachi, Black Sea region, depicting a Bactrian camel

Golden statues from the Siberian collections at the Hermitage Museum

pommel of the four-lobed dagger from Dachi on the Sea of Azov in southern Russia.

However, there is one motif that occurs so frequently in these tombs that it cannot be purely a matter of coincidence or due to the personal preference of the artists, and that is the heart motif. Be it smooth or faceted, wide or long, inlaid or not, there is not a single grave where the heart was not found in some form. These artifacts are often in turquoise and from an artistic perspective this is quite an undertaking, as it is more difficult to shape turquoise into the form of a heart than it is to produce a comma or a circle. If no one until now has noticed this omnipresence, it is no doubt because the heart has become such a common motif that we have turned blind to it. We also need to be careful not to misinterpret it. The heart here does not represent a "lady of the heart," or warm feelings. We will understand the meaning of the motif if we look closely at the back side of the handle of the dagger with the four-lobed sheath (no. 114), which shows the stem of a plant leaf. This is not the heart-shaped leaf of sarsaparilla, water lily, or poplar, but probably an ivy leaf. The question remains why this plant should have such a prominent place among the weaponry of this leader. In fact, despite what we might expect, this motif was not so common in ancient times. This motif certainly needs further investigation.

The most important question raised by this necropolis has intentionally been left aside until now: Which nomadic tribe was responsible for Tillya Tepe? Was it the Yuezhi, driven from the steppes of northwest China with the rise of the Xiongnu kingdom around the second century B.C., who destroyed Aï Khanum, and, once they had crossed the Oxus, settled there? Or was it, as the great number of connections suggests, the Sakas or Sakarauks, moving within the sphere of influence of the Parthian state, who perhaps had always been in this area? To which tribe did the nomads buried at Tillya Tepe belong? Where were the grazing lands of their parents and grandparents?

The nomads were numerous, infinitely more numerous than we might imagine, as their numbers declined steeply with the rise of the great sedentary states. We should probably interpret their movement forward less in terms of conquest and enmity and more in terms of sheer numbers. We should also remember that their world was like a sea with its waves, its eddies, its whirlwinds, which mixed up the waters; making it difficult to identify nomadic groups by name (cf. Schiltz 2002, pp. 874–877).

We are beginning to know more about the people of Kangju, a state north of Bactria (in Khorasmia and Sogdiana). But what was the situation of this Sheberghan oasis, backed by the Hindu Kush, but open to the steppes? It is true that the major centers of Bactra and Dilberjin lay less than a hundred kilometers distant, but could it not have been far enough for Tillya Tepe to escape Yuezhi influence, while the Sheberghan oasis remained active on the great trading route of the East? This would have been a situation comparable with the ethnic diversity of the present population of the area, with its many and various warlords.

Things being what they are, it is futile to look for a perfect correlation between race, language, and culture, not to mention artistic forms. And this is perhaps the most important lesson to draw from this superb collection of finds: That all art represents an alloy and that the Afghan soil was the crucible for this unique alloy.

The back side of the Tillya Tepe dagger (no. 114) from Tomb IV

Tillya Tepe, Tomb I

TOMB I LAY ON THE WEST SIDE OF THE mound, behind the walls surrounding the former temple. This was the first grave to be discovered, and it was found to be somewhat damaged before the actual excavations began. Nevertheless, it was possible to establish the dimensions of the simple rectangular pit: It was 2.5 by 1.3 meters and 2 meters deep. The body of a young female between 20 and 30 years of age and of average height (1.58 meters) lay on her back, with her arms by her body and her head to the north. It is probable that she wore no diadem or crown, but her head was richly adorned with jewelery. Seven small appliqué images of the "Man With a Dolphin" (no. 36), interpreted by the archaeologists as possibly decorating plaits of hair, were either fastened to the hair itself or to the upper outside of the clothing. A hair decoration (no. 38) lay below the neck, while a silver pin and a colored cylindrical ornament (no. 54) were found close to the left temple. A single boat-shaped earring (no. 42), lay in the area of the right ear. Two rosettes with pendants (no. 41), were found to the right of the body. Finally, she wore a simple chain around her neck, with a closure formed by two small tubes (no. 43).

Based on the remnants of gold thread and pearls found below the body it is possible that the woman wore a shawl or a cape around her shoulders or perhaps two robes. The arrangement of the threads and pearls suggests a piece of fabric embroidered with large motifs, possibly plants, similar to those on the robes found in frozen graves in the Altai Mountains, as well as Afghan coats of reversed sheepskin. This garment or over-garment was held together with a pair of round clasps of solid gold (no. 37).

Square bracteates with turquoise inlay work were sewn onto the sleeves (no. 49), as were double gold spirals in the form of volutes (no. 50), bracteates with turquoise inlay showing a heart with four droplets (no. 51) and—at shoulder level—"masks" (no. 48).

A badly damaged coin (an obol of Sanab-Heraeus), probably held by the deceased in her hand, was found in the area of the pelvis. The date of the coin is unclear, but it may come from the first quarter of the first century A.D.

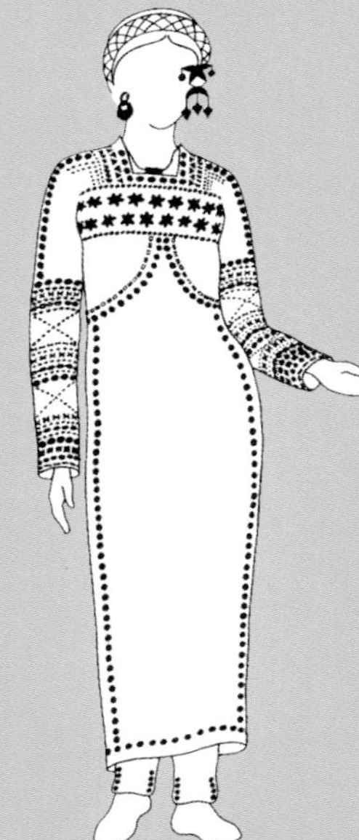

36 EACH OF THE SEVEN PLATES shows a male figure seen from the front, the head inclined slightly to the right, the upper body naked above a sort of skirt made of three large, veined acanthus leaves. Below the skirt we see an undulating double tail rather than legs, with volutes on either side, ending at the waist with a cloverleaf.

This monster—half man and half snake—bears a great fish on its shoulders, draped around the neck, with the left hand next to its head and the right hand holding the tail. The right hand also holds a tool, possibly a shovellike oar, or short paddle.

The monster's hair is indicated by dots. The broad face with its almond-shaped eyes looks flattened. The nose is wide, with pronounced nostrils. Only the left ear is shown, the earlobe marked with a recess. A double arched and hatched motif is applied in the area of the elbows and above the shoulders, broadening out as it descends. It was thought to be a plant motif but is more probably two wings.

At the base of the appliqué three rounded recesses alternate with double crescents. The simple gold leaf reliefs here show a goldsmith's arrangement found on various other jewels at Tillya Tepe (nos. 72, 73 and 129).

The plates are stamped, but may not have used a single matrix. Leaving aside the engraved details (for example the facial expression, the navel, and the breast), the attitude, particularly that of the head and the shape of the cheekbones varies between the different examples.

A comparable figure can be seen on an ivory object from Begram (no. 151), another example of which is in the collection of the Musée Guimet (MG no. 19011). There seems little doubt that the figure is a water god. The oar is one of the traditional attributes of the Tritons. The fish has the head of a dolphin but a scaly body and is comparable with the fish shown on the clasps (nos. 59 and 80) where they are ridden by cupids. This motif is inspired by a depiction of a dolphin, a very common subject in Greek art. However the great head and the flattened snout, combined with the carp-like scales, are reminiscent of the huge fish living in the nearby Oxus River (Amu Darya): a catfish or a variety of sturgeon. Could the bearer of the fish be the god of the Oxus? The most persuasive comparison brought forward as an explanation of this image is a creature whose image was quite common among the Scythian nomads living to the west of the steppes from the last third of the fourth century B.C. Its visual vocabulary derives from the "half-plant goddess"

36
Seven appliqué plates, showing the "Man With a Dolphin"
Tillya Tepe, Tomb I
Second quarter of the 1st century A.D.
Gold
4.1 x 2.9 cm
National Museum of Afghanistan
04.40.303

found in the Greek or Hellenized art of the time (including mosaics in Olynthus and Vergina in northern Greece, a column capital from the palace of Euagoras at Salamis on Cyprus, and a Thracian grave at Sveshtari in Bulgaria). Just as in the objects exhibited, the three-pointed "skirt" combined with plants and "snake-foot" forms (see Tolstaya Mogila and Tsimbalka in Artamonov 1968, pl. 186). The figure often has wings (op. cit. pl. 189, 230, 308), but it is always feminine. She is identified as the "snake woman" who Herodotus tells us (IV, 9) was believed by the nomads to be the daughter of the river Borysthenes (the Dnieper) and the mother of all Scythians. This explanation by the Greek historian tells us a great deal about the substantial role played by this creature, who belongs both to earth and to water, in the world of the steppes, and shows how important was the notion of a power renewing the forces of nature, uniting in itself both the male and the female. The Bactrian culture of the Bronze Age also had its "snake man" (Azarpay 1991). As well as the "Mistress of the Animals" from Tomb VI (no. 137) a "Dragon Master" was also found in Tomb II (no. 61). In this world of steppe and desert, where water was of crucial importance, the "Man With a Dolphin" was naturally closely associated with power over water, and with its ability to create fertility.

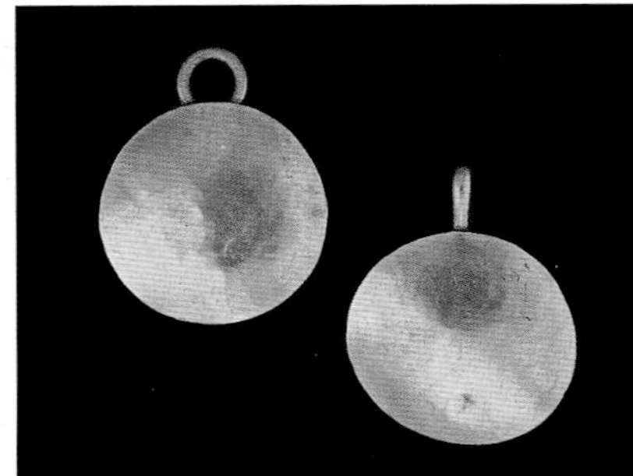

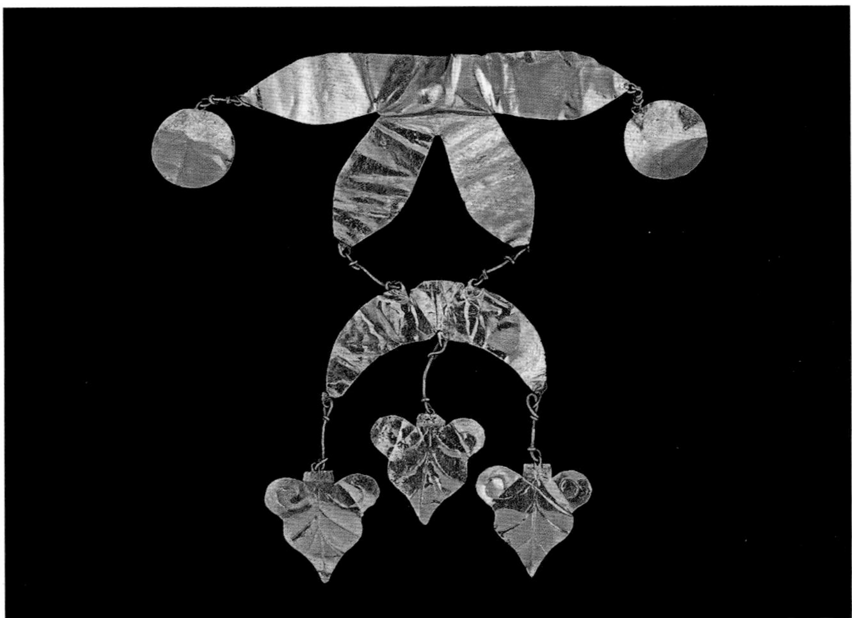

38 THIS HAIR ADORNMENT WAS MADE from gold leaf, with five excised leaves. Small disks are attached to the two outermost leaves. The two innermost leaves retain a crescent, with three pendant veined leaves. A 1 cm tube is fitted to the rear, allowing the ornament to be attached vertically to a rod. Two hairpins found in Tomb VI are broadly similar in appearance (no. 142).

37
A pair of smooth, round clasps
Tillya Tepe, Tomb I
Second quarter of the 1st century A.D.
Gold
Diam. 3.3 cm
National Museum of Afghanistan
04.40.301

38
Hair ornament
Tillya Tepe, Tomb I
Second quarter of the 1st century A.D.
Gold
H. 6.5 cm
National Museum of Afghanistan
04.40.305

39
Five-leaved brooch in the form of a flower wreath
Tillya Tepe, Tomb I
Second quarter of the 1st century A.D.
Gold, turquoise, mother of pearl
Diam. 5.0 cm
National Museum of Afghanistan
04.40.299

40
Six-leaved rosettes
Tillya Tepe, Tomb I
Second quarter of
the 1st century A.D.
Gold
Diam. 3.5 cm
National Museum
of Afghanistan
04.40.298

41
Two ornaments in the form of flowers, with a "small tree" and pendants
Tillya Tepe, Tomb I
Second quarter of
the 1st century A.D.
Gold
Diam. 4.0 cm
National Museum
of Afghanistan
04.40.297

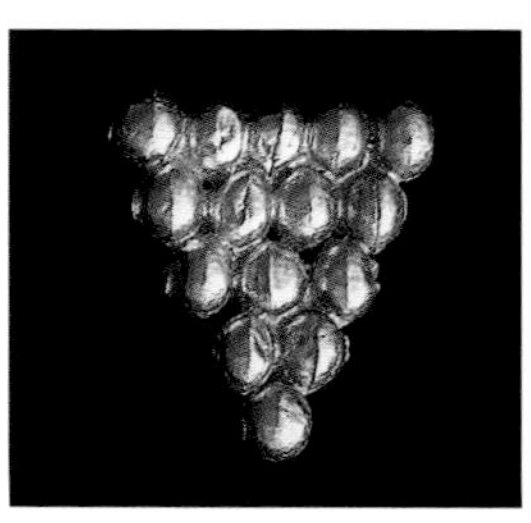

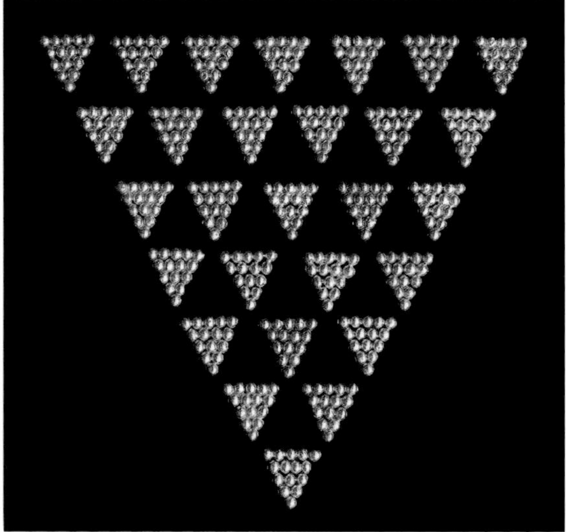

42 THIS TYPE OF EARRING, boat-shaped, with a hook, in this case hollow and granulated, is a not uncommon form of Greek jewelry and is also found to the north of the Black Sea. This example however is by itself, and an open ring has been added to the hook. This may indicate that it is an unmatched earring, reused as a hair ornament.

43 THIS SIMPLE CHAIN IS MADE from interlinking bent rings, clasped together in the middle. The fastening consists of a pair of tubes, hinged at the ends, which can be fixed together by means of a vertical rod with a nail head.

42
Earring
Tillya Tepe, Tomb I
Second quarter of the 1st century A.D.
Gold
2.9 x 2.4 cm
National Museum of Afghanistan
04.40.300

43
Chain and fastening
Tillya Tepe, Tomb I
Second quarter of the 1st century A.D.
Gold
L. 45.0 cm
National Museum of Afghanistan
04.40.304

44
Triangular granulated bracteates
Tillya Tepe, Tomb I
Second quarter of the 1st century A.D.
Gold
1.3 x 1.0 cm
National Museum of Afghanistan
04.40.323

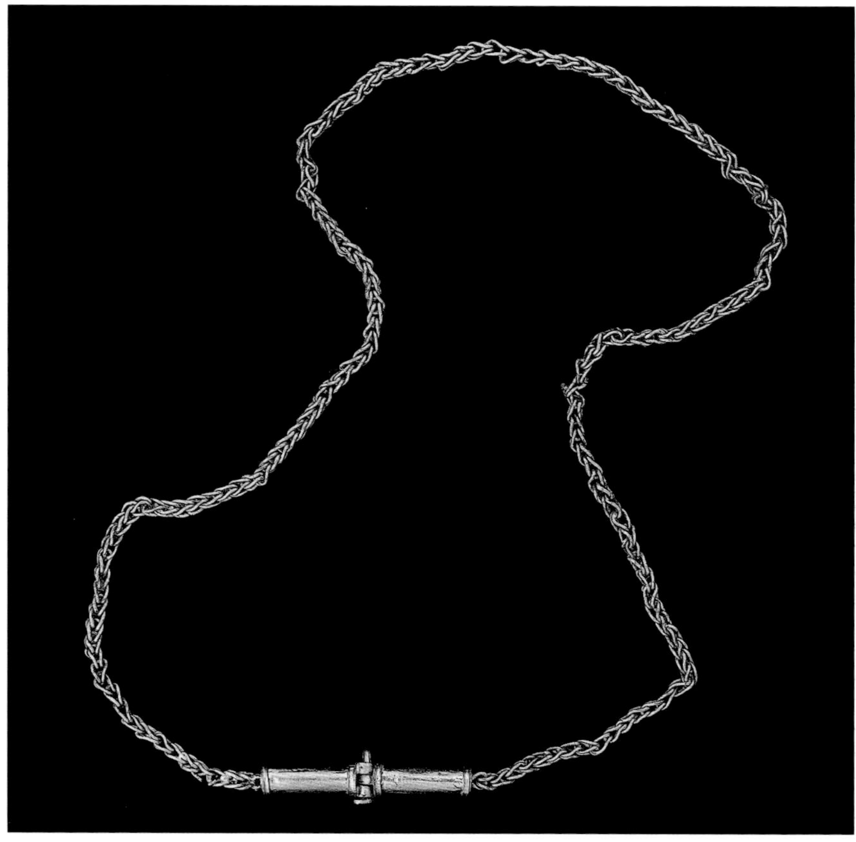

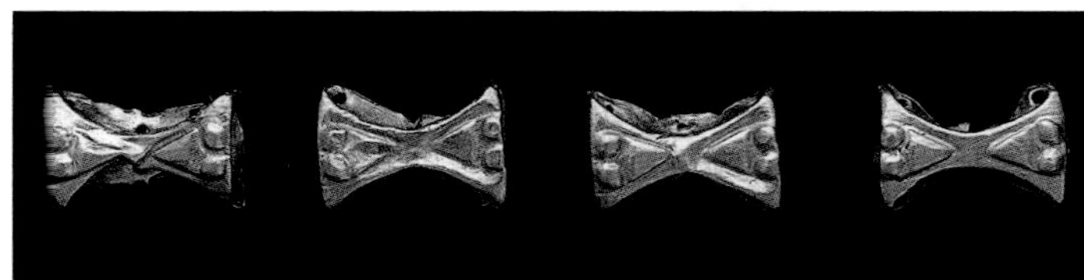

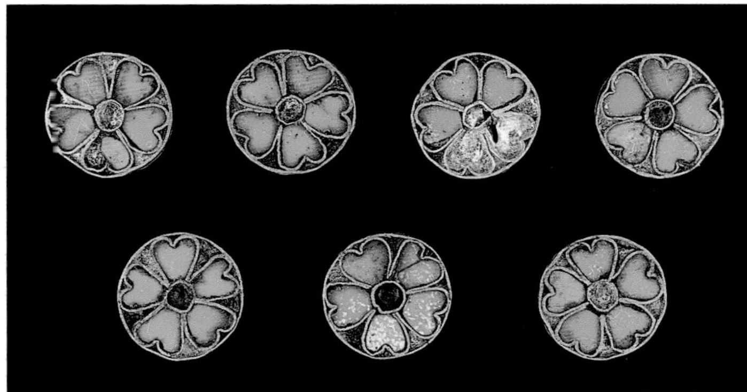

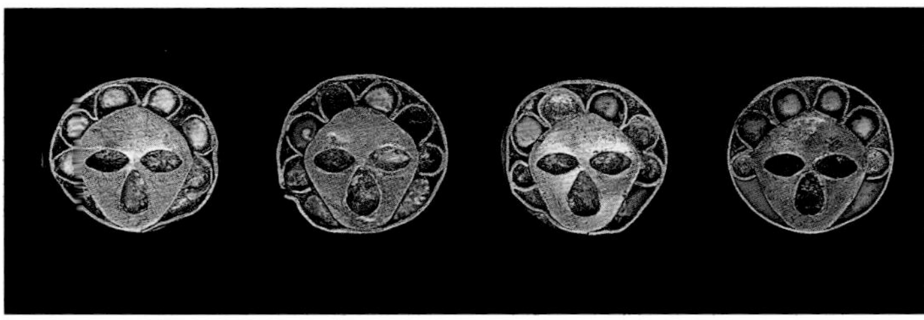

45
Bracteates made from opposed triangles with imitation granulation
Tillya Tepe, Tomb I
Second quarter of the 1st century A.D.
Gold
1.1 x 0.7 cm
National Museum of Afghanistan
04.40.309

46
Bracteates made from opposed triangles, inlaid and with a granulated finish
Tillya Tepe, Tomb I
Second quarter of the 1st century A.D.
Gold, turquoise, lapis lazuli, pyrites
0.4 x 0.35 cm
National Museum of Afghanistan
04.40.331

47
Round, five-leaved bracteates around a core
Tillya Tepe, Tomb I
Second quarter of the 1st century A.D.
Gold, turquoise, garnet
Diam. 1.0 cm
National Museum of Afghanistan
04.40.327

48
Bracteates in the shape of a "mask"
Tillya Tepe, Tomb I
Second quarter of the 1st century A.D.
Gold, turquoise, garnet, ivory (eyes)
Diam. 1.0 cm
National Museum of Afghanistan
04.40.322

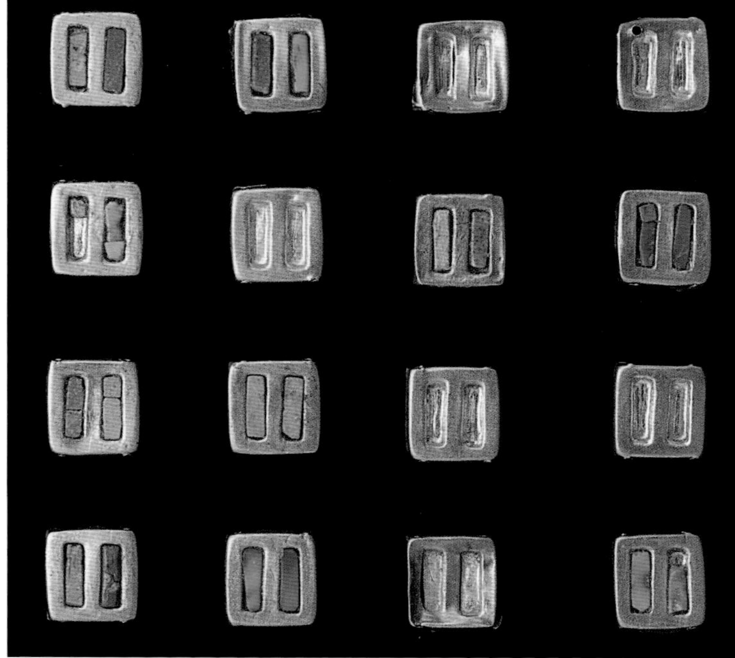

49
Square bracteates with inlay work in turquoise
Tillya Tepe, Tomb I
Second quarter of the 1st century A.D.
Gold, turquoise
0.9 x 0.8 cm
National Museum of Afghanistan
04.40.330

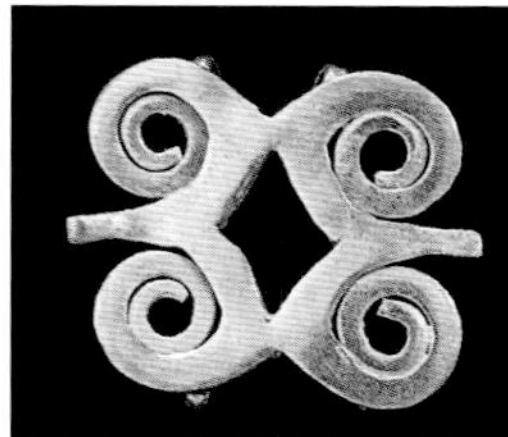

50
Volutiform bracteates (opposed ram's heads)
Tillya Tepe, Tomb I
Second quarter of the 1st century A.D.
Gold
1.1 x 1.0 cm
National Museum of Afghanistan
04.40.321

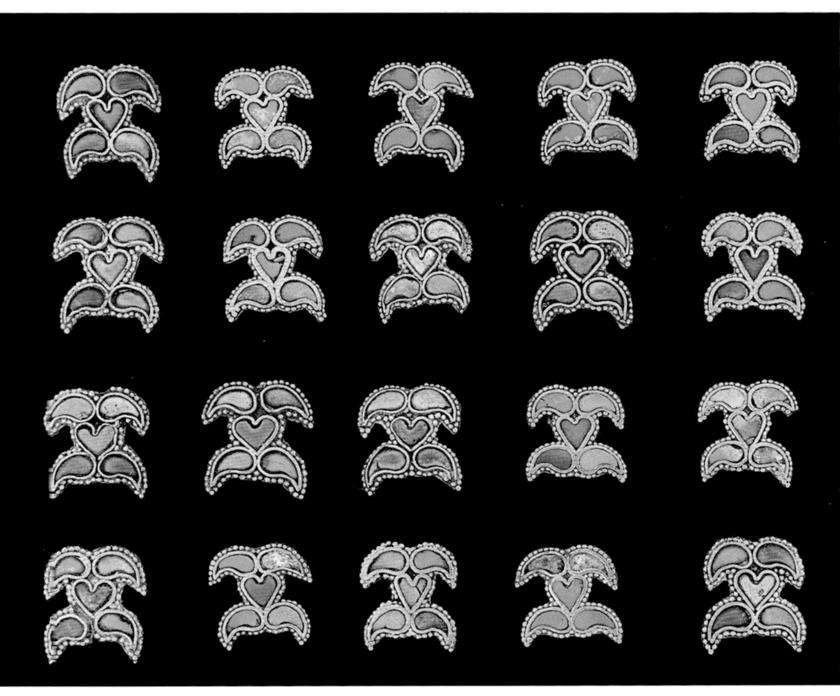

51
Bracteates shaped like a heart and four droplets with an edge lined with granulation
Tillya Tepe, Tomb I
Second quarter of the 1st century A.D.
Gold, turquoise, lapis lazuli
1.3 x 1.1 cm
National Museum of Afghanistan
04.40.312

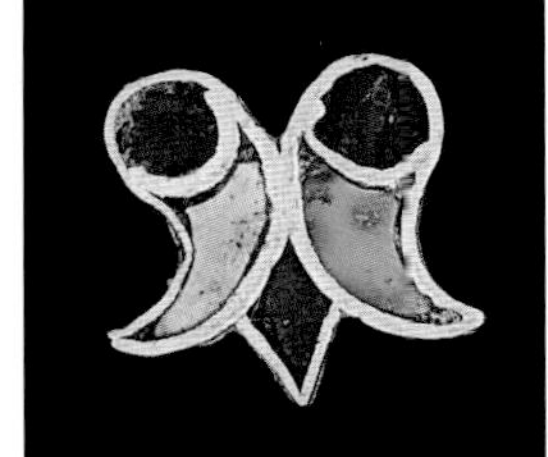

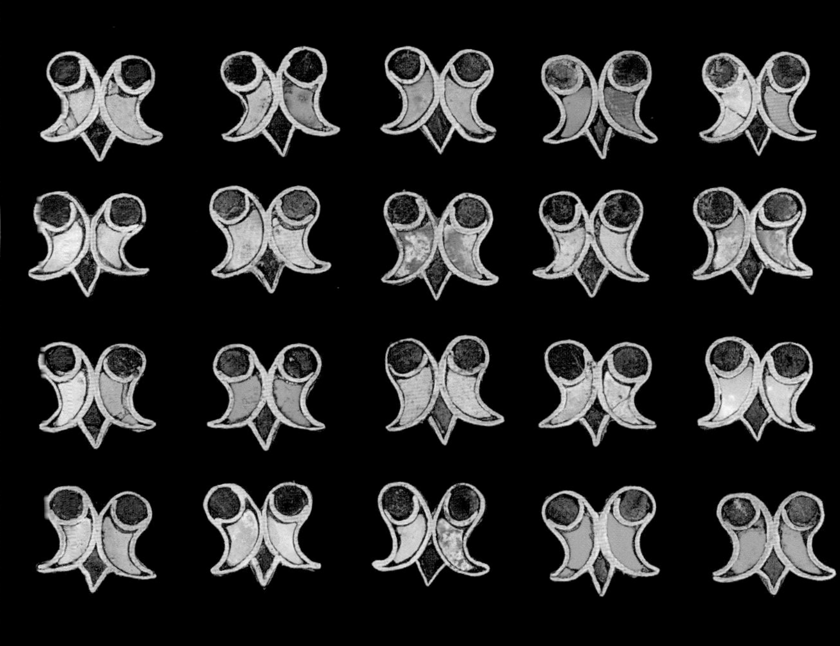

52
Three-leaved bracteates (lotus?) with inlay work
Tillya Tepe, Tomb I
Second quarter of the 1st century A.D.
Gold, turquoise, pyrites
0.9 x 0.9 cm
National Museum of Afghanistan
04.40.313

54 THE GOLDEN CYLINDER is set off above and below with a finely granulated border and edge, with a double row of bezels or stone settings placed with their convex faces together. The inlay work is arranged so that an attractive pattern of color emerges. The matte turquoises contrast beautifully with the white gloss of the mother-of-pearl lozenges and alternate with sparkling, transparent red garnets, probably of Indian origin.

The flat sides of the drum have, first, a series of five carefully placed holes to allow a thread to be inserted, and, second, four larger slots, made more crudely with a tool stuck through the object from top to bottom, damaging the gold leaf. It may be that the object originally had some other function.

A comparable golden cylinder with a granulated rim but also with pendants was discovered in grave 2 at Pazyryk in Siberia's Altai Mountains (Rudenko 1953, fig. 58 and pl. XXVII, 10); this is thought to be an earring. Cylindrical or spool-shaped earrings have also been found in Sarmatian graves along the river Don (Schiltz 2001, nos. 171, 280). A cylindrical earring was also discovered at Dalverzin-tepe in Uzbekistan (Pugachenkova 1978, fig. 77). The silver pin also found beside the woman's left temple gave the excavator the idea that the cylinder might be attached to the hair with the pin. It is also possible that this ring was directly braided into the hair, or at least reused as such a hair ornament.

This would account for the large holes, as knotted or braided hair could be passed through these, a practice encountered elsewhere among nomads.

53
Rosettes of fourteen leaves with a round pendant
Tillya Tepe, Tomb I
Second quarter of the 1st century A.D.
Gold
Diam. 1.5 and 1.2 cm
National Museum of Afghanistan
04.40.307

54
Cylindrical ornament in the form of a drum
Tillya Tepe, Tomb I
Second quarter of the 1st century A.D.
Gold, turquoise, garnet, mother-of-pearl
1.4 x 1.1 cm
National Museum of Afghanistan
04.40.326

Tillya Tepe, Tomb II

THIS TOMB WAS PLACED BEHIND the northern wall of the temple. It was oriented northeast-southwest: In other words, the corners pointed to the four points of the compass. The grave formed a rectangle of 3 by 1.6 meters. The base was 2 meters below the mound's ground level.

The coffin was 2.2 meters long and 0.65 meters wide and rested on wooden supports. There was no lid, but there were traces of plaster on the outside of the coffin. The presence of round gold and silver plates indicated that a cloth had been wound around it. The coffin was slightly out of line with the axis of the tomb, and the head of the occupant was to the north. Was this due to chance, or to the ground conditions? The orientation of the corners of the excavated grave to the four points of the compass and the position of the body not completely in line with the axis of the grave (although the head was generally to the south) are noteworthy. These features match what is found in the graves of the Alani at the time when this group appeared halfway through the first century A.D. in the steppes near the Don River and introduced a style of polychrome objects in gold and turquoise.

The deceased person, a woman in her thirties or forties, lay on her back. Judging by the location of the appliqués found, she probably wore a high conical head covering of felt or leather. High conical head coverings were generally worn among the nomads, from the Ukrainian steppes to the Altai Mountains. Some of the Saka tribes even bore names meaning "high caps" (the Tigraxauda, mentioned in an inscription by Cyrus in Behistun, Iran, and the Orthocorybantes mentioned by Herodotus). In this case, we are dealing with a head covering lacking ear flaps, so that it is comparable to those worn by the Parthians and Kushans, and even more similar to the earliest known women's headwear, found to the west of the steppes but also to the east, in Tuva, where brooches were found with lengths of 30 to 35 cm alongside a woman in a grave at Arzhan.

Framing the face lay two ornaments with pendants (no. 76), probably attached to the hair, and a pair of double-sided pendants showing the "Dragon Master" (no. 61). As well as a necklace of gold and black beads (no. 78) and three rings (nos. 55, 56 and 57), she also wore on each wrist a bracelet with antelope heads (no. 58) and rings around her ankles (no. 77).

Various pieces of jewelry were attached to her clothing. Clasps with cupids riding dolphins (no. 59) held together the two sides of a long gown at breast level. This garment had a large number of droplet bracteates in gold attached (no. 74). The "Kushan Aphrodite" (no. 60) was placed as an ornament centrally on the breast. Figures of musicians (no. 75) were found near the shoulders and probably form the two ends of a neckline ornament. The bust was covered with heart-shaped bracteates (no. 63) and appliqués in the form of vertical strips (no. 72) echoing strips on the shoulders (no. 73). The hem of the sleeves was decorated with rows of bracteates, including a ram's head (no. 62) and a stepped pyramid (no. 67). Above these were worn various types of amulet, in the form of an axe, a fish, a pomegranate, a hand (nos. 69 and 70) and a foot (nos. 68 and 71). The hem of the trousers was also decorated with a row of appliqués.

A gold cylinder, possibly a scepter, lay close to the right hand. A Chinese mirror lay on the breast, probably between the tunic and the outer gown. A woven basket decorated with round appliqué work ornaments (nos. 64, 65 and 66) had been placed on the legs. The tomb contained an iron axe and two knives of a type also found in Siberia. At the feet lay a silver box.

This tomb was apparently the only one that did not contain coins.

55 THE RING HAS A GOLD SETTING, surrounding a white gold panel depicting the goddess, sitting but lacking a seat, with her face to the left but the upper body facing forward. She holds her right arm outstretched, the hand palm down. The left arm seems to rest on the hip and at the same time to hold a lance and shield. She carries a Greco-Bactrian helmet with a plume hanging down to the rear. Her features are pronounced: A long, sharp nose extends from the forehead; she has an open mouth with well-marked lips and a prominent chin. She appears to wear a necklace. The hem of her tunic is indicated by a double row of dots at the knee.

The name of the goddess Athena is engraved in reverse at the left, indicating that the ring was intended as a seal. Athena was a very popular subject among the nomads, probably because of her warlike nature (see cat. nos. 56, 105 and 127); the same was true of the Kushan dynasty.

56 THE ATTITUDE OF ATHENA in this piece is comparable with that shown in the previous ring, except that a seat is suggested by means of a curved line, the goddess appearing to float above it. The head is barely delineated. A similar line of stippling is shown at the knees, indicating the hem of a tunic; however, the folds of the robe reach down to the ground.

The goddess radiates calm, but holds a shield before her as though she was walking forward, and the left arm reaches back as though leaning on a lance, but this is not visible. These omissions provide a good demonstration of how iconography can lose certain details over the course of time, thereby losing its meaning.

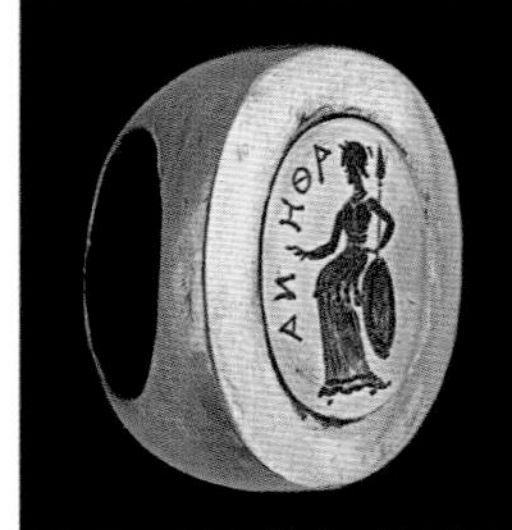

55
Ring with an image of Athena
Tillya Tepe, Tomb II
Second quarter of the 1st century A.D.
Gold
3.0 x 2.7 cm
National Museum of Afghanistan
04.40.116

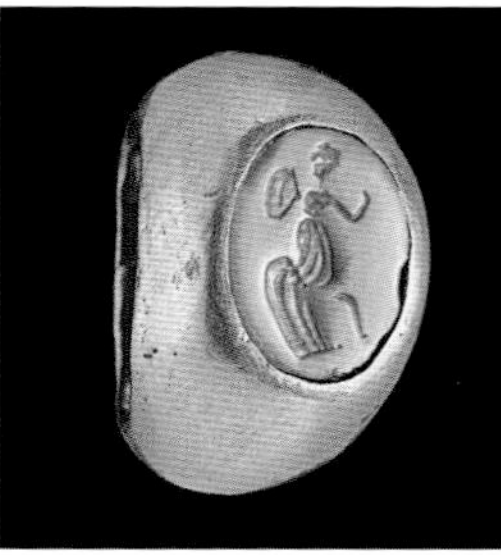

56
Ring with an intaglio depicting Athena
Tillya Tepe, Tomb II
Second quarter of the 1st century A.D.
Gold, turquoise
3.0 x 2.7 cm
National Museum of Afghanistan
04.40.117

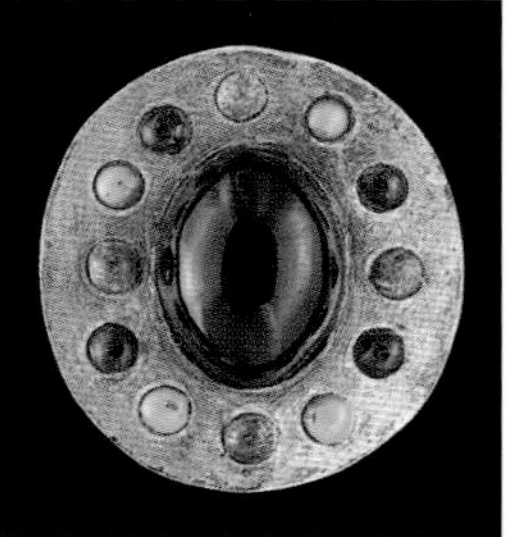

57
Ring, with an amethyst in a setting of twelve precious stones
Tillya Tepe, Tomb II
Second quarter of the 1st century A.D.
Gold, amethyst, turquoise, lapis lazuli, amber 3.3 x 3.0 cm
National Museum of Afghanistan 04.40.115

58 THIS IS AN EXAMPLE OF THE practicality of the visual vocabulary of the steppes. The animal, probably an antelope, has a bent spine, which determines the shape of the bracelet. His nose rests on his outstretched feet. The horns and ears are inlaid with turquoise and point backward as though flattened by the wind while the animal runs. Turquoise droplets inserted in the gold indicate the shoulders, hips, and hooves.

Similar brackets that were typical of the art of the nomads were also found with the Oxus treasure (now partly held by the British Museum), in the burial site at Dachi by the Sea of Azov in southern Russia (Schiltz 2001 no. 236), and in the Siberian collection of Peter the Great (now in the Hermitage in St. Petersburg). The bracelets show clear signs of wear, indicating that they were in actual use.

58
Pair of bracelets (antelopes?)
Tillya Tepe, Tomb II
Second quarter of the 1st century A.D.
Gold, turquoise, carnelian
8.5 x 6.3 cm
National Museum of Afghanistan
04.40.114

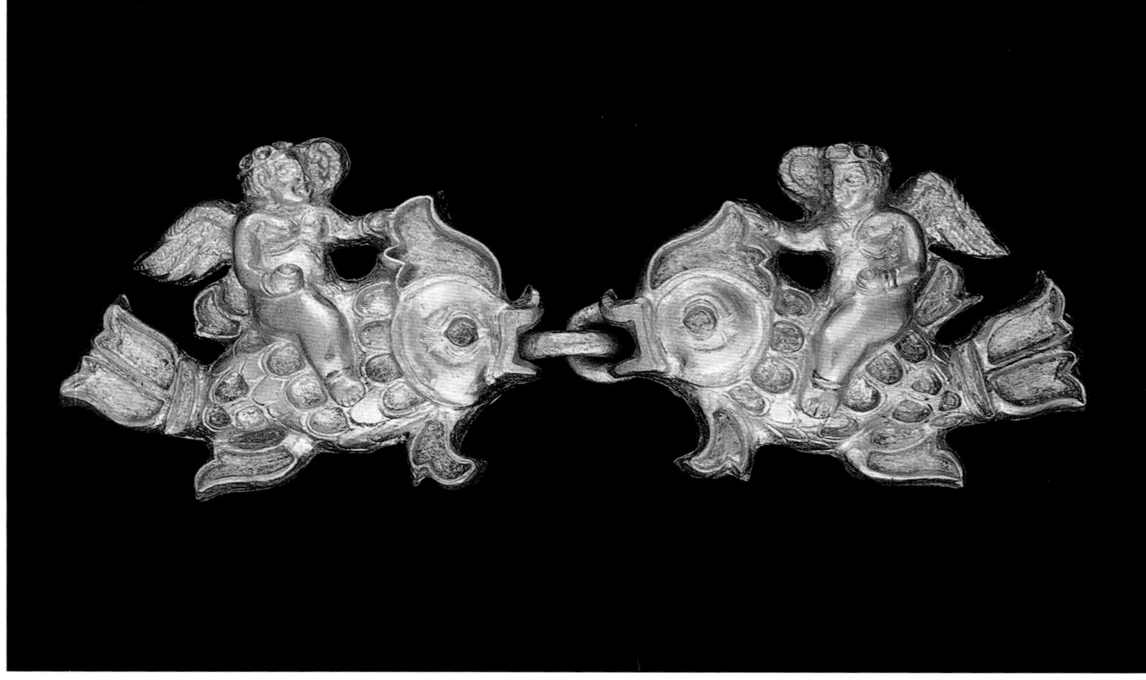

59
A pair of clasps. Cupid figures mounted on dolphins
Tillya Tepe, Tomb II
Second quarter of the 1st century A.D.
Gold
4.5 x 3.0 cm
National Museum of Afghanistan
04.40.175

59 THIS PAIR OF SYMMETRICAL CLASPS is joined by means of a hook and ring attached to the noses of the dolphins. To the rear are four attachments points. On the front are winged cupids, mounted on large fish with rounded heads. Their bodies feature deep recesses which were intended to contain inlay (see also no. 80). When carefully examined these creatures bear little resemblance to dolphins. They are unlike the animals depicted as mounts in the countless images of Taras, Arion, or Eros on the island of Delos. Neither do they resemble the dolphin shown on a stone in the fountain at Aï Khanum, where the water jet in the form of a theatrical mask was found (no. 33), or the dolphin with a cupid, which sits at the feet of Caesar Augustus in the famous statue from Prima Porta in the Vatican Museum, the bronze original of which dates from shortly after 20 B.C., the year in which the Roman insignia were returned by the Parthians, while the Indians and Scythians sent envoys to the leader of the Roman Empire. These "dolphins" are squat and scaly, and it appears that the cupid figures are holding on by one hand to the animal's dorsal fin, which has been moved forward until it resembles a tuft of hair on the head. Various other images show how this displacement was caused, like the depiction on the tap of the Trajanus's fountain in Ephesus (modern Turkey) or the tableau in polychrome stucco on a sarcophagus from Kerch in the Crimea, now on display in the Louvre. One detail is particularly notable: Three grooves radiate out from the corner of the eyes, which are out of place there unless they symbolize the barbels of a catfish, which does indeed have three on each side. The long tail fin is also characteristic of the catfish. This was a giant fish, which seemed to lord it over the other river creatures and must have made an impression on the local inhabitants, whether they were nomads or sedentary people.

The cupid figures are naked and plump; they are winged and wear crowns with recesses for inlays. They are shown in half profile: one wing is cut short in the Greek manner. They wear crossed bands on their chests, more as decoration than as straps for their wings. They have bracelets at the wrist and ankle, and one hand carries a round object, hollowed out into a cup in order to hold a colored stone.

60
Appliqué, "Kushan Aphrodite"
Tillya Tepe, Tomb II
Second quarter of the 1st century A.D.
Gold
4.5 x 2.5 cm
National Museum of Afghanistan
04.40.113

60 THIS FEMALE FIGURE, HER ATTRACTIVE name provided by the archaeologists who found her, is flanked on the right by a plump and naked cupid, a character readily associated with Aphrodite. The image of Aphrodite with a small figure of Eros on her left shoulder is, indeed, almost a cliché, particularly in goldsmith's work. Here however the butterfly wings are clearly those of Psyche. This subtle Greek distinction may have escaped the notice of the young woman who wore the ornament. Psyche-Aphrodite is accompanied by Eros, in this case a very youthful Eros. He seems to have wings; his face is barely indicated although his gender is very clear. She is rather short and squat in build and wears a kind of turban, or it may be a knot of hair, with locks falling over the left ear. The upper body is naked to the hips, apart from two strips of material hanging over the shoulders and meeting between the small breasts and then disappearing behind the back at the level of her rounded stomach. Perhaps this represents the attachment of the wings, although it was more usual in Roman art to use purely decorative breast-bands, and even more so in the art of Gandhara and India. Another odd detail is provided by the two symmetrical pillars, obviously inspired by the pedestals of a throne, although the goddess is shown standing. Two small gold appliqués of the same type and from around the same time were found among the Indo-Parthian level from Taxila in Pakistan (Marshall 1951, pl. 191, nos. 96 and 97). Like our Aphrodite, these had a flat plate with attachment points on the rear, with the attachment created by two pairs of soldered rings.

61 BOTH PENDANTS HAVE A SUSPENSION ring at the top of the middle section. The various chains and pendants, ingeniously attached and providing a tinkling sound, transform these into remarkable pieces of jewelry adding a sonorous effect to the impressive visual aspect of the object. The pendants consist of two identical plates soldered together, and they can therefore be read on either side of the face. This confirms all the more their mobile character; they can turn around.

There is a central image of a man, shown frontally, who holds two mythical creatures firmly by their front legs, his arms spread wide. His indented crown resembles that worn over his leather and felt hat by the individual from grave 3 in Pazyryk in Siberia (Rudenko 1953, pl. XCVI, 2), but it is also similar to the crowns of Achaemenid and later Sasanian rulers of Iran. The man has broad, flat cheekbones and two conspicuously slanting large eyes. He has an Indian-style dot on his forehead. He wears a neck ring or torque around his neck. The man is dressed as a nomad, in a kaftan with crossed panels fastened at the waist; the swelling folds, particularly at the sleeves, suggest that his robe is of a thick material (reversed sheepskin?). Under the spreading kaftan he wears a garment first interpreted as a kind of compromise between the Persian tunic and riding breeches, but which is now (Pfrommer 1996, Boardman 2003) seen as a "skirt" in the form of a three-lobed acanthus leaf, similar to that worn by the "Man With a Dolphin" (no. 36).

The two dragons have crests of turquoise droplets. Their supple, catlike backs form a double S. Their rear legs are reversed and seem to point upward, a typical motif from the art of the steppes, which is frequently encountered in the Altai Mountains and in Tuva in Siberia, but also in Alagou in the Chinese province of Xinjiang (Francfort 1998, fig. 6, 7 and 8), in Issyk (Kazakhstan), and also among the objects in the Siberian collection of Peter the Great in the Hermitage in St. Petersburg (Rudenko 1962, pl. VIII, 7 and 8). The turquoises at the ends of their claws resemble clogs rather than claws. The archaeologist who unearthed the object called it "the master fighting the dragons:" He saw the two creatures as horses with wings and horns, and the monsters do, indeed, have mouths that stretch from ear to ear without teeth, like horses.

But in view of their flexible backs, thin tails, and in particular the short wings and the grooved ibex horns, granulated where they join the skull, these are hybrid beings that cannot be categorized, though they resemble winged and horned lions more than dragons. We are dealing here with a very traditional eastern iconographic motif, both in the male and female varieties: The "Master" or "Mistress of Animals," with a plant motif added here by means of the "skirt," which also recurs with the (aquatic? lotus?) flowers on the round pendants.

But above all, the iconography of these pendants reflects the essence of the nomadic spirit: an attempt to seize hold of space and experience an attachment to it.

61
A pair of pendants showing the "Dragon Master"
Tillya Tepe, Tomb II
Second quarter of the 1st century A.D.
Gold, turquoise, garnet, lapis lazuli, carnelian, pearls
12.5 x 6.5 cm
National Museum of Afghanistan
04.40.109

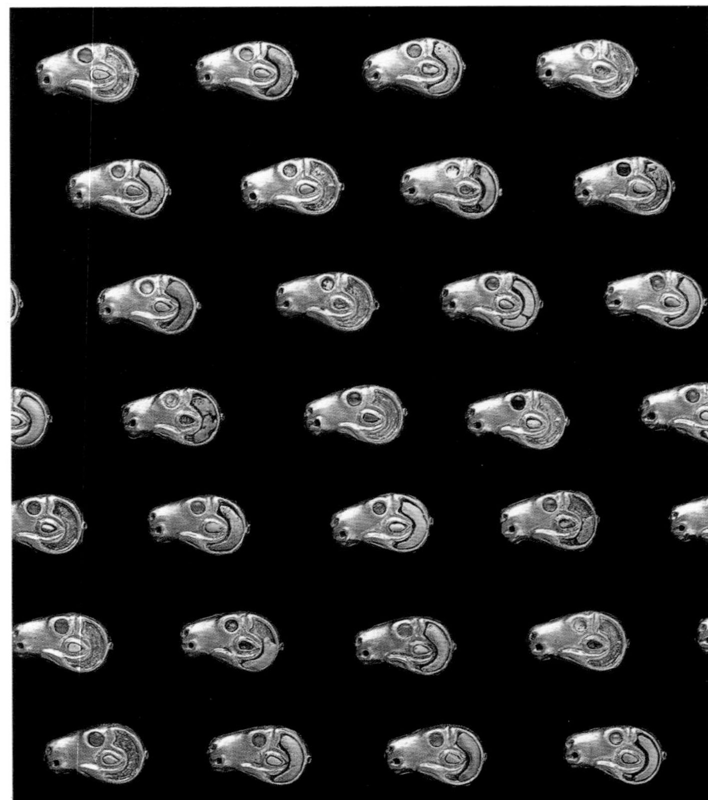

62
Bracteates in the form of a ram's head
Tillya Tepe, Tomb II
Second quarter of the 1st century A.D.
Gold, turquoise, carnelian
1.5 x 1.0 cm
National Museum of Afghanistan
04.40.81

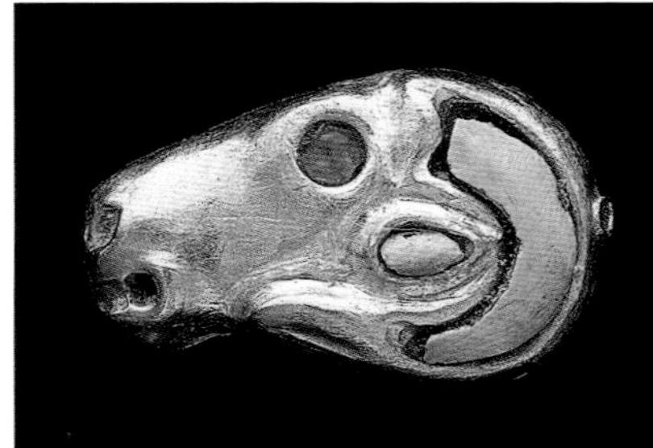

63
Heart-shaped bracteates
Tillya Tepe, Tomb II
Second quarter of the 1st century A.D.
Gold, turquoise
1.1 x 1.0 cm
National Museum of Afghanistan
04.40.89

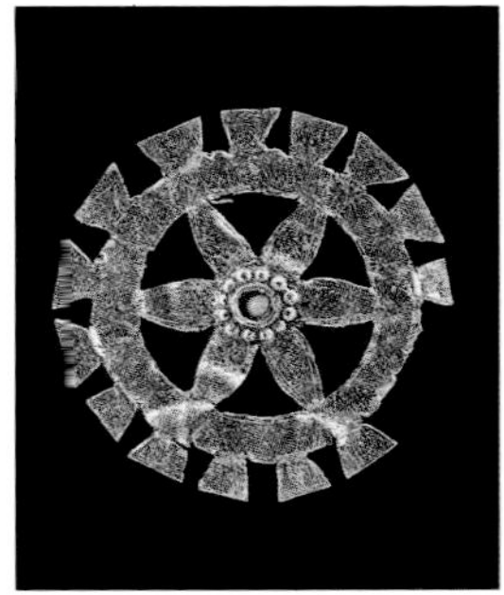

64
Bracteates in the form of a toothed disk
Tillya Tepe, Tomb II
Second quarter of the 1st century A.D.
Gold
Diam. 2.0 cm
National Museum of Afghanistan 04.40.88

65
Three bracteates in the form of toothed disks
Tillya Tepe, Tomb II
Second quarter of the 1st century A.D.
Gold
Diam. 2.0 and 1.4 cm
National Museum of Afghanistan 04.40.87

66
Two round bracteates with heart-shaped decoration
Tillya Tepe, Tomb II
Second quarter of the 1st century A.D.
Gold
Diam. 1.6 cm
National Museum of Afghanistan
04.40.86

67
Bracteates in the form of stepped pyramids
Tillya Tepe, Tomb II
Second quarter of the 1st century A.D.
Gold
1.2 x 1.0 cm
National Museum of Afghanistan
04.40.78

67 THE STEPPED PYRAMID is an architectural form with a long history in the East that was already known during the kingdom of Urartu (ninth to sixth century B.C., in modern Turkey and Armenia) and in particular in the Iran of the Achaemenids (sixth to fourth century B.C.). It was first as a defensive construction and later a decorative element, for example, in Persepolis in the battlements surmounting the walls. When applied to bracteates, this form allowed not only spatial or linear arrangement, but also a head-tail structure, where the interlinking plates could form a band, belt, or breast ribbon, as seen in objects from Taxila-Sirkap, Pakistan (Marshall 1953, pl. 194, 75). Bracteates of this toothed form are also found in Sarmatian tombs along the Don, in particular at Dachi, close to the river mouth (Schiltz 2001, no. 230). They were used here to decorate a horse blanket, in which objects with gold and turquoise decorations were wrapped. Toothed bracteates are also found on a Sarmatian gilded silver jar from Vysochino (Schiltz 2001, no. 208).

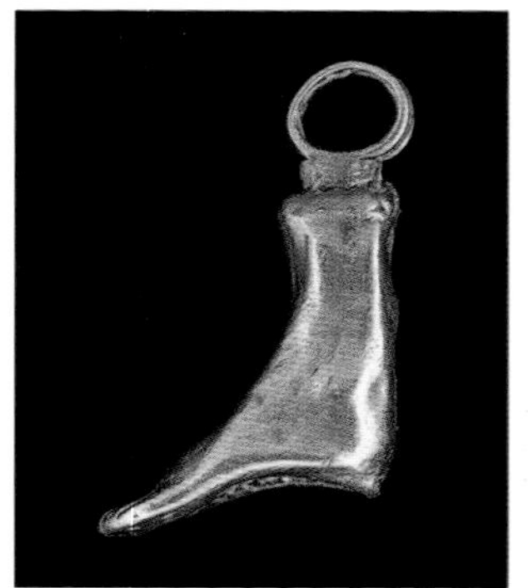

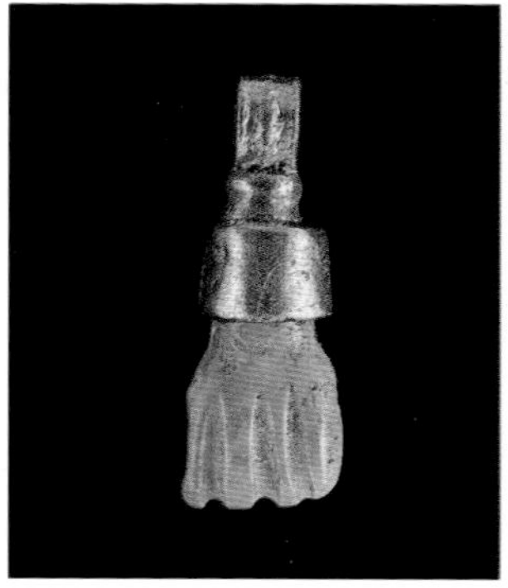

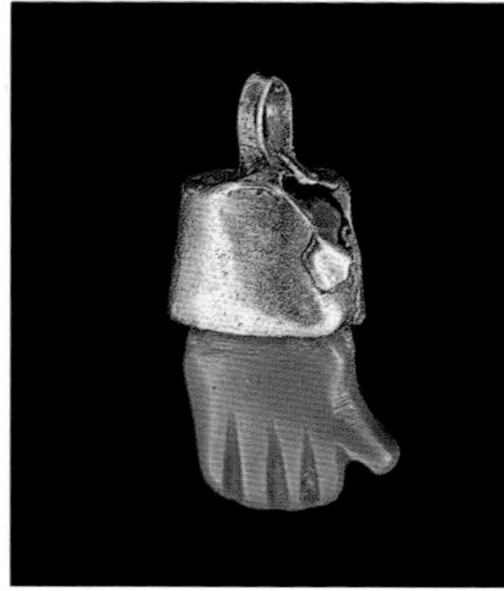

68
Amulet in the form of a foot
Tillya Tepe, Tomb II
Second quarter of the 1st century A.D.
Gold
1.5 x 0.9 cm
National Museum of Afghanistan
04.40.77

69
Amulet in the form of a hand
Tillya Tepe, Tomb II
Second quarter of the 1st century A.D.
Gold, turquoise
1.1 x 0.5 cm
National Museum of Afghanistan
04.40.99

70
Amulet in the form of a hand
Tillya Tepe, Tomb II
Second quarter of the 1st century A.D.
Gold, turquoise
1.5 x 0.6 cm
National Museum of Afghanistan
04.40.102

71
Two amulets in the form of feet
Tillya Tepe, Tomb II
Second quarter of the 1st century A.D.
Gold, lapis lazuli
0.9 x 0.4 cm
National Museum of Afghanistan
04.40.107

72
Elements of an ornamental object
Tillya Tepe, Tomb II
Second quarter of the 1st century A.D.
Gold, turquoise
20 x 3.1 cm
National Museum of Afghanistan
04.40.108

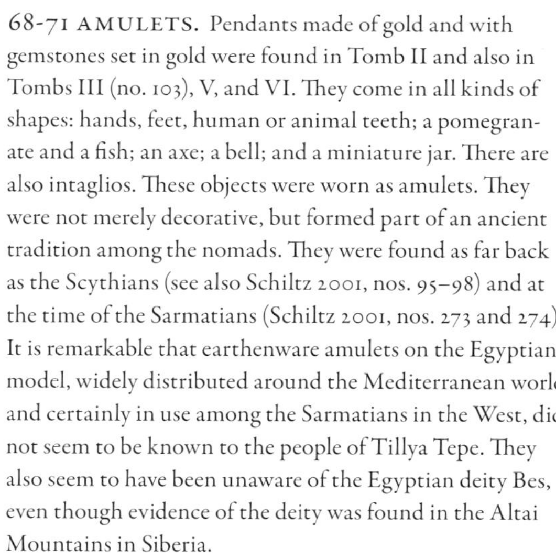

68-71 AMULETS. Pendants made of gold and with gemstones set in gold were found in Tomb II and also in Tombs III (no. 103), V, and VI. They come in all kinds of shapes: hands, feet, human or animal teeth; a pomegranate and a fish; an axe; a bell; and a miniature jar. There are also intaglios. These objects were worn as amulets. They were not merely decorative, but formed part of an ancient tradition among the nomads. They were found as far back as the Scythians (see also Schiltz 2001, nos. 95–98) and at the time of the Sarmatians (Schiltz 2001, nos. 273 and 274). It is remarkable that earthenware amulets on the Egyptian model, widely distributed around the Mediterranean world and certainly in use among the Sarmatians in the West, did not seem to be known to the people of Tillya Tepe. They also seem to have been unaware of the Egyptian deity Bes, even though evidence of the deity was found in the Altai Mountains in Siberia.

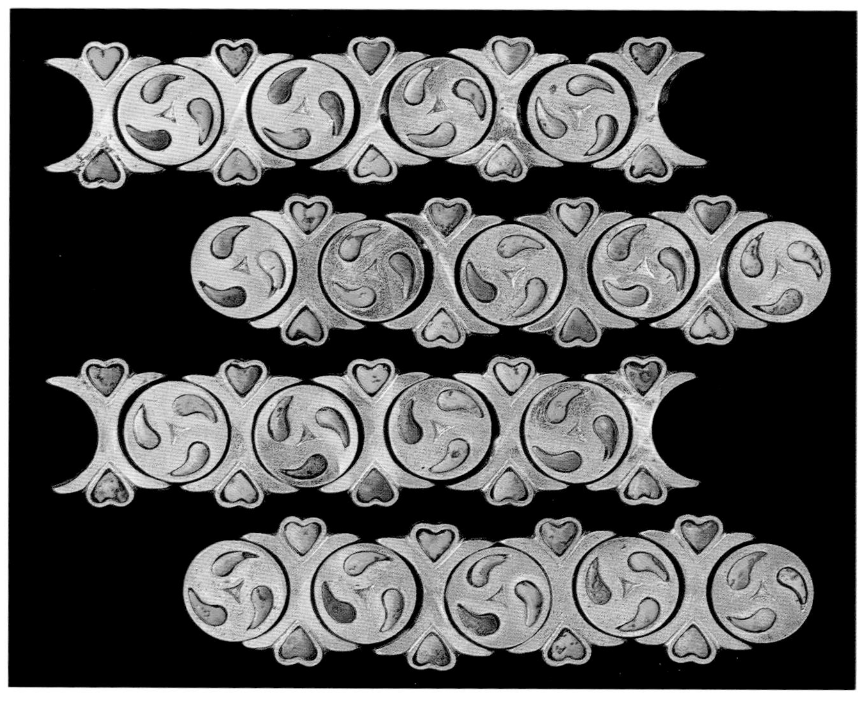

72 THIS JEWEL, WORN AS A VERTICAL BAND under the neck of the tunic, consists of a chain of gold disks inlaid with three turquoise droplets, surrounding a triangle cut out of the gold. Between the disks are dividers in the shape of double crescents decorated with hearts, also inlaid with turquoise. This type of feature, disks alternating with double crescents, can be used in a simple linked band to be sewn onto clothing, as here. It is also found as a jewel with pendants (no. 73), a necklace (no 129), and finally as a purely graphic decorative motif (no. 36). Examples of this type have been found in the Saka-Parthian layers at Sirkap-Taxila (Marshall 1953, pl. 193, 56–58).

73 THIS ORNAMENT IS OF THE SAME TYPE as the last, but with disk-pendants and the end crescents on each side end in volutes. It was probably used as a double-sided covering, possibly over the shoulder.

73
Components of an ornament
Tillya Tepe, Tomb II
Second quarter of the 1st century A.D.
Gold, turquoise
18.3 cm
National Museum of Afghanistan
04.40.95

74
Bracteates in the form of a droplet
Tillya Tepe, Tomb II
Second quarter of the 1st century A.D.
Gold
0.8 x 0.5 cm
National Museum of Afghanistan
04.40.104

75
Two musicians
Tillya Tepe, Tomb II
Second quarter of the 1st century A.D.
Gold
2.3 x 1.2 cm
National Museum of Afghanistan 04.40.82

76
Two hair ornaments
Tillya Tepe, Tomb II
Second quarter of the 1st century A.D.;
gold, turquoise, pearls, bronze (pin); diam. of the roundels: 1.5 and 2.7 cm
National Museum of Afghanistan 04.40.118

77
Pair of anklets
Tillya Tepe, Tomb II
Second quarter of the 1st century A.D.
Gold
9.5 x 9.0 cm
National Museum of Afghanistan 04.40.167

75 THE FIGURES SIT WITH THEIR LEGS crossed, plucking stringed instruments—lutes or ouds—in their right hands. Similar instruments are depicted on objects excavated at Khalchayan and Airtam in Uzbekistan. The visible navel seems to indicate nakedness. Perhaps this is the classical motif of musical cupids, like the cupid playing a lyre on a gilded copper appliqué from Takht-i-Sangin in Tajikistan. Stringed instruments of this type are also depicted on rhytons (drinking beakers) from the ancient Parthian capital of Nisa in modern Turkmenistan, and in this catalogue (from Begram, no. 207).

Music played an important role in Central Asia, particularly in the world of the nomads, a world of verbal history and heroic tales. These figures, more than simple musicians, could be reminiscent of the bards responsible for preserving the memory of the clan. One of the frozen graves at Pazyryk in the Altai Mountains of Siberia (Rudenko 1953, pl. LXXXVI, 1) contained not only drums, but also a stringed instrument, fairly similar to the instrument depicted here. The Scythians from the west of the steppes have also left us the so-called diadem from Sakhnovka in the Ukraine, depicting a kneeling lyrist taking part in a ceremony (Schiltz 1994, fig. 135 C).

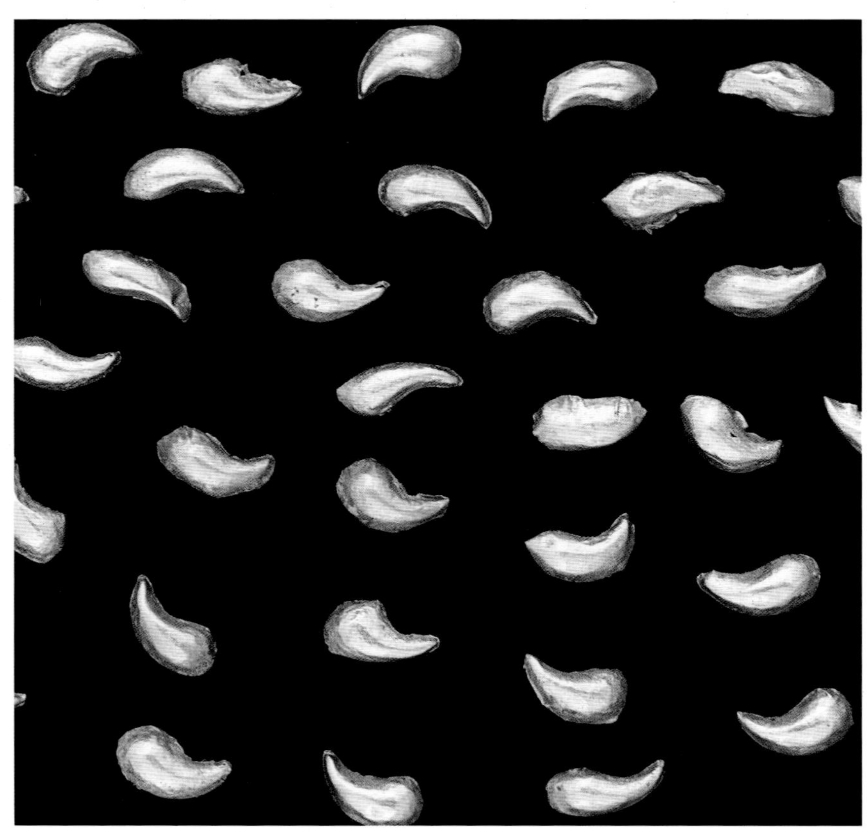

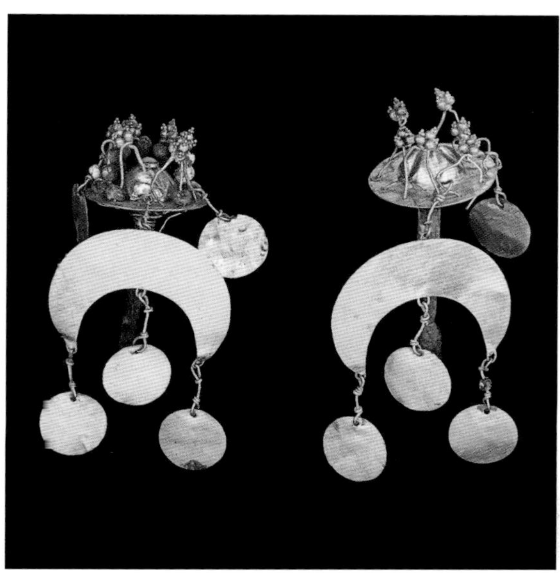

78
Necklace
Tillya Tepe, Tomb II
Second quarter of
the 1st century A.D.
Gold, organic material
(wood?)
Diam. of the beads:
1.8; 2.0; 2.4 cm
National Museum
of Afghanistan
04.40.111

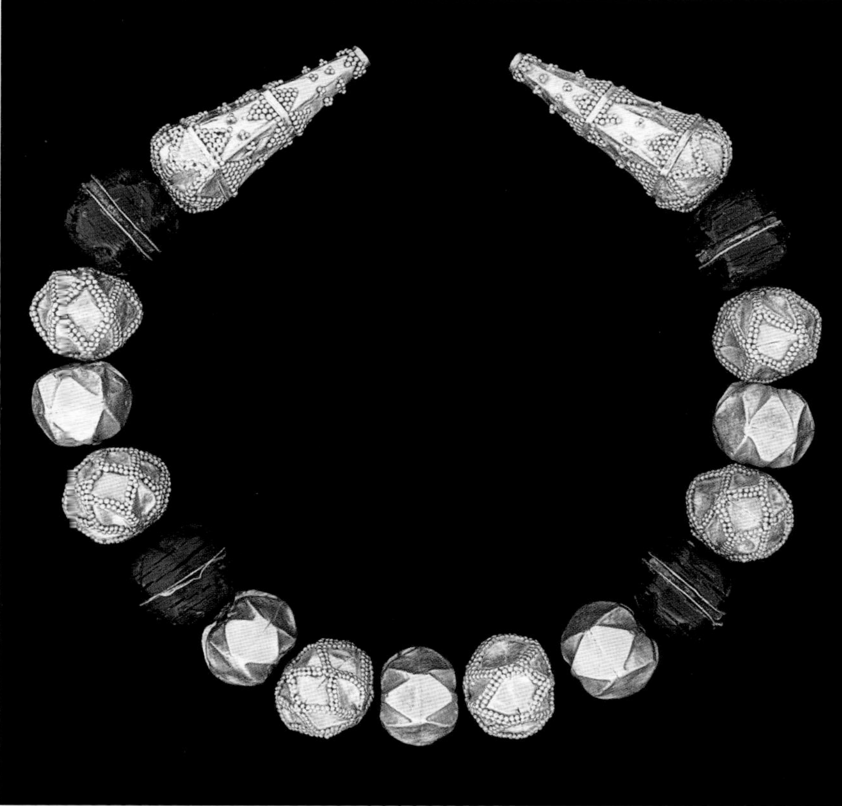

76 THESE ORNAMENTS CONSIST of a pointed rod bearing a disk with a ribbed edge. The edge bears a turquoise with a fringe of gold threads strung with pearls. The use of pearls in an ornament of this kind seems to echo a saying of the Greek-born Roman historian Flavius Arrianus, who wrote that pearls are three times as expensive as gold. The threads terminate in finely granulated pyramids. Below these hang gold roundels and a crescent, with a further three smooth disks suspended from it.

78 THE NECKLACE INCLUDES ELEVEN hollow gold beads, made of two hemispheres carefully soldered together. Their surfaces are faceted and the seams of six of the beads show a double granulated line. The four black beads are made from an organic material that is neither bone nor ivory but possibly wood; these also consist of two hemispheres with a narrow gold rim; they are stuck together with a clear adhesive. Two elongated gold beads with a granulated decoration function as closures.

Tillya Tepe, Tomb III

THIS TOMB, MEASURING 2.6 BY 1.5 METERS and orientated north-south, lay almost at the top of the mound. It was formed in one of the mud-brick walls, which separated the rooms of the former temple. The walls of the tomb were perpendicular, with the exception of the eastern wall which was slightly inclined. Analysis of the organic residues on the upper surface suggests that the boards there were covered with leather, onto which small, rounded gold appliqués had been sewn (no. 91 and 92). Another possibility is that the latter had been applied to a cloth used to wrap the coffin. Unlike the disks found in the other graves, which had only a small hole, those in this grave had a round fastening at the edge, like those from the graves at Begram and also similar to the disks on the conical head coverings and trousers worn by the leaders found at Dalverzin-tepe in Uzbekistan.

Traces of matting were found on the floor of the grave. The coffin, 40 to 50 centimeters high (and 2 m long by 65 cm wide) rested some 10 to 15 cm from the base on (wooden?) supports which have completely disappeared. The entire contents of the grave (bones, ornaments, and other items) had been gnawed and disturbed by rodents, who had dragged many items away, sometimes far into their burrows, leaving them both below the grave and above the ground. It seems very likely that the mound received its name "Hill of Gold" because of the jewels removed from the graves in this way. The occupant of the grave was probably a woman, in view of the contents of the grave, and probably lay on her back. The head was to the north and rested on a golden plate. She probably wore a headdress of fabric with gold bands and appliqués. Her jaw was held closed with a golden band. She wore hairpins (no. 98), probably decorated with pendants, like the hair ornaments with crescents (no. 87). The pendant with the horse motifs (no. 97) probably adorned her face at the temples. A gold torque encircled her neck. The pieces of a second necklace lay scattered about (no. 104).

A silver Chinese mirror lay on her breast. The various pairs of clasps, including one decorated with images of warriors (no. 79), which probably held together the panels of a heavy garment, the cupids riding dolphins (no. 80), and the almond-shaped brooches (no. 93) suggest that the woman was dressed in several layers of richly decorated clothing. It has not, however, been possible to determine with certainty the original location of four medallions, found in various places (no. 84), nor that of the ornament with the image of Athena (no. 105), the ear pendants (nos. 81, 94, and 103) and the various bracteates (nos. 82, 83 and 90) found together with various amulets and jewelry to be sewn or hung.

The young female had bracelets (no. 85), three rings, one of which (no. 101) was found outside the coffin, and anklets. The buckles and soles of her shoes, cut from gold sheet, were preserved (no. 89). The silver Parthian coin (no. 96), found in the area of the hips, was probably held in the woman's hand.

Three clay bowls were found outside the coffin at the head end. To the west lay various pieces of earthenware, silver, and ivory from bottles and cosmetics containers, as well as a tiny gold ointment box (no. 86). To the southwest corner lay a second mirror with an ivory handle and a round gold box with a lid (no. 88), the weight of which was inscribed on it in Greek script, under which the coin of Tiberius (no. 95) had been placed.

The ring close by, already mentioned (no. 101), was decorated with a depiction of a ritual offering.

Judging by its contents, which had been considerably disturbed but certainly included nearly five thousand gold objects, this was an exceptionally rich grave.

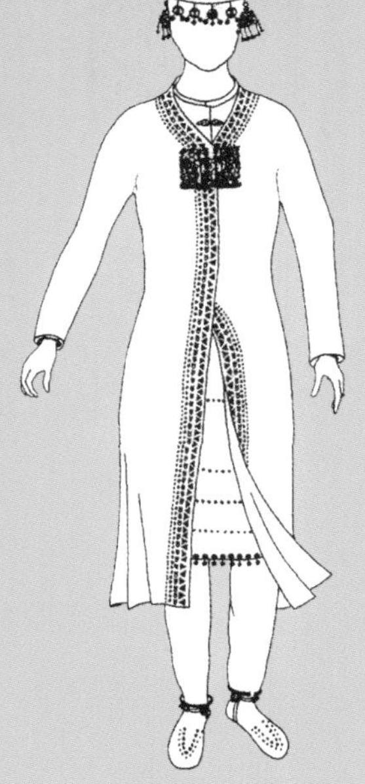

79 BOTH OF THESE CLASPS, ONE WITH TWO hooks and the other one with two loops, were covered with a smooth plate to the rear. They display almost symmetrical tableaux, with only minor differences. Within a rectangular frame of plant and animal motifs a warrior is striding forward, a lance in one hand and a shield in the other. He has the musculature of an adult male, but the long curling hair reaching to his shoulders—as originally that of the youth on the Aï Khanum relief—are those of a young ephebe (no. 34).

Some elements of the man's weapons are the same as those worn by Greek or Greco-Bactrian soldiers, but there are a few variations in the detail, which are of overriding importance. The helmet has a rippled edge, a snaking feather serving as a crest, and a chinstrap, similar to that of a Macedonian or a later traditional Greco-Bactrian helmet. However, it also has a bull's ear, similar to that seen on depictions of Alexander the Great and on the coinage of Bactrian kings like Eucratides (second century B.C.). Another detail appearing on the coins of Eucratides are the folds across the neck: These are part of a very long garment, held on the shoulders by a clasp in the form of a crescent, and looking like a *chlamys* (soldier's cloak) or *paludamentum* (a cloak

worn by a general engaged in warfare). Streaming ribbons are also shown, marking the ends of a royal diadem like the helmet ribbons of Bactrian rulers. The upper body, with the rib cage and the navel shown, is not naked, but is clad with a breastplate following the form of the body, as was worn by kings and Caesars. Below the breast is a belt, tied at the front, another emblem of power. On his left, the warrior holds a sword with a pommel in the form of a griffin's head, similar to the example in ivory from the Temple of the Oxus (Litvinsky 2001, pl. 62). In defiance of the laws of symmetry the sword is held on the correct side in both appliqués, namely on the left. The weapon is attached to a sword-belt, which runs diagonally across the trunk, below the navel. The belt is attached to the sheath with a typical vertical clip, which can be seen being worn by warriors on the bone plate from Orlat in Uzbekistan and has also been found among the Sarmatians in the west. The man wore short, laced boots revealing a toe. The ground on which the man stands is richly decorated in an architectural manner: There are rectangular recessed tiles, lozenges, and dots suggesting decorative bead-and-reel and egg-shaped recesses alternating with darts.

But the "dragon-lions" with their puckered muzzles on the Chinese model, and the plant motifs with birds (grouse?) at the corners, give the "columns" forming the frame an animalistic aesthetic, which is completely alien to Greek art, but sits very well among the aesthetic art of the steppes.

79
Pair of clasps decorated with warriors
Tillya Tepe, Tomb III
Second quarter of the 1st century A.D.
Gold
9.0 x 6.3 cm
National Museum of Afghanistan
04.40.245

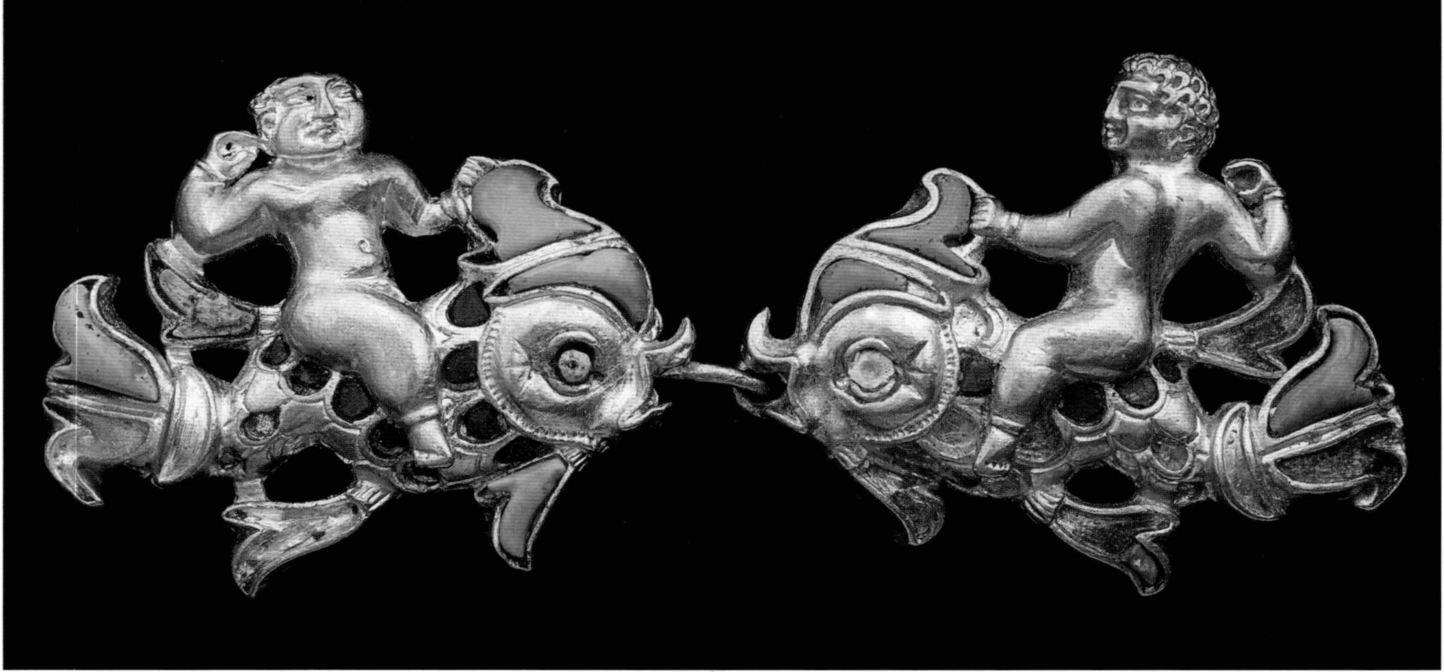

80 THESE CLASPS ARE COMPARABLE in type with those from Tomb II (no. 59). However the cupid figures here have neither wings nor a crossed decoration on the breast. They hold their upper bodies triumphantly to the rear, their arms widely spread, the knees drawn up, and the waist clearly shown. They give a somewhat airy impression, reinforced by the space below their elbows. Their postures are not entirely symmetrical: The upper body of one is shown frontally, the other is seen in semi-profile on his back. Both of these figures hold an object in their hands into which a colored stone could be fitted. The "quiff," the fins, the tail, and the scales of the "dolphins" have retained their turquoise inlay work. The eye is represented by a bead. Next to the eye is a decorative mark resembling the barbels of a catfish.

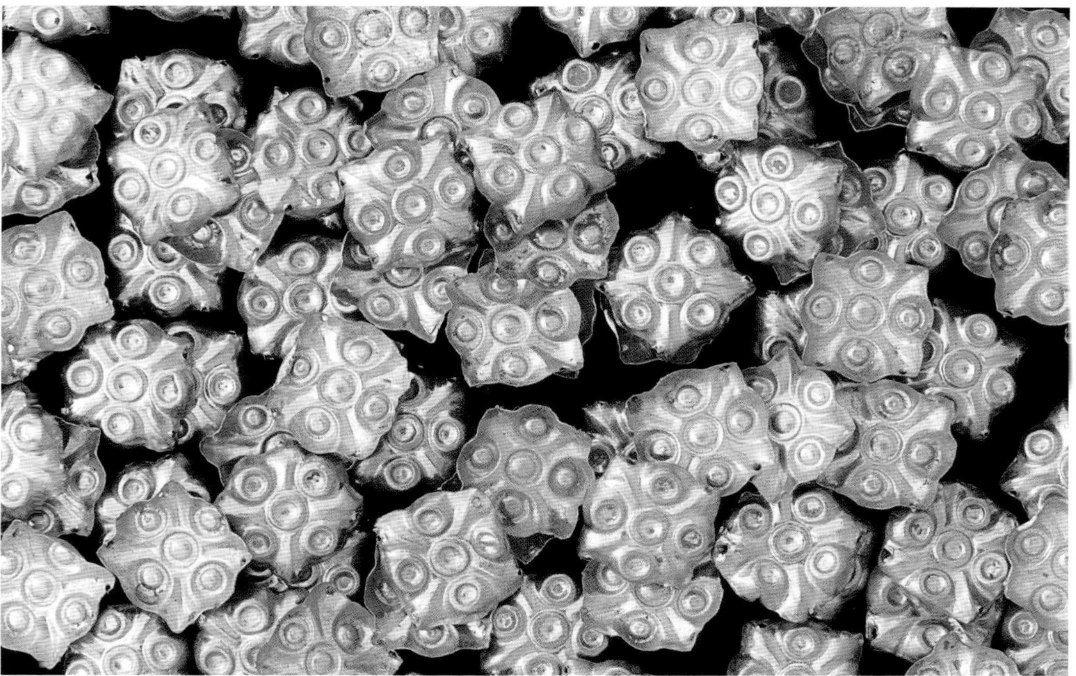

80
A pair of clasps. Cupids on dolphins
Tillya Tepe, Tomb III
Second quarter of the 1st century A.D.
Gold, turquoise, mother-of-pearl
4.2 x 4.9 cm
National Museum of Afghanistan
04.40.110

81
Ear pendants decorated with garnets
Tillya Tepe, Tomb III
Second quarter of the 1st century A.D.
Gold, garnet
L. 1.8 cm (without the disk); Diam. 0.9 cm
National Museum of Afghanistan
04.40.237

82
Bracteates with disk-shaped decoration
Tillya Tepe, Tomb III
Second quarter of the 1st century A.D.
Gold
1.1 x 0.1 cm
National Museum of Afghanistan
04.40.206

83
Heart-shaped bracteates, kinked in the middle
Tillya Tepe, Tomb III
Second quarter of the 1st century A.D.
Gold
0.8 x 0.8 cm
National Museum of Afghanistan
04.40.205

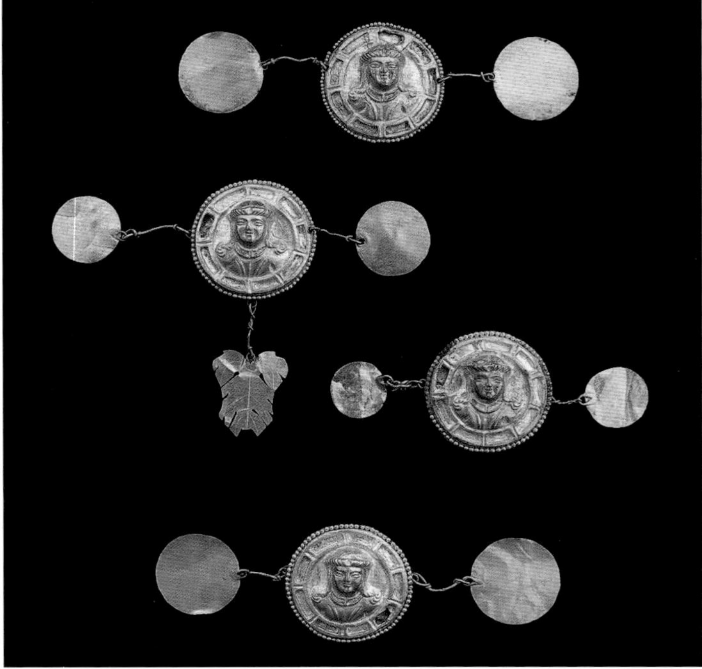

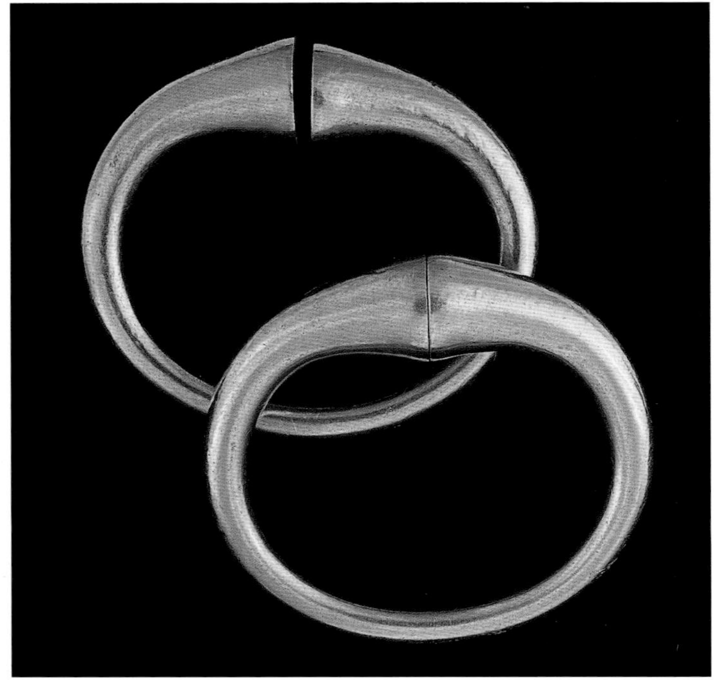

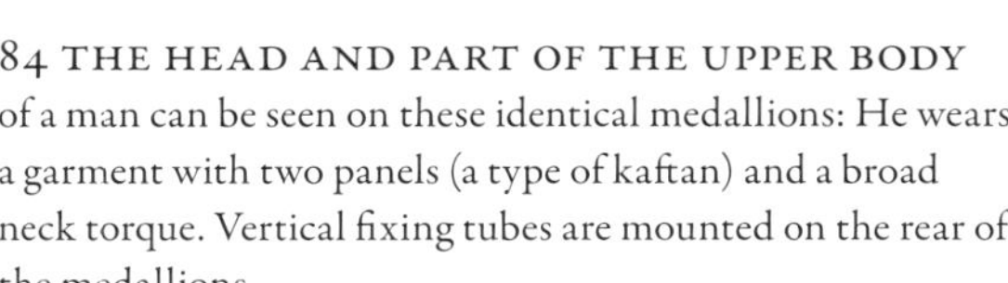

84 THE HEAD AND PART OF THE UPPER BODY of a man can be seen on these identical medallions: He wears a garment with two panels (a type of kaftan) and a broad neck torque. Vertical fixing tubes are mounted on the rear of the medallions.

The man has a short neck, a broad face with high cheekbones, a heavy chin, narrow mouth, prominent slit eyes, pronounced brows, and a low forehead. His hair is parted in the middle, with a rolled lock fastened to his head and long curls falling asymmetrically over his shoulders. These external characteristics call up associations with the representation of the young Dionysus (recognizable from the ivy), shown on a phalera of gilded bronze found in Tajikistan in the region of Dushanbe.

84
Four medallions
Tillya Tepe, Tomb III
Second quarter of the 1st century A.D.
Gold
Diam. 2.6 and 1.6 cm; L. 4.0 cm
National Museum of Afghanistan
04.40.423

85
A pair of bracelets
Tillya Tepe, Tomb III
Second quarter of the 1st century A.D.
Gold
L. 23.1 cm
National Museum of Afghanistan
04.40.166

86
Cosmetics pot with lid
Tillya Tepe, Tomb III
Second quarter of the 1st century A.D.
Gold
2.0 cm
National Museum of Afghanistan
04.40.199

87
Crescent with three pendants
Tillya Tepe, Tomb III
Second quarter of the 1st century A.D.
Gold
5.8 x 7.3 cm
National Museum of Afghanistan
04.40.234

88
Round box with lid, bearing Greek inscription
Tillya Tepe, Tomb III
Second quarter of the 1st century A.D.
Gold
H. 5.5 cm
National Museum of Afghanistan
04.40.169

88 WITH ITS ROUNDED SHAPE and its lid with a pomegranate knob secured with a chain, this little box takes the form of the traditional Greek pyxis (earthenware) or cista (clay or metal) casket.

The lid and the sides are decorated with plant leaves and three-lobed petals, from which pistils with rounded stamens protrude. It is possible that the stamens were intended for inlay work.

On the base, made separately and then soldered to the box, we can see three concentric rings and an engraved inscription in Greek script (CTA E/B); these indicate the weight of the box according to the Ionic system, which used the letters of the Greek alphabet in sequence in a decimal system so that E = 5 and B = 2. This means five staters and two drachmas. Converting that weight to the metric system, a stater (tetradrachm) comes to 15.6 grams and a drachma is 3.9 grams (see also no. 123) (Bernard 2000, p. 1427, note 144).

An interesting comparison with this object is provided by silver boxes of similar shape found in the Sarmatian grave in Kossika on the Volga.

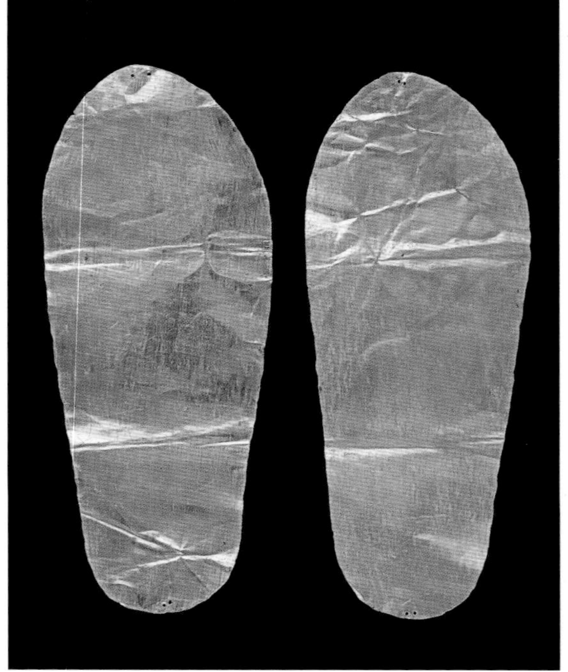

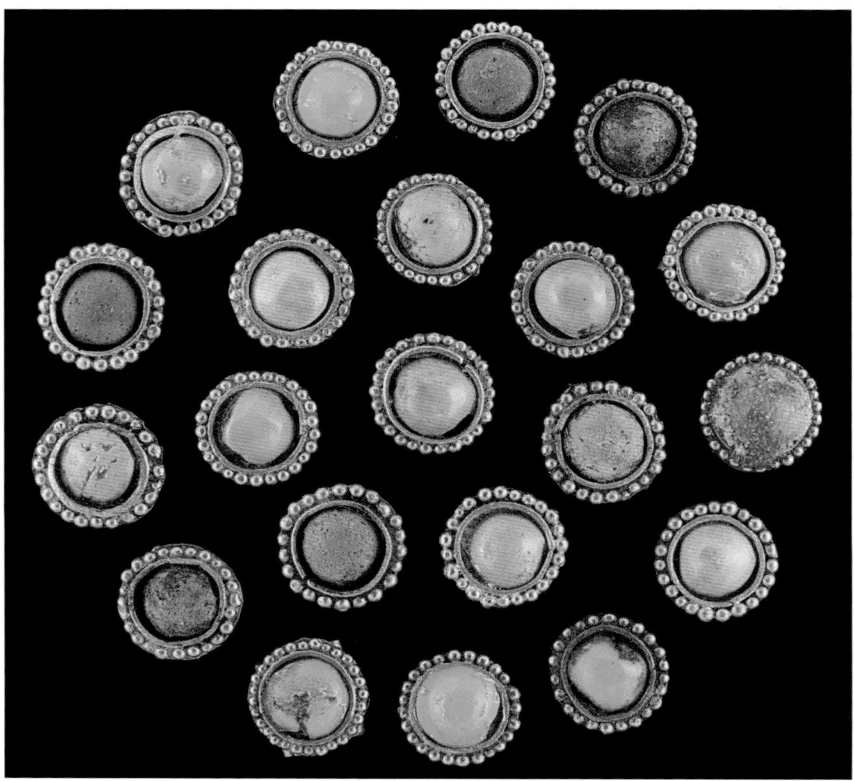

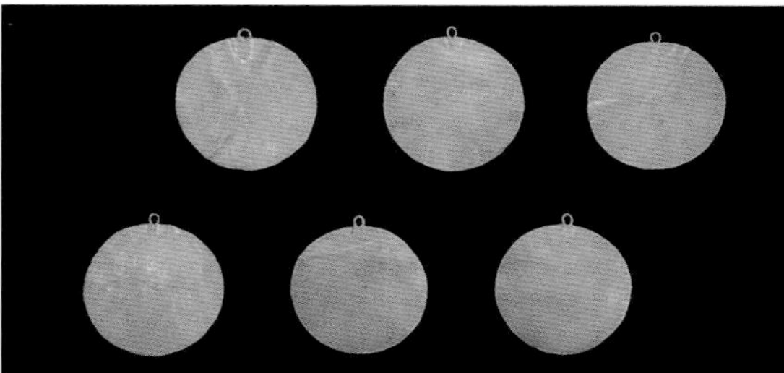

89 THESE SOLES, CUT FROM THIN GOLD SHEET and with attachment holes both on the top and at the heels, were clearly not made to be used for walking. The question is whether they were intended purely as grave decorations, as can be seen in Egypt and elsewhere. This appears not to be the case: In the mounted world of the nomads, where a person on foot might be looked at without any consideration, where the elite sat on carpets and not the bare ground, the wearing of costly or decorated soles was a sign of an aristocratic way of life. For example, boots of cloth and supple leather were found in the frozen nomad graves in the Altai Mountains of Siberia (Kurgan 2 at Pazyryk), with pyrites sewn on the soles as decoration (Rudenko 1953, pl. XXV, 2). The torque of gold and turquoise from Kobyakovo in southern Russia (Schiltz 2001, no. 240) shows a man seated in the eastern manner, with the soles of the feet outward.

89
Pair of shoe soles
Tillya Tepe, Tomb III
Second quarter of the 1st century A.D.
Gold
22.5 x 8.7 cm
National Museum of Afghanistan
04.40.174

90
Round bracteates with turquoises and a granulated rim
Tillya Tepe, Tomb III;
second quarter of the 1st century A.D.
Gold, turquoise, pyrites
Diam. 0.6 cm
National Museum of Afghanistan
04.40.209

91
Round pendants
Tillya Tepe, Tomb III
Second quarter of the 1st century A.D.
Gold
Diam. 3.0 cm
National Museum of Afghanistan
04.40.273

92
Round pendants
Tillya Tepe, Tomb III
Second quarter of the 1st century A.D.
Gold
Diam. 3.0 cm
National Museum of Afghanistan
04.40.262

93
Two almond-shaped clasps
Tillya Tepe, Tomb III
Second quarter of the 1st century A.D.
Gold, turquoise
H. 2.2 cm
National Museum of Afghanistan
04.40.231

94
Elongated heart-shaped pendants
Tillya Tepe, Tomb III
Second quarter of the 1st century A.D.
Gold
1.8 x 1.0 cm
National Museum of Afghanistan
04.40.187

95
Roman coin of Tiberius
Tillya Tepe, Tomb III
A.D. 14-37
Gold
Diam. 1.9 cm
National Museum of Afghanistan
04.40.426

96
Parthian coin of Mithridates II
Tillya Tepe, Tomb III
123-88 B.C.
Silver
Diam. 2.2 cm
National Museum of Afghanistan 04.40.172

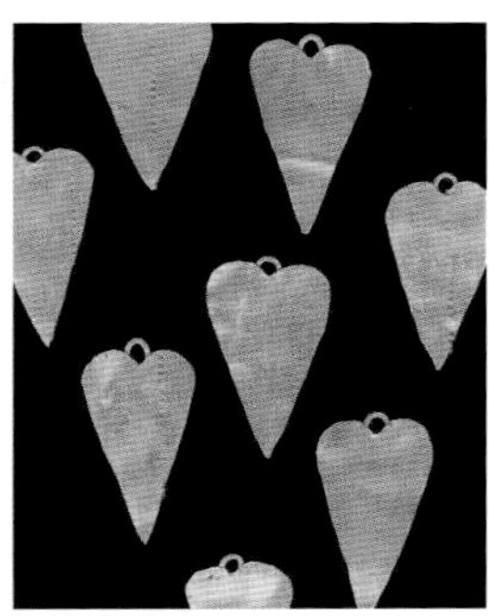

95 OBVERSE: HEAD OF EMPEROR TIBERIUS with laurel wreath, turned to the right. Inscription to the right: TI CAESAR DIVI; left: AUG F AUGUSTUS.

Reverse: Seated female figure, facing right; her right arm leans on a staff, the left hand holds a bough. To either side the inscription PONTIF[EX] MAXIM[US].

The female figure on the reverse of the coin is probably Livia, the mother of Tiberius and the spouse of Augustus, here depicted as goddess of peace. The coin was struck in Lugdunum (Lyon) in Gaul during the reign of Tiberius (A.D. 14–37); more precise dating is not possible yet (Amandry et al. 2003).

This Tiberian aureus, the oldest Roman coin yet found in Afghanistan, did not arrive here by land but rather by sea, via the south of India. Many coins of this type have been found in Central India, while a Tiberian denarius was found in Taxila in the valley of the Indus. This coin provides an important clue in the dating of the necropolis.

96 OBVERSE: HEAD OF A KING WITH BEARD and moustache, diadem on his head, in profile, and turned to the left.

Reverse: Figure in Parthian dress, seated on a throne and facing right, the right arm outstretched, and holding a bow. Inscription above: BASILEOS, right: BASILEÔN, below: MEGALOU; left, on two lines: ARSAKOU EPIPHANOUS.

Coin of the Parthian King Mithridates II (123–88 B.C.), perhaps struck at Nisa.

97 AN APPLIQUÉ IN THE FORM OF TWO HORSE protomes, placed opposite one another, the base of the necks touching, is soldered to the triangular central section, with inlay work in pyrites and a granulated decoration. Their extended forelegs rest on a broad rectangular recess; below this are further rounded recesses, which once held alternating turquoises and gold balls. The ears, manes, eyes, withers, and hooves were decorated with polychrome inlay work. Below the ornament hang flat roundels on chains, with two pendants on either side, consisting of three hearts and a cut-out leaf.

The motif of animals shown as protome was in use in antiquity and later in the East. Examples include the bronzes from the western Persian province of Luristan and the column capitals from Persepolis, the Greek island of Delos, and Mathura in India. The choice of horses was clearly a matter of status in a traditional mounted society: Other examples pointing to this include a comb with opposed horse heads, discovered with the skeleton of a woman at Koktepe in Uzbekistan, placed close to her right hand (Rapin 2001, fig. 10, no. 15). A comparable image can be seen on a leather saddle ornament from grave 5 at Pazyryk, Siberia (Rudenko 1953, pl. CV, 2).

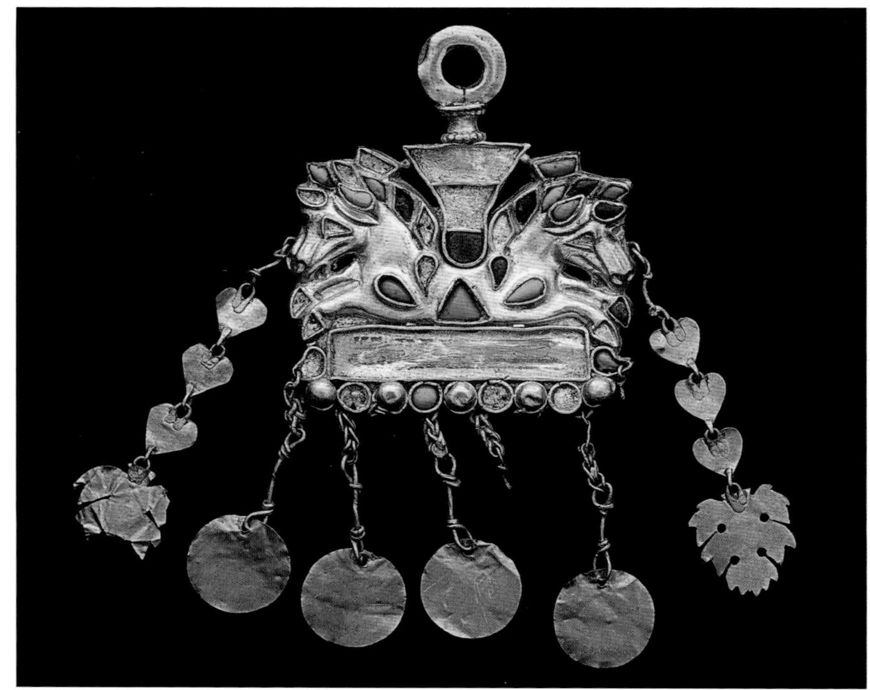

97
Hair ornament with protomes of two horses
Tillya Tepe, Tomb III
Second quarter of the 1st century A.D.
Gold, turquoise, lapis lazuli, carnelian, pyrites
8.6 x 4.6 cm
National Museum of Afghanistan
04.40.163

98
Two hairpins with a rosette
Tillya Tepe, Tomb III
Second quarter of the 1st century A.D.
Gold, bronze
Diam. 7.5 cm
National Museum of Afghanistan
04.40.165

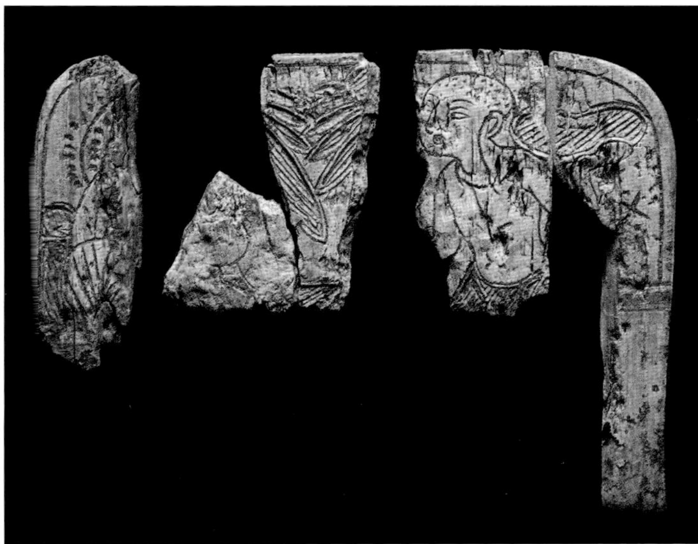

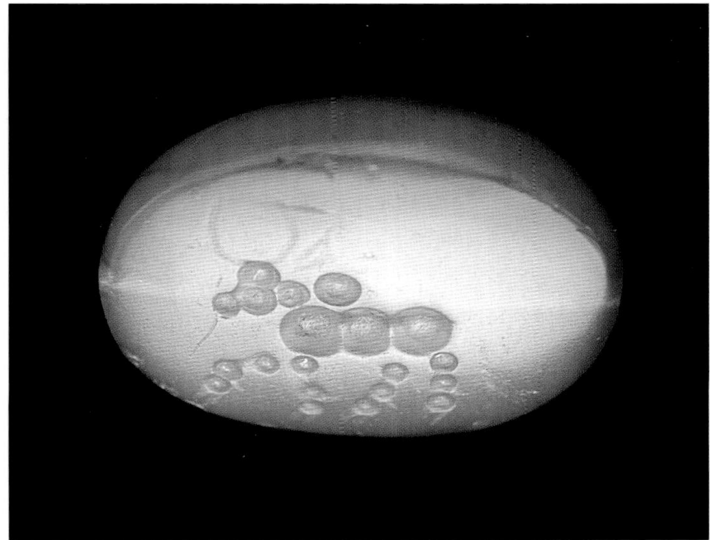

99 COMBS HAVE BEEN FOUND in other nomad graves, including a recent find in the grave of a woman in Koktepe, Uzbekistan (halfway through the 1st century A.D.) (Rapin 200[illegible], fig. 10), but this comb was the only example from the tombs at Tillya Tepe.

Only the upper part of the comb was found, albeit in poor condition. However, enough remains for some conclusions to be drawn: The form with its rounded corners, the ivory it is made from, and the stylistic characteristics of the fine engraving on both sides indicate that the comb came originally from India. The only visible decorative element is a male figure in the centre, reaching forward somewhat, and with an apparently shaved head put forward. Apart from the ivory toilet articles found at Begram, another similar comb was discovered at Dalverzin-tepe in the north of Bactria, now part of Uzbekistan (Pugachenkova 1978, fig. 65–87).

101 THE GOLD RING IS SET with a precious stone, displaying a standing figure, clad in a short tunic and with the right arm leaning on a branch. An object, probably an altar, is shown in front of his left hand, which holds a leafy branch.

To his right stands a low pillar decorated with a garland. The silhouette of the man, the thyrsus staff (proper to the cult of Dionysus) and the pillar with the double plinth and capital are clear indications that this is a religious image or a representation of a ritual sacrifice on the Greek model.

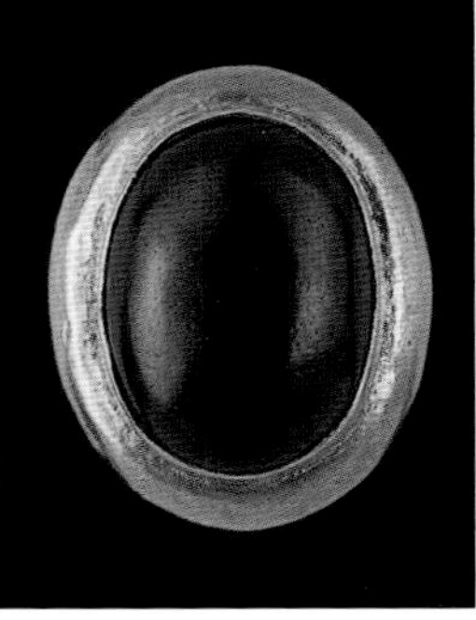

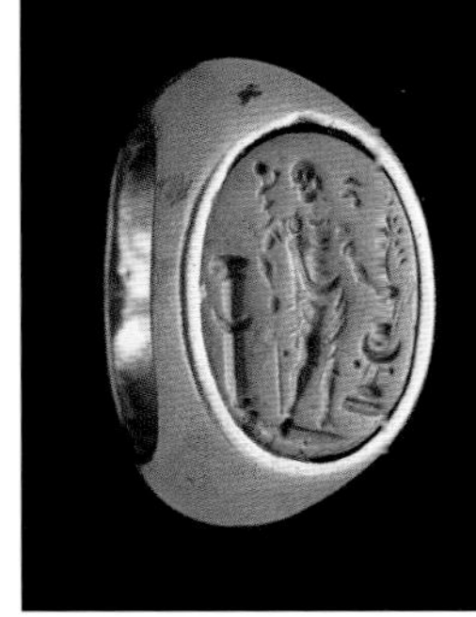

99
Comb
Tillya Tepe, Tomb III
Second quarter of the 1st century A.D.
Ivory
W. 5.0 cm
National Museum of Afghanistan
04.40.241

100
Cabochon (polished stone) in an oval setting
Tillya Tepe, Tomb III
Second quarter of the 1st century A.D.
Gold, haematite
2.2 x 1.7 cm
National Museum of Afghanistan
04.40.256

101
Ring with an intaglio, depicting a ritual offering
Tillya Tepe, Tomb III
Second quarter of the 1st century A.D.
Gold, turquoise
2.3 x 2.0 cm
National Museum of Afghanistan
04.40.227

102
Gem showing a hump-backed figure
Tillya Tepe, Tomb III
Second quarter of the 1st century A.D.
Nephrite jade
2.1 x 1.6 x 1.0 cm
National Museum of Afghanistan
04.40.242

103 THESE ARE TWO FOSSILIZED teeth of a shark (Odontaspididae) possibly from the same jaw (we are indebted to F. Poplin for his analysis). According to a later tradition these so-called petrified snake-tongues or glossopetrae were deemed to possess all kinds of magical powers.

104 THE NECKLACE CONSISTS of eight round beads with repetitive engraved decoration, five smooth rounded beads, and two elongated beads forming the fastening.

105 A STANDING ATHENA is depicted on an oval field, with a helmet with chinstrap on her head. Bracelets adorn her extended left arm, as well as a veil, which extends behind her knees to the right arm, emerging below the shield. The lance, partly hidden by the shield, slants across the figure of the goddess.

On the rear are four loops, allowing the ornament to be attached to clothing or worn as a pendant. If it is not a copy or imitation, this may have originally been the stone in a seal ring. At least, that can be inferred from the form and flat surface of the object, the name of the goddess, written in reverse, and above all from the significant wear on the engraved surface.

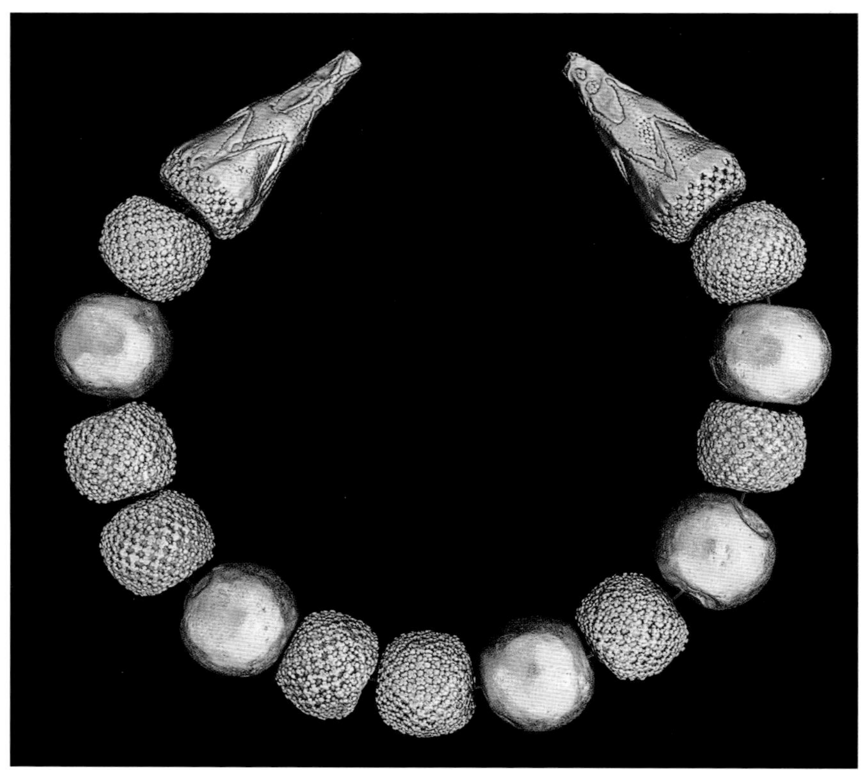

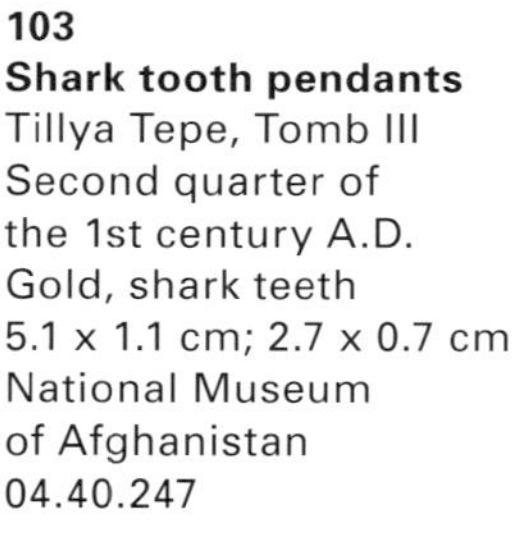

103
Shark tooth pendants
Tillya Tepe, Tomb III
Second quarter of
the 1st century A.D.
Gold, shark teeth
5.1 x 1.1 cm; 2.7 x 0.7 cm
National Museum
of Afghanistan
04.40.247

104
Necklace
Tillya Tepe, Tomb III
Second quarter of
the 1st century A.D.
Gold
Diam. of beads
2.1 x 1.9 and 1.6 cm
National Museum
of Afghanistan
04.40.162

105
Ornament with an image of Athena
Tillya Tepe, Tomb III
Second quarter of
the 1st century A.D.
Gold
1.6 x 1.2 x 0.6 cm
National Museum
of Afghanistan
04.40.197

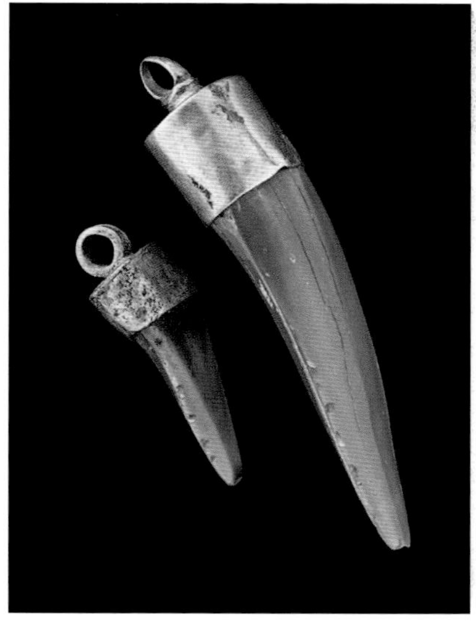

Tillya Tepe, Tomb IV

THIS TOMB WAS SET IN THE MIDDLE of the western wall of the terrace. It was dug inside the top of the former temple wall. The grave was 2.7 meters long, 1.3 meters wide, and 1.8 meters deep, and orientated north-south. At a depth of around 40 centimeters the archaeologists made a remarkable discovery: the skull and bones of a horse. This might suggest the remains of a funeral feast, but because no pottery was discovered and only the head and forelegs of the animal were found it seems more likely that the horse was a sacrificial offering, perhaps placed in the grave to watch over his master and to be ready for his use if needed. This custom has been described by such diverse authors as Herodotus (IV 72), Ibn Battuta, and Simon de Saint-Quentin (Richard, 196[illegible], p. 50), but is also associated with a continuing tradition in Siberia, and in the weakened form of the bæx fældisyn, (the "consecration of the horse"), among the Ossetes in the Caucasus (Dumézil 1978, p. 250).

The skeleton lay on its back with its head to the north, in a wooden coffin 2.2 meters long, 0.7 m broad, and 0.75 meters high, covered with red leather, with painted motifs in black and white, and sewn with gold bracteates. The coffin rested on supports about 15 centimeters from the floor of the grave, which was also covered with leather.

The deceased was a tall man, between 1.7 and 1.85 meters. His head rested on a grooved golden plate (no. 123) which, according to the archaeologists, itself rested on a silk cushion. His jaw was fastened with a double chin band. The man wore a head covering to which were attached a golden wild ram (no. 108) and a golden tree (no. 121). The man's most notable ornaments were a necklace consisting of two twisted threads with a cameo (no. 116), a braided gold belt with nine medallions (no. 107), and a number of bracelets. His clothing was removed layer by layer and carefully examined. In the opinion of the archaeologist responsible (Sarianidi 1989), the man was clad in a shirt and a short kaftan, tied to the left, with trousers below this, but it is more probable that he wore a long, single breasted jacket (Yatsenko 1989 and 2001). Thousands of bracteates (no. 117) and appliqués were sewn onto his clothes, the fabric of gold threads and pearls bearing large decorative motifs on the most visible areas, the upper body and the legs.

His footwear was probably boots or bootees of supple leather, as can be seen on the sculpted depictions of Parthian rulers and the images of Kushan kings at Surkh Kotal in Afghanistan and Mathura in India. It was beautifully decorated with buckles in gold and turquoise (no. 106) and golden rosettes with—once again, in turquoise against a golden background—a heart motif (no. 118). The gold appliqués (nos. 109, 124) were probably the ends of straps attached to the footwear or to the gaiters covering the legs. However, they may also have been attached to the belt.

An Indian medallion—not a coin—lay at the level of the ribcage (no. 119). An intaglio was also found close to the body (no. 120), with an image of the Heraclides, the sons of Heracles, casting lots to determine, which kingdom each would hold. The decorations (nos. 110 to 112) and shield-shaped appliqués (nos. 125 and 126) found on the lower body were interpreted by the excavators as elements of a harness, placed symbolically over the body of the deceased. However, it seems more likely that these were components of a sword-belt or other system for attaching weapons: The same applies to the ornament, which is probably the end of strap (no. 122). This seems all the more likely as these objects were all found set out symmetrically on opposite sides of the body, like the weapons. The deceased, the only male found in the six graves, had a number of magnificent weapons, clearly indicating his status as a leader. Apart from a long sword at his left side, comparable with an example found in the north of Bactria (Mandelstam 1975, pl. XXX,1), the man had a dagger on his right, its handle covered with gold, inserted in a four-lobed sheath decorated with gold and turquoise (nos. 113 and 115). To his left he had an equally beautiful sheath containing a short dagger with an ivory handle (no. 114) and two smaller daggers, placed head to tail. Apart from these weapons, there were two bows with quivers containing arrow-heads. These bows, long-distance weapons characteristic of the nomads and considered by them as a symbol of kingly power, lay outside the coffin, as did a further rather surprising object, which nonetheless matched the status of the deceased, namely a leather-clad seat on X-shaped metal legs. This was both a handy folding stool to take on campaign and also a dignifying sella curulis, a kind of mobile throne, on the whole.

The regal neck chain, the belt, the golden phial or libation bowl, the horseman's dagger in its ceremonial, ostentatious version, the bow as symbol of power, for a more high fashion "Parthian shot," the throne, and finally the horse: All this points to a horseman who passed from cavalry to chivalry, and one who felt it important to emphasise his high position through the emblems of settled kingship, without renouncing his pride in his nomadic origins.

106 THE PERIMETER OF EACH BUCKLE is decorated with a double row of rotating turquoise droplets. The location of the attachment hook is decorated with a large almond-shaped turquoise. The tableau in the central panel, showing a man sitting in a chariot drawn by two mythical creatures is repeated in mirrored symmetry. He has a rather elongated head, tipped back somewhat, his ear clearly visible, the eye small and round; the mouth has clearly depicted lips and seems half-opened. The neck opening of his robe, draped in the Greek manner—rather than a torque—is indicated by a border of turquoise, as is the hem of the cloak and the end of the sleeve. One arm raised, the second bent, he holds the reins. The chariot appears to be in a woven material, while the uprights of the round baldachin look like bamboo. The traditional motif of a king processing under a parasol occurs at Persepolis, while from Aï Khanum, we have the depiction of Cybele (no. 23), standing under a similar parasol in a chariot drawn by lions, but in both cases the parasol is held by a man. This two-wheeled chariot is drawn by two winged, feline animals with curving foreheads, each raising one clawed foot and showing their teeth. They are kept in check with turquoise reins running across their chests. Whether it is the mythical creatures or the strange chariot, something about this image calls up associations with the Far East. This type of chariot, a lightweight model with two wheels, did indeed occur in China at the time of the Han Dynasty (206 B.C.-A.D. 220), and depictions have been found in petroglyphs at Chanyn Chad in Mongolia. More important still was the discovery of a chariot with a ribbed parasol, found by a team from the Musée Guimet during excavations in a Xiongnu nomad necropolis at Gol Mod in Mongolia.

The buckle could be fastened at the inner ankle using four loops at the rear, and there was also a band which passed around the ankle and under the foot, and was made fast using a strap tongue. A similar gold buckle with a hook was found at Dalverzin-tepe in Uzbekistan (Pougatchenkova 1978, fig. 80).

In this case the impression of the material with the help of which the buckle was cast can clearly be seen on the unplated rear part of the object, evidence of a very specialized technique also applied in making diverse objects in the Siberian collection of Peter the Great, held at the Hermitage in St. Petersburg (Rudenko 1962, pl. XXV to XXVII).

106
Boot buckles decorated with an image of a carriage drawn by dragons
Tillya Tepe, Tomb IV
Second quarter of the 1st century A.D.
Gold, turquoise, carnelian
Both: Diam. 5.5 cm; H. 1.1 cm
National Museum of Afghanistan
04.40.383

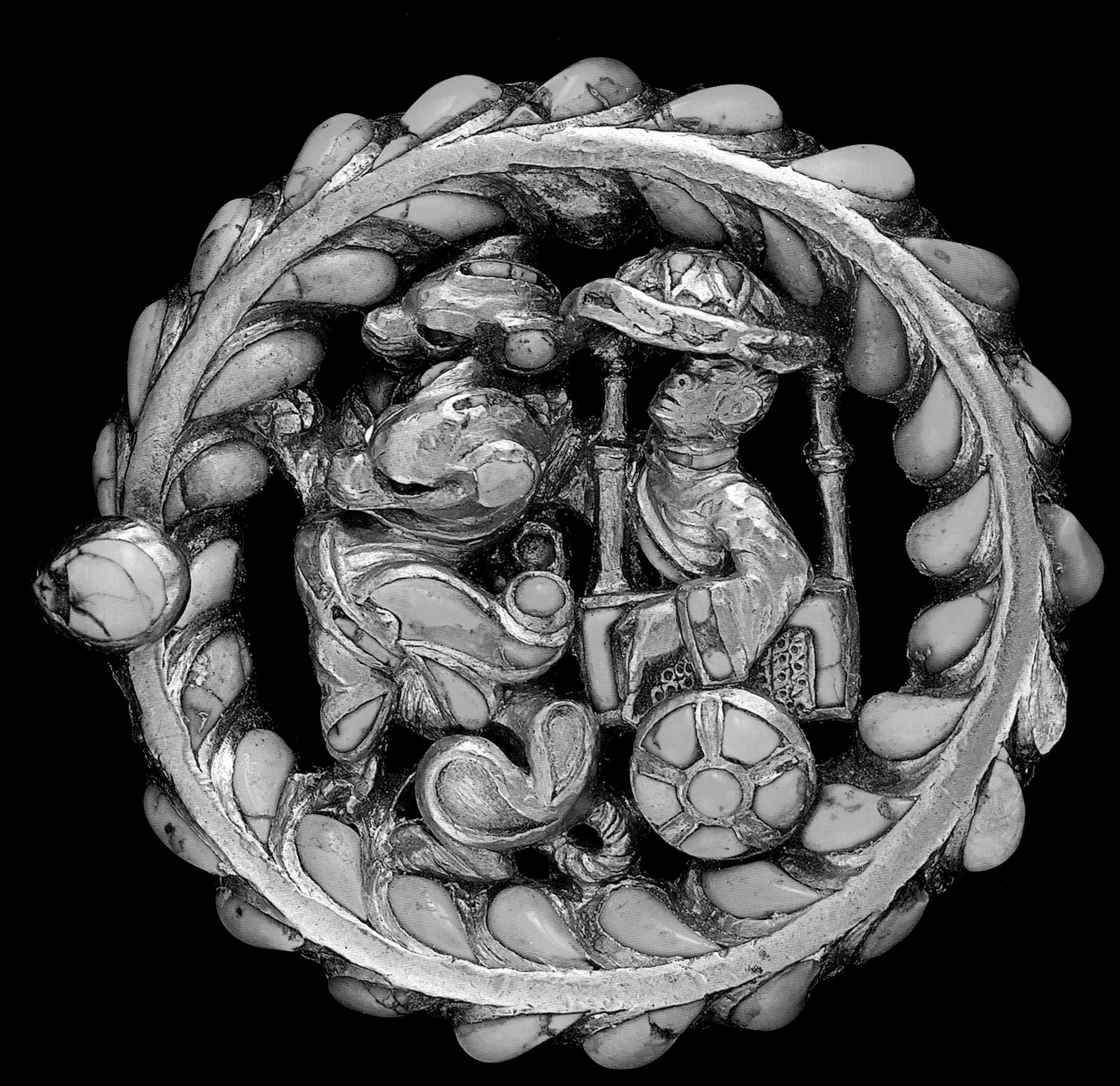

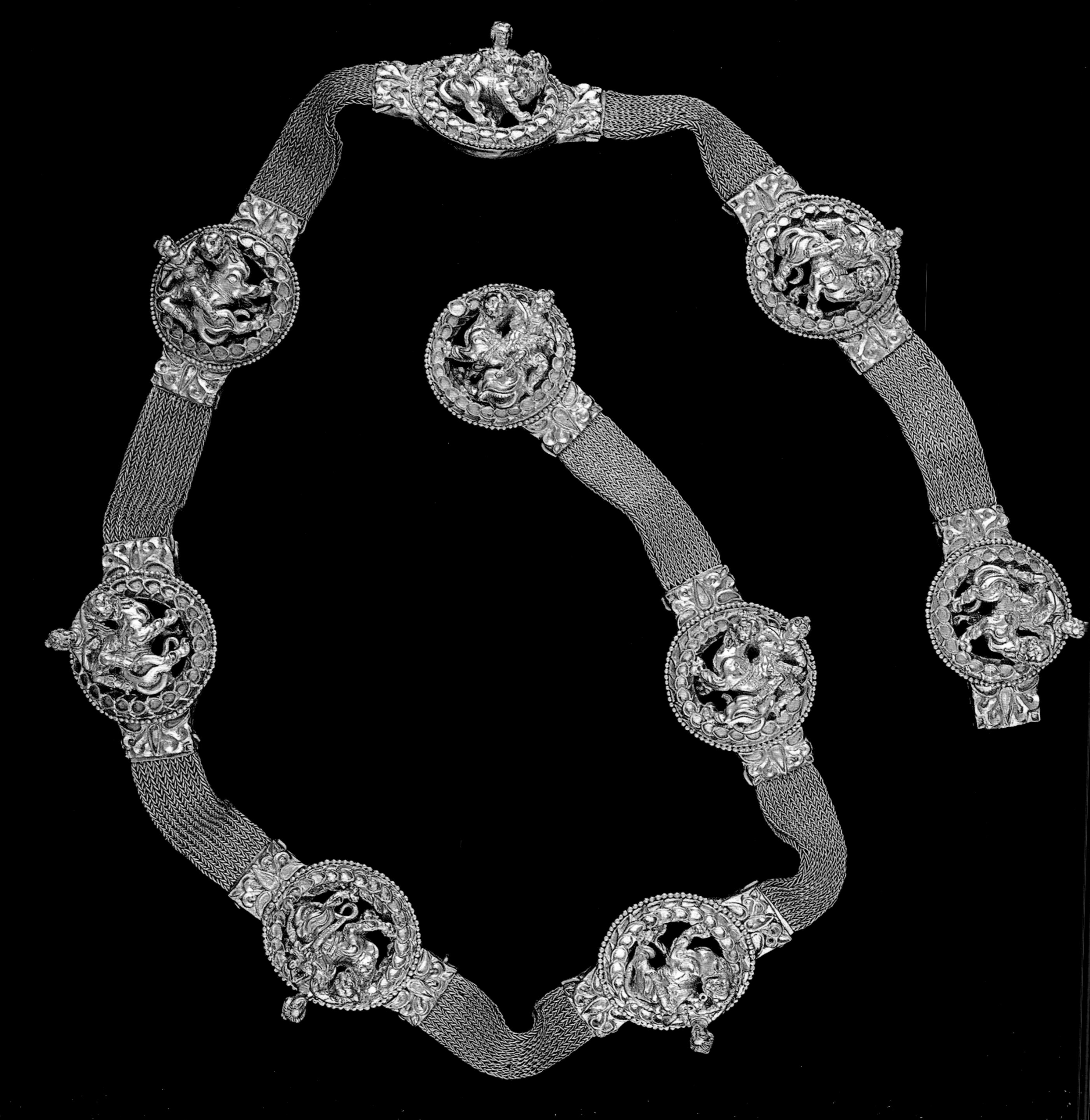

107 THE BELT CONSISTS OF A FLEXIBLE BAND of eight braided gold chains, alternating with nine medallions. Fitting marks (Greek letters?) can be seen on the rear of the medallions. Each medallion has a granulated edge and heart-shaped interlocked recesses, each showing the same tableau: A figure with a beaker in his hand sits, leaning over backward, on the back of a panther, his elbow resting on the creature's head. These images are in a pronounced relief and are all made separately and then soldered on. On five of them the animal walks to the right, while on four it walks to the left, so that they will all meet at the two medallions, which grip one another to provide the fastening. While the general arrangement is identical, there are differences in the details. The panther's attitude, the decoration of the saddlecloth placed over the creature's back, and the curves of its tail vary, as do the features of the figure sitting on the animal. He wears a torque and his hair in a high knot in each image, but on two of the medallions, the hair is held in place with a crown formed from rounded recesses, reminiscent of the hair of Dionysus on the clasps from Tomb VI (no. 136). Like the god, the figure on the panther here is clad in a short tunic exposing his knees and his boots, decorated with palmettes. He also holds a beaker with two handles, which reproduces the form of a kantharos (a Dionysiac beaker) on the third medallion from the left. Even though he is not wearing his characteristic fawn skin, there would be no doubt in the mind of any Greek: This is Dionysus, riding side-saddle on a panther, as he is shown, for instance, on a mosaic in Pella in Macedonia, and in particular on the island of Delos. However, there is one confusing detail, which seems to invalidate the Dionysus hypothesis, namely the two-fingered gesture made by the person: Milk seems to flow from "his" breast, which is nevertheless covered, to be caught by the beaker. The gaze of the figure on most of the medallions is clearly directed toward this particularly feminine gesture. Is this perhaps a case of confusion, mixing or combining different images, namely Dionysus seated on a panther, the Bactrian goddess Nana seated on her lion, and the well-known fertility goddesses who makes the same gesture? Especially puzzling is the comparison with the woman as source of nourishment, seen on a Greco-Bactrian terracotta from Susa (Iran; Louvre Sb 3800 and Ghirshman 1963, fig. 433), which is only slightly older than this belt. Equally confusing is that the so-called "Dionysus" on one of the medallions is shown with a slim neck, fine features, the hair-knot, and knees, which are closer together and more covered, giving "him" something of the appearance of the goddess Artemis. Caution, therefore, continues to be advisable: The questions raised by this image are not all answered by the notion of exchanging the male and the female.

Whatever the truth may be, and no matter what the Roman historian Quintus Curtius (III, 3, 17) may have said about the solid gold belt of the Persian king Darius III that it "looked like the belt of a woman," this object itself does clearly bear a masculine signature.

107
Belt
Tillya Tepe, Tomb IV
Second quarter of the 1st century A.D.
Gold
97.5 x 2.0 cm
National Museum of Afghanistan
04.40.384

108
Standing ram
Tillya Tepe, Tomb IV
Second quarter of
the 1st century A.D.
Gold
5.2 x 4.0 cm
National Museum
of Afghanistan
04.40.399

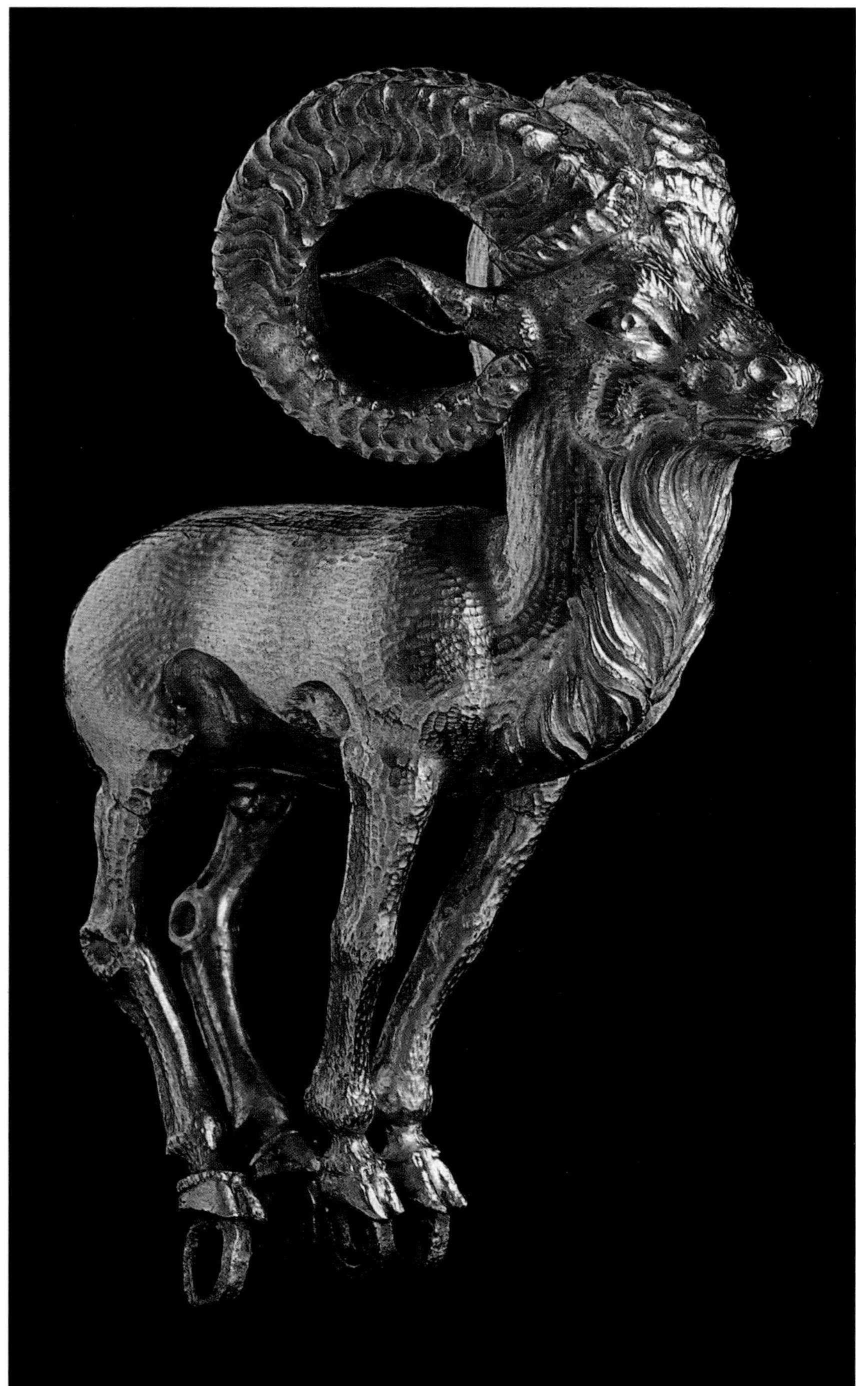

108 IT SEEMS AS THOUGH THE ANIMAL is standing on its four feet keeping watch, with its nose straight ahead and its hooves flat on the rings. This would allow it to be used as a head adornment. The ram has the large grooved horns characteristic of the mouflon breed (identification by C. Jarrige, confirmed by F. Poplin, to whom we are indebted). The animal serving as a model here may have been the urial *(Ovis vignei)* or Severtzov's argali *(Ovis ammon severtzovi),* which is often confused with it (Caprinae 1999, p. 6). There are different varieties of mouflon occurring in Central Asia, which can only be identified using DNA.

Behind the horns is a curious tube, which would allow an ornament to be attached, possibly of organic material such as wood or leather. This seems to be the upper part of a high head covering as often seen among the nomads, such as the example from the seventh century B.C. showing a deer, from the princely grave at Arzhan in Tuva or a more recent example from the Altai, where the crests of felt helmets decorated with wooden statues with leather horns have been preserved because they were frozen (Polosmak 2001, pl. XIX). The Siberian collection of Peter the Great in the Hermitage in St. Petersburg also includes various gold images, which may have had the same function (Rudenko 1962, pl. XXII).

But while the function of the animal points to its use among the nomad leaders, the realistic manner of representation, the detail of the muzzle, the beard and the wool, the depiction of the sexual organs, and the precise delineation of the hooves are quite atypical of the art of the steppes and point to an origin within a workshop working to a completely different tradition.

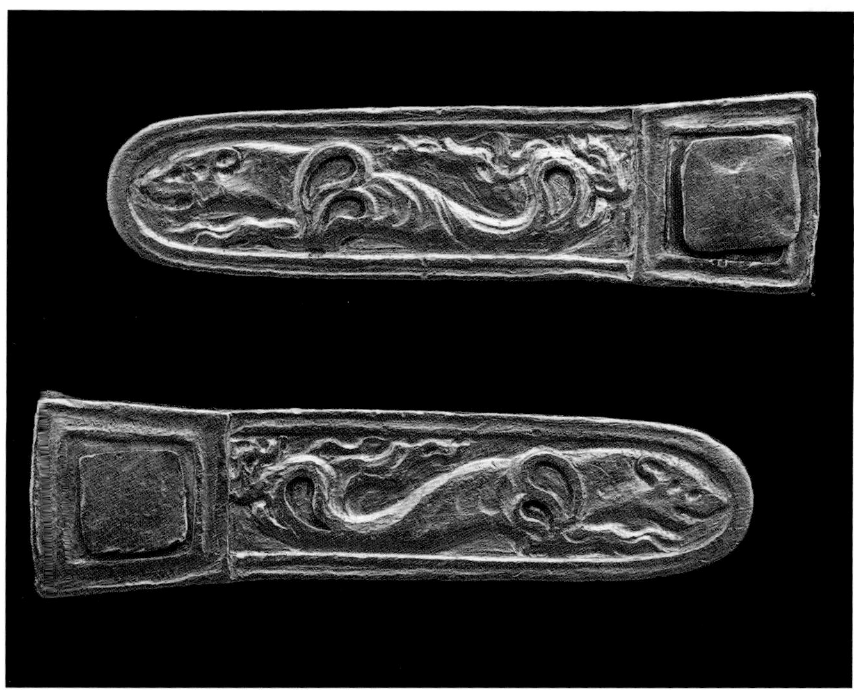

109
Two languettes showing a panther
Tillya Tepe, Tomb IV
Second quarter of the 1st century A.D.
Gold
4.0 x 1.2 cm
National Museum of Afghanistan
04.40.393

110
Strap decoration with a coiled mythical creature
Tillya Tepe, Tomb IV
Second quarter of the 1st century A.D.
Gold
Diam. 2.6 cm;
H. 1.2 cm
National Museum of Afghanistan
04.40.416

111
Strap decorations showing a coiled mythical animal
Tillya Tepe, Tomb IV
Second quarter of the 1st century A.D.
Gold
Diam. 1.8 cm
National Museum of Afghanistan
04.40.390

112
Two strap decorations showing a coiled mythical animal
Tillya Tepe, Tomb IV
Second quarter of the 1st century A.D.
Gold
Diam. 2.2 and 2.1 cm;
H. 1.8 and 1.7 cm
National Museum of Afghanistan
04.40.417

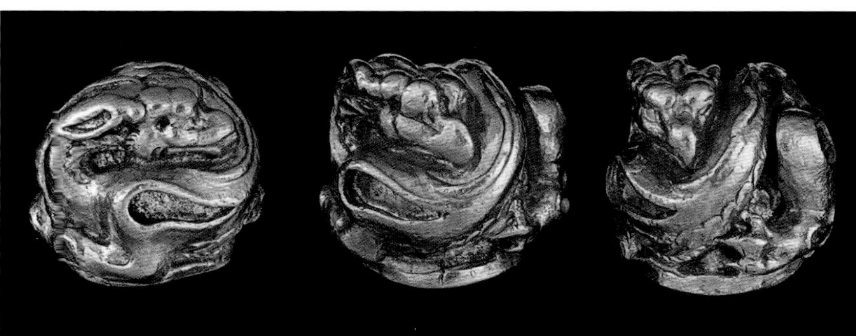

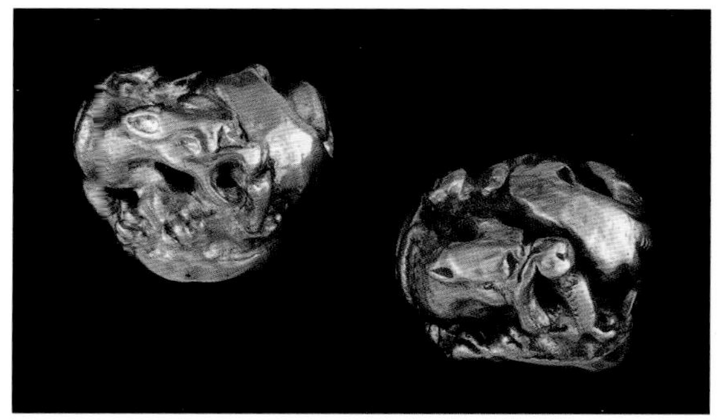

110–112 STRAP DECORATIONS The six protruding buttons are hollow. Remnants of organic materials are still present on the inside, probably from a leather band held in place by a thin piece of gold covering the rear surface at a slant. These are probably decorations used on a sword-belt from which weapons would be hung, rather than phalerae attached to horse tack.

The illustrations are of a mythical creature, rolled up and biting its own tail (no. 110), three monsters with long, doubled-over backbones and the heads of predators with powerful beaks, bumpy foreheads and long, flattened ears (no. 111), and two other more or less similar monsters (no. 112). Traces of wear can be seen, indicating that the objects were used over a considerable period.

Similar buttons are also found in the Siberian collection of Peter the Great in the Hermitage in St. Petersburg (Rudenko 1962, pl. XXIII, 24, 25, 28 to 31, 34), where they are termed phalerae, but there is no archaeological context to permit one to decide.

113 THE GOLD COVERING, which enclosed a leather sheath, had a very unusual four-lobed form, originally with a specific function. The four protruding parts in pairs on either side of the sheath were intended to fasten the weapon both to the belt, using the upper protrusions, and to the thigh, by means of a strap passing through the lower lobes, preventing it from swinging about. We have now developed (Bernard 1987, pp. 764–765; Lebedynsky 1997 and 2001, p. 135 and 2002, pp. 101–103; Schiltz 2002, pp. 853–872) a far better understanding of the origin and development of this type of sheath: Its simple prototype, in wood and leather, appeared as early as the third century B.C. in the south of Siberia, in the Altai and Sayan Mountains, and in Tuva, as well as in Mongolia. This type spread from east to west across Central Asia, across the whole Parthian area, and also among the Sarmatians in the west. We now also know the manner in which these objects changed, as in this case and in Dachi near the Sea of Azov in southern Russia, from a practical to a ceremonial weapon, an external sign that, because of his origins, a person belonged to the nomad aristocracy. The total absence of this type of sheath in the art of the Kushan Empire is interesting.

The imagery, depicting continuous devouring of one creature by another, must be seen as a representation by the Iranians of the steppes of the cycle of life and death that induces fertility. These monsters, making of themselves a "living grave" (Lucretius) as the prey they devour continues to live, fulfill exactly the same role as did the earth for the sedentary farmers, swallowing the seed into its entrails, only to allow it to germinate with greater force.

113
Cover of a dagger sheath
Tillya Tepe, Tomb IV
Second quarter of the 1st century A.D.
Gold, turquoise
23.5 x 9 cm
National Museum of Afghanistan
04.40.382

114
Dagger with gold-covered shaft decorated with a depiction of struggling animals
Tillya Tepe, Tomb IV
Second quarter of the 1st century A.D.
Iron, gold, turquoise
H. 37.5 cm
National Museum of Afghanistan
04.40.387

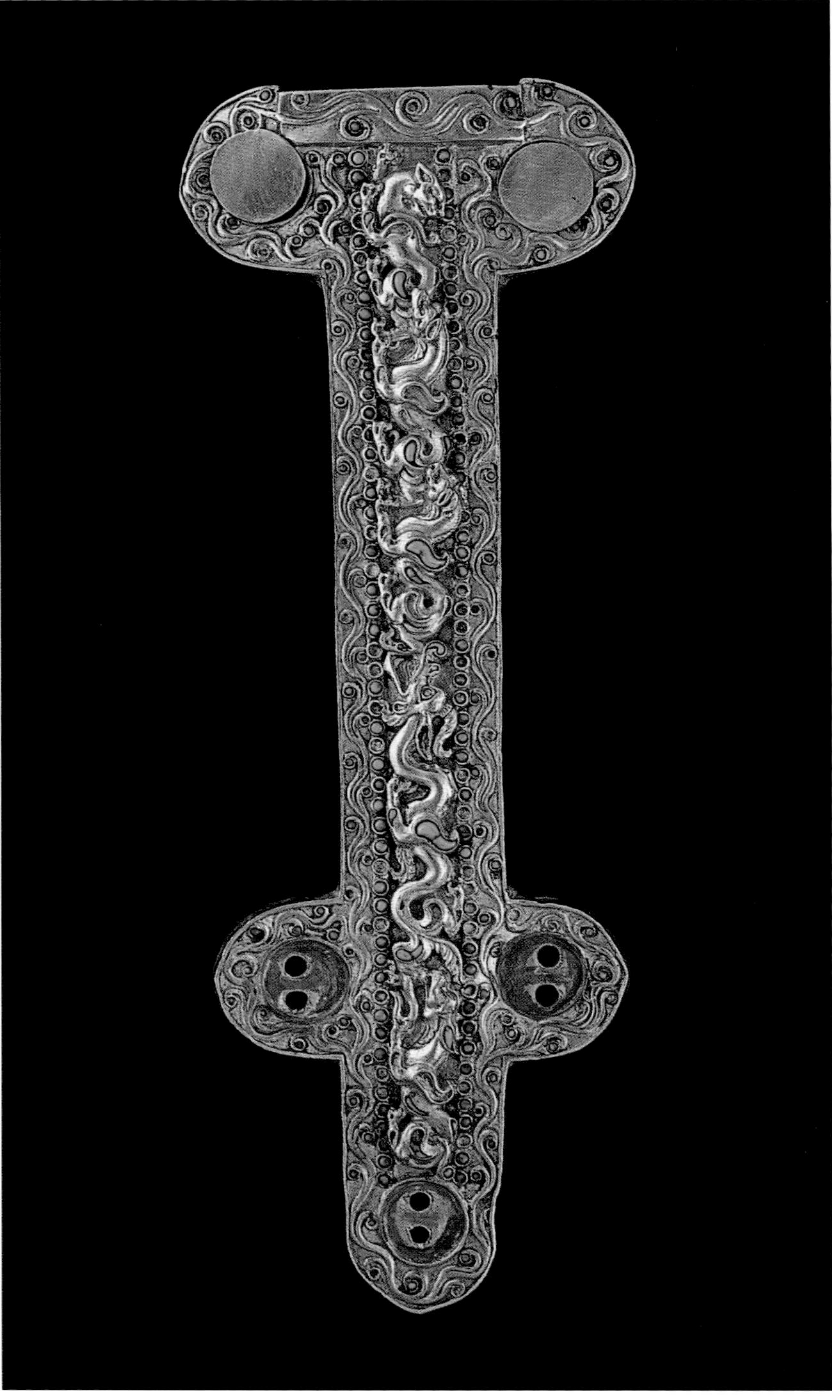

114 THE WEAPON IS A SHORT SWORD of the type known as an akinakes, characteristic of the nomads. This already appears on the reliefs decorating the staircase of the Apadana, the largest reception hall at Persepolis, showing a delegation of Sakas bringing this weapon and a rider's costume to the Great King. The iron blade is double-edged and the pommel is rounded. The long shaft with a rectangular section and the guard are covered in gold. The guard is smooth. The depiction of animals on the front must be read contiguously with the decoration on the sheath described above (no. 113). A simple foliated scroll is seen on the sides of the shaft, while the plant motifs on the rear consist of rings and veined acanthus leaves forming as it were a tree, which continues to branch over the rounded surface of the pommel. The motif of acanthus leaves with incised veins, which occurs on the capitals at Aï Khanum (third to second century B.C.), is derived from the Greek decorative tradition, in particular Megarian bowls and Hellenistic silverwork (Bernard 1968, pp. 123–124). Once again, and repeated six times, an omnipresent pattern in women's graves, the heart form appears in turquoise inlays on this major attribute of the lone dead man. However, the four recesses scattered along the length of the shaft are attached to the "tree" by an explicitly represented stem, confirming that we have before us the image of a leaf.

The clumsy silhouette of a standing bear, seeming to dance, appears on the pommel. Its triangular head with its round ears is shown frontally, its trunk from the side. In its mouth it holds a vine branch, the grapes in turquoise inlay. This fearsome carnivore is intentionally placed on the same side as triumphant life and is presented as a jolly vegetarian who eats grapes. On the rear of the handle of this deadly weapon we see the branches of the Tree of Life. It seems certain that this is no coincidence: In its form and decoration this object carries us back to the reality of the most intrinsically nomadic mode of life and belief system.

115
Sheath for three knives
Tillya Tepe, Tomb IV
Second quarter of the 1st century A.D.
Bronze, gold, turquoise (within the sheath is the iron blade of a dagger with a worked ivory handle)
H. 26.0 cm
National Museum of Afghanistan
04.40.388

115 THE BODY OF THE SHEATH consists of a bronze plate with rounded ends, covered in gold and with two side lobes. The bulbous central section contains the blade of an iron dagger with an ivory handle. On the rear of the sheath was a second tube of leather into which two smaller daggers were fitted, head to toe, reflecting a practice observed in Tuva in Siberia and also in Mongolia. Two fighting mythical creatures, one devouring the other, are shown on the covering. The attacker is a winged dragon with a waving crest, with the upper body and head seen from above, while the rear body and the feet are seen from the side. The creature being attacked has a battered head, shown side-on, with a powerful mouthful of teeth and deer's antlers with several branches, the ends decorated with turquoises. This is perhaps a reference to one of the symbolic figures of the nomads, the deer, which frequently haunts the art of the steppes, from Siberia to the Danube and beyond. Two ram's heads are shown on the side lobes (see also no. 108), depicted frontally, with horns shown as grooved volutes and a hollow triangle on the forehead. A row of hearts with turquoise inlay work runs around the entire border. Parallel to this is a frieze of alternating squares—some of a four-leaf clover with four heart-shaped leaves in turquoise—and an Indian motif, the swastika, of colored glass paste, which must originally have been bright blue.

A two-part sheath like those used by nomads, the antlers of a deer, a Chinese dragon, Indian swastikas, shoulders emphasized with inlay work using comma shapes as employed by the Achaemenids, Greek modelling, and overabundant decoration with heart shapes: This object provides one of the clearest examples of the diversity of the elements used in the art from Tillya Tepe.

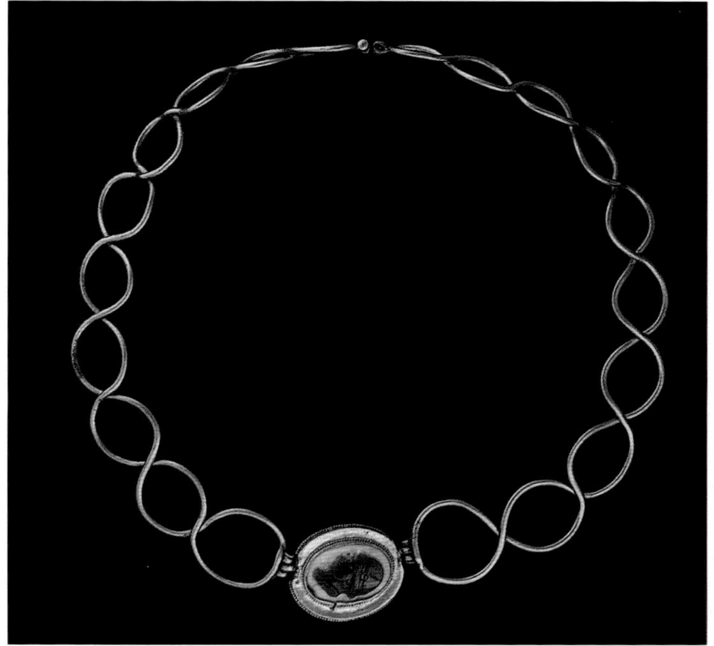

116 THE NECKLACE CONSISTS OF TWO symmetrical elements. Two thick, round gold cables, in figure-of-eight twist and soldered at the intersections, terminating above with a closure fastened with a gold nail. The size of the figure-of-eight loops steadily increases toward the bottom, so that the central ornament is shown to its best advantage. The ornament is a cameo attached by hinges to the gold cables. The two-layered stone has a white background with a head depicted in profile in brown. The figure wears a helmet characteristic of depictions of the royal Greco-Bactrian iconography. The form of the necklace, which does not occur in the art of the Kushans, is known from representations of Indo-Parthian rulers from Arachosia and the Punjab from the first half of the first century A.D. This is first noted in the case of Gondophares (ca A.D. 20–46), the founder of the dynasty, and his example was generally followed by his successors (Bernard 1987, pp. 763–764). Whether the stone was engraved in the Greek era as the archaeologist conducting the excavations believed, or if it was an imitation made to order as suspected by Paul Bernard, on the grounds of the moderate quality of the finish, it is, like the necklace itself, clearly an emblem of power.

116
Necklace with cameo
Tillya Tepe, Tomb IV
Second quarter of
the 1st century A.D.
Gold, sardonyx
L. 21.0 cm
National Museum
of Afghanistan
04.40.378

117
Bracteates decorated with four roundels
Tillya Tepe, Tomb IV
Second quarter of
the 1st century A.D.
Gold
1.9 x 1.3 x 0.2 cm
National Museum
of Afghanistan
04.40.404

119 OBVERSE: A STANDING MAN in half profile seems to be walking while pushing an eight-spoked wheel in front of him with both hands. In front of him is an inscription in Kharoshthi, the script of the Gandhara kingdom, "dharmacakrapravata [ko]," meaning: "He who brings the wheel of the law into motion."

Reverse: a standing lion, turning to the left and with the right forepaw raised. In front of the lion is the Buddhist symbol called the nandipada (a circle with a trident above); behind it, at top right of the field, is an inscription in Kharoshthi: "Sih [o] vigatabhay [o]," meaning "the lion has driven away fear."

It is possible that we have here the oldest representation of the Buddha, a forerunner of traditional Buddhist iconography.

The notion of putting into motion the wheel of the law (dharmacakra) comes from the Buddha's first sermon, delivered at Benares (Varanasi): The eight spokes symbolize the the route to enlightenment.

The lion is the symbol of the spiritual power of Buddhas and Bodhisattvas; the lion's roar makes everyone aware of the call of the dharma, the truth at the core of existence.

120 THIS OVAL APPLIQUÉ has a tube at the rear allowing it to be attached to a garment. On the front, a granulated border surrounds an intaglio showing three helmeted warriors, two of whom carry shields. They are standing around a pillar surmounted by an eagle; one bends toward an amphora resting on the ground. Comparison with other engraved stones suggests that this image may be interpreted as showing the Heraclides, the sons of Heracles, drawing lots to determine their future kingdoms, next to an altar dedicated to Zeus. The (admittedly rather uncertain) hypothesis might be formulated that such a scene, showing warriors casting lots, may be applicable to the prince entombed here. We do not know the circumstances in which he acquired his territories.

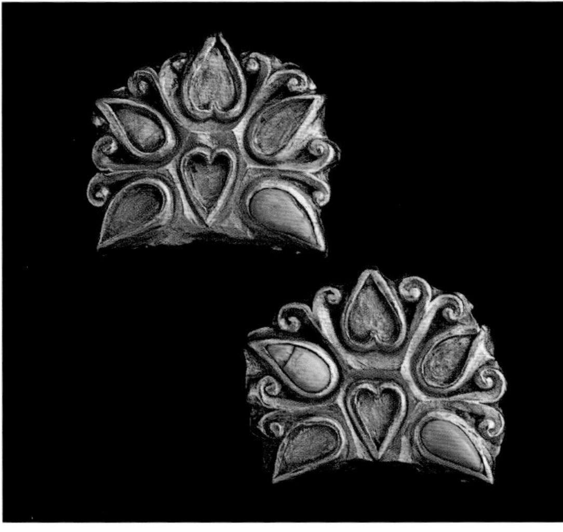

118
Two shoe decorations (hearts and leaves)
Tillya Tepe, Tomb IV
Second quarter of the 1st century A.D.
Gold, turquoise
2.5 x 2.7 cm
National Museum of Afghanistan 04.40.402

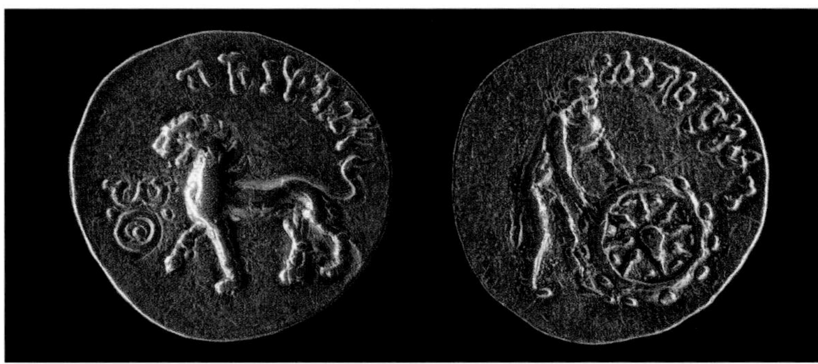

119
Indian medallion
Tillya Tepe, Tomb IV
Last quarter of the 1st century B.C.
Gold
Diam.1.6 cm
National Museum of Afghanistan 04.40.392

120
Appliqué
Tillya Tepe, Tomb IV
Second quarter of the 1st century A.D.
Gold, glass paste
1.8 x 1.3 x 0.6 cm
National Museum of Afghanistan 04.40.18

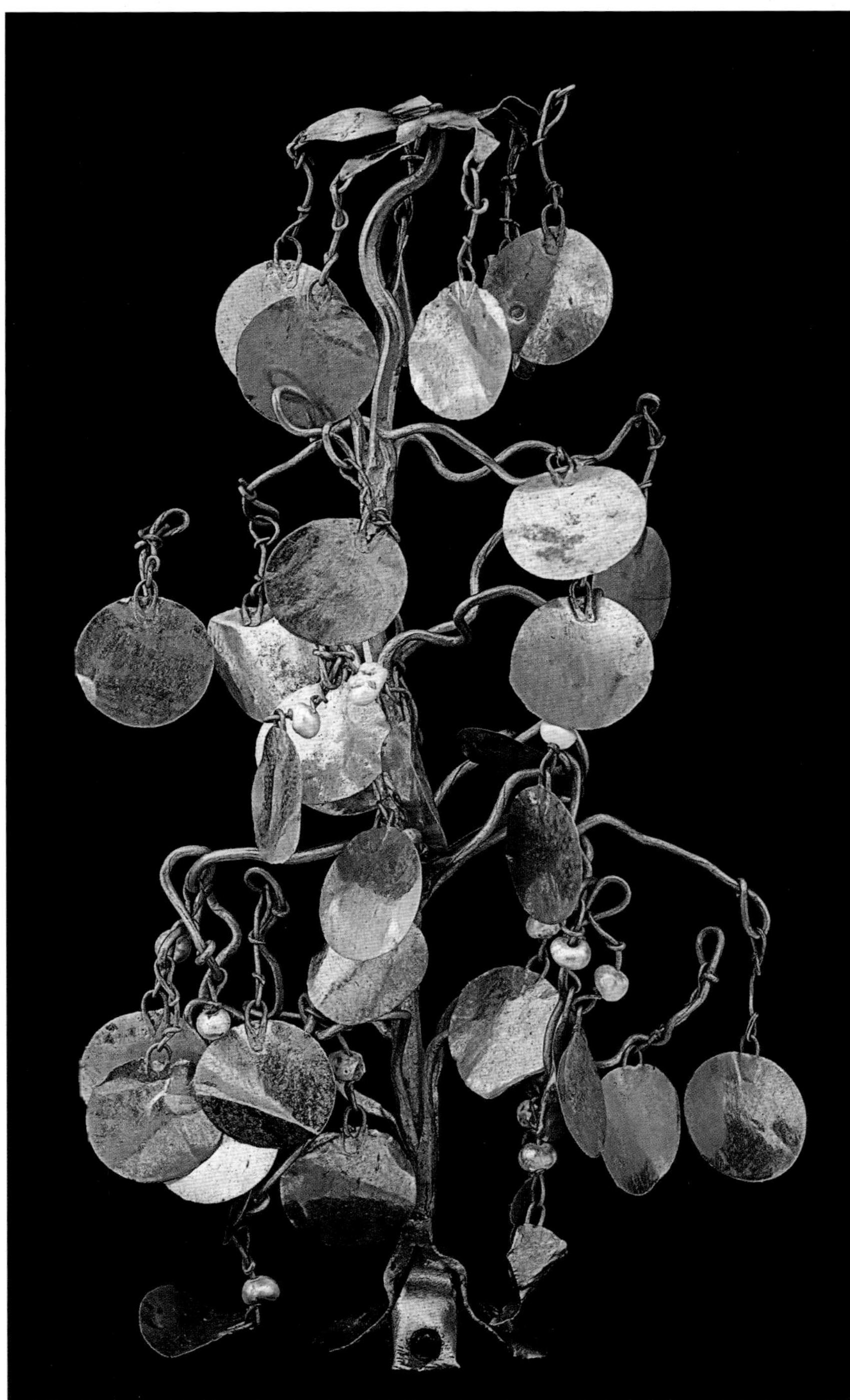

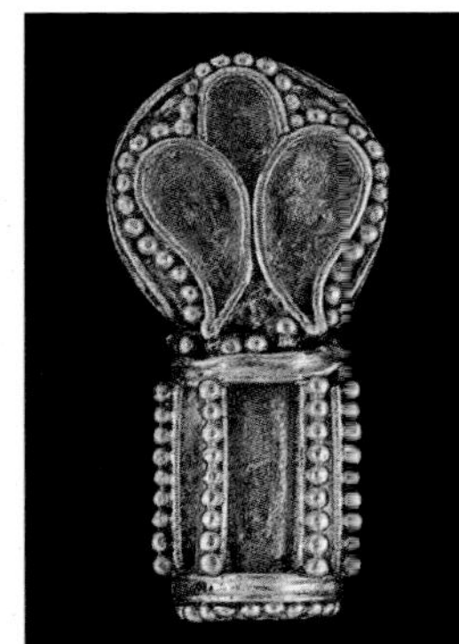

121
Headdress shaped like a tree
Tillya Tepe, Tomb IV
Second quarter of the 1st century A.D.
Gold, pearls
H. 9.0 cm
National Museum of Afghanistan
04.40.400

122
Ornament with oval head
Tillya Tepe, Tomb IV
Second quarter of the 1st century A.D.
Gold
H. 2.6 cm
National Museum of Afghanistan
04.40.377

121 THE "TREE" CONSISTS OF A VERTICAL STEM of quadrangular section to which round threads with pearls and flat disks have been attached. The crown of the "tree" consists of a horizontal leaf cut into six smaller leaves, each bearing six disks.

The Siberian collection of Peter the Great in the Hermitage in St. Petersburg includes three examples of similar golden trees (Artamonov 1973, p. 209), consisting of a stem, branches, and pendants, one of which (fig. 275) has leaf pendants with the exact shape of a heart. This is notable, and probably carries some significance, but the meaning of these hearts is not yet known.

Together with the ram (no. 108), this Tree of Life forms part of the man's head covering, following a tradition into which the woman's crown (no. 134) from Tomb VI also fits.

122 THIS ORNAMENT HAS AN OVAL HEAD and a hollow, half-oval central section with recesses intended for inlay work. It is probable that this piece formed the end of a belt, and probably a sword-belt. A similar ornament was found near a sword with a four-lobed sheath at the archaeological site at Dachi close to the Azov Sea in southern Russia (Schiltz 2001, no. 237).

123
Phial (bowl)
Tillya Tepe, Tomb IV
Second quarter of the 1st century A.D.
Gold
Diam. 23.0 cm; H. 4.0 cm
National Museum of Afghanistan
04.40.381

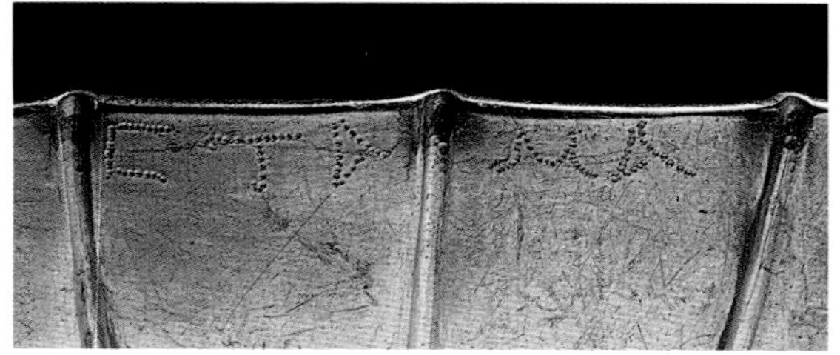

123 THE CONVEX OMPHALOS ("navel," or more generally "center") of this drinking bowl is accentuated by a number of roundels and forms the center of 32 radiating ribs. On the outside of the rim, five punched Greek letters—CTA MA—indicate the weight of metal in staters (tetradrachms), employing the Ionic system, which used the letters of the Greek alphabet in a decimal system. M indicates 40 and A is 1, giving 41 (staters). Taking account of the weight of the bowl, which can hardly have changed, a stater (tetradrachm) therefore has a value of 15.56 grams (Bernard 2000, p. 1426).

It is tempting to link the location of this bowl, under the head of the deceased, with Herodotus's observation about the phial (IV, 10): He regarded such bowls as symbolizing royal authority among the Scythians. However, it would probably be wiser to regard the bowl simply as a head-rest, a more luxurious version of the wooden cushions, curved to hold the deceased person's headdress, which are found in graves in the Altai Mountains of Siberia. This would seem to be confirmed by the fact that the heads of two of the women (from Tombs III and VI) lay on metal vessels.

124 THIS IS A PURELY LINEAR DEPICTION of a mythical animal, lacking perspective and employing incised lines. Its long, undulating body has more of the Chinese dragon about it than the Greek sea monster the ketos (see Boardman 2003).

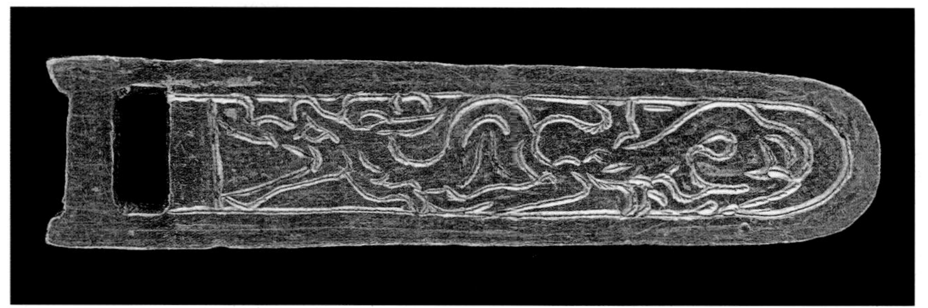

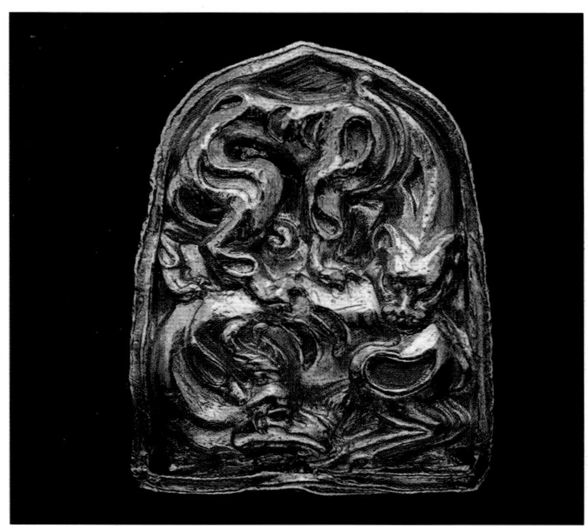

125 THE SHIELD-LIKE SHAPE of this appliqué, with five hooks on the rear and two fixing holes below, occurs frequently in ornaments of carved wood or leather found in the Altai Mountains of Siberia, but also on ivory sword sheaths from the Greco-Bactrian era, as found in the Temple of the Oxus at Takht-i Sangin in Tajikistan (Litvinsky 2001, pl. 72). It shows a winged panther standing on the back of a fallen antelope: The panther's claws are pressed into the flesh of its prey, and it is biting the antelope's rump with wide opened jaws. This is a leitmotif of nomad art from the Yellow River to the Danube. The manner in which the predator is represented, as though from above, with the body from the side and the head front on or more precisely from above; the attitude of the victim, with the head turned back and the legs folded beneath the body; and the use of comma-shaped recesses to accentuate the shoulder and the thigh, all fit within the purest tradition of the art of the steppes.

126 THIS APPLIQUÉ, OF THE SAME TYPE as the previous example, still retains its turquoise inlay work. It shows a tableau of two winged wild beasts with three sharp claws to each foot. Their bodies are shown vertically; one bites the rump of a horse, which has fallen and is shown horizontally; the other bites its neck. The theme and the manner in which the picture is inscribed in the field are characteristic of steppe art. Nevertheless, with its modelling, the delineation of the fur and the manes, and the realistic details, this image shows more clearly than the last example that the goldsmith who made it was familiar with another tradition, which in the west led to the creation of Greco-Scythian art.

As with so many other objects from the necropolis, the presence of heart-shaped inlay work on the upper and lower surfaces of the plate cannot be mere coincidence. In this particular case the motif does appear to have an explicit significance: It looks like a signature.

124
Appliqué showing a dragon
Tillya Tepe, Tomb IV
Second quarter of the 1st century A.D.
Gold
3.5 x 0.8 cm
National Museum of Afghanistan
04.40.403

125
Shield-shaped appliqué
Tillya Tepe, Tomb IV
Second quarter of the 1st century A.D.
Gold
4.7 x 3.6 x 0.5 cm
National Museum of Afghanistan
04.40.386

126
Shield-shaped appliqué
Tillya Tepe, Tomb IV
Second quarter of the 1st century A.D.
Gold, turquoise
5.1 x 4.3 x 0.7 cm
National Museum of Afghanistan
04.40.385

Tillya Tepe, Tomb V

THIS TOMB, MEASURING 2.05 to 2.10 by 0.80 meters, was inserted in the Achaemenid period mud-brick rampart on the north side of the mound. Since no metal clamps or nails were found, it seems that, in contrast to the other coffins made from wooden boards, the person buried here, at a depth of 1.65 meters, was probably interred in a coffin hewn out of a solid tree trunk, as was the practice in the Altai Mountains of Siberia.

Taking account of the manner in which the numerous small silver appliqués, round or in the shape of a vine leaf, lay below, as well as on top of the coffin, it seems that this 2 by 0.65 meter lidless cist was entirely wound round by a cloth (possibly in several layers), onto which the decorations had been sewn.

The deceased was a girl or young woman aged up to around 20. She lay on her back, with her head to the west. When we consider the robe, probably decorated with some tiny beads, but without appliqués or bracteates, the relative simplicity of her adornments and the moderate quality of the grave furnishings, this is the least wealthy grave in the necropolis.

As well as the golden band used to bind her jaw, the deceased also wore heart-shaped earrings (no. 128). She wore a polychrome necklace (no. 129) at her neck, more precisely along the neckline of her robe, a bracelet with sliding ends at her left wrist (no. 127), and rings at her ankles (no. 130). A pendant in the form of a lion (no. 131) and two gems (nos. 132 and 133) lay in a heap to the top right in a corner of the coffin, together with other amulets, including a small bell. Close to her right hand lay a silver mirror with a stand, together with the remains of a small case in gold brocade, sewn with tiny beads. Within the reach of the same hand was a woven basket containing a lidded silver cosmetics box and an iron hook. Her feet seemed to be resting on a silver dish of low silver content. However, there was also an object that appears to contradict this general air of simplicity: Just as with the deceased in Tomb VI, a long hollow cylinder reminiscent of a scepter—in this case in silver with remnants of wood inside—lay beside the woman, close to her right shoulder.

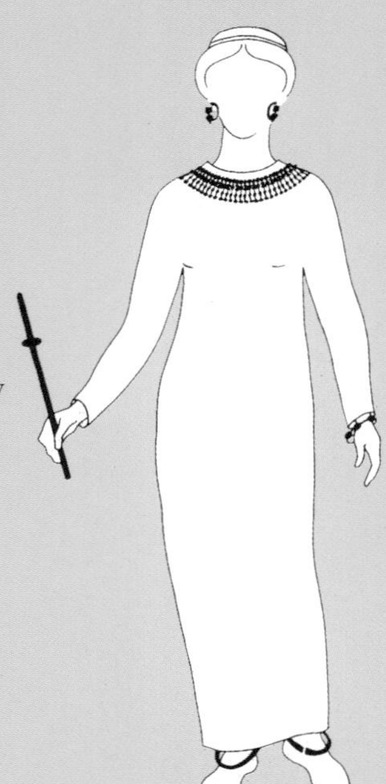

127 THE BRACELET IS MADE from a bent thin gold thread, with the spiralled ends twisting together as a fastening, which allows the ornament to be adjustable. This type of bracelet has also been found in the north of Bactria, particularly in Dalverzin-tepe in Uzbekistan (Pougatchenkova 1978, fig. 74), and at Taxila in Pakistan (Marshall 1951, pl. 195b). The two adjacent rings suggest that there must have been another stone, lost at a much earlier stage. The final setting is once again oval and includes an amber cabochon. There are two loops to the rear, showing that the stone has been reused.

The whole assembly appears to be a collection of reused elements mounted on a bracelet. These disparate elements were valuable, and it is probable that a variety of magical properties were ascribed to them.

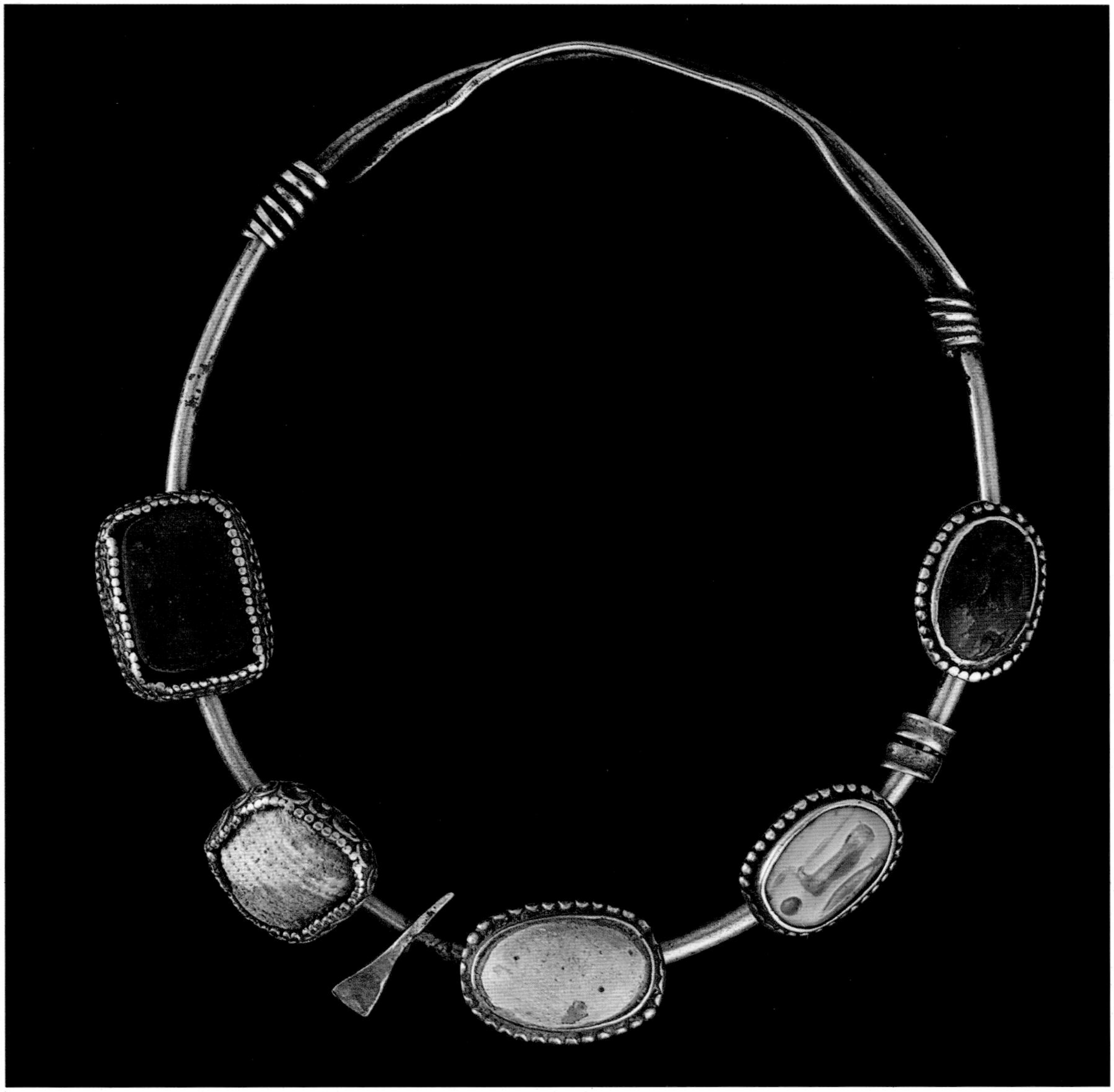

127
Bracelet with sliding ends
Tillya Tepe, Tomb V
Second quarter of the 1st century A.D.
Gold, turquoise, amber, lead glass, deteriorated stones
Diam. 6.7 cm
National Museum of Afghanistan
04.40.134

128
A pair of heart-shaped earrings
Tillya Tepe, Tomb V
Second quarter of the 1st century A.D.
Gold, turquoise
Diam. 7.2 cm
National Museum of Afghanistan
04.40.137

128 THE TWO ELEMENTS ARE IDENTICAL. An oval rod, bent into a ring, ends in a square box originally inlaid with a turquoise in both cases. Below this is a heart-shaped setting which also held a turquoise.

129
Ornament for the neck of a robe
Tillya Tepe, Tomb V
Second quarter of the 1st century A.D.
Gold, turquoise, garnet, pyrites
L. 29.1 cm
National Museum of Afghanistan
04.40.140

129 THIS ORNAMENT IS NOTEWORTHY both for the repetition and alternation of forms and also the sophisticated effect of the striking polychromy. It is a combination of two types of pendants. One type consists of smooth, hollow beads under which a round setting of semi-precious stones (garnet or turquoise) has been soldered; an almond-shaped setting with a dark semi-precious stone hangs from this, with a round disk of smooth gold suspended from that in its turn. The other type of pendant consists of granulated rings with a spacer in the form of a double crescent attached; below this hangs a similar almond-shaped setting with a dark stone, and below this the same smooth golden roundel. Similar compositions occur at Taxila in Pakistan, while at Tillya Tepe itself two other ornaments were found (nos. 72 and 73), displaying a series of rounded forms enclosed by crescents. The motif of precious stones in an almond-shaped setting with a granulated border is fairly widely used: It is notable that a very similar design was found in a grave at the mouth of the Don, and was part of an adornment similarly sewn to the neck of a robe (Schiltz 2001 nos. 275 and 278). The two conical elements with their milled edges function as fastenings. However the small tubes soldered to the rear of the crescents, through which a thread could pass, indicate that this ornament, like so many others of its type, was intended as an ornament to be sewn to the neck of the wearer's gown.

130
A pair of anklets
Tillya Tepe, Tomb V
Second quarter of
the 1st century A.D.
Gold
L. 27.0 cm
National Museum
of Afghanistan
04.40.85

131
Pendant in the form of a lion
Tillya Tepe, Tomb V
Second quarter of
the 1st century A.D.
Amber
2.6 x 2.2 x 1.0 cm
National Museum
of Afghanistan
04.40.141

132
Intaglio with depiction of a griffin
Tillya Tepe, Tomb V
4th century B.C. (?)
Chalcedony
3.1 x 2.8 cm
National Museum
of Afghanistan
04.40.161

133
Intaglio with a representation of Nike
Tillya Tepe, Tomb V
Second quarter of
the 1st century A.D.
Silver, malachite
Diam. 1.0 cm
National Museum
of Afghanistan
04.40.143

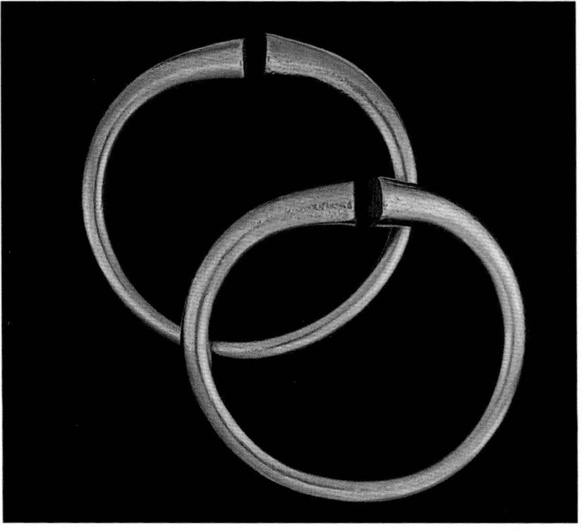

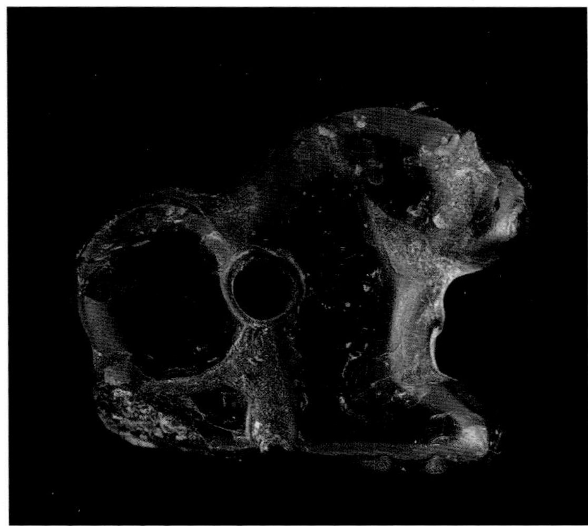

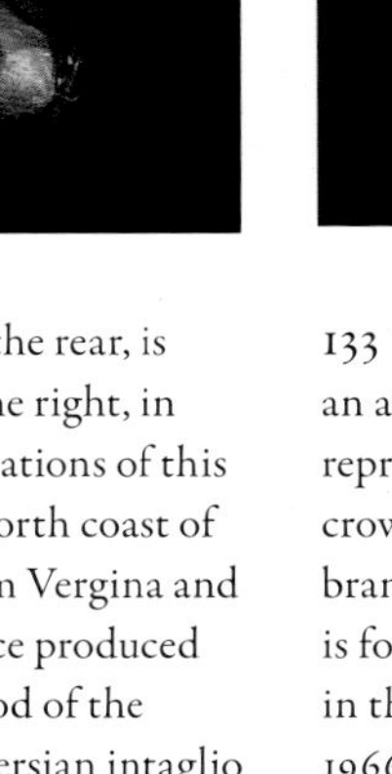

132 THE MILKY-BLUE STONE, domed at the rear, is longitudinally pierced. The griffin, leaping to the right, in many respects resembles the common representations of this monster seen in Greco-Scythian art from the north coast of the Black Sea, as well as in Macedonian art from Vergina and from Tarentum (Taranto). Possibly this is a piece produced by an experienced artist in the blossoming period of the Greco-Bactrian Empire, or it may be a Greco-Persian intaglio reused as an element of a necklace and then finally as a separate jewel which retained great significance for the nomads.

133 THIS GEM IS PLACED in a round silver setting with an attachment point to the rear. It is a green stone with a representation of a winged Nike, holding in her left hand a crown with long ribbons, while the right hand holds a palm branch, which rests on her shoulder. A similar representation is found on a brass ring in the nomad necropolis at Tulkhar in the north of Bactria (now in Tajikistan; Mandelstam 1966, p. 121).

Tillya Tepe, Tomb VI

THE SIXTH TOMB WAS LOCATED in the western section of a corridor which encircled the former temple. It was well preserved, and at the top took the form of a 3.0 by 2.5 meter rectangle, narrowing to 2.5 meters by 1.2 meters at a depth of 1 meter and then continuing down for a further meter. The shelf so created had an earth-covered mat, similar to that of Tomb IV. Free space remained between the ceiling and the cist. The coffin was made of boards and was 2 meters long, 50 centimeters wide, and about 40 centimeters high. It rested on brick supports, placing it at around 20 centimeters above the base. The coffin was probably unlidded and like the other was probably wound in a cloth decorated with gold and silver roundels.

The occupant, a young female of around 20 and of average height (1.52 meters), lay on her back with her head to the west. An unusual detail was that, like the woman in the grave at Koktepe near Samarkand, Uzbekistan, her skull was intentionally deformed, in accordance with a practice then current among the upper levels of society in Central Asia.

Her head, bearing a tall golden crown (no. 134), rested on a small silver plate. Pins with pendants had been attached to her hair (no. 142), while on either side of her face was a large gold pendant with a depiction of a goddess with two animals (no. 137). The woman wore earrings showing winged cupids (no. 138). Her jaw was held closed with a golden band. In her mouth lay a silver Parthian coin bearing a countermark, probably coming from Margiana, a region in the present border area of Turkmenistan, Uzbekistan, and Afghanistan. Around her neck was a chain of gold beads inlaid with turquoise (no. 143), and around each arm was a bracelet with a lion head (no. 140). In her right hand she held a sort of gold scepter, in her left hand, which bore a gem ring (no. 139), a Parthian coin (no. 146). She wore gold anklets, inlaid with turquoise (no. 141). Her clothing consisted of either a long robe or more probably a tunic and trousers, and was decorated at the breast, shoulders (no. 145), and sleeves with rows of numerous appliqués and bracteates bearing various motifs. The central ornament in the middle of the chest was the "Aphrodite of Bactria" (no. 135), covered by a smooth molded appliqué and with three attachment rings, two in the region of the wings and one by the feet. Clasps showing an embracing man and woman (no. 136) closed the neck of the garment. The bracteates found in the area of the feet indicate that the deceased was dressed in leather or felt slippers.

A silver Chinese mirror lay on her breast. A second mirror with an ivory handle lay at her feet, next to a large silver vessel.

Outside the coffin lay a woven basket containing a clay vessel, the remnants of iron toilet articles, three glass bottles, two ivory boxes, two miniature silver pots, and a cosmetics plate with a file and pins.

134 THE CROWN CONSISTS OF A BAND in the form of a diadem, with five elements attached, which together form "trees." The band is cut out of gold leaf and decorated with 20 six-leaved rosettes from which hang gold roundels. Each rosette has a round recess with a granulated finish, containing a turquoise. To the rear of the band are five vertical tubes made of rolled gold leaf, securing the five "trees" to two identical tubes attached to each of the five "tree branches," and also joining the trees together. This ingenious system allows this superb nomadic headdress to be dismantled and transported.

Four of the "trees" are identical and spread their branches symmetrically on either side of the trunk, which is decorated with an excised motif of two opposed hearts with a crescent between them. On the upper branches are two birds, their wings extended, reaching up with their head to the top of the tree, appearing to touch it with their bill. Each tree is decorated with six rosettes with six leaves, bearing round pendants. The fifth (middle) tree lacks the birds, but is decorated with rosettes and pendants; on either side of the broad trunk ascend two branches, which meet above, forming a round opening in which a rotating ornament is placed.

This type of crown has many parallels among the nomads, but it is not found among the Greeks, the Parthians, or the Kushans. As early as the end of the fourth century B.C., the high headgear worn by the young warrior from the kurgan mound at Issyk in Kazakhstan was decorated with birds in the crown, which undoubtedly represented the Tree of Life. The same combination of tree and birds is found at the start of the modern era at the Sarmatian site at Khokhlach near Novocherkassk, and also on the diadem of the princess from Kobyakovo, a little to the west near the mouth of the Don River. Similar headdresses, consisting of a diadem decorated with tree and bird motifs, were also found from fifth and sixth century sites on the eastern edge of Asia, in the burial mounds at royal Silla in the southeast of Korea.

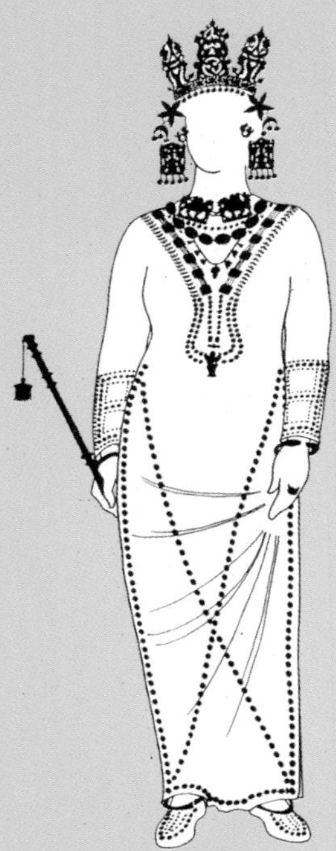

134
Crown
Tillya Tepe, Tomb VI
Second quarter of the 1st century A.D.
Gold, imitation turquoise
45.0 x 13.0 cm
National Museum of Afghanistan
04.40.50

136 THE CLASPS ARE BOTH provided at the back side with a smooth appliqué, but one bears a loop while the other is fitted with a hook. On the front they each have almost identical tableaux, one a mirror image of the other. A man and a woman are shown in an embrace, seated on a monster who is striding forward, one forepaw raised. The man sits astride, the woman side-saddle. He wears a short robe which exposes his knees, she has a long robe reaching to her feet. The man is turning tenderly toward his companion, placing an arm around her shoulders. However, it is to a hairy figure with pointed ears and a flat nose, half slumped on the ground, that he passes a ribbed, two-handled chalice. In one hand this figure holds a shepherd's staff, which has fallen to the ground, with the other hand he lifts a rhyton (drinking horn) toward the chalice, as though asking for more; at the same time the precious liquid runs into his mouth from the bottom end of his cup, which is shaped like a horned head, like rhytons found in the old Parthian capital of Nisa. For a Greek there would be no doubt: This balding figure's bushy face, here dressed in an animal skin secured with a Hercules knot, is Silenus, a god who makes prophecies during his frequent bouts of drunkenness, and who was regarded in Nisa as the foster-father of Dionysus. Here, Dionysus himself gives him a drink. The god is clad in the nebrid, his characteristic fawn-skin. The spots of the animal's skin can be seen below his arm, and even its foot is shown. His features are Asian, in his long curling hair is a wreath, probably of ivy, and he is shod in short boots decorated with palmettes, with a heart-shaped recess in the toe. His companion, with less slanted eyes, is none other than Ariadne. She also wears a wreath. Around her neck is not so much a necklace as a decoration of the neck opening of her robe, as worn by the women in the tombs at Tillya Tepe (no. 129), which extends to a round ornament on her shoulder. Behind her hovers Nike, in both cases holding in her left hand a palm branch, which rests on her shoulder, while with the right hand she holds a wreath above the heads of the couple. The goddess wears a tunic, belted in tightly at the waist, with a long robe beneath. She is barefoot and has bracelets on her wrists and upper arms. This tableau, decidedly Greek in inspiration, bears witness to the success of Dionysiac motifs from Bactria to India. On the other hand, Parthian period bronze belt buckles found in Sakastan (now the border area between Iran, Pakistan, and Afghanistan) show a man and woman, sitting facing or beside one another and embracing (Ghirshman 1979, pl. I and pl. III, 1). This kind of explicit unity between man and woman is unknown in the iconography of both the Greeks and the settled Iranians, but seems to fit more naturally into the world of the nomads, where women played an important and recognized role. Perhaps we can take this unity of man and woman on their animal mount to symbolize the woman's status as consort to the leader, and her apotheosis in death.

Leaving aside the meaning of the clasps and their gold and turquoise ornamentation, there is a further element connecting them to the world of the steppes, namely the unusual mount ridden by Dionysus and Ariadne, which is also given a saddle-cloth decorated with turquoises, with two round turquoise pompoms at the corners. Neither a bull, nor an ass, nor even an Indian panther, the monster has its ears pointing ahead, a pointed tongue protruding from two rows of sharp teeth. It has the folded muzzle of a lion, the beard of a goat, the crest of a dragon, a long tail with a plume, and the clawed feet of a predator. It provides a nice example of the hybrid monsters that were a favorite motif in the art of the steppes.

136
A pair of clasps showing Dionysus and Ariadne
Tillya Tepe, Tomb VI
Second quarter of the 1st century A.D.
Gold, turquoise
Both 6.5 x 7.0 cm
National Museum of Afghanistan
04.40.53

135
Appliqué "the Aphrodite of Bactria"
Tillya Tepe, Tomb VI
Second quarter of the 1st century A.D.
Gold, turquoise
5.0 x 2.6 cm
National Museum of Afghanistan
04.40.9

135 THIS APPLIQUÉ SHOWS a winged female figure. Her left elbow rests on a pillar with two recesses, one of which still contains a turquoise. With stretched fingers she loosely holds the garment falling over her right hip, which leaves her lower belly largely bare. This seductive figure, clearly inspired by Hellenistic models, might indeed pass for Aphrodite. While her posture suggests that, nevertheless in reality she conforms to a quite different and non-Greek ideal of beauty, as witness the rounded face, lengthened eyes, the rather squat posture and the folds that give the neck and body a certain plumpness. Furthermore the goddess has short sickle-shaped wings, she wears various bracelets on her wrist and upper arms, her hair is parted in the middle and she wears a woven hair-band decorated with sequins. Accentuated hollows (dimples?) emphasise the corners of the mouth. On her forehead between the eyebrows is a dot in the Indian way. Should she therefore be given an Indian name rather than 'Aphrodite', or perhaps she is Parthian or Iranian? Surely not; and yet it is certain that she had a real significance, and that the nomad's daughter or granddaughter whose breast she adorned believed strongly in her powers.

137 **THESE TWO PENDANTS** show identical images in a rectangular frame, with a rosette of four heart-shaped leaves, top center, and a bird, shown in profile, at each corner. With their claws, their imposing heads and their large eyes they remind us of owls. At the lower corners are two fish heads, greatly reminiscent of the "dolphins" described earlier (nos. 59 and 80). The world above is therefore populated by birds, the world below by fish. The ordering of the world is illustrated by animals. It is therefore no great surprise that the panel within the frame shows a "Mistress of the Animals." She is shown frontally, just like her male peer the "Dragon Master" (no. 61), and exhibits a femininity confirmed by her breasts, decorated with an X-shaped ornament, as well as the diadem from which her curling locks emerge, and her bracelets. The large, heart-shaped turquoises behind her shoulders may represent wings. Her robe, which is really more like a veil, spreads out at the bottom into a tripartite ornament with a slash in the middle, reminiscent of the Dragon Master's acanthus leaf "skirt."

With a gesture that appears more a fond caress than a restraint, the goddess has placed her hand on the belly of one of these strange beasts. With the other hand she holds a round fruit, an apple or pomegranate, seeming to offer it to us.

Nana? Anahita? Ardokhsho? With this figure, too, it is for the present impossible to identify a deity described or depicted in any pantheon which this might represent. However, in view of the gesture of offering made by the goddess, together with her accentuated nakedness and her surroundings, including both plants and various kinds of animal, she is clearly associated with productivity, fertility, and rebirth, themes which underlie the conception that all Iranian peoples and especially the nomads have of the world.

138 **THESE IDENTICAL EARRINGS** consist of a bent gold rod, terminating at one end in a small horn and at the other end in a winged cupid figure, backward arched putto (cherub) with a crescent above the forehead.

This type of earring, depicting a bent body, is familiar from Greek goldsmiths' work, particularly that from Tarentum (Taranto). Each earring is surrounded by a ring consisting of two circles of beads.

These adornments show clear signs of wear.

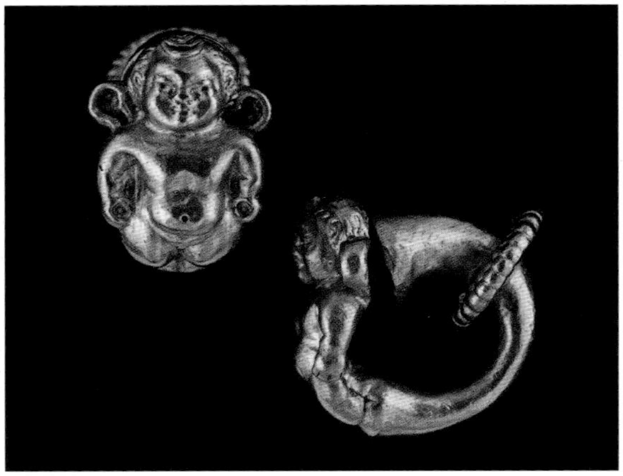

137
A pair of pendants showing the "Mistress of the Animals"'
Tillya Tepe, Tomb VI
Second quarter of the 1st century A.D.
Gold, turquoise
5.8 x 4.6 x 0.5 cm
National Museum of Afghanistan
04.40.52

138
A pair of earrings decorated with cupids
Tillya Tepe, Tomb VI
Second quarter of the 1st century A.D.
Gold
7.0 x 1.5 cm
National Museum of Afghanistan
04.40.7

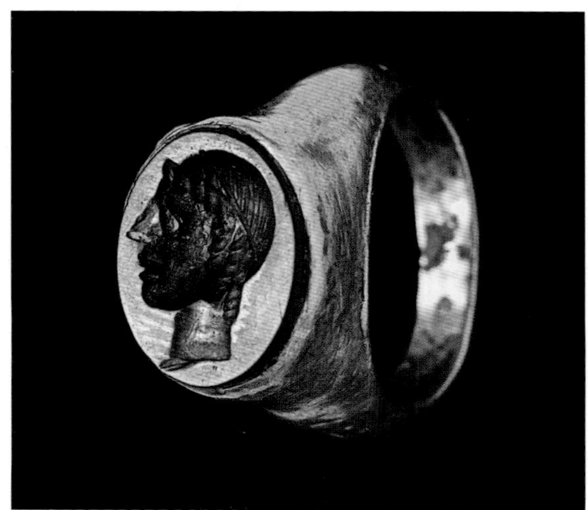

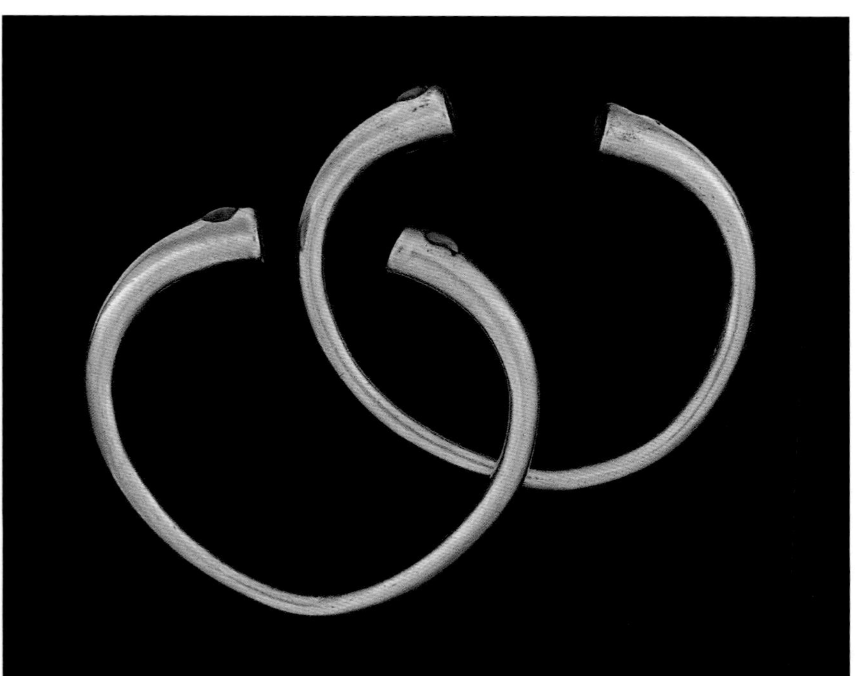

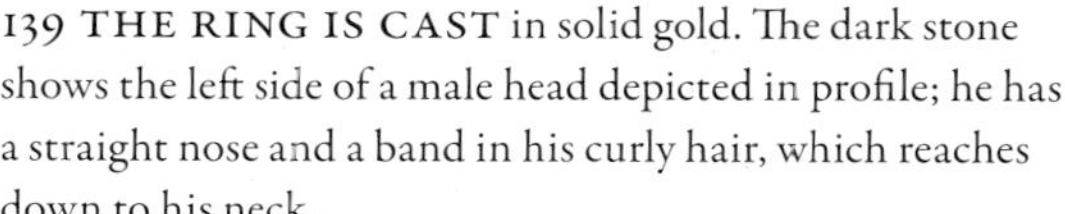

139 THE RING IS CAST in solid gold. The dark stone shows the left side of a male head depicted in profile; he has a straight nose and a band in his curly hair, which reaches down to his neck.

140 THESE TWO IDENTICAL BRACELETS, cast in gold, have lion heads at each end; they have wide eyes, gaping jaws and clearly indicated teeth, and flattened ears and horns. Like the bracelets from Tomb II (no. 58), these objects show marked similarities with bracelets from the Siberian collection of Peter the Great in the Hermitage in St. Petersburg (Rudenko 1962, pl. XIII and XV) and with others from Taxila in Pakistan (Marshall 1951, pl. 182, nos. 133–136).

139
Ring with gem
Tillya Tepe, Tomb VI
Second quarter of the 1st century A.D.
Gold, carnelian
2.0 x 1.7 cm
National Museum of Afghanistan
04.40.45

140
A pair of bracelets with horned lion heads
Tillya Tepe, Tomb VI
Second quarter of the 1st century A.D.
Gold, turquoise
L. 18.5 cm
National Museum of Afghanistan
04.40.5

141
Pair of anklets
Tillya Tepe, Tomb VI
Second quarter of the 1st century A.D.
Gold, turquoise
L. 21.2 cm
National Museum of Afghanistan
04.40.3

142
Two hair ornaments
Tillya Tepe, Tomb VI
Second quarter of the 1st century A.D.
Gold, silver
Diam. 7.0 and 1.8 cm; L. 4.0 cm
National Museum of Afghanistan
04.40.1

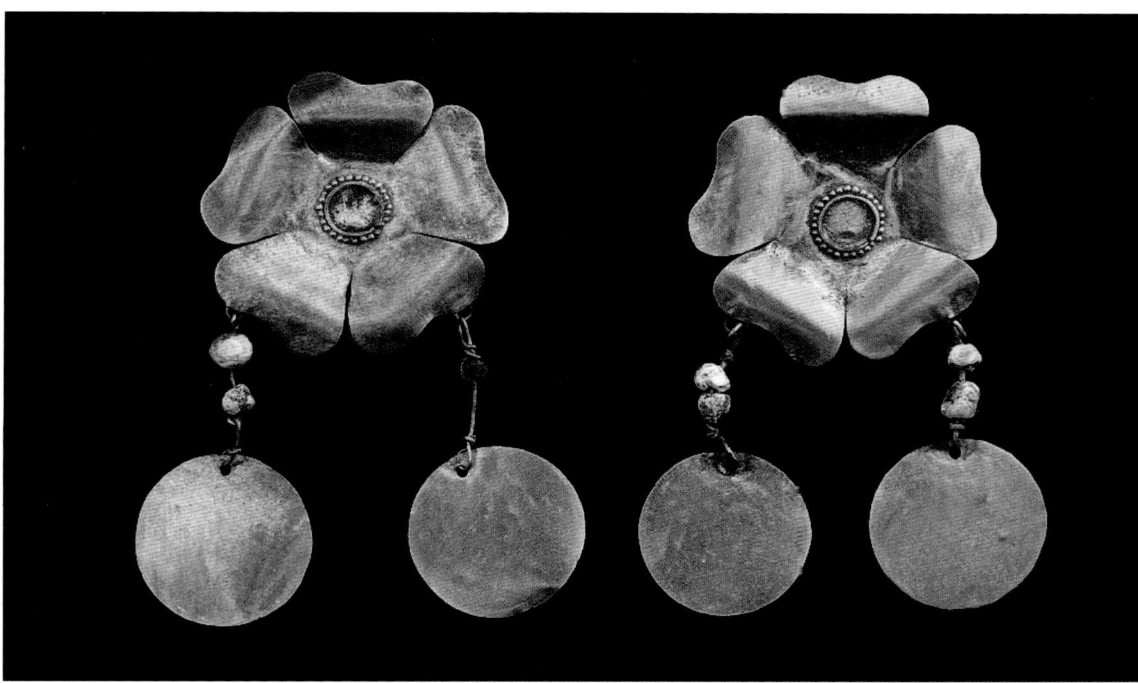

142 EACH ORNAMENT, comparable to one found in Tomb I (no. 38), consists of a gold ornament on a pointed silver rod of low silver content. The object is made from thin gold leaf cut into the form of a flower with five petals. The center of the flower is an open disk with a granulated border, holding a tube in rolled gold leaf. The rod was to be inserted in this tube. Round pendants are attached to two of the petals. The petals at the front are held together with a thread, to which are attached a crescent and a further three roundels. Decorative beads are still attached to some of the threads.

143 THE NECKLACE consists of ten round and two elongated beads, the latter serving as a fastening. The beads are divided into segments by granulated lines. Alternate segments contain a rosette with five heart-shaped leaves inlaid with turquoise.

144 THE FLOWERS have five heart-shaped petals and two pendants.

145 THIS ORNAMENT is a combination of roundels alternating with double crescents, similar to finds from Tomb I (no. 36), Tomb II (cat. nos. 72 and 73), and Tomb V (no. 129). The only point of difference is that the disk here is decorated with a motif of four hearts arranged in a cloverleaf pattern and inlaid with turquoise. The heart motif can also be found as the spacing pieces between the opposed crescents.

146 PARTHIAN COIN. Obverse: A bearded king, turned to the left, wearing a horned tiara, its points indicated by three rows of dots. The lower outline of the hair is also indicated with dots. At the front of the coronet is a prone deer, a motif which probably also appeared on top of the crown, but cannot be seen properly because of defective stamping of the coin. An oval countermark is visible behind the head, with a face depicted frontally.

Reverse: A figure on a throne, turned to the left, holding a bow in his outstretched right hand. There are traces of an inscription, which can be reconstructed as follows: above is BASILEÔS, to the right MEGALOU, below ARSAKOU, and left, on two lines THEOPATOROS/NIKATOROS.

The coin is a local imitation of silver Parthian coins of Gotarzes I (95–90 B.C.), probably issued halfway through the first century B.C. It is made of gold, rather than the silver or bronze which was generally used for Parthian and Greco-Bactrian coinage; this suggests that minting currency was not of much commercial importance, but rather a symbol of prestige for the lesser rulers within the sphere of influence of the Parthian Empire and of the Arsacid dynasty.

143
Necklace
Tillya Tepe, Tomb VI
Second quarter of the 1st century A.D.
Gold, turquoise
Diam. of the pearls 2.8 x 2.5 cm
National Museum of Afghanistan
04.40.51

144
Two ornaments in the form of flowers
Tillya Tepe, Tomb VI
Second quarter of the 1st century A.D.
Gold
Diam. 3.0 cm; L 5.7 cm
National Museum of Afghanistan
04.40.2

145
Part of an ornament
Tillya Tepe, Tomb VI
Second quarter of the 1st century A.D.
Gold, turquoise
Diam. 1.7 cm; L. 4.6 cm
National Museum of Afghanistan
04.40.47

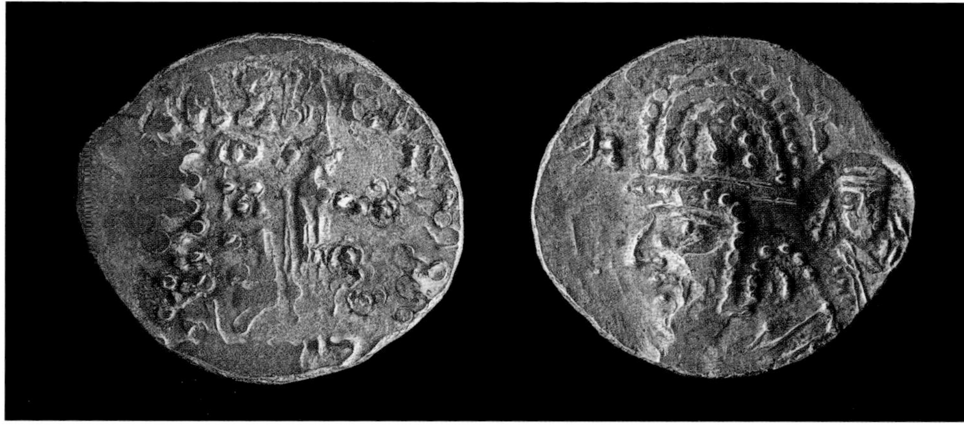

146
Parthian coin, imitation of coin of Gotarzes I
Tillya Tepe, Tomb VI
Middle of the 1st century B.C.
Gold
Diam. 1.8 cm
National Museum of Afghanistan
04.40.16

KABUL

Kabul, view of the citadel, Charles Masson, 1842

GENERAL TITLES

Allchin, F.R. and Norman Hammond, eds. *The Archaeology of Afghanistan from Earliest Times to the Timurid Period.* London : New York: Academic Press, 1978.

Cambon, P., ed. *L'Afghanistan, une histoire millenaire,* Paris: Musee Guimet, 2002.

Cribb, J. and G. Herrmann *After Alexander: Central Asia before Islam.* Oxford: Oxford University Press, 2007

Dupree, Louis. *Afghanistan.* Princeton: Princeton University Press, 1973.

Dupree, Nancy Hatch, Louis Dupree, and A.A. Motamedi. *The National Museum of Afghanistan.* Kabul: Afghan Tourist Authority, 1974.

Gorshenina, S. and C. Rapin. De Kaboul à Samarkand. *Les archéologes en Asie centrale.* Paris: Découvertes Gallimard, 2001

History of Civilizations of Central Asia, Paris: UNESCO. Published in five volumes, 1992-2005.

Tissot, Francine *Catalogue of the National Museum of Afghanistan, 1931-1985.* Art, Museums and Monument series. Paris: UNESCO Publishing, 2006.

EXHIBITION CATALOGUES

Barrett, Douglas E., and Ralph H. Pinder-Wilson. "Ancient Art from Afghanistan: [exhibition] at the Royal Academy of Arts, 6 December, 1967 to 28 January, 1968." London: The Arts Council, 1967.

Gullini, Giorgio. *L'Afghanistan dall preistoria all'Islam : capolavori del Museo di Kabul.* Torino: La Galleria, 1961.

Rowland, Benjamin. *Ancient art from Afghanistan; treasures of the Kabul Museum,* New York: Asia Society, 1966.

LOOTING OF THE KABUL MUSEUM

"Afghanistan Cultural Heritage." UNESCO, 2001. Available online at http://www.unesco.org/opi2/afghan-crisis/.

"An Endangered Heritage." Archeology (online magazine content), 1998. Available online at http://www.archaeology.org/online/features/afghan/list.html.

Tissot, Francine and Dominique Darbois. *Kaboul, le passe confisque. Le musee de Kaboul 1931-1965.* Paris: Editions Findakly, 2002.

Dupree, Nancy. "Museum Under Siege." Archeology, Volume 49 Number 2, (March/April 1996), 42-51.

Lawler, Andrew. "Saving Afghan Culture." National Geographic (December 2004), 28-41.

"Lost and Stolen Images: Afghanistan." The Huntington Photographic Archive of Buddhist and Related Art, Ohio State University, 1998. Available online at http://kaladarshan.arts.ohio-state.edu/loststolen/lsafgh.html.

Lovgren, Stefan. "'Lost' Treasures of Afghanistan Revealed in Photos." National Geographic.com, November 2004. Available online at http://news.nationalgeographic.com/news/2004/11/1117_041117_afghan_treasure.html.

"Museum Under Siege: The Plunder Continues", Archeology (online magazine content), 1998. Available online at http://www.archaeology.org/online/features/afghan/update.html.

SPACH Newsletter, Vol. 1 – 7 (May 1996 – July 2001). Available online at http://spach.info/epublications.htm.

FULLOL TEPE AND THE BRONZE AGE BACTRIA-MARGIANA ARCHAEOLOGICAL COMPLEX

Hiebert, Fredrik and C.C. Lamberg-Karlovsky. "Central Asia and the Indo-Iranian borderlands" Iran XXX (1992), pp. 1-15.

Jarrige, Jean-Francois, G. Quivron. "The Indus valley and the Indo-Iranian borderlands at the end of the 3rd and beginning of the 2nd millenium BC." *South Asian Archaeology 1999,* edited by K.R. van Kooij and E.M. Raven, International Institute of Asian Studies (IIAS), Leiden, Netherlands. In press.

Sarianidi, Viktor I. *Margush: Ancient Oriental Kingdom in the Old Delta of the Murghab River.* Ashgabat: Turkmendowlethabarlay, 2002.

Sarianidi, Viktor I. *Gonur-depe. City of Kings and Gods.* Ashgabat: Miras, 2005.

Tosi, M., and R. Wardak. "The Fullol Hoard: A New Find from Bronze Age Afghanistan." East and West, 22, Rome 1972, 9-17.

AI KHANUM

Bernard, Paul. "Aï Khanoum: Campagnes 1965, 1966, 1967, 1968 / rapport préliminaire " Mémoires de la Délégation archéologique française en Afghanistan (MDAFA), vol 21, 1973.

Bernard, P. "An ancient Greek City in Central Asia", *Scientific American* (1982) vol. 246 no. 1 pp. 148-159.

Bernard, Paul. Aï Khanoum: "Les monnaies hors trésors : questions d'histoire gréco-bactrienne" / MDAFA, vol 28, 1985.

Francfort, Henri-Paul. "Aï Khanoum: Le sanctuaire du temple à niches indentées. [pt.] 2." Les trouvailles / MDAFA, vol 27, 1984.

Guillaume, Olivier. "Ai Khanoum: Les propylées de la rue principale" / MDAFA, vol 26, 1983.

Guillaume, Olivier, and Axelle Rougeulle. "Aï Khanoum: Les petits objets" / MDAFA, vol 31, 1987.

Holt, Frank Lee. *Thundering Zeus: The Making of Hellenistic Bactria,* 1999 Berkely: University of California Press.

Lecuyot, G. "Ai Khanum reconstructed," *Proceedings of the British Academy,* no. 133 (2007), pp. 155-162.

Leriche, Pierre. "Aï Khanoum: Les remparts et les monuments associés" / MDAFA, vol 29, 1986.

Rapin, Claude. "Aï Khanoum: La trésorerie du palais hellénistique d'Aï Khanoum" / MDAFA, Vol 33, 1992.

Veuve, Serge. "Ai Khanoum: Le Gymnase : architecture, céramique, sculpture" / MDAFA, vol 30, 1987.

BEGRAM

Davidson, J LeRoy, "Begram ivories and early Indian sculpture" In: *Aspects of Indian art. Papers presented in a symposium at the Los Angeles County Museum of Art, October, 1970.* Ed. by P. Pal. Leiden 1972, 1-14.

Errington, E., "Charles Masson and Begram" *Topoi* Volume 11, 2001, 357-409.

Hackin, Joseph, and J.R. Hackin. "Recherches archéologiques à Begram: chantier no. 2." MDAFA, vol .9, 1939.

Hackin, Joseph. "Nouvelles recherches archéologiques à Begram, ancienne Kâpicî, 1939-1940; rencontre de trois civilisations, Inde, Grèce, Chine." MADFA, vol.11, 1954.

Di Castro, Angelo Andrea. "Cultural interaction in Afghanistan, c. 300 BCE to 300 CE." (Working paper no. 5). Clayton, Australia: Monash Asia Institute, 2005.

Ghirshman, Roman. Bégram; "Recherches archéologiques et historiques sur les Kouchans." MADFA, vol. 12, 1946.

Goswami, Jaya. *Cultural history of ancient India : a socio-economic and religio-cultural survey of Kapisa and Gandhara.* Dehli: Agam Kala Prakashan, 1979.

Mehendale, Sanjyot, "Pilgrim's Process: Begram and a Reexamination of Hsuang-Tsang's Kapisa", *Res Orientales* VIII (1994), 93-103.

Mehendale, Sanjyot. "Begram: New Perspectives on the Ivory and Bone Carvings," PhD dissertation, UC Berkeley, 1998.

Mehendale, Sanjyot, "The Begram Ivory and Bone Carvings : Some Observations on Provenance and Chronology" *Topoi* Volume 11, 2001, 485-514.

Musée Guimet. *Paris-Tokyo-Begram: hommage à Joseph Hackin (1886-1941).* Paris: Editions Recherche sur les civilizations, 1986.

Veyne, Paul. *L'Empire gréco-romain,* Paris: Seuil, 2005.

Whitehouse, David. "Begram, the Periplus and Gandharan art." *Journal of Roman Archaeology* 2 (1989), 93-100.

Whitehouse, David. "Begram: the glass." *Topoi* Volume 11, 2001, 437-449.

TILLYA TEPE

Boardman, John, "Three Monsters at Tillya Tepe", *Ancient Civilizations from Scythia to Siberia*, 2003 Brill, 133-146.

Sarianidi, V.I. "The Golden Hoard of Bactria." National Geographic (March 1990), 50-75.

Sarianidi, V.I. *The Golden Board of Bactria: from the Tillya-tepe excavations in northern Afghanistan.* New York : H.N. Abrams ; Leningrad : Aurora Art Publishers, 1985.

Sarianidi, V.I. "The Treasure of Golden Hill." American Journal of Archaeology, Vol. 84, No. 2 (Apr., 1980), 125-131.

Sarianidi, V.I., *Khram i Nekropol' Tillyatepe,* Moscow :Nauka, 1989.

Schiltz, V. "Les Sarmates entre Rome et la Chine: nouvelle perspectives" Comptes rendus des séances de l'Académie des Inscriptions et Belles-Lettres, (July-October 2002), 845-887.

Curtis, V.S. "Parthian Belts and Belt Plaques." Iranica Antiqua, Vol. 36, (2001), 299-328.

Davis-Kimball, J. "Enarees and Women of High Status: Evidence of Ritual at Tillya Tepe (Northern Afghanistan)." In Kurgans, ritual sites, and settlements : Eurasian Bronze and Iron Age, ed. Jeannine Davis-Kimball ... [et al.]. Oxford : Archaeopress, 2000, 223-229.

Liu Xinru. "Migration and Settlement of the Yuezhi-Kushan: Interaction and Interdependence of Nomadic and Sedentary Societies." Journal of World History - Volume 12, Number 2, (Fall 2001), 261-292.

Zeymal, E. "Tillya-Tepe within the context of the Kushan chronology" In Coins, art, and chronology : essays on pre-Islamic history of the Indo-Iranian borderlands, eds. Michael Alram & Deborah E. Klimburg-Salter. Vienna: Verlag der Österreichischen Akademie, 1999, 239-244.

Transitional Islamic State of Afghanistan
Ministry of Justice Official Gazette
Law on the Preservation of Historical
and Cultural Heritage
Issue n. 828 Sawar 31 st 1383 May 20th, 2004

To:

The Minister of Justice, The board of the directory of the Revolutionary Council of the Democratic Republic of Afghanistan in its historical session on 29/8/1359 ratified and recommended, within 87 articles, the law for the Preservation of the Historical and Cultural Heritage, which was decided by the council of the Democratic Republic of Afghanistan in its decision n. 2602 dated 24/8/1359.

Approval circumstances of the aforesaid has gained the view of his Excellency the Head of the Revolutionary Council of the Democratic Republic of Afghanistan, and under n. 1311 dated 6/9/1359 of the directory board of the Revolutionary Council, which has reached the Prime Minister, you are informed to publish the mentioned Law in the official Gazette.

Sultan Ali Kishtmand
Deputy to the Head of the Revolutionary Council
and Deputy Prime Minister

Law on the Preservation of the Historical and Cultural Heritage

Chapter 1
General Orders

Article 1
This law is adopted pursuant to article (9) of the constitution for the Preservation of the Historical and Cultural Heritage.

Article 2
The Historical and Cultural Heritage of Afghanistan belongs to the people of Afghanistan and is the manifestation of their participation in the evolution of the cultural heritage of mankind. It is the duty of the State and the people of Afghanistan to protect their historical and cultural heritage.

Article 3
In this law, the Historical and Cultural Heritage means:
1. Any product of mankind, movable or immovable, which has an outstanding historical, scientific, artistic and/or cultural value, which is at least one hundred years old.
2. Products which are less than one hundred years old, but which because of their scientific, artistic and cultural value, are also recognized as worthy of being preserved.

Article 4
The scientific, artistic and cultural value of products afore-mentioned in article 3 shall be determined by the Archaeological Committee and is applicable after the approval of the Minister of Information and Culture.

Article 5
For the purpose of study and research of the Historical and Cultural Heritage, a committee will be formed and will be named the Archaeological Committee. This committee will consist of:
1. The Director of the Institute of Archaeology, designated as the Head of the Committee.
2. Two scientifically competent archaeologists chosen by the Ministry of Information and Culture.
3. One scientifically competent member of the Museum chosen by Ministry of Information and Culture.
4. One historian, from the Academy of Science, chosen by the Director of the Academy.
5. [A lecturer from the Faculty of Social Sciences from the University of Kabul at a higher rank than (Poohandoi)].
6. [One engineer, from the Department for the Preservation of and Rehabilitation of Historical Monuments, chosen by the Minister of Information and Culture].

Article 6
In the case of ambiguity, as to whether a historical and cultural heritage object is genuine or forged, the decision of the Archaeological Committee will be final.

Article 7
The Institute of Archaeology [and the Department for Preservation and Rehabilitation of Historical Monuments] is bound to survey and register all historical monuments and sites, specify their limits, collect and organize all the documentation and references pertaining to them.
No person can build or allow another to construct a building within the registered limits of an archaeological area, without the permission of the Institute of Archaeology.

Article 8
All historical and cultural properties, movable or immovable, in Afghanistan, discovered or hidden in the earth (or to be discovered], are classified as property of the State, thus the transformation of such object without permission is prohibited.

Article 9
The owner of the land cannot take possession of unearthed, or excavate hidden, historical and cultural properties by the virtue of ownership.

Article 10
Whenever, municipalities, urban housing building corporations, irrigation projects, and any other government or private corporations, in undertaking construction, expansion and improvement projects, come across valuable historical and cultural objects, they are bound to stop their work and inform the Institute of Archaeology [the Ministry of Information and Culture on the issue.

Article 11
In the case that construction work endangers an archaeological property or its site, the project is suspended until a definitive solution is found for their protection.

Article 12
Any modification of the structure of a registered monument of historic value is prohibited, without the authorization of the State [Ministry of Information and Culture].
The State [Ministry of Information and Culture] takes proper arrangements for the protection of such monuments.

Article 13
The Archaeological Committee will fix and pay reasonable compensation to those who help the State in the discovery of historical and cultural heritage [after the approval of the Ministry of Information and Culture].

Chapter 2
Immovable Historical and Cultural Properties

Article 14
1. Registration of immovable historical and cultural property will be undertaken, after the ratification of the Archaeological Committee and the approval of the Ministry of Information and Culture, and will be published in the State Newspapers for public knowledge.
2. The Institute of Archaeology is bound to attribute a registration number to the registered historical and cultural property and send copy to the related provinces and municipalities.
3. The boundaries of the immovable historical object should be measured by the Archaeological Committee.

Article 15
Sacred places or historical buildings, which have been registered as historical and cultural property, remain in the custody of the owner, custodian of pious legacies, [Department of Historical Monuments], Institute of Archaeology or the local administrative authority. In this case, the person or the administration [Department of Historical Monuments] is bound to protect them and take advice for the preservation of their authenticity from the Institute of Archaeology.

Article 16
Burial of the dead, digging wells, drains and ditches, quarry mining with dynamite, building chimneys, driving heavy vehicles or any other operation, which cause loss and damage to the historical and cultural property, within the limits of the archaeological territory, is not allowed without the permission of the Institute of Archaeology

Article 17
The State can, if necessary, at the instigation of the Ministry of Information and Culture and upon approval from the Council of Ministers, acquire, at a reasonable cost, the ownership of immovable historical and cultural properties and sites.

Article 18
The claim of having been in possession (Zulyadi) of immovable historical and cultural properties, for a long period of time, is not acceptable and is not a proof of ownership.

Article 19
1. The finder of immovable historical and cultural properties, or the owner of the land, or rightful user of landed properties, where such heritage properties have been discovered, are bound to inform the administrative authority of their discovery within one week, in urban areas, and within two weeks, in rural areas, and the administrative authority shall inform the Institute of Archaeology without delay. Such properties are known as Public Property. The State shall acquire, at a reasonable price, the ownership of the land and the habitable premises, on which the historical and cultural property is situated or constitutes a part of.
2. If the discovered immovable historical and cultural property includes movable historical and cultural property, such properties are regarded as State properties and the owner will be given reasonable compensation under article 12 of this law.

Article 20
The Institute of Archaeology can study, draw, photograph and mould all immovable properties. The owner is bound to provide necessary facilities to the archaeological representatives for this purpose.

Article 21
If a private property is contiguous to that of historical or cultural property, in case of construction or modification of a building, prior permission must be obtained from the Department for the Preservation and Rehabilitation of Historical Monuments.

Article 22
The transfer of ownership of a registered immovable historical and cultural property will take effect one month after the Institute of Archaeology has been informed. The notification will include the identity and a photocopy of the title of the new owner.

Article 23
The immovable historical and cultural object that comes under the public properties cannot be sold.
Chapter 3 Movable Historical and Cultural Properties

Chapter 3
Movable Historical and Cultural Properties

Article 24
Movable historical and cultural properties, which have been in the custody of a real or legal person, before the application of this law, are registered by

the Ministry of Information and Culture. The owners of the movable heritages are bound to inform the Institute of Archaeology, in the capital. In this case, the private ownership of these properties is preserved.

Article 25
The Directorates of Information and Culture are to inform the Institute of Archaeology officially and send an inventory of the properties for registration, within 15 days. Also, the Institute of Archaeology is bound to send the copy of registration card to the relevant administration of Information and Culture, within 3 months.

Article 26
The finder of movable properties is bound to inform the Institute of Archaeology, within one week in the capital, and the Office for the Preservation of Historical and Cultural Heritage or to the local administration in the provinces, within two weeks. The administration is obliged to inform the Institute of Archaeology in the shortest delay. Rewards will be given to the finder of the historical or cultural property according to the Article 13.

Article 27
In case, the Institute of Archaeology feels it necessary to own a movable historical or cultural property, for scientific purposes, it has the right to buy it by preemption. If the owner does not agree, the Institute has the right to take the case to court.

Article 28
1. The Institute of Archaeology can request a registered historical or cultural movable property, which is in the custody of private persons, for the purpose of studying, drawing, molding, photographing and for scientific and technical use. After the completion of this research, the Institute must return it to the owner within a reasonable delay. Also, the Institute of Archaeology can publish such historical and cultural properties. 2. The Institute of Archaeology can mold and take photo from any historical and cultural object within the country.

Article 29
Historical and cultural properties that are in the custody of private persons can be entrusted to the researchers of the National Institute of Archaeology for the purpose of scientific use. The researcher is bound to mention the name of the owner as the main reference in her research.

Article 30
The owner of a registered movable cultural property is obliged to inform the Institute of Archaeology and the National Museum in the case of change of the place of preservation.

Article 31
All persons, legal and real, that possess registered movable properties, are bound to preserve them according to the instructions of the Institute of Archaeology and the National Museum.
In case of damage to this heritage by negligence of the owner, the Institute of Archaeology can repair it scientifically at the cost of the owner.
If it is proved that the owner of the heritage is not capable of its preservation, the Institute of Archaeology can buy it at a reasonable price.
In the case of disagreement upon the price, the Institute of Archaeology has the right to approach the court.

Article 32
Selling registered movable cultural properties is not permitted to foreigners.
If a person wants to sell a registered movable property to an Afghan, he is bound to inform the Institute of Archaeology about complete particulars of the buyer.
If the Institute of Archaeology refrains from buying the heritage, the owner can sell it to a third person.

Article 33
The officers of the Department for the Preservation of Historical and Cultural Heritage and the persons from the Institute of Archaeology do not have the right to buy or sell historical and cultural properties.

Chapter 4
Archaeological Excavations

Article 34
The right of excavation for the discovery of cultural heritage is limited to the Institute of Archaeology.
No other government offices, private organizations or private persons have the right to excavate, even on their own land, without the permit, which is issued for this purpose according to the provisions of this law.

Article 35
The Institute of Archaeology can give a permit, after the approval of the Council of Ministers, to local, foreign and international scientific organizations upon their application for a permit for archaeological excavation. This permit is not transferable.

Article 36
1. The organization requesting a permit to excavate should forward the application, with the following elements to the Institute of Archaeology:
i. object of the excavation and work programmed;
ii. fix the excavation site and its limits;
iii. complete particulars of the head and members of the excavation delegation.
2. The head and the members of the excavation delegation cannot be changed without the prior agreement.

Article 37
The validity of the permit is for five years; the organization requesting the permit to excavate cannot delay the excavation, without prior permission of the Institute of Archaeology, for more than one year. The period of delay is counted in the contract period. If the excavation is delayed, due to accidents or due to the work capacity, the extension of the excavation period is contracted on the basis of a new contract, according to the provisions of this law.

Article 38
The excavation council is bound to observe the laws, customs and habits of the country, and the area of their excavation.

Article 39
Settlement of torts and compensation of any damage caused to the land of the person where the excavation is performed is the responsibility of the excavation council.

Article 40
The foreign board of excavation is exempted from paying any kind of customs duties for the importation of goods, scientific and technical

instruments, vehicles for their need, provided that after the completion of the work, it is either reexported from Afghanistan or left to the government organizations gratuitously.

Article 41
The right of investigation and supervision of all archaeological excavation is reserved to the Institute of Archaeology.
Without the presence of the representative, or representatives of the Institute of Archaeology, the contractor organization does not have the right to undertake survey and excavation

Article 42
Excavation should be performed by the most modern methods of scientific instruments.

Article 43
The excavation board is obliged to present, within six months after the end of each season of excavation, its preliminary report including plans, sketches, photographs, drawings and the contents of the discovered heritage, to the Institute of Archaeology.

Article 44
Information relating to the results of the research and development of the work of one season of excavation can be published or written electronically. The Institute of Archaeology can also publish the report of the board in the name of the excavation board.

Article 45
All cultural properties, which are discovered during survey and excavation, belong to the State of Afghanistan.

Article 46
The protection of the excavation site and transportation of the discovered properties, under the contract, is the responsibility of the contractor organization.
All the discovered movable properties are to be delivered to the Institute of Archaeology before the end of contract.
The Institute of Archaeology after studying the discovered properties must deliver them to the National Museum within six months.

Article 47
Temporary, exportation of discovered cultural properties for the purpose of research, maintenance and restoration, in case of lack of scientific instruments and specialized laboratories in the country, and for the completion of information and publishing the results, will be allowed upon the request of Archaeology Committee and approval of the Minister of Information and Culture.

Article 48
The excavation board cannot transport discovered cultural properties, for temporary research, out of its central office without the permission of the Institute of Archaeology.

Article 49
The right of publication of the results of scientific excavations and survey is reserved for the board of excavation.
The excavation board is bound to publish its final research within three years. After completion of excavations in the name of Afghanistan's Historical and Cultural Heritage, after three years the board will lose the right of monopoly of publishing.

Article 50
The excavation board is bound to officially deliver 50 copies of all its publications, such as the preliminary report, final report, articles and pamphlets [written or delivered electronically] relating to the excavation and research, free of cost to the Institute of Archaeology.

Article 51
The terms of revocation of the excavation contract are clearly assigned from both sides in the related contract.

Chapter 5
Museums

Article 52
1. Establishment and administration of museums, for the purpose of preservation and maintenance of historical and cultural properties and for their scientific use, is the responsibility of the State.
2. This order in section 1 of the article should not hinder the real and legal persons, who possess such properties or collections.

Article 53
In Afghanistan, museums are divided into three categories:
1. The National Museum, which is located in the capital of the country.
2. Local Museums, whose number, place and location are fixed by the suggestion of the Institute of Archaeology and the approval of the Minister of Information and Culture.
3. Special Museums are established at the suggestion of the Ministries, desirous organizations and ratification of the Council of Ministers.

Article 54
In the National Museum, all the n. 1 valuable scientific and artistic properties, and all other properties of which there is a unique example available in Afghanistan, are conserved and put on display.
All the historical and cultural properties, of which there is more than one example available, are kept in local museums where the mentioned properties were discovered.
The distribution of the available and discovered properties among different museums of the country is decided by the Archaeological Committee with the participation of the national and local museum officers.

Article 55
Except for the case, mentioned in article 54 of this law, shifting the National Museum or a part of its collections, without excessive need and the ratification of the Council of Ministers from its specific place to another place is prohibited. Transportation of the properties takes place under the supervision of the Institute of Archaeology, under the best possible conditions to protect them from being stolen, broken, spilled or suffering any other damages, and the best conditions are provided for its preservation in the new place.

Article 56
Transfer of a local museum's collections takes place under excessive need on the basis of joint ratification of the local officer, information and Culture Minister's officer and education and training officer by observing the rules of article 55 of this law.

Chapter 6
Trading of the objects similar to the Historical and Cutural Heritages

Article 57
1. No one can engage in trading of similar properties to

historical and cultural objects, without obtaining trading permit. Trading permit of section 1 of this article contains the following information:
i. complete particulars of the applicant; n. address and location of business;
iii. full identification of trader should be kept by the National Museum;
iv. the validity of the above-mentioned permit is only two years and it is extendable. The transfer of the permit to other persons is not allowed.

Article 58
Selling and buying of properties that have a historical and cultural value, is permitted according to this law, under the condition that they are registered and recorded on the basis of this law.

Article 59
A person who holds a permit for the trading of historical and cultural properties is obliged to offer for a sale the mentioned properties only in the areas mentioned in the license.
The holder of the permit can buy heritage from any place in Afghanistan.

Article 60
A trader of cultural properties if bound to: t. fix the trade permit in the trading place;
2. to register all dealings, sales and purchases of historical and cultural properties in the register book, which is given to the trader, at a cost, by the Institute of Archaeology;
3. during an investigation by the representative of the Archaeological Institute (or Museum) the trader should show any historical and cultural properties, which he possesses to the investigator for verification;
4. he has to inform the seller about provisions of this law.

Article 61
In case of violation the Archaeological Committee has to cancel the permit of the trader. The trader can approach the court if he is not satisfied.

Article 62
The license for the trade of historical and cultural properties is issued against four thousands Afghani and in case of renewal a rate of one thousand Afghani will be charged for the duplicate.

Article 63
The Institute of Archaeology while registering historical and cultural properties has the authority to purchase, at a reasonable rate, any heritage, which has a scientific value and is in the custody of the merchant.
In case of disagreement over the rate, the Institute of Archaeology can approach the court.

Chapter 7
Export and Import of Historical and Cultural Heritage

Article 64
Export of the registered historical and cultural properties by a merchant, or all other persons, is prohibited except in conformity with this law.

Article 65
In the following conditions, the State can send historical and cultural properties abroad:
1. for international exhibitions;
2. for scientific research, according to the provisions of this law;
3. for maintenance of the property;
4. in exchange for historical and cultural properties conserved in foreign museums, upon the approval of the Council of Ministers.

Article 66
No historical and cultural property can be sent abroad, unless fully covered by insurance and presence of the representatives of the Archaeological Committee and the National Museum.

Article 67
An object is considered to be exported, when the process by which it is to be removed from Afghanistan has commenced even though it has not left the territory of Afghanistan.

Article 68
1. For the return of the historical and cultural heritage a commission should be appointed as follows: Minister of Information as a Head of the Commission, representatives of the Ministry of Justice, Head of Institute of Archaeology and Head of the National Museum as members.
2. The above mentioned Commission has the authority to take decision regarding the return of the stolen and illicitly imported historical and cultural heritage according to the provisions of the chapter two and three of the UNIDROIT Convention.

Article 69
Where an object considered by a state party to the UNESCO Convention on the means of prohibiting and preventing the illicit imports export and transfer of ownership of cultural property to be part of its cultural heritage and whose export is prohibited is exported contrary to the prohibition and is imported into Afghanistan it is prohibited import and liable to forfeiture.

Article 70
Request from return of cultural heritage alleged to have been unlawfully exported from a state party to the UNESCO Convention on the means of prohibiting and preventing the illicit import export and transfer of ownership of cultural property shall be directed to the Ministry of Information and Culture.
The appointed tribunal in the section 1 of article 68 has the authority to order the seizure of the objects liable to forfeiture through the relevant organs, which will be placed under the control of the Ministry of Information and Culture.

Article 71
The historical and cultural properties, which are imported by the State, are exempt from custom duty.

Article 72
Persons, scientific and derivate organizations importing historical and cultural properties, are bound to deposit them along with a detailed inventory with the custom office and receive a receipt.
The custom administration sends a copy of the inventory, as soon as possible, to the Institute of Archaeology.
The Institute of Archaeology, as soon as checks and photographs of the contents are made, gives customs clearance, after comparing the inventory with the contents.

Article 73
If a foreigner imports his own historical and cultural property to the country, he is exempt from paying custom duty, on the condition that the property is re-exported with the foreigner. In case the owner sells the property inside Afghanistan, he is bound to inform the custom's administration and the Institute of Archaeology before selling it.

Chapter 8
Penalties

Article 74
Any person, who deliberately destroys or damages a historical and cultural property, in addition to paying compensation, is sentenced to imprisonment, from one month up to ten years.

Article 75
If the persons mentioned in articles 19 and 26 of the law, omit to inform the related authorities of the discovery of a cultural property within the fixed period, they are sentenced from one month up to three months imprisonment.

Article 76
Whenever, the owner, custodian or protector of historical and cultural properties does not take care of their protection, or when there is a violation to article 31, and in effect, damage is caused to the property, in addition to compensation, the viola -tor is sentenced to one year up to three years imprisonment.

Article 77
A person, who contrary to article 66, exports or takes a cultural property out of the country, in addition to seizure of the property, is sentenced to six months up to ten years imprisonment.

Article 78
A person who resorts to stealing, abducting or forging properties from museums or excavation sites, in addition to paying the price of the properties, is sentenced to six months up to ten years imprison -ment.

Article 79
For all violations of the rules of this law, the court fixes a proper penalty according to the nature of the crime.

Article 80
Any person who imports the prohibited historical and cultural objects to Afghanistan will be sentenced to the penalty of article 346 of penalty law.

Chapter 9
Miscellaneous Orders

Article 81
Bilateral contracts and agreements concerning historical and cultural properties, and whose articles are contrary to this law, are with the agreement of the parties put into conformity of the provi -sions of this law.

Article 82
Fixing and hanging (for exhibition) original historical and cultural properties, belonging to the State, outside the museums, is prohibited, including in palaces and the State authorities.

Article 83
The establishment of the voluntary associations for conservation and preservation of historical and cultural properties can be established after the permit which will be issued by the Ministry of Information and Culture.

Article 84
For the best implementation of this law, the Ministry of Information and Culture can adopt a regulation and put it for further processing.

Article 85
The present law will come into enforcement, after its publication in the Official Gazette. And this law shall abolish the Law on the Preservation of the Historical and Cultural Heritage Published in the official Gazette n. 469 dated 30/09/1359.

AFGHANISTAN

Hidden Treasures

EDITED BY FREDRIK HIEBERT AND PIERRE CAMBON

Founded in 1888, the National Geographic Society is one of the largest nonprofit scientific and educational organizations in the world. It reaches more than 285 million people worldwide each month through its official journal, NATIONAL GEOGRAPHIC, and its four other magazines; the National Geographic Channel; television documentaries; radio programs; films; books; videos and DVDs; maps; and interactive media. National Geographic has funded more than 8,000 scientific research projects and supports an education program combating geographic illiteracy.

For more information, please call
1-800-NGS LINE (647-5463)
or write to the following address:
National Geographic Society
1145 17th Street N.W.
Washington, D.C. 20036-4688 U.S.A.

Visit us online at
www.nationalgeographic.com/books

For information about special discounts for bulk purchases, please contact National Geographic Books Special Sales: ngspecsales@ngs.org

For rights or permissions inquiries, please contact National Geographic Books Subsidiary Rights: ngbookrights@ngs.org

Library of Congress Cataloging-in-Publication Data is available upon request.
ISBN: 978-1-4262-0295-7
Printed in China

The original catalogue accompanying this exhibit is titled *Afghanistan, les trésors retrouvés,* co-published by Editions de la Réunion des musées nationaux, Paris, 2006 and musées des arts asiatiques-Guimet, Paris

All images are from *Afghanistan, les trésors retrouvés,* co-published by Editions de la Réunion des-musées nationaux, Paris, 2006 and musées des arts asiatiques-Guimet, Paris © Thierry Ollivier/musée Guimet except for the following:; 10-11, Kenneth Garrett; 12, Kenneth Garrett; 14-15, Kenneth Garrett; 20-21 32-33 musée Guimet; 22, Kenneth Garrett; 26-27, Viktor Ivanovich Sarianidi; 28, Michael Yamashita; 32-33 musée Guimet; 34 32-33 musée Guimet;44, Fred Hiebert; 52, Kenneth Garrett; 100, Paul Bernard; 104, Fred Hiebert; 130, Délégation Archéologique Française en Afghanistan (DAFA); 144, musée Guimet 210, Viktor Ivanovich Sarianidi; 211, Viktor Ivanovich Sarianidi; 212, Viktor Ivanovich Sarianidi; 216, Viktor Ivanovich Sarianidi; 218, National Museum of Afghanistan; 219, Viktor Ivanovich Sarianidi; 294-295 32-33 musée Guimet.

Chapter 6: The chapter text is an abridged version of the previously published essay by Pierre Cambon. The full version is found in: *Afghanistan, les trésors retrouvés,* RMN, 2006 and the musées des arts asiatiques-Guimet, Paris

Exerpt of "Eurasian Empires" produced by NHK, Executive Producer, Masahiro Kikuchi with collaboration of Osamu Ishizawa, Taisei*Co. and Guy Lecuyot, ENS, copyright : NHK